FOURTH EDITION

BRIEF TREATMENT AND A NEW LOOK AT THE TASK-CENTERED APPROACH

LAURA EPSTEIN

Late Professor Emerita
University of Chicago

LESTER B. BROWN

California State University, Long Beach

Allyn and Bacon

Boston ■ London ■ Toronto ■ Sydney ■ Tokyo ■ Singapore

Series Editor, Social Work and Family Therapy: *Patricia Quinlin*
Editor-in-Chief, Social Sciences: *Karen Hanson*
Series Editorial Assistant: *Alyssa Pratt*
Editorial-Production Service: *Omegatype Typography, Inc.*
Composition and Prepress Buyer: *Linda Cox*
Manufacturing Manager: *Suzanne Lareau*
Cover Administrator: *Kristina Mose-Libon*
Electronic Composition: *Omegatype Typography Inc.*

Library of Congress Cataloging-in-Publication Data

Epstein, Laura.
    Brief treatment and a new look at the task-centered approach / Laura Epstein, Lester B.
Brown.—4th ed.
        p.   cm.
    Includes bibliographical references and index.
    ISBN 0-205-29150-3 (alk. paper)
    1. Social case work—United States.   2. Task-centered social work—United States.   3.
Social work administration—United States.   I. Brown, Lester B.   II. Title.

HV43 .E67   2002
361.3—dc21

                                                                                            2001022110

Printed in the United States of America

10   9   8   7   6   5   4   3   2   1   06   05   04   03   02   01

CONTENTS

CHAPTER FOUR

The Task-Centered Model: The Problem-Solving Paradigm in Action   91

PART II   GUIDELINES FOR BRIEF TREATMENT   109

CHAPTER FIVE

Starting Up: Receiving Referrals and Applications   111

CHAPTER SIX

First Step: Problem Identification   126

CHAPTER SEVEN

Second Step: Contracting: Plans, Goals, Tasks, Time Limits, and Other Agreements   164

CHAPTER EIGHT

Third Step: Implementation: Problem Solving, Assessment, Task Achievement, and Problem Reduction   191

CHAPTER NINE

Fourth Step: Termination: Discontinuance, Extension, and Monitoring   228

CHAPTER TEN

Interviewing Techniques for Brief Treatment   237

CHAPTER ELEVEN

Adaptations of Task-Centered Treatment: Balance and Flexibility in Practice   267

■ ■ ■ ■ ■

Before she died of pancreatic cancer in 1996, Laura and I had several discussions about how to revise her book, *Brief Treatment*. I have followed her guidelines as well as I can. Reviewers of our suggested revisions made one very strong proviso: that I maintain the clarity of Laura's writing style. I thank them for their suggestions, and I hope that I have accomplished what we all wanted.

Most of Laura's content remains intact in this edition. I have updated references, added content in numerous places, and made changes sparingly in Parts I and II. All of Part III is new.

Part I of the book covers the basic frameworks of brief treatment. These chapters compare and contrast the fundamental characteristics of the major models of brief treatment, including the task-centered model, which was developed at the School of Social Service Administration of the University of Chicago.

Part II of the book lays out in detail the steps for implementing the task-centered model with a range of clients and in various settings. In this section getting started, identifying problems, contracting, implementing problem-solving strategies, and termination are covered in detail for those wanting the most recent guidelines for using short-term treatment and, specifically, the task-centered model. Short-term interventions are ideal for first-line intervention: they are more sensitive to client concerns and help clients deal with issues now. Task-centered treatment has the advantage of also being culturally sensitive to the world views and cultures of most groups, so the model may enhance a worker's abilities in that regard. These interventions are all that many people, if not most, need and want as they deal with everyday problems of living. Most of the chapter on eclectic practice has been eliminated, because there is now a body of literature devoted to the subject.

Part III is new to this edition. This section contains three new chapters that detail the use of task-centered therapy in three different and new settings. Chapter 12 covers the use of task-centered treatment with surgical patients. Using a single subject design, the effectiveness of the model is evaluated in a hospital setting with surprising results.

Chapter 13 is a report of the use of task-centered therapy with HIV/AIDS hospice patients. Again, using a single subject design, the model was found to be especially useful in this hospice setting. The last chapter reports a yearlong study of task-centered treatment with homeless clients, individuals, and families. This last single subject design study may be the largest effectiveness study ever done on the task-centered approach. Almost all of the homeless individuals and families made significant changes in their identified problems in living contiguous with intervention. This study also provides an example of what an agency can do when the staff wants to systematize and to evaluate their own effectiveness.

ACKNOWLEDGMENTS

Numerous people have helped me in this endeavor to revise Laura's book. Those who continue with Laura's inquiries into researching effective helping efforts deserve the most thanks, for they are the ones who continue her tradition of combining practice and research and, more importantly, client-centered work. May your efforts continue to be successful.

I would like to thank American Indian Studies, College of Liberal Arts, and the Department of Social Work, College of Health and Human Services, both at California State University, Long Beach, for their tangible and intangible help in this effort. I would especially like to thank Craig Stone, John Oliver, Jean Granger, Nancy Oliver, and Debbie Repp for their encouragement and assistance. For their intrepid word processing, I would especially like to thank Leticia Govea and Evelyn Calderon. I would also like to thank the reviewer, Andrew Bein, California State University, Sacramento.

For direct contributions to this edition, I would like to thank the flexible, inquiring, and encouraging staff of Shelter Network of San Mateo County, California. I would also be remiss not to mention the contributions of Michael Radding, William Cotton, Missak Parsseghian, Debra Moriarty, and, especially, Glen Alley, a friend and colleague who helps keep my mind agile. Aeree Yoon is the person most responsible for maintaining the delicate chemical balance in my body, which keeps me going, and, for this, I am grateful, although I frequently don't behave in such a manner.

Mostly, I continue to thank Laura for being my teacher, my colleague, and my friend. You lived your own way, were an inspiration to many, and will always be missed.

—*Lester B. Brown*

PREFACE TO THE THIRD EDITION

This book has grown out of experience and research on psychosocial treatment focused on helping people deal with current problems in living. Typically these problems involve distressful and disturbed personal feelings, attitudes, anxieties, and moods; they also involve interpersonal relationships characterized by dissension and strife. These conditions may, in certain circumstances, be identified as psychopathology, although such a designation is not always necessary and is never sufficient to put important interventions in place. Problems in living nearly always reflect the effects of stress produced in the environment and in the social context within which persons live.

What Is Brief Treatment?

Brief treatment is above all other things a practice, a way of mediating between the universal and the particular. This means that there are many ways to build the bridge from the general to the specifics of a case, and there are many equally convincing explanations of what transpires within the controlled time limits of brief treatment. Based on a variety of theoretical propositions, brief treatments are usually derived from psychodynamic approaches in altered forms. Modified by rearrangement, subtractions, and additions from other approaches, such as behaviorism and cognitive treatment, brief treatment approaches are prime examples of the modern turn toward integrative-eclectic systems of treatment. They are sophisticated methods, embedded in research and characterized by pragmatic and analytical thinking. They are regarded as cost effective.

Brief treatments have certain ideas held in common: *planning, focus,* and *brevity.* There are areas where the different approaches diverge significantly, such that practitioners need to understand several viewpoints and make reasoned choices among them. Even within an area of consensus, some approaches lean a bit more in one direction than in another.

Frameworks for Brief Treatment

Brief treatment approaches are structured around two major types of governing ideas or frameworks. They tend to emphasize a problem-solving paradigm or an interpersonal/intrapsychic change process. In real life, however, this emphasis is relative because eclecticism is widely practiced.

Interpersonal and intrapersonal emphases are usually referred to as *psychotherapy.* However, problems can also be located primarily in the environment and in the social context. It is even more likely that problems can be found within the interactional field of person/environment transactions or within the social context. This is the ecological arena where persons and environmental conditions and events face each other and undergo reciprocal exchanges. Where the helping process is concerned with environmental circumstances, it is customary to name it *counseling, casework,* and *social work,* or simply *clinical work;* but some would call it *psychotherapy.* The fact that many names are used to designate similar or related types of clinical problem solving does not mean that we are recognizing distinct entities or sharp boundaries. Rather, there are different histories during the course of which names were affixed and changed repeatedly. These ambiguities in naming the processes reflect the perpetually evolving nature of the treatment enterprise.

The concept of *problem solving* is a familiar framework for psychosocial helping. The task-centered approach to treatment organizes a set of problem-solving rules into a treatment technology. Research and development on this project was conducted at the University of Chicago during the 1970s. During the 1980s, this approach underwent changes and transformations as the developers and their associates moved into new areas, and as the major ideas of the model merged with other ideas.

Problem solving, a central feature of the task-centered approach, is not the only metaphor available to denote the essence of psychosocial treatment. Different branches of knowledge about individuals and the social environment generate diverse paradigms for organizing and directing practice. As a result, besides problem solving, or in addition to it, there are treatment frameworks that take into consideration cognitive processes, learning, behavior modification, psychological growth and development, and ecological adaptation.

In a field that is rapidly changing and responding to new problems of a society in transition, there is no firm consensus today that can guide decisions about what framework to adopt. We are on solid ground to emphasize the overall important themes of *planning, focusing,* and *brevity.* Treatment organizations and funding sources are concentrating on treatment effectiveness and cost control. These characteristics are primary components of brief treatments in general and of the task-centered approach in particular.

Organization of this Book

Readers beginning the study of practice can benefit from learning how to manage the boundaries of brief treatment because they can see the treatment process in a nutshell. They can experience getting results in a reasonably short time. Those who are trained and experienced in long-term treatment, or in some specific models of treatment, may be uncertain how to make technical changes in their practice repertoire fit within the constraints of brief treatment. This book concentrates on the techniques of managing the structures of brief treatment. It explains the fundamentals of brief treatment and provides a manual of guidelines about the process, emphasizing the common features and showing where differences exist among the systems. The primary mission of this text is threefold: (1) to elaborate on the common features; (2) to put those common features into a perspective that is based on the task-centered approach; and (3) to identify adaptations and variations across the spectrum of brief treatment so as to provide a framework for rearranging, subtracting, and adding components to create an individualized fit with client need, and with agency and practitioner preferences and styles.

What follows in the text is first an analysis of concepts, or a discussion of fundamental ideas about brief treatment. Issues that confront practitioners, especially students setting out to learn to be clinicians, are highlighted. Information and discussion of pertinent treatment issues lay the foundation for using the guidelines with understanding and sensitivity. The actual guidelines in Part II of the book combine a revision of the second edition of *Helping People: The Task-Centered Approach* (Merrill, 1988) and *Talking and Listening: A Guide to the Helping Interview* (Merrill, 1985). The guidelines explain how to put planned, focused, and brief practice into effect. The text establishes general rules for a method of practice that works; a method that is generally validated as capable of good outcomes, as well as economical and within the reach of many clients. New material in this edition considers who is most likely to benefit from planned, focused, and brief treatment, and suggests avenues that might be pursued in situations in which other means of intervention need to be considered and applied. The text will highlight both the common techniques and important variations among the various models.

Acknowledgments

With the publication of this third edition, I would like to thank Dean Jeanne Marsh and Associate Dean Sharon Berlin, both of the School of Social Service Administration, the University of Chicago, for their encouragement and for providing me with the administrative resources to get the work done. Special thanks are due to three colleagues who carefully read the manuscript, giving me excellent suggestions to make the book better: Lester B. Brown, California State University at Long Beach; Martha Morrison Dore, University of Pennsylvania—Philadelphia; and Ronald H. Rooney, University of Minnesota—Minneapolis.

PREFACE TO THE SECOND EDITION

Practitioners and students in human service occupations have some dominant concerns, among them how to make plans of action specific enough to guide their cases and how to provide service that is client-oriented and also in harmony with the operations of complex organizations. The most urgent question practitioners ask is *What do I do?*

This book offers guidelines for deciding what to do in many of the usual circumstances of general practice. It attempts to explain how characteristics of agencies, belief patterns of the professions, and social sanctions and expectations of the public affect the results of direct work with clients.

The task-centered model of practice is the base on which this book is built. Presently, the term *task-centered* is affixed to many different ideas about intervention, but when the Task-Centered Project was established in 1970, it was only coming into professional usage. The project was sponsored by the School of Social Service Administration at the University of Chicago, originally through a small start-up grant from a private foundation. The development of the task-centered model was aided by a grant from the Federal Department of Health and Human Services (SRS Grant 18–P–57774/5–03). The work began and continued through the collaboration of William J. Reid and myself, with valuable support from Dean Harold A. Richman and Associate Dean John R. Schuerman.

Research on the model at the University of Chicago occurred between 1970 and 1978. During those years, the project enrolled about 125 graduate students. They suffered through the trials of the model, testing and refining the work. Doctoral students were exceptionally helpful in conducting studies, supervising students, and developing the task-centered model in new, ingenious ways. Thirteen social agencies in Chicago collaborated by affording fieldwork placements for students and research case material. These agencies included medical and psychiatric hospitals and clinics, school social work departments in public elementary and high schools, child welfare agencies, and others. The project tests of the task-centered model included approximately 1,300 cases handled by students in Chicago agencies between 1970 and 1977. Of this entire group, a smaller number became the sample for the research on processes and outcomes. The practitioners in the American project were nearly all graduate social work students. A number of studies were undertaken in England, using experienced practitioners.

The mission of the Task-Centered Project was to develop technologies that could be learned efficiently, increase the effectiveness of direct services, and increase the ability to conduct research on treatment practices. The first three years of the project, roughly from 1970 to 1973, saw the design of the basic task-centered model. Its processes and effects were studies in actual case practice. With the publication of *Task-Centered Casework* (W. J. Reid and L. Epstein, New York: Columbia University Press) in 1972, the model attracted interest in agencies throughout the country and abroad. Practitioners and researchers from many settings began to test and develop the model. A specialized literature began to appear. References can be found at the end of each chapter in this book.

Many of the case examples I have used have come from actual cases handled in the project. Others are from practice supervised by former doctoral students. All cases have been disguised; the names of the agencies have been withheld to prevent improper disclosures.

The technical guidelines described in this book are my attempt to distill and arrange the product of years of model building and practice. Wherever possible guidelines are derived from practice research conducted in the project and from published practice research conducted elsewhere. Since the end of the project in 1978, it has been necessary to rely on personal contacts and published reports from numerous sources to obtain new information. A good deal of practice experience and innovation occurs in day-to-day work and is not published. Sometimes, it is possible to get such information by word of mouth.

The origins of the task-centered model are varied and represent selections and revisions from a host of ideas and practices that preceded it. Although many questions about the task-centered model remain, years of research-based practice and evaluations of that practice support the conclusion that task-centered practice is effective in reducing many of the problems encountered in a range of agencies.

Many central ideas of the task-centered model have combined with ideas of practice that have other origins. The task-centered model has been adapted to coexist within an eclectic practice framework. This second edition of the book explains how the task-centered approach can be used flexibly. This means considering more settings than originally conceived, and harmonizing the task-centered model with additions and rearrangements by mixing and matching other compatible approaches.

The many clients, students, and agencies who cooperated by giving their effort and resources to this endeavor have been indispensable in making the work possible. Helen Mansfield, the Department of Health, Education, and Welfare (predecessor of the Department of Health and Human Services), aided in shaping the early presentation of this model.

I am indebted to colleagues from the original project: Professor William J. Reid of the State University of New York at Albany; Associate Professor Lester B. Brown, Wayne State University; Associate Professor Ronald Rooney, University of Minnesota at Minneapolis; Associate Professor Anne E. Fortune, Virginia

Commonwealth University; Associate Professor Eleanor R. Tolson, University of Illinois (at Chicago); and Assistant Professor Robert Basso at the Wilfrid Laurier University in Waterloo, Ontario, Canada. To Gwendolynn Graham, who put the original manuscript into readable form, my very great thanks. Also, I sincerely appreciate the constructive comments and suggestions I received from reviewers at different stages in the development of this text: Ronald H. Rooney, University of Minnesota; Craig W. LeCroy, Arizona State University; Jack F. Finley, Portland State University; and Debbie D. Hoffman, Belmont College. I am extremely grateful to Dean Laurence Lynn, and Associate Deans Jeanne Marsh and William Pollack for the resources they provided so that I could carry on this revision.

—*Laura Epstein*

PART I

FUNDAMENTALS OF BRIEF TREATMENT

Brief treatment is prominent in the repertoire of psychosocial clinicians in the present and the foreseeable future. The gist of brief treatment is that many, perhaps most, contemporary clients want to put in a reasonable amount of time and money in return for a demonstrable result that seems to "do good." People today are result-oriented and tend to view therapy as a humane technology directed at acquiring a relatively measurable degree of definable well-being. A great deal of clinical work is done in the public sector or is subsidized by government and philanthropy. The agencies that underwrite and fund treatment want to have some assurance that what is done and paid for in the name of treatment is reasonably effective, relatively harmless, and modestly priced. That is what authorities mean when they say they want treatment that is "accountable."

Long-term treatment has been slowly acquiring a "bad name," which it does not deserve. A great many different problems and issues concerning psychotherapy have been collected under the disparaging rubric of "long-term treatment." Problematic issues emerged as psychotherapy became established as an integral part of the social landscape. As its novelty and fascination have worn off, it has become relatively commonplace instead of an unusual, mysterious happening behind closed doors. The print and television media have thoroughly publicized what occurs in therapy, even though some of what appears in public information channels is not as accurate as it should be and tends to be oversimplified. Questions have arisen about the value of the results of therapy, the quality and training of practitioners, and the ethics of providing psychotherapy to impoverished populations without also enabling them to possess the necessities of modern life, such as proper education, good job opportunities and housing, and wholesome social environments.

Long-term treatments are mostly associated with and in some way based on the theoretical foundation of psychoanalysis. For decades, these treatments were the most desirable, provided by a small elite cadre of therapists, originally medically trained psychoanalysts. Later other types of therapists developed, including psychiatrists, social workers, psychologists, and various types of counselors.

These original or traditional therapies were based on the idea that human problems were deeply embedded, hard to perceive and understand, and hard to change. Psychoanalysis was hailed in the United States by new therapy professions—social work, psychology, and psychiatry—to which it offered sets of flexible methods to change people's minds and presumably also their actions. Mind-changing had become an important idea in the conduct of the world's affairs.

Long-term treatments provided a reason for the existence and expansion of new therapy professions and their offshoots. Particularly for women, the therapy profession as practiced in social work offered a career option that was new, newsworthy, and interesting, and that provided entry into uncharted territory that was considered valuable and virtuous. Long-term treatments originally offered post–World War II society a means to develop oversight structures to subdue dysfunctional and anti-social behaviors that were at odds with social norms and that threatened progress.

A chastened and skeptical post-modern society today wonders about its not too subtle devotion to the ideals and customs of the therapeutic ideal as it evolved in the last several decades. A better informed citizenry and a more sophisticated professional establishment, after 50 years of experience with modem psychotherapy, have raised knowledgeable questions about psychotherapy and its discontents. Thus it has come about that brief therapy, once regarded as a second-rate practice, has been rediscovered as a way to tighten up treatment, remove excess baggage, improve it realistically, and make it fit within a lean and cost-conscious modern world that was no longer capable of being easily swayed by romantic ideas about human perfectibility.

Brief treatment is basic psychotherapy and basic psychosocial intervention in individual and family lives. It exists to help people improve their social relations in any relevant sphere, and to obtain and use the skills and resources this society has available to achieve a satisfactory mode of living.

The amount of time used in therapy is not an issue. It is illogical and incorrect to assume that more is better in psychotherapy, because what is at issue is not the measured amount of therapy but the quality and contents of therapy. It is also illogical and incorrect to assert that less is better. There is no evidence on either side of this conundrum. What is at issue is what is done, whether it is done systematically and in accordance with standards, and whether what is done is targeted on some problem of importance that should be and can be improved by the end of the treatment.

This is not to say that questions about the appropriate amount of therapy are unimportant. Rather it is to face up to the fact that it is not presently known with any exactness just what amount and what type of therapy is best, or is the treatment of choice. The questions of amount and time need and undoubtedly will receive in the future serious attention by the researchers and developers of therapies. For the present, there are useful indications, many of which will be suggested in this book. There remains the necessity for using solid professional judgment in making clinical decisions.

Brief therapy is fundamentally a matter of reducing the impact of a problem or set of closely related problems. Brief treatment is a means of reducing the impact on a person, or a set of related persons, of a problem or set of closely related problems: that is, problem solving. It does not matter whether the problem is perceived as being located primarily in the inner person—an intrapsychic problem, or whether the problem is one of interpersonal conflict of any sort, or whether the problem is located in the environment—in the arena of the person-environment transactions. Any type of problem may be formulated so as to be capable of being subjected to the methods of brief treatment. There are no inherent reasons for limiting brief treatment to a single sequence. If a good case can be made for the need for additional treatment, additional sequences can be planned. Also therapy can be intermittent, meaning clients can return for "booster shots" or for further work on the same or different problems if they are interested and able to do so.

Brief treatment today is a practical, modern approach that aims to reduce and ameliorate problems in living of many sorts. It is not a restrictive modality. It has considerable research support. It is adaptable to many types of situations based on client interests and clinical judgment.

CHAPTER ONE

PROBLEMS

Where Services Start

PROBLEMS AND PROBLEM DEFINITIONS: THE IMPORTANCE OF PROBLEM DEFINITION IN BRIEF TREATMENT

When we approach the professional process of clinical intervention, or treatment, we take for granted the idea of problem as some intricate unsettled issue, a source of perplexity, distress, and vexation. We are less accustomed to the view that problems are social constructions (Kitsuse & Spector, 1973; Spector & Kitsuse, 1974).

The degree of consensus about what problem definitions should be tends to be weak in some areas and strong in others.

Customarily, therapists have assumed that the diagnosis or assessment formulated in any case is the problem definition, in the sense that the assessment presumably directs the practitioner toward the focal issues of treatment. Traditionally the assessment has been a judgment of what the problem is, plus a condensed evaluation of the people and social situation in which the problem is found (Siporin, 1975, pp. 219–249). A typical psychodynamic formulation of the assessment holds that we "make a psychosocial assessment to ascertain what is troubling the client and what personal and situational variables are contributing to the distress" (Strean, 1978, pp. 131–132). In brief treatment, the problem area that is to be the focus is more narrow and constrained than in the traditional formulations. The assessment made in brief treatment is pulled together and organized to produce a problem definition that is a short description and the focus of treatment.

Historically, there has been confusion in terms used to conceptualize the nature of the unit or thing meant by the term *problem*. We have talked and written about presenting problems, underlying problems, real problems, basic problems, requests, focal problems, and target problems. There are no clearly distinguishable delimitations of these various terms. *Presenting problem* appears to refer to a *presenting complaint* or the client's or referral source's specific view at the time of first contact about what is wrong, what should be done, and what is wanted. Thus, common usage seems to define *presenting problem* as a combination of problem as perceived by the client and request. But the term *presenting problem* contains a connotation of superficial overlay, a cover for the real or underlying problem which is the crucial problem that the practitioner has to discover. Once uncovered, the practitioner is supposed to try to lift the real problem to the center of attention, to the "focus." The term *basic problem* is sometimes used as a synonym for the *underlying problem* that has yet to be discovered, or the *real problem*. *Requests* are usually associated with the diminished meaning of *presenting problem,* and used as a representation of the underlying problem that has to be discovered. *Focal problem* and *target problem* are similar in that both refer to the problem that will be the focus of attention for the treatment.

Target problem, a term usually associated with the task-centered approach, also includes the idea that the problem has been agreed to by the client and represents the problem as perceived by the client.

In today's practice world, there are no hard rules about what kinds of problems are suitable for brief therapy and what problems are ruled out. That issue has been supplanted by a drive for cost-effectiveness and interventions that are effective under particular circumstances. It is now recognized that the value of treatment is not related to how long a person spends in treatment, but rather to what goes on during the treatment to enable clients to feel understood and hopeful; to better understand themselves, their problem, and their circumstances; and to achieve some modest and desirable goal in changed behavior and social circumstances. The changes may not be world-shaking but will surely make a difference in how the client gets along and achieves the personal relationships and the practical things needed.

Problems that are the focus of clinical work are those that have immediately discernible impact on an individual person and on the immediate family and intimate friends. These problems are thought of as being inside the person (intrapsychic), outside the person (environmental, social context), interpersonal (between individuals). For example, a central problem of pervasively low self-esteem may be located entirely within the individual; but a problem of low self-esteem may be a product of discriminatory and hostile attitudes toward women, toward ethnic groups, toward people with disabilities, and thus be a problem produced or maintained by an exploitative relationship with a parent, spouse, or authority and by sociocultural structures, such as racism and patriarchy.

This example of a common problem illustrates how important it is to define the problem carefully in order to create a focus for treatment. In brief treatment, where we are so much interested in efficiency, it is very important that the problem be defined as specifically as possible so as to be a boundary for both client and practitioner, delimiting just what areas of a problem are to be the focus and how the goal is to be visualized. In this way, a push can be created to get things accomplished.

In brief treatment, problem definition is a prerequisite to planning the treatment. There are various methods available for defining problems in brief treatment, as we shall see later on, and no one method is superior for all conditions. But without an understandable and relatively specific problem definition, focus will wander widely, time and energy will be dissipated, clients will become dissatisfied, and brief treatment will be ineffective or lose its verve. In terms of the three central ideas of brief treatment—planning, focus, and brevity—a reasonable and sensible problem definition is a condition of achieving the time limits, formulating a workable plan, and implementing a sturdy focus.

All models of brief treatment define the problem focus at the start, meaning somewhere within the first to third interview. However, the specific details about what is included in the problem definition vary according to the terms of the model. For example, Mann, in the model he calls time-limited psychotherapy, focuses on a life central issue, that is, the chronic pain which has pursued an individual over a life course (Mann, 1981). Sifneos, a pioneer of brief treatment in the psychodynamic genre, in his model named short-term anxiety-provoking psychotherapy (STAPP), defines the problem for which his model is to be used as the client's enduring maladaptive relationship in an unresolved, chronic oedipal conflict (Sifneos, 1987). Bauer and Kobos (1987) define the problem for work in their model as "any assessed psychopathology" connected to a selected core conflict. The Parad and Parad (1990) crisis intervention model defines the problem for work in their approach as a threat and disequilibrium associated with a precipitating event.

Other writers on crisis intervention suggest a wide variety of types of problems that are defined as the focus for crisis interventions (Roberts, 1990). Beck and his collaborators have been developing and testing for many years a brief treatment model for treating the focal problems of depression and anxiety (Beck, Rush, Shaw, & Emery, 1979). Klerman, Weissman, Rounsaville, and Chevron (1984) have a well-developed and well-regarded brief treatment model addressed to the focal problem of depression. Strupp and Binder (1984) define problems for work in the model developed by them and their associates, time-limited dynamic psychotherapy, as "an interference with current living."

The task-centered model is unique in having emerged from the clinical practices of social work rather than from psychology or psychiatry. Its guidelines call for concentration on the *target problem*, which the client determines and the practitioner accepts. Target problem concentration is intended to minimize deadlocks when clients are resistant or reluctant to accept the practitioner's problem focus, and to maximize motivation by adhering to what the client wants and is willing to do. The client's focus may be, and often is, changed in the course of the client-practitioner work.

The main criterion for defining the problem and focus is congruence with the client's interests. Attention to the problem in the client's own terms is an ethical consideration. The task-centered model's position is based on respect for the client's independence and rights to exercise choice about what is going to happen. As in all models of brief treatment, the problem definition and formulation in the task-centered model (TC hereafter) defines the condition or state that is to be affected by the intervention program. The problem is the target of change.

TC is addressed to the problems in everyday living. Thus, constantly encountered psychological, environmental, and social interaction problems become the subject of professional intervention. This occurs when people request help voluntarily, are referred by an agency, or are required by courts or other authoritative bodies to take help, and when they cannot carry out effective problem-reducing actions on their own or through informal helpers. The purpose of TC is to enable and empower clients to solve or ameliorate their problems by assuming appropriately formulated tasks with proper support. How the problem is formulated influences the focus selected and the treatment plan. TC may overlap with or be integrated with many of the types of problem definitions in the various psychodynamic brief treatment models referred to already. But TC differs in undertaking problem-solving programs with clients whose problems can be worked with only or primarily in terms of interpersonal conflicts or conflicts and dysfunctions in relation to the environment and in the client's immediate social context.

DILEMMAS OF PROBLEM IDENTIFICATION

Which problems do I work on? Who decides? How is it decided? What is the rationale for a particular choice? How much change is necessary? According to what criteria? How much change is sufficient? What are the consequences of failing to solve a problem? These questions are uppermost in the minds of practitioners as they approach each helping situation. Answering these questions requires judgments about goals, priorities, assessment, and feasible focus. Practitioners need to pursue several trains of thought to make an appropriate judgment that leads to a focus. This chapter and Chapter 2, "Intervention Frameworks," discuss the basis for deciding on a focus and planning the implementation. Most dilemmas of problem identification may be perceived as falling into three areas: the indeterminate quality of personal problems, the relativity of problem definitions, and the complexity in the process of problem defining.

The Indeterminate Quality of Personal Problems

The types of personal problems that arrive in the offices of human service practitioners are associated with multiples of problem conditions. Some of the more prominent problem conditions are lack of resources or skills, often the results of real deficits or deprivation; personal unhappiness in feelings and interpersonal relationships; disturbing consequences of ineffectiveness and failure in major and important life tasks, such as work, love, friendships, and self-respect; and deviance, which places the person in conflict with himself or with family, peers, and authorities.

Personal problems can be viewed in varying ways. One of the ways problems can be thought of is that they are predominantly the result of unfairness and insensitivity of social institutions, for example, inequality in the distribution of educational, health, housing, and vocational opportunities. Inequalities of social status and wealth complicate these issues. Problems can be viewed as the result of poor schools, racial prejudice, stigma, and discrimination. From a different viewpoint, some of us think that unhappiness and ineffectiveness may be the result of emotional disturbances, cognitive disturbances, poor performance skills, and threats and challenges to a more or less steady state in life.

Personal problems may result from or be associated with *deviance,* that is, behavior departing markedly from accepted norms and that has a public character calling for intervention by authorities. Deviants significantly depart from approved behaviors and lifestyles. They develop conflicted interactions with those around them, especially families, teachers, and employers, and also with organizations and staffs authorized to help and control them. The etiology of deviance, however, is subject to considerable controversy. However, the labeling of deviant individuals or groups is relative. Not everyone agrees on particular designations. Furthermore, conditions deplored at one period of time become less important under other historical circumstances; and conditions that have been dormant for long periods of time later emerge as social crises (Kitsuse & Spector, 1973; Merton, 1971; Piven, 1981; Spector & Kitsuse, 1974).

When persons with problems are widely spread out in a neighborhood, region, or society, their individual conditions may become aggregated and packaged into discernible patterns of social life, for example, "the underclass," "single moms," "drug related," "perpetrators," and "victims." To acquire public recognition, the community has to be prepared to understand the condition. That is likely to be the case if the public perceives the problem as being intrinsically real, observable, and having some understandable cause, and if they are willing to act collectively to protect themselves or the problem bearers. In addition, the public has to believe or have faith that it is possible to correct the problem now or in the near future (Thio, 1978).

Individual problems experienced by a single person or by a small group are aspects of wider social problems. Individual problems are affected by and in turn influence a family, peers, and formal or informal organizations with which the individual is in contact. Individual problems (for example, depression, anxiety, or low self-esteem) have common features that make it possible to classify or at least label them descriptively and communicate about them. However, individual problems also have distinctively particular aspects, leading to the perception of a high degree of uniqueness in problem experiences. No two persons experience depression in identical ways. Depression is always an individual experience even though it partakes of many common elements.

Sociologists prominent in the study of social problems who adopt the social interaction perspective (Becker, 1966) consider opinion to be the essence of a social problem. They believe that conditions become defined as problems by a complex and fluid process. The process of problem definition centers on the issue of who defines the problems and how the problem definers decide on the definition. Problem definers are those who give voice to an issue and who exercise power to declare the existence and parameters of a problem. Problem defining takes place in social interactions. Decisions that identify some condition as a problem emerge in a variety of contexts. Problems get identified in interactions within families and among peers; in a community, labor, or special-interest organization; between the readers and writers of newspapers and magazines; between the viewers and the producers and commentators of television accounts; between teachers and students, workers and supervisors, and management and labor; within professional organizations; among scholars and researchers and their various publics; and among politicians or between politicians and their constituents. In other words, throughout varied and multiple social interactions, the nature of and the opinion about some behaviors and conditions produce the perception that a condition is a problem.

The Relativity of Problem Definitions

Defining problems is a continuous and changing process. Who defines and what is defined reflect how a social order is functioning at a particular time. Social problems are defined and redefined in the process in which individuals, families, groups, and organizations experience the stresses produced by modern living with its industrialization, urbanization, and technological, political, and ideological movements. This process produces changes in the ways that agencies organize services and methods for the control, treatment, and alleviation of individual and family problems. Over time there develop varying emphases by government, research, and practice organizations to change and develop content of treatment methodologies and their applications (Allen, 1981). Even particular individuals change the way they perceive their own problems.

A recently and highly publicized social and individual problem is child abuse, a subject formerly given so little public attention that it did not appear in the *Reader's Guide to Periodical Literature* until 1968. Before that cruelty to children was indexed intermittently. The Library of Congress changed its primary entry to "child abuse" in 1968 and most of the major indexes followed suit (Nelson, 1984). Similarly, recent additions to the roster of important social terms noting problems are the "feminization of poverty," and "single mother" (earlier labeled as "unmarried mother," with a different set of beliefs about causes and treatment). Other fairly recently identified problems, or problems identified differently from their earlier versions, are "homelessness" (formerly regarded as mainly the problem of skid row alcoholics, or "stranded men" as they were known), and "battering" or "spousal abuse" or "domestic violence" (what used to be known as "wife beating"). Having an abortion was once considered a problem; then, after the Supreme Court decision in *Roe v. Wade*, 410 U.S. 113 (1973), abortion for many became a solution. Now abortion legislation has become a problem for some people—a new problem. Homosexuality is a condition that has and has not been considered a problem, depending on the historical era.

The changing nature of problem defining is, in part, a result of a constantly increasing and improving quality of social science knowledge about the human condition in the modern world. It is also the result of fads that rapidly infiltrate professional thought and behavior and spread by effective dissemination in the media. The perception and importance of problems also change under different political, ideological, and cultural conditions. Furthermore, the wide dissemination and approval of therapeutic intervention offer the expectation of problem reduction for problems when they are conceived as individually rooted psychological or emotional disturbance or illness.

Reporting on a study of the process of problem formulation, Proctor and Rosen (1983) state, "In nearly every approach to systematic treatment, thorough and accurate problem formulation, or the assessment of what constitutes the client's problem, is a basic component of planning the overall intervention and is considered central to the success of treatment" (p. 22). Nevertheless, clinical judgments are not sufficiently reliable, and problem formulations vary widely among practitioners.

Many, if not most practitioners, believe that change in any domain of a client's functioning will affect other areas of functioning. Along with this belief is the notion that any treatment must deal with the core, covert, basic, or underlying problem for effective change to occur.

However, the empirical evidence available fails to support beliefs about the significance of particular underlying causes (such as specific family environment, dramatic or traumatic experiences, or constitutional abnormality) thought to give rise to a particular pattern of disordered behavior (Kanfer & Saslow, 1969, p. 423).

There is also no evidence in the empirical literature of a direct link between insight and symptom relief (Fisher & Greenberg, 1977, p. 412).

Complexity of Defining Social and Personal Problems

Defining the target problem calls for exercising informed and discriminating judgment about persons and the important features of their *social context*. The physical and social environment and surroundings, cultural, ethnic, age, socioeconomic, and status considerations, and sometimes the politics of the community, may together produce a context that decisively shapes the appearance, content, and meaning of a client's problems.

The context may also figure in the practitioner's deciding what interventions to use. For example, the problem may be defined in such a way as to make a good fit with a known and preferred intervention program already organized and supported by some elements among the public or within the helping professions. Some interventions may have better reputations than others at various times, and, accordingly, will tend to be preferred, and so the problems tend to be defined to fit the capabilities of the preferred intervention program. Some problems are of greater interest to the public, clients, the media, and professionals. Naming the problem, describing and specifying it, attributing importance, deciding on goals to shoot for, making realistic plans, selecting interventions with a good track record—all these call for judgments that are difficult to make. So many things have to be considered, and often there is insufficient information or knowledge to underpin firm decision making. At the same time, there is almost always pressure to make fast judgments decisively.

The tension that exists in making judgments about problem definition is between focusing primarily on the individual person, individual traits, attributes, character, personality, and psychopathology, and focusing primarily on concrete changes in the environment and/or in the habitual patterns of social interaction. It is not uncommon to view a problem as being primarily within the general social structure that provides work, health, education, housing, opportunity, and so forth, and yet find that professional preference and style concentrate on a portion of an individual's dysfunctional behavior or attitudes and feelings. It is also common to take a global approach to personal dysfunction, that is, to define a problem with excessive breadth. These tensions always exist and are based on the nature of the helping disciplines. Attempting to tackle these issues makes counseling difficult, challenging, and important and develops the background of experience and professional thinking that is the distinction of the helping disciplines.

To illustrate the dilemmas facing the professional attempting to define a problem, three major social problems—poverty, child abuse, and mental disorder—are briefly described in the following section. They vividly reveal the kinds of issues that typically appear as one attempts to define problems falling into the broad categories of poverty, child abuse, and mental illness. Some general guidelines will be suggested; the balance of this book develops these and other techniques in greater detail.

MAJOR SOCIAL PROBLEMS

POVERTY

DEFINING THE PROBLEM WHEN THE CLIENT IS POOR

Poverty exerts strong influence on lifestyle and is a condition impossible to ignore. Problem definitions must take it into account in every instance. The practitioner's framework of thought should have taken into account the influence on behavior, attitudes, and lifestyle of poverty and its associated conditions, such as poor housing, poor schooling, and limited neighborhood childcare and recreational facilities. This framework needs to include numerous elements:

- A specialized knowledge about poverty and its consequences.
- An attitude of openness in order to observe and understand, without condescension, the realities of low-income and minority lifestyles and culture.
- A special attentiveness to the conditions of many women with children but without spouses, of working women earning unfair and inadequate wages and salaries, lacking adequate affordable daycare, and of elderly women, never married or widowed.
- A sensitivity to clues about the client's attitudes and feelings, such as suspiciousness resulting from experiences with hostile authorities, including other professionals; resistance, reluctance, caution, or protectiveness about making disclosures for fear of being misunderstood, criticized, humiliated, frustrated; mistrustfulness of the professional relationship leading to denial, misstatements, and similar distortions; readiness to be angry and respond quickly or suddenly out of experiencing unbearable frustration or humiliation that may have been accumulating over hours or days; a dependent and demanding attitude, often a strategy for minimizing resentment or appealing to the practitioner.

In addition, women, single mothers, and members of ethnic minorities have unique patterns of response to discriminatory and impoverished conditions, to personal relationships, and in the way they view themselves. These patterns are related to their particular status and to stereotypes about them. In such complex circumstances, the problem definition has to be simplified. If not, the problem exploration will go on interminably, or may result in a stereotypical evaluation that is useless or harmful.

The key to formulating a problem definition that takes account of poverty, race, gender, and ethnic factors is to avoid scrupulously any prepackaged definition. Instead, having general knowledge about poverty and the other relevant conditions, one should carefully and thoroughly explore in detail just how it is that the client defines the problem, that is, what the client thinks the problem is. Once the client's perception has been established, it is possible to shape a useful problem definition. Professional knowledge guides the process through specific steps to clarify the problem, makes sure it has been stated accurately, makes sure the definition takes into account the way the problem reflects poverty (and race or gender), sifting through the information to identify, explain, and make some judgments about the problem's nature. (See Chapter 6.)

This means, for example, that poor clients ought to be provided not only with material resources but also with needed and wanted counseling, planning, support, and social services. It means that poverty will not be misinterpreted as psychosocial pathology and treated as an illness. It means that psychosocial maladjustments should be treated in ways that are acceptable to the clients and that reflect the best available professional knowledge.

CASE 1–1   *RITA AND JOSEPH*

Presenting Problems

Rita and Joseph were children of a welfare mother. Public assistance benefits (cash payments plus food stamps and Medicaid) maintained the family, but at a level below the poverty line. Joseph is 11; his sister Rita is 8. They are black children living in a deteriorated neighborhood. Before Joseph and Rita were born, this neighborhood was crowded. Two main business streets were heavily trafficked and noisy. There were lots of shops. The merchandise was overpriced. Bright, ugly signs grabbed you. The "El" train ran on top of one of the main streets. Every block had some variant of tavern, gyp joint, greasy spoon, welfare office, bank, gambling and drug joint, or mental health clinic. Gangs fought. For ten years the neighborhood burned; today, empty lots are cluttered with bricks. Buildings are shells; here and there a block or a building stands in the rubble. The streets are dangerous. The two main streets are deserted. Urban renewal high-rises and town houses show up strangely. The real estate speculators are there. The urban renewal experts are there. The school attended by Joseph and Rita used to be a loud, teeming place. Now it has empty rooms and lots of special education classes.

Joseph and Rita live in an apartment with their 31-year-old mother and two younger sisters. Their mother is on welfare. She came to this northern city from the South twelve years ago. She has never had any paid employment; she has been on welfare during most of her years in the city.

Joseph and Rita were referred to the school social worker because they were dirty. This is a mandated problem but of relatively low power: that is, no one is likely to be deprived of liberty or subjected to police action for poor body hygiene. But this problem raises potentially more important ones: the mother might be labeled "neglectful" and become subject to investigatory procedures; the children and mother might be pressured by school officials, reported to the welfare department, and so forth. Because cleanliness is a high priority in our society, it is sometimes believed that a parent who fails to keep children clean may be doing worse things, may be guilty of neglect, even abuse, for instance.

The teacher who referred Joseph and Rita for a dirtiness problem had both children in her room, an ungraded learning disability (LD) class. The two children were first interviewed by a social worker. Joseph was a spontaneous, lively, talkative child; Rita was his follower, quiet, shy, and depending on big brother to talk for her and fight for her. When Rita wanted to add something or change something Joseph was telling the social worker, the girl would gesture to Joseph and whisper.

The social worker told the children the reason for the referral. They denied the accusation. They were only dirty from being on the playground. They had different woes (target problems): the teacher was unfair to them, singling them out for criticism when they acted no differently from the other children; they did not know why they had been put in an LD class; and they did not know what to do to get out of the class.

The children agreed that the social worker visit their mother. She did and found the apartment clean, the laundry facilities adequate, the quantity of clothing adequate. The mother showed the social worker her things to defend herself against the false accusation of uncleanliness. The mother's target problems were that she had never been informed her children were to be placed in an LD class (a violation of law in that state if true) and that the white teacher was prejudiced against black kids.

The practitioner's judgment was that Joseph and Rita were, in his experience, average in cleanliness and in their mother's attention to cleanliness. What came through was the family's distress and indignation at the children's being labeled LD—dumb. The family blamed the school officials; they thought the teacher was prejudiced and generally unfair.

Environmental Context

Rita and Joseph are poor and black. The combination of ethnic minority status with poverty is a powerful conditioner. "To be poor in America is to let America down—to let that Pepsi image down; to let the American dream down; to not do your share, carry your weight, lift up your corner of the flag" (Sidel, 1986, p. 9).

Low-income and minority clients are not a homogeneous group. Minority populations are represented at all economic levels, but whites outnumber non-whites among the poor. Life in poverty and minority status is not stereotypically bleak, disadvantaged, deficit-ridden, or meager. It is different from the lifestyle ordinarily pursued by the majority, and it is unfair and overstressed. It is sometimes full of justified fear, anxiety, and suspicion. It is generally understood among scholars that observing, acquiring knowledge about, and resisting stereotypical thinking are among the most important conditions for making accurate and fair assessments of minorities and poor people (Lorion & Parron, 1985; Solomon, 1976).

It takes immense effort, planning, and resourcefulness to provide for oneself and a family on food stamps, welfare, unemployment insurance, or minimum wages. Poverty is an endless series of unpredictable crises, calling for shifting meager resources from one necessity to another. Everything needs repair. Credit at stores is rarely available. Borrowed funds have to be taken out at exorbitant rates and no money can be saved because it is all spent on current necessities. Daily decisions are necessary to survive the reality of economic hardship. One can often see the resourcefulness, or at least the rationale, behind apparent "impulsiveness" and short-term planning.

In the case of Rita and Joseph, neither the family nor the school raised any problems having to do with financial matters, housing, health, employment, or other conditions related to socioeconomic status. Nor was adequacy of the children's education dealt with directly.

We are left with a number of unanswered questions: Was there prejudicial intent in perceiving these children as dirty and possibly neglected? Was there lack of sensitivity to the stress the mother was under, managing on her welfare grant? How did that stress affect the children? Did the fact that the family was black lead to an assumption that the children were not clean enough and were mentally inferior?

These questions were not thoroughly explored. Should they have been or how might they have been explored, because at no time did the mother raise any question about her economic circumstances? The practitioner needed to rely on observations and sensitivity. The economic facts, the low-grade housing, and the unattractive, dangerous neighborhood all suggest that many of the stresses described earlier existed to some extent and that, if they did not actively produce or exacerbate the presenting problem, they created tensions that added weight to the problem.

Interpersonal and Personal Features: Are Poor People Special?

Contemporary scholarly research and theory in the specialized psychological and interpersonal characteristics of ethnic minorities and the poor are not well developed. Interculturally skilled counseling is a priority of the National Institute of Mental Health, the American Psychological Association, the National Association of Social Workers, and other professional and public organizations. The governing ideas about personality theories and human development represent core values of the Western industrialized world of Europe and North America and are middle-class values at that. The available ethnic-sensitive literature, although voluminous, is widely distributed among many sources, some of them not well known, and much of it has been criticized as being of poor quality (Pedersen, 1985).

Are Joseph and Rita Special?

Joseph and Rita are black, and some distinctive psychosocial features of black culture noted by contemporary observers are seen in their case. For example, the majority of black children have never been able to have a protected childhood, and black children know and understand this. Black children early confront a reality that contains racism and illegal and violent events in their immediate neighborhoods and perhaps even in their own homes. Exposure to harsh conditions often speeds the development of adaptive behaviors that enable them to survive in a hostile environment. And there is among blacks a tradition of older children caring for younger siblings and being given jobs and chores as a way of preparing for an adult work life (Jones, 1985). Elmer (1981) has graphically detailed the association of poverty conditions with problem attitudes and behaviors of children, such as chronic fearfulness and sadness, apathy, and lack of energy.

Joseph and Rita's mother seems a strong person, able to fend off official criticism about her childcare and personal hygiene. She probably approved of Joseph's baby-sitting job, wanting to help him grow independent in a society that will not make things easy. She probably encourages Joseph and Rita to stick together and encourages the older boy to take care of and protect his more vulnerable sister.

However, when the mother was summoned to school to confer about the children's academic problems, her strength may have failed her, and she may have turned to her manfriend to take care of something she feared to confront. Or, perhaps she thought a man would be more respected by the school authorities than a woman. Perhaps her manfriend tried to protect her by not telling her all that had transpired at the school when he authorized the children to be placed in the LD classroom. Perhaps he told her and she forgot. Still, why had the school accepted approval of the transfer to an LD classroom by a person not known to be the children's guardian? The tenor of the case referral from the school suggests rather strong disapproval of the mother. She must have been suspicious of the school authorities and revealed her situation only in the smallest bits absolutely necessary without volunteering much. All these behaviors and interpersonal transactions can be understood as normal reactions to real and perceived threats in the situation and as careful attempts to deal with a threatening bureaucracy.

The school may have misinterpreted the children's home life because of inadequate perception of adaptive or normal behaviors common among some, or perhaps many, black families. Problems may have been perceived where there were none, or the problems of concern to the family may have been different from the ones identified. Tensions about contradictory views of the problem were understood by the practitioner in this case. She eventually used a conference of all parties to separate facts from supposition and accusation.

CHILD ABUSE

Protective services are the basic means for intervening in cases of abuse. Family problems that result in the neglect, abuse, or exploitation of children normally are channeled into *protective services,* that is, services sanctioned by law in state and federal statutes, requiring investigation and interventions, including services to persons who do not want intervention and are involved involuntarily. In fact, services are often initiated by a third party report, that is, a complaint coming in over a hotline operated by officially designated public child welfare organizations. The obligation to protect is in conflict with a basic theme of the task-centered model, namely to legitimate client voluntarism. This is a conflict that cannot be easily reconciled; it can be glossed over, or in some circumstances, ignored, but it will not go away.

Child abuse is a public issue. A study sponsored by the National Center on Child Abuse and Neglect reported 652,000 maltreated children out of a child population of children under 18 of 61,900,000, or an incidence rate of 10.5 per 1,000 children. Sexual abuse, which receives high publicity, accounts for a small number of abuse cases involving 44,700 children, or an incidence of 0.7 per 1,000 children (Gelles & Cornell, 1985).

Child abuse is now accepted by the political, legislative, and administrative apparatus of government as a social problem about which public consensus has been developed. The press and television regularly disseminate information, some of it oversimplified or melodramatic. Keen public interest has linked child abuse to public issues of violence and personal autonomy (e.g., rape, wife battering, incest, sexual abuse, pornography, and attacks on the elderly, for example). The policy-making process has turned toward the social-psychosocial underlying problems (Nelson, 1984).

The intense media and legislative attention to child abuse creates its own dilemmas. Aware of the limitations of treatment technology to reduce or eliminate child abuse within the short time span often demanded by the public, professional practitioners develop harried, defensive, or evasive tactics.

Intervention in child abuse is multidisciplinary. Because child abuse is a medical, legal, and social problem, protective service workers work with judicial, police, medical, and legal personnel, as well as with professionals from social service agencies and community representatives. It has become common for protective services to be organized by a team of personnel, and to consist of packages of services put together to fit the individual characteristics of each case. Teams have broader access to numerous types of knowledge about interventions and consequently are thought to have access to comprehensive evaluations perceived to increase the validity of assessments and problem definitions.

Because there are so many actors involved in most child abuse cases, and because of the participation of several disciplines, there easily develop differences of opinion about how treatment should be designed. Professional jealousies and struggles over turf push and pull the decisions on problem definition, assessment, and intervention strategy in different directions. These differences must be compromised. A cooperative intervention calls for an eclectic posture.

Numerous social, environmental, and psychological factors are involved in child abuse problems. There are no simple generalizations about types, signs, and patterns of social, individual, and family problems involved in child abuse (Kadushin & Martin, 1988).

There are several types of explanations of family violence, but none of them is conclusive.

- The *psychiatric explanation* holds that the abusing parent is mentally disturbed, even though the prevailing impression is that only a small portion of family violence is attributable solely to personality traits, mental illness, or psychopathology.
- The *social-situational explanation* proposes that the personal problems of violent parents arise from interpersonal conflict, unemployment, isolation, unwanted pregnancy, and stress.
- *Social learning theory* suggests that people learn to be violent by growing up in violent homes.

- *Resource theory* suggests that persons of low status who lack resources may become violent as a way to assert power and dominance.
- *Ecological perspectives* explain family violence by society's support for the use of physical force to discipline children and the absence of public and private resources for family supports (Gelles & Cornell, 1985).

Some authorities hold that, despite the appearance of child abuse in middle-class and upper-class families, the problem is largely found among impoverished and deprived families. Their circumstances are thought to make them vulnerable to the stresses and deprivations that provide the necessary conditions to develop patterns of child abuse. Still, poverty in itself does not explain child abuse without mediating conditions such as individual particularities that create unusual vulnerability to stress and recourse to violent behavior (Pelton, 1981).

What are the recommended interventions? Currently, the theory and research available do not provide firm conclusions about what kinds of interventions are most likely to achieve desired results in cases of child abuse. Involuntary cases taken on to protect children and families are characterized by only modest success. The most successful approach may be one that is directed to situational changes. Parents seem to be helped by learning homemaking and parenting skills, developing regular routines, accepting a firm, supporting attitude from the practitioner, receiving highly structured statements of unambiguous expectations, with the practitioner demonstrating willingness to effect some concrete improvements in the client's living situation (Kadushin & Martin, 1988). Task-centered casework is recommended by Horowitz and Wolock (1981). There would seem to be a good case for using the task-centered approach because of its emphasis on providing resources and enhancing social skills.

Gelles and Cornell (1985) assert that intervention must protect the victim while preventing further violence, if possible, by strengthening the family (p. 134). It would follow that immediate crisis intervention is called for when children are at risk. Beyond crisis abatement, interventions that could be expected to protect victims or predicted victims should include homemaker services to augment the role of a poorly functioning or nonfunctioning mother, a hot line for on-the-spot assistance in parent-child crises, transportation, child care, counseling, health care, clothing and shelter, access to self-help groups, and other resources to ease the burdens of children and parents involved in such critical situations (Gelles & Cornell, 1985; Stein, 1981; Schuerman, Rzepnicki, & Littel, 1994).

Defining the Problem When Child Abuse Is Confirmed: The Task-Centered Approach

The problem definition in a protective case in which the client is involuntary or semivoluntary has two parts.

- The *target problem,* that is, the problem exactly as it is perceived by the client, and may be modified by the practitioner to the extent agreed by the client. Mandated problems should be defined according to the general task-centered rules for pinning down the individualized interests and concerns of the client. (See Chapter 6.)

■ The *mandated problem,* that is, the problem specifically as it is perceived by the governing authority, agency, court, law enforcement, or other duly sanctioned organization. Mandated problems are formulated according to the style and preferences of the authority responsible for stopping or preventing abuse. (See Chapter 6 for further discussion.)

In most instances, the two parts of the problem definition will contain the same or similar issues but probably in different form. To obtain the most impact, the target problem should contain as exactly as possible what the client sees as the feature or condition most troublesome. Often the client's problem will be lack of resources and the negative or harmful actions of others. The mandated problem must be kept in place by the practitioner's authority. The likelihood is that improvement in the target problem will either spill over into improvement in the mandated problem or will release some motivation for the client to work on the mandated problem.

MENTAL DISORDER

Mental disorder is a psychosocial-medical problem and is revealed in personal behaviors that deviate substantially from consensually understood norms. When deviations are channeled into the medical classification and treatment system, they are defined as *disease.* The disease formulation of mental disorder has two essential components: a given symptom or syndrome that is a recognized pattern of cognitive-affective-behavioral abnormalities, and an actual biological abnormality or belief that biological causation is a distinct possibility to be eventually confirmed or refuted by research.

However, mental disorder is more than a disease in the narrow medical sense. It is a set of ideas and personal-social actions that are presently unacceptable or incomprehensible. The presence of a known biological abnormality may or may not be discerned. Mental disorder is part of the whole social-psychological context in which a person lives (Wing, 1978).

Problems of mental illness are distributed throughout the human services system and can be dealt with in a wide variety of settings. They are often handled without the direct intervention of a psychiatrist when the problem is minor. If the problem is more severe or is chronic, the patient may need social support, resources, and skill enhancement, instead of, or in addition to, psychiatric treatment.

Mental illness is often treated in specialized clinics, particularly in community mental health clinics where the chief authorities are psychiatrists although they are the fewest in number. Professionals from the other helping disciplines carry most of the day-to-day treatment. It is common for psychologists, social workers, and nurses to acquire major responsibility for psychotherapy, short of prescribing and dispensing drugs.

Special Features of Defining Target Problems in Instances of Mental Disorder

If medical personnel are in charge, the diagnostic and treatment processes will normally follow a medical model. The central client will be viewed as a patient afflicted with an identifiable symptom or syndrome having a known or suspected underlying biological abnormality. The medical organization will define the problem in accordance with the classification system approved by the American Psychiatric Association in the fourth edition of its *Diagnostic and Statistical Manual of Mental Disorders* (1994). The standard procedures advocated in the *DSM IV* provide for appraisal of the client's pathology, physical condition, and social-environmental stress. These procedures legitimate the formulation of a problem definition that will include the relevant aspects of the problem in addition to the focus on psychopathology. Nevertheless, the usual procedure results in a strong focus on the disease aspects of the problem. The *DSM IV* is firmly oriented to the medical disease approach to psychopathology.

If nonmedical personnel are in charge, the style of work may nevertheless be dominated by the medical model that is influential throughout all the helping disciplines. There is no set of consensually approved rules for classification of psychosocial problems, making it likely that the *DSM IV* will be used even though not entirely applicable, if at all. However, the principle of making a problem definition that reflects the relationship between people and environments, the person-in-situation context, is well accepted. The individualized target problem definition recommended in the task-centered model, concentrating on what the client perceives, how he perceives it, and what people want to and can do about their problems, can be made perfectly clear. Even if the dominant practice preferences put high value on attending to theoretically determined underlying problems or classified psychopathology, practical professional common sense usually prevails.

Conflicts of opinion often develop when disputes arise between disciplines about how cases should be processed. Professional practitioners, colleagues, and supervisors may differ about how the client problem is to be defined and how the work is to be focused. Differences of opinion come about because of differences in professional education; contending value systems; and differentials of status, power, and authority.

The exception to emphasis on the target problem occurs when the client is incompetent, incapable, homicidal, or suicidal, and when action must be taken at once on his behalf to prevent clear and present harm.

The crucial decision about problem definition is to answer these questions: Which problem of major concern to the client, if ameliorated, would make the most difference in quality of life, and what are the feasible solutions to the problem?

DEFINING PROBLEMS FOR CLINICAL WORK

Defining the Problem: Describing, Specifying, and Naming

The problem definition delimits and succinctly explains the problematic issue at hand. The statement should describe, specify, and name the problem. To construct the problem definition is to make decisions, to the extent possible, about what is to be included or excluded and why.

Problems should be described clearly and specifically, and in sharp, exact, and vivid detail so they will be comprehensible to the client and to other professionals and collateral persons. Everybody involved should be able to comprehend what is being talked about and meant. It should be possible for another similarly trained professional observer to duplicate or repeat the same processes and extract the same or a similar description. Ambiguity is expected because of the complexities described and discussed earlier, but the practitioner's aim is to minimize ambiguity and to be clear about the uncertainty that does exist. Clarity pays off by making interventions better and more efficient. Though it is possible to leave some questions open, working closure is needed to implement an intervention program. If an inappropriate target has been decided upon, the plan will change.

There are yet other reasons for achieving closure, even though tentative, on the problem definition. We want to construct interventions to fit the problem, and we want to perceive the problem in sufficient detail to see at intervals whether it is abating, getting worse, or staying the same. Clarity and detail provide points of reference for comparing where we began and where we are now in the intervention and to help us determine whether or not the intervention is working. To perceive a change in the situation over the time of the intervention sequence encourages the client, collaterals, and professionals. Monitoring the ongoing process is an early warning system for ascertaining that all is not well and that the plan needs to be revised.

The specification component of the problem definition defines the essential characteristic or quality of the problem that pinpoints the focus. Specifying the problem helps client and practitioner convert the larger problem into pieces or bits that can then be utilized to fit into the concentrated work to reduce the problem.

Naming a problem is a communication device. The name is shorthand for a longer problem description and refers to some key distinguishing feature of the problem. The name of the problem is *not* the same as the problem classification adapted from the task-centered or any other typology, but rather is an individual characterization that comes from the particulars of the client and the client's situation.

Locating the Focus

The *focus* of the intervention work is the concentration point. If we review the case of Joseph and Rita, we can see the relationship between problem definition and focus.

First, the problem definition will *describe, specify,* and *name* the problem. Then the focus picks out a distinct image that captures the chief site of the problem. This site should conform to the client's perception and should generate specific tasks that can be worked on with a reasonable expectation of success and a reasonable amount of client motivation. The focus is obtained directly from the problem specification. The focus may be the same as the specification, but if it is different, it will vary in convenience of expression or style of the formulation, not in substance.

- *Problem described.* Joseph and Rita, and their mother, are seriously distressed and troubled. They all believe the school is unfair and discriminatory and has thus deprived the children of proper education (because the children have been placed in the learning disabled class). They think the teacher is unfair, singling the children out for criticism when they act no differently than other children. They do not know why they were put in the learning disabled class; and they do not know how to get out of it and into a regular class. Note is made of the school's view that the children may be neglected because they come to school dirty.
- *Problem specified.* The children fear the teacher and are shamed by their placement. Children and mother want this wrong rectified by placement in a regular class.
- *Problem named.* Conflict with school authorities.
- *Focus.* Clearing up why the children are in LD.

Combining Problem Definition and Focus

As we have seen, the focus is drawn out of the problem definition and is actually the problem definition put into operational terms. It is the problem to be ready for or in condition to be affected by problem-reducing work. For example, the focus with Joseph and Rita is *clearing up why the children are in LD.* When this is done, it is expected that the focus will change to *making an educational plan that is proper and satisfactory.*

The term *focus* is used in this book to refer to the concentration of the whole intervention. (Sometimes we speak of the focus of a single interview, but that is a temporary matter and a convenient expression.) At times it refers to the concentration point of a single interview or portion of an interview. The focus of intervention should be stable until the problem definition alters. An unstable case focus will lead to an inefficient drift in the work and may jeopardize effectiveness.

Managing Client–Practitioner Disagreement

Disagreement on focus can create an impasse that slows or stops the work. Avoiding the impasse or arriving at a compromise can minimize the obstacles. Disagreement can be avoided or reduced satisfactorily by achieving congruence between client and practitioner on the focus. Achieving congruence is more complicated if client and practitioner have very different perspectives or ideas and a struggle starts about whose ideas will prevail. The likelihood is that the practitioner will prevail in a straight power struggle because the practitioner has more power. However, the client may ultimately win by handling the practitioner skillfully, artfully, possibly deviously, and by discontinuing contact (Tolson & Brown, 1981). Compromise is the best way to ensure that the client's interests are genuinely attended to and the practitioner's professional judgments and recommendations are clearly given along with adequate opportunity for the client to give them proper consideration.

Identifying Mandated Problems

Mandated problems must be attended to by law, court order, or public sanction and should be placed in a focal position. Doing this often means that the case situation will be worked on with two foci: the client target problem and the mandated problem.

Problem Definition and Assessment

Problem definition and assessment are related concepts. The assessment is a set of observations, explanations, and interpretations that places the problem definition within an understandable context. General information about the client's life circumstances and major interpersonal relations compose the context.

The relationship between assessment, problem definition, and focus can be thought of as one of increasing specificity. The assessment is the most comprehensive and inclusive and attempts to formulate an answer to the question, "What is the trouble, the whole trouble?" The problem definition proceeds to narrow the terrain by answering the question, "What exactly is the trouble here and now?" The problem definition attempts to say, "The trouble here is this." The focus makes a statement, saying "Here is what we concentrate on." (See Chapters 6 and 7 for more about assessment and focus.)

Problem Definition and Practical Judgment

Practitioners in the human services professions need to be broadly knowledgeable about human conditions and the social contexts of living. No one ever knows enough, but an individual can have sufficient knowledge to take beneficial action. All instances require a practical judgment, and in defining problems, a practical judgment means deciding what problem to put in focus and what is the problem definition for the work at hand.

Knowing what to do is specific and particular—not general. Specific knowledge for doing purposes is set within the context of a whole, concrete situation. The act of taking professional action, "doing treatment," as they say, has no theory in and of itself and cannot have a theory. That is because the professional act itself is not explaining, analyzing, or hypothesizing anything. Applying a theory, doing something suggested by knowledge and theory, is not simply making some clear and logical jump from the theory to practice, like making some kind of calculation. Application is not simply derivative. Application involves making a decision based on judgment (Jonas, 1966).

Practical judgment is a reliable mode of balancing out a variety of observations, information, intuition, and pressure to arrive at an individualized conclusion about problem definition, focus, and treatment. It is based on experience of many sorts, but particularly on experience with similar types of conditions. Parts of that experience can be adapted and applied to new and novel circumstances. Almost always, in the human service organizations, there are colleagues, supervisors, and consultants whose wider knowledge can be obtained to bear on a particular judgment. Texts, such as this one, contain a quantity of guidelines, both general and specific, that are based on empirical knowledge to the extent it exists and on the practice wisdom of the author or the group of practitioners with whom the author identifies. What remains to be put into effect is the practitioner equation, namely the work the practitioners do within their own minds to think about what is best and what is rational and logical, and what is relevant and makes sense.

Problem Definition and Psychopathology

Assessing the existence of psychopathology is a part of the work to arrive at a workable problem definition. Making an appropriate psychiatric diagnosis requires specialized training ranging from course work and seminars to on-the-job training and student field work. *Psychopathology* is the technical term for psychologic and behavioral dysfunction occurring in mental disorder. The term is sometimes used to designate *social disorganization;* but that usage is questionable because social disorganization involves impairment in the structures of social institutions of all kinds. Law, custom, and history dictate that the treatment of mental illness is the domain of the medical profession, particularly the specialization of psychiatry. However, current developments in the licensing of social workers and changing perceptions among legislatures and professionals are starting to legitimate non-medical personnel making diagnoses of psychopathology.

Disease theory, a basic concept in the medical model, influences how we think about psychopathology. Disease theory has two components: (1) the identification of symptoms, and (2) the attempt to discover an underlying biological abnormality. To qualify as a mental disease, the abnormality must be a condition that has existed over time. In other words, transient and perhaps fleeting feelings and emotions, or even temporary and occasional aberrant behaviors do not in themselves signify mental disease. Persons whose problems in living qualify them for an appropriate diagnosis of mental illness usually also suffer from impairments in social and physical health, all interacting to produce severe problems. The *disease* label should be applied only to those persons who meet the diagnostic criteria in *DSM IV* (American Psychiatric Association, 1994). Suffering because of stress in its many varieties does not in itself define a problem as mental illness or disorder. Pain and stress are the human condition.

It is likely that mental disorder will be found in many clients, because the signs of such disorders are found widely throughout our society. To give some idea of the extent of mental illness, it has been estimated that 30 to 35 million people in the United States suffer a definable mental illness. Approximately 50 million people contend with adverse, disabling life events that do not qualify for a *disease* label. And large numbers, impossible to estimate, have problems in living and desire to increase their well-being (Klerman et al., 1984).

Brief treatment offers various ways to weave psychopathology into the problem definition that is the focus. Although later in this book, in Chapters 3 and 11, more detail will be given on the different approaches taken by various models, at this point it is enough to mention that models associated with the medical framework, models organized and authored primarily by psychiatrists, put a particular psychopathological diagnosis in a central place in forming their problem definition focus; and they tend to apply their particular model only to those patients whom they judge conform to that particular diagnosis. Some of the medically inclined models allow for inclusion of psychiatric diagnoses of a mild to moderate sort, and eliminate for brief treatment those with severe psychopathology. Other models, including the task-centered model, emphasize the psychiatric diagnosis only if it is severe enough or noticeable enough to be an important obstacle to problem solving around a life problem issue that can otherwise be worked with. The idea in TC is not to cure or repair a mental illness. The idea is to work out some suitable improvement in the practical life conditions of the person. The idea of TC is also to teach and influence the individual to adopt a line of reasoning and set of attitudes toward some troublesome conditions that are interfering with a decent quality of life.

Problem Definition in Relation to Underlying Problems

There is a long-standing philosophical belief that it is preferable to solve the underlying cause of a present problem, that is, its basic, fundamental, and prior cause, because anything less is not worthwhile. This view holds that unless the underlying problem is solved, if therapy resolves a "symptom" in medical parlance, or the "presenting problem" in nonmedical language, the expected therapy result will be short-lived; the problem will "break out" somewhere else.

There are several difficulties with this view. First, it is almost impossible in the real world to point with exactness to the particular cause of a problem in living. Too many variables are involved in human events. Much of what happens is probably random. Modern thought suggests that to decipher a causal chain in any single human life incident is beyond the present ability of social science.

The notion of the importance of treating the so-called "underlying problem" in therapy gained strength from certain positions taken in traditional psychoanalytic theory, although these ideas have been revised over the years (Edelson, 1988, pp. 278–308). In a nutshell, dating from 1905, Freud considered that aversive sexual influences in childhood (not necessarily only erotic but also broadly emotional) were a necessary precondition to mental illness in adulthood and predisposed an individual to mental disturbance. Later, the original theory held that troubling life events would give specific form to an illness-to-be. Then, some present problems would put stress on the individual; and all it would take was a precipitating event to cause the illness to make its appearance (Sulloway, 1979, pp. 92–93). There is no serious empirical evidence to support this theory. There is no evidence either to support the idea of "symptom substitution," that is, that if the present problem is solved then the underlying problem will break out in some other symptom, as if the mental apparatus were a stockpot of boiling trouble seeking a way out.

The idea of an underlying problem is also found in a different context. It is held that problems in living arise because of environmental stress and disadvantage, discrimination, substandard housing, education, health care, and the like, and that present problems are the result of severely problematic relationships with families and friends. Viewing the underlying problem thus as products created by transactions in the social environment opens up possibilities of an immense number of variables that are not hidden from view, as in the case of unobservable intrapsychic difficulties. Many of the hazards of the social environment are pretty plain; and most observers are clear that on a case-by-case basis it is extremely unlikely that alteration can occur in a hazardous social environment without community and political action. It is also difficult to understand what exactly in the social environment causes a personal problem. But even assuming that one's theoretical persuasion justifies a belief that a certain pattern of life, a certain family constellation, type of marital relationship, or what have you, underlies the appearance and maintenance of a certain problem in living, then even so the various therapy fields are not now in a position to offer exact treatment programs to repair specific underlying problems.

Rather than putting forward the concept of an underlying problem as central to the problem definition, it is more practical to define the problem in terms of its current appearance, having in mind that it is likely to be of great benefit to a client to have relief from the impact of the current problem. In later chapters of this book, there will be more detail about the techniques for holding the focus to current problems, while at the same time allowing for some explorations into the past, particularly the recent past, so as to give texture and context to the client's and our own understanding.

Problem Definition in Relation to Socioeconomic Status, Age, and Gender

In the process of defining problems, the client's socioeconomic status, age, and gender form an inherent part of the social context in which the client lives and which shapes the client's lifestyle and problems. Socioeconomic status, age, and gender issues complicate the process of defining social/personal problems.

Studies of the influence of socioeconomic status on therapeutic experiences suggest that persons classified as lower in socioeconomic status are less likely than those of middle or higher socioeconomic status to be accepted for treatment, are less likely to be assigned to intensive therapy, and are more likely to drop out of therapy early. For those who remain in treatment, there does not seem to be much evidence of differences in outcome clearly related to socioeconomic status (Parloff, Waskow, & Wolfe, 1978, pp. 258–259.) That is, if poor people are not passed over in the screening process and if they do not drop out, they are likely to do as well as their better-off counterparts.

Persons classifiable as of lower socioeconomic status are substantially over-represented among clients who are authoritatively referred or mandated to therapeutic social intervention. These are clients found among groups judged to be deviant and coming before the police, the courts, and the public child protective agencies in order to achieve changes in thoughts, feelings, attitudes, and behaviors intended to cause their actions and lifestyles to become more in keeping with social norms.

There is no firm empirical knowledge about best techniques specifically for treating persons of lower socioeconomic status. There is practice information and theory concerning sound approaches to work with involuntary clients (Rooney, 1992). Indications are that practitioners may be uncomfortable with clients whose experiences and lifestyles are different from their own. Poor clients have particular experiences relating to what they do for a living, where and how they live, what they value, how they feel about those who have more or different advantages, and how they react to negative public portrayals of their circumstances in the media, in legislative halls, in advertisements and literature, and the like.

In the process of selecting, prioritizing, and formulating the problem focus in brief treatment, the preferred stance of the practitioner would be to hew as closely as possible *first* to the problem as it is perceived by the client, in the client's own terms, to get that position clearly put on the table and to be careful not to impose a definition. The focus on a problem to be the center of a treatment sequence should relate closely to the adversity as experienced and interpreted by the client. Thus, stereotyped thinking about the poor, about their psychology and personal traits, about what should be the aims of poor people—all these are traps that need to be avoided in order to get a clear picture of the problem as perceived by the client.

The client's age shapes the form that the problem takes. This is not because of the meaning of any particular number of years. Rather, people construct their personal attributes and roles over time and in the course of their social and personal development. Public attitudes about how persons of various age groups ought to live, think, and act become formed into group consensual norms, resulting in expectations of age-appropriate behaviors and attitudes. These public expectations about how older people are supposed to behave, look, feel, and react often bear little resemblance to the facts of how older people really live. Because of the substantial increase in the number of older people in the population, there is a need to be sensitive to the wide variety of their individual characteristics, and to be attentive to the need to find out how a particular older person perceives a problem, to avoid lumping all or most problems of the elderly into catch-all categories. At the same time, there are circumstances about older people that are characteristic of their life stage, such as their sense of time, sense of the life cycle, tendency toward life review, tendency toward making reparation for wrongs and resolution of problem issues, a certain conservatism and attachment to the familiar, a desire to leave a legacy and to transmit their power to the young, a sense of fulfillment, as well as continued growth (Butler & Lewis, 1982).

The age of a young or younger child influences how a treatment problem is defined. Most work by human service professionals with and on behalf of children is not psychotherapy (in the narrow sense) as much as it is problem-solving work. This means providing resources and social skills in which the child may be deficient; and it means enhancing the child's opportunities to obtain and use education, to form personal relationships, and to develop satisfactory attitudes toward the self and the world. Usually family members will be the central actors in such problem-solving efforts.

Teenagers are another group whose issues pose special problems for practitioners assigned to provide them with therapeutic services. As is the case with the other groups discussed in this section, the technical problem involved in problem definition for pinning down the focus of brief treatment is the necessity to avoid stereotyping and imposition of adult bias in determining the focus of a treatment sequence. Teenagers are subject to bad press, to the suspicion, fear, and hostility of a good many adults. Teenagers know how they are publicly regarded, and they react to negative stereotypes with resentment. Here again it is wise to refrain from a priori judgments on problem definition and to attend as much as possible to the individuality of the young person and the needs and views from that person's own perspective.

Problem Definition in Relation to Human Diversity

Another area that poses complexity for defining problems for treatment is the effect of an increasingly diverse population in this country. Changes in immigration law and practices, as well as population movements developing out of vast economic and political changes occurring in the world of the 1990s, have brought to American shores large numbers of Asian and Latino immigrants, and also Central Europeans, Soviets, and others. This influx is requiring us to understand the culture, needs, and experiences of new immigrants and refugees. We also need to be adequately sensitive to new problems experienced by ethnic groups, who have been part of the American scene for hundreds of years, such as African Americans and Native American Indians.

Much has been written in the past decade about ethnic and culturally sensitive clinical practice (Bromley, 1987; Brown, 1996; Brown, Oliver, & Klor de Alva, 1986; Devore & Schlesinger, 1996; Franklin, 1985; McGoldrick, Pearce, & Giordano, 1996; Morrow-Howell, Lott, & Ozawa, 1990; Mortland & Egan, 1987; Neighbors & Taylor, 1985; Oliver & Brown, 1983; Taylor, Neighbors, & Broman, 1989). All authors recommend that priority should be given to immediate current problems. There is a difference of opinion about what issues in the past should be stressed and also about whether the pacing of the treatment should be slow or rapid. The typical focus of brief treatment on the present and on the problem as perceived by the client makes a good fit with the conditions that seem advisable when working with persons of a different or minority culture. The other key point stressed by all writers on this subject is the necessity for the practitioner to understand and be sensitive to the clients' cultures and world views.

The literature suggests that minority group clients will only respond to clinical work that incorporates empathic awareness of the particular group's belief systems and usual ways of behaving. For example, it is vital to understand the special patterns families of a foreign culture normally reveal in how they relate to each other. It is necessary to know about such factors as the culturally specific sex and age roles; the way newcomers have experienced the overwhelming impact of immigration traumas, cultural dislocations, loss of the familiar, prejudice and racism, disappointments after immigration, and unaccustomed expectations of them by the culture into which they have transferred; and a host of similar and related stresses.

The technical issue is how to achieve congruence between clients of a different culture on what the problem is and what it means. This is a general problem in doing treatment with all groups, but it is a special problem when trying to work with clients of a different culture and ethnic background and history. Achieving practitioner–client congruence on the problem definition is also the hallmark of brief treatment. As explained by Brown (1996):

> Congruence between clients and practitioners on the problem situations and the strategies for change is essential if one is to be sensitive to clients from other cultures, particularly those groups traditionally oppressed in this country. The implementation of intervention requires a constant awareness of the fit between the practitioner's actions and the client's culture and belief system. When the practitioner is sensitive to those issues, the intervention selected can be designed so that cultural conflict is minimized or obviated altogether. Practitioners can become ethnically and culturally sensitive by learning about their clients and by learning about the ways that they operate in their daily living. Such knowledge will help to understand how clients solve problems together with others in their support networks so that interventions designed for such client groupings will utilize existing structures to the greatest advantage.

It is probable that the problems perceived by many, if not most, clients who are immigrants or members of vulnerable minorities concern parent–child conflict, getting an education of high quality, locating employment in a field that has a future, mitigating the distress caused by immigration or discrimination experiences, coping with communication problems, isolation due to language barriers, and the like.

Problem Definition in Relation to Environmental Deficits

As mentioned earlier, there is a historical debate among scholars and the public about the cause of major social problems over whether the basic causes should be attributed to the structures in society, that is, to environmental and social context, or whether the causal agent is some deficit, dysfunction, psychological illness, moral, or characterological maladjustment. The issue is essentially moot, because all of these are the usual suspects.

Sometimes the driving force in the production of a problem is clearly environmental and the client may see it that way. Such a perception is difficult for clinical practice, which is well developed for intervening in psychological matters and weakly developed for interceding in environmental matters or which limits the view of the environment to immediate family and immediate peers. Practitioners are put in the position of having to deal with social policy and social institutions without the kinds of techniques available on a purely one-to-one interactional basis. Thus, it is frequently the case that clients' perceptions of their problems as being "out there" are put aside in favor of defining the problem as a mental or emotional problem. The possibility of dealing with the problem as environmental deficit or malfunction is thus not operational.

The techniques of environmental change generally involve negotiating with other persons and social agencies on behalf of the client to provide concrete resources; open up access to the client's obtaining resources; find and develop resources for appropriate education, vocational and job training, and job finding; secure medical and psychiatric care or alcoholism, family, and drug counseling; find low-cost housing; find and develop recreational and friendship resources; repair family estrangements; and the like. Broadly speaking, these interventions may be subsumed under the terms *advocacy, negotiations, mediation,* and *community action.* Germain and Gitterman (1980, pp. 137–202) list the skills needed as assessing needs, mobilizing motivation and interests, identifying and supporting natural leaders, locating and securing resource persons, and facilitating mutual aid.

Homelessness is a current example of a problem universally recognized as located primarily in malfunctioning social policies and institutions. Although also attributed to personal difficulties and psychopathologies, there seems to be considerable consensus among experts that social structural problems are the underlying problem in homelessness. Recent research on the nature of contemporary homelessness reveals a complex set of problems. Sosin, Colson, and Grossman (1988) concluded that homelessness is essentially a condition of being very poor, so that the homeless are predominately poorly educated men and women, more often than not of a minority ethnic background, locked out of employment because of the reduction in low-skilled manual labor that characterizes the contemporary labor market, excluded from a regular domicile because of a severe shortage of low-cost housing, and lacking family with whom they can comfortably double up in living arrangements. Mental illness appears to be somewhat more frequent among the homeless than among the domiciled very poor, but it cannot be established whether they are ill because they are homeless or homeless because they are ill. A crucial factor is that while the homeless do turn to social agencies for help, the agencies are not well organized for the provision of the kinds of intensive supportive services needed, such as basic education, retraining, outreach, and follow-up, or for providing adequate public income maintenance benefits.

The problem of homelessness is particularly useful to illustrate the array of environmental problems that may become the focus of brief treatment. However, other problems in which the environment is implicated are not always so clearly portrayed and understood. Techniques for intervening in the environment are not well developed and they may need longer times to work out than is reasonable within a brief treatment program. This is an important area in which there are as yet few specific guidelines; thus, practice must depend on the judgment of individual practitioners and their agencies. See, for example, the last chapter in this book which is a study of the effectiveness of task-centered work with homeless clients.

SUMMARY

The dilemmas of problem identification occur for three reasons. First, personal problems are indeterminate. They are associated with various combinations of: lack of resources or skills, unhappiness, ineffectiveness, failure, and/or deviance. Just exactly what components constitute the problem is a matter of what observations happen to be made and what viewpoint is applied in interpreting those observations. Second, personal problems are relative and there are no absolute criteria for establishing their presence. Problem defining is a continuous and changing process. Finally, problem defining itself is a complex process, relating to the state of knowledge about social problems and varying public and professional views about them. These complexities are illustrated by the number and quality of factors that have to be considered in problems involving poverty, child abuse, and mental disorder.

After the client and practitioner make a judgment on the problem definition, the focus must be found within that definition. Client–practitioner disagreement about focus has to be negotiated. Mandated problems have to be considered and fitted into the focus. The problem definition process is best considered as a part of focusing and assessment. Considerations of psychopathology; perceptions of underlying problems; the client's socioeconomic status, age, and gender; issues relating to understanding and managing cultural diversity; and difficulties in locating the problem in the environment all enter into the totality of getting a grasp on the problem definition and shaping it so that it can be an effective framework for structuring brief treatment.

■ ■ ■ ■ ■ ▬▬▬▬▬▬▬▬▬▬▬▬▬▬▬▬▬▬▬▬▬▬▬▬

CHAPTER TWO

INTERVENTION FRAMEWORKS

CLINICAL PRACTICE DEFINED

The term *treatment* is used in association with practicing medicine and ordinarily refers to curing, healing, medicating, and similar activities. However, *treatment*, broadly interpreted, refers to acting upon something with an agent for the purpose of improvement or alteration. It is the latter, nonmedical meaning that applies to the services nonmedical practitioners perform to help people with problems in living.

Intervention means "coming between." When providing a social welfare re-source, such as residential care for a child or financial assistance to a single mother, we come between the condition in which the child is lacking proper care and the opposite condition of having proper care; or we may come between evic-tion and being at home. Psychotherapy in any of its varieties comes between, for example, drinking oneself out of a job and keeping that job, or between depressed loneliness and reasonable companionship. Intervention is an interference in a state of affairs.

Intervention is a modern term that has come to identify a certain activist pos-ture in treatment. There is a nuanced difference between *treatment* and *intervention*. *Intervention* suggests deliberate and immediate interposing of some relationship, action, counsel, behavior, or treatment "in-put" intended to change something at once, or be part of a chain of acts that will change something in the situation. Using the term *intervention* is a way of departing from the medical aura of the term *treatment;* but in the end, both mean about the same thing.

TREATMENT/INTERVENTION FRAMEWORKS

Interventions, including treatment, have purpose, objectives, and goals. These three—purpose, objective, goals—have similar meanings and are used inter-changeably; all refer to intentions. In this book we try to say *purpose* when we mean a broad, general, far-reaching intent or expectation; we tend to say *objective* when we mean an end to which our effort is directed; we use *goal* as a technical term to mean specific and particular behaviors, conditions, thoughts, and feelings that are actively sought to be the end product of the intervention sequence. The main purpose, and objective, of intervention is to cause desired actions to occur. Other purposes are to restrain, control, or hold back certain actions; to maintain or alter a condition; or to permit or encourage actions. These purposes are viewed within a matrix of principal or grand purposes, such as social control and therapy.

When performing *social control functions,* practitioners are attempting to help people attain normative functioning on the grounds that the individual is better off who can fit in with the generally accepted modes of acting in society. The person will be happier personally and less difficult to deal with in society. Basic social control is the accepted role of police, but human service professionals are often responsible for meeting society's needs to reduce conflict and ensure that the general welfare is not endangered by harmful acts. Protective services in cases of child abuse and neglect is an example in which human service practitioners, especially social workers, have a major responsibility for social control.

Therapeutic functions include remedial treatment of emotional disease or dis-order and of dysfunctional interpersonal relationships in families or among peers and other important people. Therapeutic functions include a wide variety of activities, organized according to numerous models of practice. Their purpose is to correct personal disturbances of many sorts, to enhance the individual's ability to engage in satisfactory interpersonal relations, to enhance self-esteem appropriately, to increase skills for personal problem solving, and, generally, to reduce unhappiness and dissatisfaction and to improve the quality of personal relationships. According to some usages, therapeutic functions may also include resources and educational counseling to enhance social skills.

GENERAL TYPES AND MODELS OF TREATMENT

The terms *types, models,* and *approaches* are somewhat interchangeable. *Types* and *approaches* refer to broad categories of technical guidelines that have strong similarities or are based on similar intellectual grounds. We speak of cognitive-behavioral types or approaches, psychodynamic types or approaches, group treatment types or approaches, task-centered types, brief treatment, crisis intervention, and so forth.

Model is a more contemporary term that refers to collections of practice guidelines, derived from a specified body of knowledge and often from identified research work. Models offer organized sets of related interventions that are stated and described with a high degree of specificity. They do not displace professional judgment and they cannot account for all possible occurrences. They guide the practitioner through a process that is in harmony with the real practice conditions, cutting down on some drift and trial-and-error. They depend on sensible professional judgment to adapt the model as necessary and encourage flexible use. Models are a product of the development of technologies in the helping occupations. They help organize input and identify results that are specific and possibly measurable, capable of being described, and replicated.

GOALS

What Are Goals in Clinical Services?

Goals are powerful instruments for determining intervention. The present and particular interests of clients shape intervention goals. By themselves, however, a client's goals are not the only factors that determine the substance of intervention programs such as, for example, those found in a mental hospital, a juvenile court, or a welfare agency. Public outcry in the newspapers and on television shape the goals of intervention by establishing the public, or society in general, as influences that decide what goals should be. Decisions at a professional conference and the information and opinions expressed in professional books, journals, and training programs also shape intervention goals. Because all these influences come from different directions, goals become tangled, complex, and ambiguous.

Some of the influences shaping goals are in conflict. The conflict may be muted; that is, the operational goal may be a compromise among contending factors. For practical purposes a practitioner may focus on one or two aspects of the whole goal situation, yet uncertainty and ambiguity will remain a natural condition of the goal-setting process. To reduce the ambiguity, goals should be explicit. *Unstated, vague, hidden goals are powerful and elusive and may often work against the overt goals, complicating intervention unnecessarily.*

What Are Goals in Social Welfare Services?

The idea of a goal is straightforward. It is the end toward which effort is directed; it is a point beyond which something does not or cannot go. A goal is *not* a practitioner's, agency's, or client's wish. A wish is something desired and is the same thing as a goal only if it is attainable or potentially attainable. It takes the application of resources and social skills plus real, favorable opportunities and some luck to convert wishes to goal achievement. Furthermore, to be realizable a goal must be real, tangible, and concrete. A therapeutic goal that visualizes the achievement of a set of behaviors, for example, fewer family fights, can easily be made concrete by making a baseline measurement of the current undesirable number of fights and formulating what lesser number will do. Simply to assert a goal of "improvement in communication," or "more positive relationships," however, is rhetoric and not readily visualized or capable of specific definition. For example, what I consider improved or positive in my life you may consider highly unsatisfactory.

Rhetoric, however, serves a purpose. It encourages communication about a subject, and useful ideas arise from communication. Rhetoric can be a shorthand way to clarify—or obscure—a subject. Notions such as "improvement in communication," "positive relationships," or "personal maturity" are shorthand for expressing a wide variety of attitudes about what is desirable. To be loved, employed, or promoted; to graduate, have a good income, live in a nice place, have healthy children—all these are understandable goals because they refer to conditions in the commonsense real world; they are not abstractions. On the other hand, unlimited or nonspecific rhetoric can blur understanding and lead nowhere.

Therapeutic goals can include changes in feeling, thinking, beliefs, and attitudes that are not visible to the degree that "fewer fights" or "a better job" are. But cognitive goals are tangible if they deal with real, internal events such as fears and anxieties, lack of appropriate self-esteem, painful or depressed moods, excessive suspiciousness, unfocused anger, misperceptions of one's own or other's attitudes and behaviors, misperceptions of the reality of events, and so forth.

The notion that social services have goals is old and commonplace, but in contemporary practice the professional perception of goals in practice has undergone a change. Since the mid-1960s, a climate of thought has developed that has put high value on programs and techniques that could demonstrate "payoff." Results are desirable if they are in accord with defined objectives and produced by efficient, economical, and accountable methods. Hence, there has been an attempt to formulate goals in concrete, finite, and measurable terms. The anticipated payoffs from using goal-directed interventions are that clients will benefit from direct, rapid action to cut down a problem; accumulated information about goal achievement (results) can be used to improve service by distinguishing among better or worse interventions; staff can be rewarded and their morale improved by seeing client change; and it is possible to shed light on the characteristics of problems and interventions, enabling better quality research to take place.

Goals Are Not a Panacea

Goal-directed interventions are not cure-alls for the ills of the social welfare system. Intervention methods to reach goals have to be constructed and learned, and that takes time, energy, and money. Issues of values emerge and create conflict among staff, agencies, and the public. Some goals may seem better or more important than others, depending on a person's viewpoint, habits, and beliefs. Techniques have to be constructed to monitor outcomes and effectiveness of interventions, that is, to measure the performance of clients, staff, and agencies. Studies of outcome, whether for a single case or a total agency clientele, have to be interpreted, and interpretations can be complex, inconsistent, or contradictory.

The complexity of economic and social problems often retards straight-line goal achievement. Incomplete and inadequate goal achievement raises questions about how much goal attainment is enough. Is the work a failure if some ultimate condition is not obtained? Is the work a success if a limited useful gain has occurred?

It has for decades been an ideal to *maximize* help to clients. To this end, the tendency developed to formulate goals that were broad, inclusive, and multiple (Siporin, 1975). Such an ample approach, however, cannot be put into practice readily, given the limitations of technology, staff, funds, and constraints in the general climate of public opinion and in norms of society. Maximization is an ideal that seems logical and desirable, but lack of resources and technology to achieve this ideal as well as lack of consensus about the definition of an ideal precludes achieving it. The present trend to simplify, reduce, make concrete, and put limits around intervention reflects the practical meaning of goals, an end set of client behaviors and attitudes, and conditions in the environment.

Goals should be achievable in a reasonably short period of time, and as economically as possible. They should result from relatively specific actions that the client and practitioner can and do take to alleviate a specified target problem.

Why Goal-Oriented Practice?

Cost and Efficiency Considerations.   The social welfare system of the United States has grown to billion dollar proportions. It is financed through the uniquely American combination of taxation to pay for government-operated services and employer–employee paid fringe benefits. In 1980, the private sector (employer–employee) provided $433.5 billion to welfare fringe benefits. In the same year, government costs were $493 billon, which rose to $641.7 billion by 1983. Private philanthropy provided only a minute portion to supplement the large-scale benefit plans (National Association of Social Workers, 1987, pp. 49–63). It is apparent that issues of cost and efficiency are priorities in administering service programs.

The size of public and private sector expenditures justifiably arouses intense scrutiny, debate, and considerable acrimony among influential sectors of the public. People want to know what is being accomplished by social welfare expenditures and whether the results are worthwhile. These questions disturb everyone. Today computers make it possible to collect detailed information and to conduct increasingly sophisticated data analyses that put out more and more information in an attempt to deal with the questions of "What exactly is the welfare system doing? How is it doing it?" and "What are the results?" There are no simple answers, of course, but the data do help human service professionals and administrators understand what the system is doing and how it is operating.

To control costs and enhance efficiency it is necessary to state the goals of intervention processes clearly and to specify what is to be done and what results are to be accomplished. Formulating goals is one of the accepted ingredients in setting up interventions that can be monitored to find out with some exactness what was done and what resulted. Such straightforward planning and implementation, in and of itself, is considered to improve efficiency. In addition, the gradual accumulation of information about the relative merits of different interventions may, in time, provide usable information about what kinds of interventions should be emphasized and what kinds de-emphasized, and what kinds dropped from the repertoire. This kind of specificity and measurement in human services is only just beginning, but there is every reason to believe the trend will persist and produce, within a few years, interesting and potentially useful data.

Administrative and Policy Considerations. Decades ago concern developed about administrative practices in social welfare, which were thought to be partly responsible for poor results (Comptroller General, 1973). Since then, great strides have been taken in upgrading the training of administrators and in developing business practices for the purpose of increasing efficiency, controlling costs, and enhancing effectiveness of the services.

Former policy was often based on assumptions that the social services should make major alterations in family lifestyles and individual behaviors that would enable disadvantaged and deviant people to achieve economic independence and to reorganize and "normalize" their personalities and family relations. From a contemporary viewpoint these aspirations not only sound naive, but also fail to give enough consideration to structural problems in society that engender and maintain these problems, no matter how much effort is expended for individual "rehabilitation." Revisions in practice and innovative practices directed at goal-oriented results are today seen as potentially capable of reducing limited, specific problem conditions and behaviors of substantial importance without necessitating attempts at major overhauls of personality and relationships.

The Issue of Congruence. The question of what goals to pursue is not the sole responsibility of the agency and the practitioner. The client is an important, probably the most important, actor in the situation. Agencies and practitioners often feel they are in an adversarial relationship with clients; and clients often share that feeling. The issue of differences between the professionals and the clients about what goals are proper consumes a good deal of time and energy.

What About Differences between Client and Agency over Goals?   Differences of opinion between clients and helping practitioners and their agencies have long presented difficulties in the helping process. A good deal of theorizing has gone into explaining why clients will circumvent, oppose, ignore, and obstruct supposedly beneficial efforts. The most prominent explanation for the unwillingness of clients to accept a practitioner's appraisal is the theory of resistance. That hypothesis assumes a mostly unconscious tendency to cling to habitual perceptions, ideas, and behaviors, and thus to resist change.

Professional practice that relies on the resistance explanation has a tendency to extrude an impasse that slows down problem solving. There may be a concentration on dissolving the resistance rather than getting rid of the problem. The problem may become a struggle between client and practitioner over problem definition. The working through or working out of this impasse extends treatment time, and may develop client dissatisfaction, dropout, or other unwanted events.

Resistance is thought to be activated and maintained primarily by the presence of feelings, attitudes, and habits of mind that go back to earliest childhood, and by transference and repression. The process of "working though resistance," derived from psychoanalysis, is used to resolve transference and repression.

Transference is the tendency to project feelings, thoughts, and wishes onto the psychoanalyst, who becomes in the patient's mind a representation of persons from the past, primarily parents. *Repression* is the process of keeping unacceptable ideas or impulses out of consciousness. "Working through" in psychoanalysis is thought to enable the patient gradually to relinquish accustomed but dysfunctional ways of thinking, feeling, and acting, and also the assumed satisfaction possibly attached to the illness. It is thought that slowly pushing away at the impasse develops insight and enables the patient to experience new perceptions and appropriate conflict-free affects (Hinsie & Campbell, 1970, pp. 662 and 814).

The theory of resistance and guidelines for working through are influential in treatment practice and have been popularized in novels and movies, on TV, and on the stage. Many practitioners think in these terms about the reluctance and unwillingness of clients to accept and consent to the focus determined by the practitioner. However, there are other, probably more practical, approaches with a problem-solving purpose.

It stands to reason that, if practitioner and client were working on the same problem and headed in the same direction, such cooperation would increase pressure to achieve good task performance. In fact, research evidence supports this commonsense idea. Reid and Hanrahan (1982) reviewed controlled experimental studies of direct social work interventions published from 1973 to 1979. The most clearly successful interventions were those in which the clients' motivations were directed toward what the social workers were attempting to provide. Research in the University of Chicago Task-Centered Project indicated that target problems worked on at the initiative of the client or as a result of close client–practitioner agreement were those that showed the most successful results (Reid, 1978). One study of task-centered work found that dropout/discontinuance was reduced to 11 percent, compared with other studies at the time with much higher dropout rates, from 20 percent to 75 percent. This same study attributes most of the dropouts to there being no agreement on a target problem; practitioners seem to get only so much time to accomplish this agreement (Tolson & Brown, 1981). This kind of "motivational congruence" between practitioners and clients was missing from most of the intervention programs with poor outcomes. Videka-Sherman (1988) offers additional substantiation in her larger meta-analysis of thirty-eight studies and suggests that clients' commitment to working on the problem defined may be a critical component of effective practice.

There are differing perspectives about dealing with conflicts between clients and practitioners on problem definition and focus of problem solving. There is steadfast adherence in American society, shared by many human service practitioners, to *psychic determinism,* the belief that early and unconscious psychological patterning causes present unhappiness, misbehavior, deviance, and inadequate self-fulfillment. It is assumed that it is best to tackle underlying problems to achieve desired results, and long-standing views contend that intervention dealing primarily with presenting problems is inferior and insufficient. The aspiration to resolve deep psychological problems at the foundation of personal character and lifestyle conflicts with the pervasive observations that people do not change readily, if at all, that social structures change very slowly, and that causes of problems are as much in the realm of society and culture as they are in the realm of psychology.

It is obvious that problems underlie all areas of life—history, economics, and politics as well as psychology. The question for problem-solving therapists is not whether or not there are underlying problems that should be eradicated, but rather what problems are accessible to change and what immediate, contemporary problems ought to be addressed to make a difference in the life of the client. Changes of importance are never trivial and are often hard to effect. However, when the client's interests can be meshed with the practitioner's expertise, so-called "resistance" can often be reduced to manageable dimensions, and there can be a significant release of client effort.

We may be uneasy when clients concentrate on defining problems that put the blame or responsibility on some other person or on some large environmental, political, or economic structure. Ordinarily, in a direct service agency, neither the client nor the agency has an immediate ability to change anything in the macro-economic-political system, or in the behaviors of persons they do not know and who are not present in the problem-solving effort at hand. An agency may have an advocacy function or a social action function, but normally proceeding in those ways is too slow to have an immediate impact on a particular client's troubles.

Placing blame for a problem is quite common and need not be an obstacle to work. For example, I might say the chair of my department is to blame for my poor student teaching evaluations; if he had given me the courses I like to teach my ratings would have gone up. Don't I still have to deal with potentially more poor teaching ratings in courses I like as *obstacles* to showing everyone that I am right? If each family member blames another, the overall problem might be that the family members are "unhappy about their interactions." The ways all are blamed become the specifications of the problem. Each family member then must deal with another's complaint as obstacles to solving their problem and the overall problem. In order to get the son to stop yelling, mother may have to stop doing her annoying habit. Father will need to do such and such if the daughter is to do something the father desires, and so on.

Clients focus on matters of great interest to themselves, regardless of how they formulate the problem statements. Their formulations are legitimate and deserve respect. They probably indicate the surest direction for problem-solving work that will be taken seriously and has a good chance of success.

Sometimes, the dissonance between practitioner and client is exacerbated by public pressure, particularly from the various media, demanding results beyond the present capacity of the helping professions. The practitioner may feel squeezed between the resistant client on one hand and the critical, demanding public on the other. This tension is natural in present-day political democracy where human service issues are among the most important concerns of the society, but systematic public education could help alleviate this stress.

Psychodynamic types of brief treatment make use of psychoanalytic principles such as helping the client "uncover, experience, and work through repressed emotional conflict by means of analysis of defense, resistance, and transference. Through this experience the [client] is helped to learn new ways of functioning," explain Bauer and Kobos (1987, p. 6). Adequate congruence between the therapist and the client is managed in psychodynamic models of brief treatment by a fairly tight set of criteria for whom is to be offered this type of treatment. By and large, the various psychodynamic models devise selection criteria that tend to bring in only those clients who are most likely to have views similar to the views held by the therapists as to what kinds of problems should be the focus. Even though the clients may be resistant, at bottom, they want something out of treatment that is in the same arena that their therapists want to give and believe in; clients are often prepared for working through resistance by having taken courses in psychology and having read psychoanalytic works.

On the other hand, therapists take into treatment in problem-solving modes clients who are not often prepared for and/or do not want to engage in much uncovering of the past. Clients are not so much concerned with repressed emotional conflict as they are with warding off and overcoming the demands of problems in living that are felt to be primarily or solely in the present, often the doings of other persons or social forces. Actually, many of the issues of concern to clients can be understood by therapists in either psychodynamic or problem-solving schemes of thought. Nevertheless, some clients are clearly neither interested in nor candidates for psychodynamic treatment. They may be willing participants in problem-solving treatment if the therapist's mind-set encompasses an outlook that validates the clients' own perspectives. Such an outlook permits the treatment to be planned so there is congruence between clients and therapist to minimize the altercations, dissonances, disagreements, and hostility aroused when the therapist is pushing on one set of problems and the clients on a different set.

Types of Goals

Agency Goals.   Agency goals are established formally by the service organization. They chart a direction for the administration to accomplish a whole program. Agency goals cannot be directly applied to individual cases because they are too abstract. Their accomplishment does not depend on single individual cases but on the collective results of all the cases considered together.

Agency goals determine case goals only indirectly. There is usually no straight-line connection between broad, abstract agency goals and individual case practice, and there is no technology for applying broad agency goals to individual clients. Only individual intervention techniques apply to individual cases. The programmatic interventions of an agency with large aggregations of individuals require macro-system interventions, such as community organization, social planning, and social action.

The character of agency goals is normative; that is, agency goals express conviction about ideal abstract intentions, and intentions implicit in law and custom. They also reflect political aims. For example, an agency is operating to carry out a law to protect victims of child abuse. The agency goal may be stated as protection of children, rehabilitation of disorganized families, or prevention of multiple problems. No individual case goal can be visualized to carry out such lofty aims, although many a case plan, to its folly, does frame its individual goals in such rhetoric. An individual case goal would more likely be, "to eliminate physical abuse of Bill; to place Bill in a foster home; to teach the parents to control their rage; to get the father a job," and so forth. Accomplishing individual case goals can be measured: Bill's mother either does or does not stop beating him with an electric cord; she does or does not stop taking out her rage on her son; her husband does or does not get a job; Bill does or does not go to a foster home; he either does or does not thrive in the foster home.

Professional Goals.   Professional goals are *opinions* of what is good, effective, and valuable in furthering the well-being of people and society. Professional goals may be abstract or specific. If espoused by powerful leaders, teachers, and supervisors, they may exert substantial power over the opinions and actions of practitioners. Professional goals, like expert opinions, vary over time, vary from one locality to another, and rarely offer a firm consensus to guide individual case action. Professional techniques can guide action directly. Professional goals are indirect influences on actions and tend to be long range, philosophical, and political.

Psychotherapy Goals.   The goals of psychotherapy occupy a special place. These goals are pertinent to clinicians who treat clients in private practice or in settings such as outpatient psychiatry clinics with voluntary clients. Persons coming for treatment to such settings under their own initiative usually perceive their problem as lying within themselves, as being a kind of illness. Or a practitioner may persuade a client in any setting to view his or her problem in terms of therapeutic ideals. In such instances, in addition to all of the socially determined considerations about goals, there are also the consensual goals of psychotherapy, which are to change the person's perception of self, others, the world, and their relationships with important other people, including to change the behavior.

Personal Practitioner Goals.   These goals reflect the private opinions of individual workers, their own views of life and their own biases. These may be highly individualistic and unexpressed; they may also reflect the cultural, religious, and socioeconomic background of the practitioner. Strongly held personal goals of which the practitioner is not sufficiently aware can exert the strongest influence on how the practitioner leads the client and sets up or imposes unrealistic and irrelevant goals. Such procedures are obviously detrimental to the client's well-being, and sophisticated professionals attempt to control excessive personal influence to avoid distorting the goal-setting process.

Client Goals.   Client goals are the most practical way to carry out a goal-oriented strategy for individual case action. A forthright expression of what the client wants to achieve provides a relatively clear idea of what the focal problem is and to what the client is ready and able to give the most attention and effort. When the professional doubts the relevance or feasibility of the client's expressed goal, discussion can explore, evaluate, and possibly alter the client's goal, with the client's participation and genuine agreement. (See Chapter 6.) When an agency or the courts authoritatively prescribe goals, these may need to be negotiated. The likelihood is that clients will not be motivated to work for goals of which they disapprove or that are counter to their strongest beliefs and wishes. The direct way to minimize dissonance between practitioner and client goals is to accord the client's goals a prominent place in the intervention strategy. This is also the activity most likely to result in a satisfactory outcome.

FROM GOALS TO RESULTS: DEVELOPING A PLAN

Elements of a Plan

Most contemporary approaches to treatment advocate planned, systematic procedures because they are generally the most efficient and effective (Epstein, 1985; Rosen, Proctor, & Livne, 1985). Planning consists of designing or outlining the intervention components by

1. Defining the problem(s): "What is to be tackled or changed?"
2. Identifying goal(s): "What outcome will be looked for?"
3. Choosing intervention activities: "What will be done?"
4. Formulating a sequence: "In what order will the intervention activities take place; where, with whom, and for how long will the work take place?"
5. Making the contract: "What are the client and practitioner committed to do?"

Exercising Choice of Components

At each step in planning, choices have to be made that involve judgment (Meyer, 1983; Mullen, 1983; Thomas, 1984). Deciding on the components of the plan involves subjective factors, including the practitioner's value orientations, preferred habits and ways of working, and attained level of skills. Other more objective factors, in the sense that they are easier to observe and confirm, include the client's problem and condition, the style and aims of the practice setting, and the guidelines for practice incorporated into various practice models.

Interventions are categories of action expected to ameliorate a problem. Purposefully selecting intervention activities (rather than relying on trial-and-error or happenstance) is essential. As much as possible, intervention activities should be selected from among those that have been tested in research or in codified practice, published in reputable sources, and that have achieved verifiably good records of success. Experimental and innovative interventions should be encouraged with the informed consent of clients.

General Types of Interventions

The general categories of interventions can be outlined. Each general category, however, includes a large number of separate and specific intervention items too numerous to list here. The intervention types listed here are not mutually exclusive and tend to overlap considerably.

1. *Practical help.* Straightforward informing, advising, arranging, and expediting in such matters as financial assistance, housing, clothing, referrals and applications, employment-seeking, daycare centers, clubs, and outings (Goldberg & Warburton, 1979).
2. *Referral and linkage.* Connecting clients with other agencies, such as physical and mental health facilities, educational and vocational services, financial assistance agencies, and the like.
3. *Negotiating, advocacy, and bargaining.* Dealing with other agencies through conference, discussion, and compromise on behalf of the client to settle conflicts between the client and other agencies, especially regarding such matters as eligibility for benefits and terms and conditions of the client's relationships and behavior with other agencies.
4. *Task formulation and guided performance.* Moving along in a relatively orderly manner to pinpoint tasks, identify obstacles to task performance, overcome obstacles, and acquire skills for task performance, all focused on actions to reduce the target problem.
5. *Emotional support.* Providing an empathic helping relationship in which adequate and relevant compassion, responsiveness, encouragement, and reinforcement are displayed and conveyed.
6. *Teaching and enhancing social skills.* Conveying needed information and directing, guiding, enabling, modeling, rehearsing, providing feedback, encouraging,

and supporting in order to make possible the acquisition of behavioral skills needed to have an impact on the target problem.

7. *Psychotherapy (including counseling).* Helping individuals develop themselves and their personal resources in terms of interpersonal relationships, self-regard, problem-solving skills, moods and tensions, handling of stress, mental and emotional conflicts, and the like, using professional relationships and interviewing skills and other selected and combined processes described above.

Sequencing

The sequence is the order of the activities in the plan and includes such related matters as where the work will take place, with whom, in what order, and for what duration (time limit). In some settings, administrative regulations limit the length of contact and may also influence or prescribe the location and participants.

Contracting

The idea of a practitioner–client contract has wide currency in the human services field even though there is much variety in actual practice. Contracts vary from complex to simple, from general to detailed, and from written to verbal. As explained by Rothery (1980):

> Increased interest in contracts reflects the influence of a number of beliefs about practice, including: (1) that people can and should make informed choices about the nature and goals of the services they receive; (2) that this carries with it a concomitant share in the responsibility for their treatment and its consequences; (3) that this responsibility includes full participation in the process of making decisions and choices and acting on them; and (4) that there is value in maximizing a client's cognitive involvement in problem-solving from the outset of the helping process. (pp. 179–180)

METHODS: IN GENERAL AND IN BRIEF TREATMENT

Problem-Solving Methods

Problem solving is essential to the practice of science, including scientific approaches to dealing with social and psychological subjects. People and their predicaments can be approached by systematic methods of reasoning, or cognitive processes. Despite the prevalence of problem-solving ideas in human service practices, these views have critics. Applying technology to the human sciences meets with resistance because some fear that important moral, ethical, and value considerations will be put aside (Whan, 1986). Some fear that applying technological ideas to human services may lead to manipulation and covert social control (Castel, Castel, & Lovell, 1982).

In 1933, John Dewey's work, *How We Think,* was published; in that book, he worked out an analysis of problem solving that underpins contemporary approaches used in the helping disciplines.

In the mid-1950s, a steady development of emphasis on problem solving and problem-solving methods occurred. In 1956, Dartmouth College was host to a conference on the problem-solving potentials of computers, which ushered in studies on problem-solving methods uncovered in the development of artificial intelligence (Gardner, 1985). In 1957, the publication of *Social Casework: A Problem-Solving Process* established the idea of problem solving firmly in the professional consciousness of social work (Perlman, 1957). In 1971, D'Zurilla and Goldfried published an outline for problem-solving steps in behavior modification (D'Zurilla & Goldfried, 1971), followed by the development of task-centered casework in 1972 (Reid & Epstein, 1972).

What becomes apparent is that there was growing belief in the merits of problem solving as a key concept for the helping disciplines. A similar development was occurring in the administration of social institutions, government, and business; there it took the form of "management by objectives" that had a central theme of solving management problems and arriving at desired goals by structured, planned means.

There are many ways to classify problem-solving methods. The present discussion will group the common methods into "families" that have some essential features in common. Actually, each author explains methods differently; however, lack of uniformity among the adherents of a particular school or family of treatment reflects the flux characteristic of the field, the constant search and experimentation, the responsiveness to new ideas, and the influence of social pressures and fads.

Task-Centered Problem Solving

The task-centered model (TC) emphasizes the construction of interventions to reduce the impact of specified problems that are its focus. Specifically, it aims to decrease the frequency of the problem occurrences, the intensity of the problem, and the problem's undesired effects on behavior, relationships, rewards, and lifestyle. The reduction in impact is expected to decrease the impediments to the individual's or family's adequate social functioning and also to increase desired behaviors, relationships, rewards, and quality of life.

The major means of problem solving in TC are: (1) the provision or acquisition of resources with which to do effective problem solving, (2) the teaching and learning of social skills and problem-solving skills, and (3) the actual performance of tasks that do in fact produce demonstrable improvement in the direction sought. It is assumed that in most environments the person with the necessary resources and the necessary skills will be in the best position to manage. Resources and skills may be acquired by direct receipt of material funds and goods, and by combining various types and amounts of advice, guidance, instruction, therapy, and counseling.

The problems that the task-centered approach attempts to reduce are "problems in living," by which is meant conflict between persons (interpersonal conflict), dissatisfaction in social relations, difficulties with formal organizations, difficulties in role performance, reactive emotional distress, or inadequate resources (Reid, 1978).

Psychodynamic Approaches

Psychodynamic approaches have undergone considerable revision in recent years as theorists responded to criticism and questioning from such varied sources as, for example, the women's movement, sociologists, historians of science, and the helping professions themselves (Castel, Castel, & Lovell, 1982; Sulloway, 1979). Psychodynamic approaches, which are adaptations of classical psychoanalytic treatment theories, reflect powerful intellectual trends in the modern world and have many strong adherents, especially in the United States. Furthermore, some of these ideas have saturated modern international culture, literature, drama, art, and everyday habits of thought, as well as human service programs.

Psychodynamic approaches emphasize interventions to enhance and restore personal well-being, to help people meet their needs for self-actualization and self-fulfillment more fully, and to promote more adequate functioning in social relationships. The improvements intended are envisaged in broader terms than the target problem defined in the task-centered model. In the psychodynamic approach, the changes hoped for are personality growth and development, reduction in current life pressures, and correction of poorly functioning ego and superego (resulting in a distorted perception of the outside world or the self, poor judgment, excessive anxiety, insufficient ability to control impulses or to direct behavior, poor reality testing, and inappropriate uses of defenses) (Woods & Hollis, 2000).

The major means of problem solving in psychodynamic therapies is the therapeutic relationship in which the helping practitioner guides the client through processes of acquiring insight, that is, understanding oneself, significant others, and the social environment; acquiring resources and skills along the way; or achieving diminution or resolution of intrapsychic conflicts as a means to self-fulfillment and improved relations with others. Benefit from these processes is expected to decrease the impediments to adequate social functioning.

The problems that psychodynamic approaches attempt to affect are the same ones that TC formulates; but the ideal or preferred form of the psychodynamic approaches considers that the internal (i.e., the private mental or intrapsychic) reflection of the problem takes priority in the treatment. However, if the client and/or the circumstances bar effective attention to underlying problems, psychodynamic practitioners are realists and settle for limited goals.

Cognitive-Behavioral Approaches

Cognitive-behavioral approaches are relatively new on the scene and were first formulated and published in the 1970s. As is the case with other treatment models, various writers, based on their different experiences and interests, have made unique contributions to the ideas that are now called cognitive-behavioral approaches. These writers emphasize interventions to help clients cope with immediate, pressing problems and acquire knowledge and understanding useful in managing future life problems (Berlin, 1983). Some evidence suggests, for example, that clients who learn problem-solving skills achieve more gains in treatment than clients who receive only treatment (Brown, 1980).

Cognitive-behavioral approaches relate to cognitive theory, a developing body of knowledge that is enlightening while still tentative and speculative (Gardner, 1985). These approaches offer new possibilities for the clinical practitioner. They suggest that the client come to understand and appraise the essential nature of the situation and its options and then take steps to improve those options and reduce those problem states. Berlin (1983) suggests a wide range of activities that may facilitate change. How a client thinks and feels about problems may be changed by constructing more adaptive meanings and expectations and providing experiences that support changed views. New behaviors may be developed through modeling, rehearsing, and repeated enactments. Relevant social-environmental strategies may achieve new social supports for clients, enhancing their abilities to solve problems. Berlin (1983) suggests increments of change: helping clients to increase their skills, mastery, and support systems so they can handle more and more difficult problem-solving work.

The problems that cognitive-behavioral treatments attempt to affect are those of central concern to all the intervention models, problems in living. Cognitive-behavioral approaches, like others, are addressed to how people think, feel, and believe, in other words, to psychological or mental aspects of their situations, but also to interpersonal transactions and transactions with the environment, in much the same way as the Task-Centered Model.

Crisis Intervention

Quick, immediate responses to emergencies and to acute, sudden onset of problems, often resulting from some outside agent (for example, a sudden beating or rape), are included within a broad, general category of crisis intervention. Sometimes included are acute emotional crises, such as grief. Crisis intervention approaches are responsive to public events, such as natural disasters and wrecks, and to traumas induced in special populations by newly emerging or newly recognized social problems such as child abuse and wife battering. There is no single unified crisis theory or intervention method. Crisis intervention is in fact a variant of planned brief treatment adapted to the circumstances of particular intervention programs (Lemon, 1983; Parad & Parad, 1990).

Family Approaches

Family treatment represents another collection of related but dissimilar approaches. Problems in living are explained as an expression of the way the family system functions. There are numerous views about the processes involved in the family system. Walsh (1982) has summarized the activities of various family intervention approaches as follows:

- Reorganizing the family structure (structural approach)
- Resolving the presenting problem (strategic approach)
- Improving concrete, observable behavior (behavioral-social exchange approach)
- Developing insight into and resolving family conflict and losses, reconstructing relationships, and stimulating individual and family growth (psychodynamic approach)
- Modifying relationships in the family system (family systems therapy)
- Enhancing clear, direct communication and individual and family growth through immediate shared experience (experiential family therapy)

These various approaches overlap. Available research does not indicate the superiority of any one approach over any other, and it is not established in what circumstances family treatment is the treatment of choice. Many practitioners, however, prefer treatment to include all or part of the family when several members are involved in the problem. The problems that are the focus of family treatment are the same array of problems that are the focus of other treatment models. The psychodynamic approaches concentrate upon theoretically identified internal conflict areas in the family treatment mode as they do in the individual treatment mode.

From its inception, the task-centered model has included family treatment within its scope (Reid & Epstein, 1972; Epstein, 1985; Reid, 1985) with respect to both focal problems and methods of intervention adjusted to take account of multiple participants. Adaptations of the task-centered approach have been worked out to enhance permanency planning for children in foster care (Rooney, 1981; Rzepnicki, 1985).

Group Approaches

A *group* is a collection of unrelated persons who have some explicit connection to one another that makes them interdependent. Groups consisting of individual adults, parents, children, or couples are formed in human service organizations. People facing similar illnesses or social problems, or seeking increased competence in social skills, are typical examples of those who might constitute problem-solving groups.

Groups may be effective in ameliorating problems in living. Their problem-solving processes are augmented by group processes such as convening the group; integration and disintegration; the development of intragroup conflicts; and subsequent reorganization of the group (Epstein, 1985; Garvin, 1981; Yalom, 1985). Groups are complex phenomena that are difficult to research. Available information comparing group and individual treatment does not indicate that either is more effective than the other. Like individual treatment, group treatment may result in casualties (Bednar & Kaul, 1978; Lieberman, Yalom, & Miles, 1973; Parloff & Dies, 1977).

The task-centered model has been applied to work with groups since its inception, adapting the steps and processes to take account of multiple participants and group processes (Fortune, 1985b; Macy-Lewis, 1985; Newcome, 1985; Rooney, 1977). Some of these adaptations include:

- Selecting group members whose target problems and anticipated tasks are similar
- Using group tasks as well as individual tasks
- Using visual aids to clarify actions and keep attention on goals
- Using formats for achieving task performance, such as consulting pairs and buddy systems

Blending Approaches: Eclecticism

Intervention practice cannot get along without developing and using technology. Real practice, however, must be eclectic. But this does not mean a hodgepodge; it *does* mean a reasoned selection from a number of sources of what seems or is judged best at a particular time under specific circumstances. What is best depends on one's viewpoint and philosophy of practice. Many today are persuaded that the best techniques are those most closely connected to the target problem, having a published record of effectiveness, developed from empirical testing and research, and making sense.

Eclecticism is the selection of elements from different systems of thought, without regard to contradictions between the systems. It differs from syncretism, which tries to combine various systems while resolving conflicts. Eclectics are frequently charged with being inconsistent. The fact is that practitioners are habitual borrowers and continual developers of their own practice procedures, based on experience; personal preference; loyalty to influential agencies, teachers, and supervisors and to their own therapists; and attention to keeping up-to-date.

After a decade of muddle during the 1970s, when followers of various schools of therapy engaged in combat with followers of other schools of therapy, a wiser atmosphere emerged. Many contemporary practitioners do not "belong" to any particular system of psychotherapy, although they seem to have preferences or habits. They sometimes elevate their preferences by calling them "principles" or even "theory"—rhetoric that is not always deserved. However, many of today's practical and result-minded practitioners attempt to put some organization into collections of what they believe to be significant phenomena, based on their experience and the experience of trusted colleagues and relying on research data whenever possible (Garfield, 1980; Norcross, 1986; Tolson, 1988).

Present-day eclecticism is based on an awareness that no one model or approach can be universally applied, cover any and all circumstances, or produce an effective outcome across the board. Although little is known with any certainty about what procedures work best in the multitude of practical circumstances, there is nonetheless an awareness that useful strategies and ideas may be found in many various sources.

The problem-solving lens reveals what is common among the approaches, namely, that they all deal with the same or similar problems in living and that they all use verbal discourse in which one person (the practitioner) helps the other person (the client) overcome difficulties. The differences among the basic categories of models are in the different emphases put on defining or focusing the problem; formatting an intervention into individual, group, or family mode; determining the comprehensiveness or specificity of goals; or deciding on the nature of the structure of the intervention sequence (for example, from the manifest steps of the task-centered model to the intricate constructions of the psychodynamic approaches).

Observation and available research findings suggest that practice in the real world is eclectic. Kolevson and Maykranz (1982) obtained information from 670 responding clinical educators (mostly field instructors) in ten graduate schools of social work. The results indicate that their ideas about intervention action were only slightly influenced by their model preferences. Garfield and Kurtz (1976) surveyed 855 clinical psychologists and found that over half indicated they were eclectics. An additional study of a sample of these eclectic psychologists showed they thought that relying on only one psychotherapeutic approach was inadequate for working with the wide variety of problems they encountered (Garfield & Kurtz, 1977). Jayaratne obtained information from 515 respondents to a questionnaire sent to a random sample of clinical social workers. Of the total respondents, 267 (or 54.6 percent) identified themselves as eclectic practitioners (Jayaratne, 1978, 1982).

What seems important at the present time is a commitment to what is most effective to the extent that can be ascertained from research and analysis of various theories of practice and practice reports from reliable sources. It is possible and practical to blend the task-centered approach with a wide variety of other approaches. In fact, the increasing literature about the task-centered model suggests that this kind of adaptation is constantly occurring.

THE ISSUE OF EFFECTIVENESS

The Effectiveness of Treatment in General

The effectiveness of helping others using psychotherapy and other approaches has been of significant concern since early in the twentieth century. Experimental studies from the 1950s through the 1970s were not encouraging. More recently there are grounds for optimism.

Multiplicity of Treatment Models or Approaches.   In the last thirty years, there has been an explosion of systems, models, approaches, and techniques ranging from traditional approaches (usually meaning based on psychodynamic/psychoanalytical techniques) to cognitive and behavioral approaches, to problem-solving approaches, to other approaches not so easily classifiable (Germain &

Gitterman, 1980; Norcross, 1986; Patterson, 1986; Pincus & Minahan, 1973; Reid & Epstein, 1972; Roberts & Nee, 1970; Roberts & Northern, 1976). A diverse cadre of professionals—psychiatrists, psychologists, social workers, nurses, and pastors—are practicing in the field (Strupp, 1986).

Accountability, Including Third-Party Payers' Interests.   Insurance companies, employer- and union-operated health plans, group health plans, health mainte-nance organizations (HMOs), government-funded health benefits (Medicare), and means-tested benefits (Medicaid) have increased the demand for accountability. The growth of a large group of researchers able to engage in evaluative outcome and process research has enhanced the capacity of the helping disciplines to under-take increasingly sophisticated research. Divisive issues exist about methodology and the philosophy of research in these fields (Berlin, 1990; Mullen, 1985). Nev-ertheless, there appears to be no slackening of effort in the research enterprise devoted to identifying activities and results of the far-flung treatment enterprises.

The effectiveness of treatment has become a priority issue as the sums in-vested in therapy and social remediation of all sorts have risen to unprecedented levels. There have developed widespread expectations that psychotherapy and counseling should improve personal and social well-being. Questions about the worth of programs and practices, about their ability to deliver what they promise, about whether or not they "work," and about their cost effectiveness demand cred-ible answers.

Methodological Issues.   Both outcome research and process research about what actually is done in intervention practice are difficult for technical and conceptual reasons. It is complicated to pinpoint, operationalize, observe, confirm, and mea-sure the events of treatment as they occur within the major unit of activity, the interview. Compounding the complexity is that therapeutic events have connec-tions to the situations of family, peers, work and school, culture and community, socioeconomic status, gender, the avowed norms of society, the influence of eco-nomic recessions, unemployment, war, and politics. In fact, the contextual com-plexities are so unwieldy as to induce scholars and practitioners to avoid them.

The tendency is to regard intervention as presumably capable of being ana-lyzed as a technical operation. On the other hand, it is possible to view the treat-ment enterprise as primarily a matter of human and social relationships, that is, compassionate, realistic, caring interactions in the client's behalf, bringing to bear such influence as is reasonable, and providing necessary resources and skills to enable people to negotiate the risks and dangers, the demands and requirements of contemporary life.

What Works?   Given the complexity of this subject, it is necessary to be cautious about summarizing what is known about the active ingredients of the intervention process and about the question of what works, in what circumstances, for whom, as implemented by what type of personnel in what settings, and under what con-ditions. The state of knowledge about the efficacy of treatment is in flux and can be expected to be changeable for the foreseeable future. Briefly stated, the basic points about effectiveness at this point in time appear to be these:*

1. *Psychotherapy, counseling, and social interventions are beneficial and better than no treatment or intervention.* Many psychotherapies have been shown to have demonstrable effects. Psychotherapy adds to natural healing, helps people cope and learn strategies of use to them in the future. Improvement tends to be lasting, even though some problems tend to recur, such as addictive disorders. Generally, psychotherapy is shown to have better results than no therapy (Bergin & Garfield, 1994; Janowsky, 1999; Lambert, Shapiro, & Bergin, 1986; Reid & Hanrahan, 1982).

2. *There is not at present, nor can there be expected in the near future, agreement on any one single model or set of techniques as the most superior.* Research to date is unable to identify a particular all-embracing superior model or models, despite many comparative studies. Within these studies there appear tendencies that suggest that an approach may be preferable under certain conditions, but these findings are highly varied and difficult to implement. More fine-grained analysis of practice is striving with some success to observe, define, and describe packages of techniques that appear to be particularly useful when addressed to bounded problems or problem areas. Thus, the existing research is creating new developments in practice that are relatively problem-specific. Rather than look for one model or one set of unifying effective principles, practitioners need to be familiar with the literature on basic common principles (see below) and also with specialty journals and workshops that organize what is known about problem-specific techniques.

It is argued that the apparent similarity of results emerges from comparative research on models due to the inaccuracy and insensitivity of research procedures. It is also argued that the practices studied in research do not properly represent the best practice. To tackle this problem, research methods are constantly becoming more sophisticated. However, some sectors within the broad field of psychotherapy are strongly persuaded of the correctness of their own beliefs. They are not swayed by evidence to the contrary or by competing beliefs.

3. *It seems possible that there may be common or similar activities across models, and that these activities may be the most powerful or among the most powerful.* Certain practitioner attributes appear to be common across models: warm involvement with the client and communication of a new perspective on the client's situation. Contemporary research has not contradicted the strong contribution of these relationship attributes to achieving good outcomes. However, researchers have found it difficult to specify and measure these attributes and trace their role during the treatment process. Different theoretical viewpoints tend to shape the relationship and new perspectives according to their particular explanations of behavior and values.

*Bednar & Kaul (1978); Bergin & Lambert (1978); Garvin (1981); Johnson (1986); Koss, Butcher, & Strupp (1986); Lambert, Shapiro, & Bergin (1986); Newman & Howard (1986); Reid (1978, 1985); Reid & Hanrahan (1982); Rubin (1985); Strupp & Binder (1984); Videka-Sherman (1988); Wells (1982); Wood (1978).

A recent development is intended to increase uniformity of practice across practitioners, thus to enhance the standardization of common techniques. Such standardization is being attempted by training therapists to use treatment manuals that prescribe how to do the basic techniques. This book is one example of a manual. (See also Beck, Rush, Shaw, & Emery, 1979; Klerman, Weissman, Rounsaville, & Chevron, 1984; Luborsky, 1984.) Therapists trained according to treatment manuals have shown that they practice in line with the manuals' specifications, thus minimizing the variations that make practice research so difficult. Even therapists who merely assert their allegiance to a school of therapy have shown appropriate, systematic particularities in their practice. Comparative-outcome studies have had difficulties in making clear comparisons, because such studies are generally deficient in describing both in detail and comprehensively what practices were actually carried out. Practitioner behavior is so individualized that it is rarely exactly clear that procedures have been carried out in accordance with the rules of the approach or its best practice recommendations.

4. *Beyond the common features, certain attributes of practice tend to be associated with the likelihood of good outcomes.* These attributes include:

- *Structured approaches addressed to specific problems, behaviors, or social skills.* *Structure* means planned content, order, and arrangement of the design and conduct of the intervention program. *High structure* means the quality of strong, tight specificity and uniformity of the treatment plan. *Low structure* means a diminished degree of specificity and uniformity, together with a high degree of practitioner independence in selecting and arranging the treatment components, their timing, and their type. The extremes of structure—high to low—are sometimes referred to as being *tightly focused* or *diffuse.*
- *Task-centered problem solving and behavioral contracting.* Behavioral contracting and the task-centered model call for securing from clients commitments to undertake specific problem-solving actions. What is to be done and what is to be gained from doing it are laid out clearly, and the client is engaged as a voluntary participant. According to Reid and Hanrahan (1982), "Within this arrangement are apparently potent ingredients for bringing about change in human problems" (p. 338). Rubin's review of research (1985, p. 474) confirms that

  Most of the studies with unequivocally positive outcomes tested forms of practice that relied heavily on problem-solving and task-centered methods, usually in conjunction with behavioral methods, such as social skills and training. These forms of practice were found to be successful with such diverse groups as mildly to moderately retarded adults; chronic schizophrenics in aftercare; young, nonchronic psychiatric inpatients; women on public assistance; and low-income children experiencing school problems.

  Videka-Sherman (1988) found that conveying the structure to the client and preparing the client for intervention and for a personally responsible role in the change process (all part of contracting) were effective interventions associated with good outcomes.

- *Motivational congruence.* Achieving and maintaining a focus in keeping with the client's own interests has the effect of improving the probability of a good outcome. The need is minimized for engaging a client in a long process of uncovering resistance to the practitioner's mind-set or way of formulating a problem, and influencing the client to give up his or her own views in favor of those put forth by the practitioner. This kind of impasse is eliminated or shortened. The client senses the empathic thrust of being taken seriously in her own terms, and the healing power of the treatment relationship is probably enhanced. Particularly in dealing with involuntary clients, getting into the way the client perceives the situation and what the client wants and can do releases a valuable degree of client commitment (Rooney, 1992).

- *Sharp focus.* Sharpness of focus is characterized by pinpointing the area to be worked on and putting related or distant issues in the periphery or background. As will be seen later in this book, sharp focus is the hallmark of brief treatment. There is every reason to believe that sharpness of focus, when attainable, is a significant attribute of effective treatment of any length.

- *Case-management techniques.* Brokering, linking, advocating, and referring are activities designed to select, obtain, and monitor community services. Such techniques have been judged successful with both physically and chronically mentally disabled clients. These techniques hark back to the origins of social work and to the work done in settlement houses earlier in the twentieth century. It is interesting that in their modern form evidence has been obtained as to their value and effectiveness. These techniques are the surest avenue we have to induce and make changes in environmental stress and to make those changes directly by selecting, obtaining, and applying resources that already exist in the community but are not being properly distributed and used.

- *Comprehensive treatment packages in aftercare of chronic schizophrenics.* There has been a great deal of research and development in connection with the problem situations of chronically mentally ill persons. There is evidence for the value of structured, brief treatments that focus on problems of role performance and basic living skills, provide material resources and social support, and reach out into the community to arrange the best possible, least stressful environmental and social network conditions. Long-term "talking" programs do not appear to succeed with these clients and seem to have no real place.

  Treatment packages include restoration of major role performance, instruction in basic living and social skills, drug therapy, support system development, family education, and provision of material resources. Distinctive in these successful approaches was a practice orientation emphasizing support, linkage, education, and rehabilitation and avoiding psychodynamic and cognitively arousing approaches. Successful approaches sought to facilitate role performance and living conditions (Rubin, 1985; Videka-Sherman, 1988). Studies are going forward suggesting the possibility that biological deficits in schizophrenics may limit their ability to problem-solve to the point where they may need continuing open-ended assistance from professional helpers (Hogarty, 1989).

■ *Socialization of the client for intervention.* Informing the client thoroughly and understandably about what will occur in treatment and what are reasonable expectations has been shown to be strongly associated with good outcomes.

■ *Short-term treatments.* Treatment programs that have a set, relatively brief time limit are associated with effective interventions. It is not known what duration of treatment is best in particular circumstances. It is possible that the successful outcomes of brief treatments are the result of the structured effort induced by time limits or deadlines. In order to comply with deadlines, it is advisable to rely heavily on task-centered, problem-solving, behavioral, and cognitive approaches. Successful outcomes in brief treatment may be due to the fact that these therapies have been introduced through handbooks and manuals that provide fairly detailed instructions as to how to apply the techniques. Short-term treatments tend to be focused and active, perhaps accounting for their good results.

Surveys of length, or duration, of treatment consistently show that most outpatient therapies last no longer than twenty sessions, and the average ranges from five to seven sessions. A growing body of research supports the effectiveness of brief treatments in work with families, in mental health out-patient treatments, in cases of marital conflict, in problems involving children and adolescents, in crises and depressions, in social and interpersonal relationship difficulties, and in some forms of treatment for drug and alcohol addiction. Brief psychotherapy is today considered to be an effective and efficient treatment option (Koss & Butcher, 1986).

■ *Behaviorally and/or educationally oriented family interventions.* Despite continuing and growing interest among practitioners in family-oriented interventions, few studies meet the criterion of adequacy in research. A formulated family-problem-solving approach based on the task-centered model is promising, depending on a variety of empirical findings from a number of research sources (Reid, 1985).

■ *Group treatment of various types.* There is no clear evidence as to the superiority of group or individual modalities. Clear goals and use of contracts appear to be valuable aids in achieving satisfactory results.

■ *Practitioner activity, including advice and direction.* Practitioner activity refers to verbal behaviors such as directing, guiding, advising, instructing, and modeling, and to actions (such as obtaining resources, advocating, linking, referring, negotiating, and the like) taken on behalf of the client. On the whole, the frequently noted effectiveness of such treatment activities may be a part of the more general effectiveness of support and case-management processes. By and large the conclusion about the effectiveness of techniques in this category is based on limited research and logical inferences.

5. *A proportion, perhaps a fourth, of cases shows little or no improvement.* With some types of problems, the proportion of poor outcomes may be greater, as in the situ-

ations of persons addicted to drugs, or persons revealing severe deviation from social norms, or persons who are socially disadvantaged to a serious extent.

This fact has caused considerable debate in all the helping disciplines. The extent of the problem and why it occurs are issues that are far from settled. The tendency has been to attribute poor outcomes to practitioner errors such as insufficient personal behaviors (for example, a lack of warmth, empathy, and genuineness), insensitivity of various sorts (such as lack of time, adequate supportive relationships, hostile behaviors, and aggressive actions), or lack of training and relevant knowledge (Mays & Franks, 1985). However, analysis indicates additional factors are probably at work, suggesting that the practitioner's characteristics may not be the only or primary factor involved in negative outcomes. Thoits (1985) states that substantial research supports the commonsense idea that undesirable life events and chronic strains have deleterious psychological effects upon individuals. Recent work confirms that these negative effects may be reduced when individuals possess adequate social support or use coping strategies to buffer the impacts of events and strains (Camasso & Camasso, 1986). The likelihood is that negative outcomes result from a combination of factors including those already mentioned as well as constraints imposed on the helping situation by the structure of agencies, by value and ideological positions, by political factors influencing the availability of resources and opportunities, by features of practice methods, and by the plain and unadulterated pain and stress of living.

The Effectiveness of Brief Treatment

Based on the current state of knowledge, Janowsky (1999) concludes that

- Clients typically come to psychological treatment seeking specific problem resolution for which brief treatment is well suited.
- It appears that brief treatments have approximately the same success rates as longer-term treatment programs.
- Most insurance companies or prepaid health programs recognize the benefits of psychotherapy but limit payment to brief treatment.

Treatment programs are expensive. The combination of limitations of funds, together with pressure from clients and insurers to get results in a focal problem, push therapy into brief treatment modes. Brief treatment is justified by the positive findings of research and practice experience. Insurers are slicing reimbursements for psychiatric care, often by half or more. Insurance companies are giving priority to short-term therapy focused on one single problem (*New York Times*, 1990).

Deficiencies in the methodology of the studies and fragmented coverage of important features of brief treatment create puzzles and gaps in knowledge. Methodology defects are being corrected in newer research. Research methods and the credibility of the results are improving but progress is slow because research of high quality is expensive and time consuming. Some of the key problems in evaluating brief therapy are:

1. *Omnibus comparative studies of brief and extended treatment have emerged with seemingly contradictory findings.* This happens when studies confuse the different effects of the passage of time and the amount of treatment. It is far from clear whether to measure the amount, or "dose," by time in treatment, that is, weeks, months, or years; whether the amount is the number of sessions, number of hours, or what? Ratings of improvement are usually made by therapists themselves who have shown strong preference for long-term treatment, thus introducing prominent bias. In addition, samples contain clients who dropped out and whose situations confound the results (Luborsky, Crits-Christoph, Mintz, & Auerback, 1988). In spite of some contrary findings, the overall outcome research indicates that the results of brief treatment are at least as good as those of time-unlimited treatments, and there does not seem to be a significant relationship between duration of therapy and outcome (Garfield, 1989). Why this has turned out to be the case is not understood definitively. The most common explanations suggest that the research methodology creates the finding; perhaps a better explanation is that the benefits of brief therapy derive from the particular features of brief therapy, particularly, its structure, focus, and ability to secure the cooperation of clients.

A small number of studies that have carefully and directly compared time-limited versus unlimited approaches show equal effectiveness (Reid & Shyne, 1969). As is true in the general field of psychotherapy outcome research, studies comparing different models of brief treatment fail to show clear superiority for any of the approaches studied to date. However, comparative studies so far do not cover the range of available models. And some types of comparisons are impossible to make. For example, one could not compare a psychodynamic model with strict selection criteria permitting inclusion of a narrow band of a particular diagnosis, such as the Sifneos (1987) model, with a general problem-solving model that accepts people with difficult diagnostic categories or strong environmental deficits and people sent or ordered to treatment involuntarily.

2. *Many of the older data on brief psychotherapy outcome were derived from only a few studies, but newer studies have begun to cover typical client groups.* The older studies represented a limited sector of the range of clients seen in day-to-day treatment practice; thus, caution is advisable in generalizing the results of those studies to the population of clients as a whole (Koss & Butcher, 1986). Nevertheless, brief treatments are now being used widely throughout treatment programs. Recent studies supporting brief treatment have been coming from a broader population and from some basic treatment settings where typical client groups are seen (Elkin et al., 1989).

A list of the range of current applications indicates how wide the usage is. A handbook by Wells and Giannetti (1990) includes reports on brief treatment with depressed patients, families, married couples, sexual dysfunctions, single persons, groups, social skills training groups, and schizophrenics. Other reports give details on using brief therapy methods with alcoholics and drug-addicted persons. In fact, particularly under the influence of finance-driven and client-preference pressures, the practice of brief therapy is increasing in all areas, except where public policy underwrites long-term care, as in child welfare and care of the aged and severely handicapped.

3. *How long is brief therapy?* The available research does not provide definitive standards for determining what the optimum or desirable length of treatment should be. In present practice, time limits are set rather arbitrarily. The usual time limits of brief treatment do not exceed sixteen to twenty sessions. These usual brief treatment time limits turn out to exceed the median number of interviews in most unlimited treatments. One meta-analysis (Howard, Kopta, Krause, & Orlinsky, 1986) indicates the probability that 10 to 18 percent of patients could be expected to show some improvement while waiting to be seen for their first session. By eight sessions, 48 to 58 percent of patients would be expected to have measurably improved. About 75 percent in all likelihood would show improvement in twenty-six sessions, and 85 percent by the end of a year of treatment.*

In modern brief treatment, eight sessions is a common time limit, although much present practice seems to prefer a time limit a bit longer than that. Present research indicates that it can be expected that the majority of clients will have achieved satisfactory demonstrable results by eight sessions. After that, it is likely that if the client continues there will be small incremental increases reaching a slowly ascending plateau after fifty-two sessions. The relationship of number of sessions and patient improvement is graphically shown in Figure 2.1.

This analysis speaks to average expectable results for most clients. In commenting on this meta-analysis, Orlinksy and Howard (1986) state:

> Improvement is proportionately greater in earlier sessions (during which time patients commonly experience considerable relief), and increases more slowly as the number of sessions grows (and the patients' less tractable problems become the focus of treatment). This analysis also suggests a course of diminishing returns with more and more effort required to achieve just noticeable differences in patient improvement. (p. 361)

However, there will be failures in brief treatment as there are in long-term treatment. The best results in brief treatment, as in any other kind, will be among those clients who have the least serious problems and who have the most personal, economic, and social resources. The Howard et al. (1986) meta-analysis indicates that depressive patients appear to respond at the lowest dosages of psychotherapy, anxiety neurotics at somewhat higher dosage, and borderline psychotics at a still higher dosage. The challenge is to extract knowledge from research and experience that will maximize results within definable brief treatment durations.

---

*Many studies have attempted to review the relationship between time in treatment and treatment outcome. These studies yield somewhat varied results. They are not readily comparable because of differences in methodology and in the way they are interpreted. The Howard et al. study is the first one based on sophisticated meta-analysis.

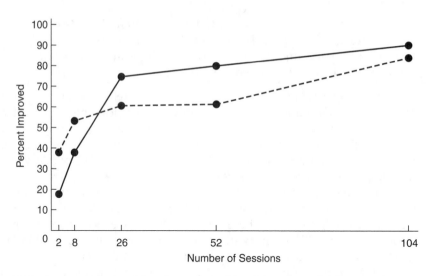

FIGURE 2.1   Relationship of number of sessions of psychotherapy to percentage of patients improved

Note: Objective ratings at termination are shown by the solid line; subjective ratings during therapy are shown by the broken line.

Source: From K. I. Howard, S. Kopta, M. Krause, & D. E. Orlinksy, "The Dose-Effect Relationship in Psychotherapy," *American Psychologist, 41*(2), p. 160. Copyright © 1986. Reprinted by permission of the American Psychological Association.

Who Can Benefit from Treatment, Especially Brief Treatment?

Increasing numbers of people are finding psychotherapy helpful in controlling clear-cut, mild to moderately severe mental disease of a temporary or chronic nature. Large numbers of people find therapy useful in reducing the impact of depression, anxiety, under-achievement, low self-esteem, and lack of satisfactory interpersonal relationships—all the accumulated unhappiness related to problems in living. Problems in living are often classified by a diagnostic category in the range from mild to moderate to moderately severe mental disorder. Problems in living are sometimes treated by direct targeting of circumscribed pathological behavior, as in the case of phobias, depression, unresolved oedipal problems, and other diagnostic categories that have developed protocols for intervention.

Most problems in living, whether or not they are tagged with a diagnostic label, are most often treated today by some program of support, increased understanding, emotional release, and new learning about better ways to negotiate relationships and the social environment. It is this large population of distressed people who are treated in outpatient psychiatric clinics, in private practice, and in many social agencies, such as family and adult service organizations. From this population are drawn most of the data concerning the outcomes of therapy and its effectiveness.

It is fair to say that the majority of this population can be expected to benefit from therapy and to be better off with than without therapy. This population can be expected particularly to benefit from brief therapy. The less disturbed people are, the more personal resources they have, and the more recent the onset of their trouble, the better off they will probably be as a result of therapy.

Other large populations of distressed persons have problems that are more severe, more intractable, and more difficult to work with. Some are chronically mentally ill. Controversy surrounds them. Some reports indicate that such clients do well with brief treatment that is supportive by including large amounts of advocacy and brokering, by obtaining and providing social resources, and by teaching social skills (Videka-Sherman, 1988). Other reports suggest that long-term care is necessary (Hogarty, 1989).

Large numbers of clients in the treatment system are considered socially deviant to a serious degree, such as persons addicted to alcohol and drugs, persons who suffer from substance abuse and psychopathology together, perpetrators of child abuse, spouse batterers, overusers of medical care, persons with eating disorders, violence-prone persons, and sex offenders. The effectiveness of treatment for these difficult populations poses research problems that have been solved only in a rudimentary way. Most recent studies focus on the effectiveness of treatment with specific populations or for specific problems or diagnostic categories (Janowsky, 1999).

A great deal of the responsibility for dealing with these more difficult groups falls to the social work profession, which pioneered in inventing methodology for research with these populations. However, progress was set back when, during the 1970s, there were unearthed considerable difficulties with designing and implementing solid programs that were effective to the degree desired (Mullen, 1983; Mullen, Dumpson, & Associates, 1972). A new generation of research, building upon the original efforts, has come up with support for treatment effectiveness in some of these difficult areas, including support for brief treatment (Reid & Hanrahan, 1982; Thomlinson, 1984; Wood, 1978).

A recent study that takes advantage of improved methods of research is the Health Care Utilization and Costs study of the Hawaii Medicaid Project (Cummings, Dorken, Pallak, & Henke, 1990). This study reports that different forms of psychological treatment had dramatically differing effects on overall medical usage and costs among the study populations, who included persons receiving Medicaid, which is the government program for medical assistance to persons in poverty, and another population of federal employees. The application of targeted, focused brief treatment had a more profound impact on reducing the costs of medical usage than did the application of traditional forms of mental health treatment. The project used an eclectic type of brief treatment that assumes it could be intermittent, that is, resumed for brief additional periods on an as-necessary basis.

Recently Elkin et al. (1989), Blatt (1999), and Shea, Elkin, and Sotsky (1999) published analyses of a unique and complex study. The study, under the auspices of the National Institute of Mental Health (NIMH), was carried out under carefully controlled conditions in multiple sites by twenty-eight well-trained therapists, psychiatrists, and psychologists. This landmark study succeeded in standardizing the procedures for the two forms of brief therapy for depression, interpersonal psychotherapy (IPT), and cognitive therapy for depression (CT-D). Both these forms of brief psychotherapy were shown to be capable of successfully treating patients who met the models' criteria for depression. The IPT model appeared possibly better for the more severe depressions. The study also suggests that for mildly depressed patients, a meaningful initial approach can consist of monthly or biweekly "watchful waiting," attention, and sympathetic curiosity, with encouraging support or drugs in addition.

The Effectiveness of Task-Centered Treatment

The task-centered approach is a generic type of brief treatment model designed for use with problems in living where the problem issues can be framed in terms of interpersonal relationship difficulties and difficulties in the social environment. The design of the model does not make a good fit if the problem targeted is conceived of in medical terms. The problem has to be framed in terms of interpersonal, intrapersonal, or person–environment terms. The task-centered model recommends many practices similar to those recommended by the whole group of short-term or brief treatment approaches: time limits, limited goals, focused interviewing and present centeredness, activity and directiveness, rapid early assessment, and therapeutic flexibility.

There have been numerous studies of the task-centered model in the United States and England. Some are concerned with research and development of the model and some with evaluation of outcomes. A wide variety of settings, clients, and problems are represented, for example, medical and psychiatric settings, public schools, corrections, services for the aged including residential care, child guidance clinics, public welfare, family service, child welfare, hospice, homeless programs, sex offenders, and employee-assistance programs.*

These reports recount venturesome efforts at developing a general practice model. Developers used as much empirically tested information as could be assembled at the time to design and formulate descriptions of techniques or guidelines for practice.

---

*Alley & Brown (2000); Bass (1977); Bailey-Dempsey (1993); Blizinsky & Reid (1980); Brown (1977, 1980); Brown, Alley, Radding, & Cotton (1999); Butler, Bow, & Gibbons (1978); Diekring, Brown, & Fortune (1980); Donohue (1996); Epstein (1977); Ewalt (1977); Fortune (1977); Garvin, Reid, & Epstein (1976); Gibbons, Butler, & Bow (1979); Gibbons, Butler, Urwin, & Gibbons (1978); Goldberg & Stanley (1978); Hanrahan (1986); Hari (1977); Hofstad (1977); Jackson (1983); Kilgore (1995); Larsen & Mitchell (1980); Macy-Lewis (1985); Moriarty (1990); Naleppa (1995); Naleppa & Reid (1998); Newcome (1985); O'Connor (1983); Parsseghian (1993); Reid (1975, 1978, 1981, 1985); Reid & Bailey-Dempsey (1995); Reid, Bailey-Dempsey, Cain, Cook, & Burchard (1994); Reid & Epstein (1972); Reid, Epstein, Brown, Tolson, & Rooney (1980); Rooney (1977, 1978, 1981); Rzepnicki (1982, 1985); Salmon (1977); Tolson (1977); Toseland & Coppola (1985); Weissman (1977); Wexler (1977); Wise (1977); Wodarski, Marcy, & Malcolm (1982).

The basic outcome research showed that the task-centered model was effective with a wide array of problems. In most instances, the model was able to reduce a set of related problems that clustered around the target problem. The model was less effective if the problem was broad in scope, global, or loose in focus. Some "ripple effect" was observed; that is, good results sometimes fanned out to other problems. Although the quality and rigor of the studies varied, and despite the absence of desired results in some instances, the model was useful as a basic set of interventions for many, if not most, problems in living as they appear in ordinary practice. Taken altogether, the research reports on task-centered work indicate it produces satisfactory results over a wide area of problems. It does this efficiently, in a cost-effective manner satisfactory to clients.

TREATMENT IN COMPLEX, NATURAL CIRCUMSTANCES

The Nature and Limitations of Treatment in Complex Circumstances

It is the nature of the helping disciplines to expect more and better solutions through technology. However, social science is not capable of producing technologies to solve all problems. Although some problems lend themselves to clear-cut assessment and relatively neat and straightforward solutions, others are difficult or intractable.

In live, natural circumstances, personal and social problems are often obscure in their origins, confounded by multiple circumstances, and resistant to quick fixes. Knowledge may be fragmented or lacking. Practice has to take place without the certainty of thorough, complete, valid, and reliable knowledge. This is the essence of problem solving in complex, natural circumstances.

The daily encounter with clients involves methods that comprise the technology, theories, and values. In our technologically minded society, practice— doing, acting, intervening—is underpinned by technology. That underpinning is the problem-solving process. Of equal importance is *prudence,* that is, practical wisdom or practical common sense, with which one mediates between the universal and the particular, between the theories and their application, between the practice guidelines (as in this book) and the live case. Practice decisions get made by applying theory or principles with judgment, choice, and reflection on what constitutes the good for which one acts (Whan, 1986). In spite of many different motives that may coexist when defining problems or deciding on intervention strategies, the final, legitimating value is the concerned judgment about what is best for the client.

The Influence of Helping Organizations

Except in the case of individual private practice, intervention is conducted in bureaucratic organizations, such as welfare agencies of various types, clinics, hospitals, schools, housing authorities, employment and training facilities, or correctional facilities. The organization influences the way practice is conducted. It usually affects the selection of practice models. Policy decisions may direct the specific ways models are used. The types and training of personnel hired will strongly influence the way practice is conducted. The organization emphasizes work in a particular service domain and makes decisions about what interventions are appropriate for the problems or sets of problems over which it assumes responsibility. The organization establishes the terms and conditions for the availability of resources needed in the helping process.

The Role of Organized Professional Judgment

Clients of human service professionals are vulnerable because they must reveal personal, intimate information in order to be helped. Consequently, they have no choice but to depend on and trust the practitioner. They must have greater confidence than if they were using a service with more technical control over its processes, for example, engineering. However, not everybody can be comfortable with that amount of dependence and many lack confidence.

To protect the clients and to maintain their authenticity before the public, the human service professions support a wide variety of mechanisms that organize professional opinion. The organized professional associations collaborate with universities in sanctioning professional education. Through publications and conferences, the professions formulate preferred views and practices; that is, they set standards. Professions are not immune to being influenced by prevailing winds on the political scene and in the funding organizations. They are not immune to the dominant directions of their culture and the body of opinion about what norms to uphold, what priorities to set, or what goals and results to shoot for.

Organized professional judgment makes itself felt at the level of the client's personal problem solving through what the practitioner has learned or selected from the whole body of shifting professional judgment. The power of that judgment is strong because professionals acquire much of their status, security, power, authority, and prestige from identification with their own profession. Because the helping professions are divided into numerous parallel and subsidiary strata, they diverge in general outlook and specific practice rules and recommendations. This creates some confusion, but professionals in these fields learn to live with that confusion as a regular part of their professional work.

Effects of Environment

It is all too obvious that the characteristics of the environment are a major determinant of problems in living. The physical environment comprises both the natural world and the man-made world. The social environment encompasses the system of socioeconomic stratification, the distribution of equality and opportunity, the repressive mechanisms of discrimination, the advantages enjoyed, and the micro-environment—the network of family, friends, community and neighborhood, resources, work, and school. Enfolding all environments are culture, values, knowledge, and beliefs that guide our choices and form our consciousness.

The immensity of the environment, the multiple sources of information and knowledge about it, and the complexity of intervening to change the environment have all combined to turn the attention of helping professionals to more manageable sectors of problems in living, namely the individual and the most immediate environment, the family. Furthermore, the environment is enmeshed in politics, in conflicts between management and labor, and in crucial conflicts over domestic and foreign social policy. It is difficult for any profession sanctioned by law, society, and custom to put itself in a position where it is actively participating in working out large-scale social conflicts, played out mostly in the political arena. Most persons in the helping professions do not have the taste for such conflicts; instead they see themselves as mediators at most. A stream of social activists surfaces at various historical times, the latest being during the civil rights struggles of the 1960s and 1970s. But for the most part, helping professionals attend to the individual and the close family–neighborhood environment.

Within that small arena, the profession of social work has historically possessed a special expertise in connecting people to resources through referral, linkage, and advocacy. This service is highly valued by clients and of growing interest to other helping professions such as nursing.

In the live case, the environment saturates the problem circumstances. For purposes of practice, that is, for practical judgments about problem identification, focus, and intervention design, assessments ought to be attempted that judge the degree to which environmental factors are dominating the problem. Understanding those factors or intervening in some of the environmental circumstances may ameliorate the situation. Should that be the case, even partly, the intervention may be efficient and successful.

Effects of the Personal Characteristics of the Client and Practitioner

The client's response to the helping process is only partly a product of the techniques of problem solving used. Clients' responses are conditioned by who they are and where they come from and are shaped by their expectations and their views of themselves, other people, and social institutions arising from their ethnic background, culture, social class, personal traits, values, and circumstances.

Mental or physical illness, handicaps, and background affect the manner in which clients present themselves and perceive the practitioner's intentions and actions. A client's characteristic mood, anxiety level, education, cultural background, talkativeness, interests, and expectations all combine to produce the individuality that each person contributes to the treatment situation.

The individual characteristics of the practitioner also influence the process. The practitioner acquires a professional posture or professional "self" that is the result of knowledge, experience, discipline, and socialization. At the same time the practitioner is an individual with unique personal characteristics. Personal and professional selves coexist, however; we do not do away with our personal self and substitute a cardboard character, scripted and made up to look "professional." Like the client, the practitioner has ideas about what to expect, what is preferred, and how to appear. These ideas are personal, derived from the practitioner's background, culture, values, and circumstances. The importance of self-awareness lies in appreciating that practitioner characteristics are present and affect the process of interacting with the client.

SUMMARY

Intervention in human service work means acting on the client's problems in such a way as to improve or alter them for the better. The main purpose of intervention is to cause desired actions to occur.

Numerous types of intervention models and approaches exist: cognitive-behavioral types, psychodynamic approaches, group treatment, task-centered approaches, brief treatment, crisis intervention, and so forth.

Goals are powerful in determining intervention content and substance. Goals include changes in feelings, thinking, and beliefs and attitudes, and in environment, social relations, and behaviors. Goals are important in controlling work to produce results that are as economical as possible and efficient. The contemporary view of goals is to visualize them as reductions in limited, specific problem conditions and behaviors of substantial importance without necessitating major overhauls of personality and relationships.

Differences between clients and helping practitioners and their agencies present difficulties in the helping process. It is advisable to minimize these differences as quickly as possible. The most direct and feasible way is to accept the client's statement of target problems as a straightforward focus for the work, modified, to the extent necessary and possible, on the basis of professional judgment and with client understanding and agreement.

There are several types of goals, all of which may be present: agency, professional, personal practitioner, and client goals. Goals need to be explicit and lead into the development of a plan. Planning involves making choices about interventions and selecting types of interventions expected to be effective in the particular case circumstances, choosing from types of practical help: referral and linkage; negotiating, advocacy, and bargaining; task formulation and guided performance; emotional support; teaching and enhancing social skills; and psychotherapy. The intervention plan includes a plan for the sequence or order of the activities and for contracting, which is primarily a way to assure that the client is well informed about the nature of the intervention and the client's part in the process and is willing and agreeable to proceeding.

The helping professions have only recently developed research means for evaluating the effectiveness of interventions. Although there are no absolutes that will guarantee results, some major findings suggest the kinds of interventions most likely to succeed: structured, planned sequences that are congruent with the client's own perceptions and interests and are sharply focused.

Most practitioners and theorists agree that certain aspects of intervention are important to effective interventions: for example, a satisfactory professional relationship or therapeutic alliance and the presence of facilitating conditions (and absence of strongly limiting conditions) in the environment and in the helping organization or agency. The intervention program may be affected by prevailing professional opinion and by unique effects of the client's and practitioner's personal characteristics.

Problem-solving methods provide the means to get from goals to results in intervention practice. An eclectic repertoire, organized around an effective core, can be organized to fit the perceived needs of particular clients and the style and preferences of agencies and practitioners. The task-centered approach is a way to conceptualize problem solving to make it applicable to human service practice. Psychodynamic, cognitive-behavioral, planned brief treatment and crisis intervention, family, and group techniques contain theories, viewpoints, and techniques which may be used to compile an eclectic program, tailored to particular circumstances of many types.

.....

CHAPTER THREE

FEATURES OF BRIEF TREATMENT

HISTORY AND BACKGROUND OF BRIEF TREATMENT

Brief treatment is not a new subject in psychotherapy; it has emerged slowly and gradually to its present position in the forefront of available modalities. Brief treatment developed in psychotherapy as a modality for treatment in outpatient psychiatry. Its early history was part of the whole movement to develop psychoanalysis and the various related psychodynamic approaches. Later, when the helping disciplines began using new knowledge achieved through outcome and process research, it became evident that it was impractical to conduct research on long-term treatment, because such research was too time consuming and too costly, and its methodological problems were immense. Thus, it came about that treatment research began to occur with brief treatment. Research in long-term treatment became the province of a small specialization in research on psychoanalytic types of treatment (Luborsky et al., 1988).

In clinical social work, brief treatment is found in outpatient psychiatry; in addition, brief treatment has long and distinct roots as a social work specialty. It developed in practice areas that were uniquely the province of social work, that is, crisis intervention, task-centered treatment, Traveler's Aid services, and practical interventions focused on person–environment mismatches and dysfunctions.

Modern individual verbal psychotherapy has been constructed around a basic adherence to the doctrines of psychoanalysis, specifically directed to the belief that changes in behavior, attitudes, and affects can be accomplished under certain therapeutically designed conditions. These conditions involve the patients in talking about their difficulties in relatively well-defined ways—in free association, in psychoanalysis proper, or in psychoanalytic psychotherapy—using relatively unconfined speech within a positive relationship with a trusted therapist. Moreover, the developers of psychoanalysis taught that behavior and affect changes could be made to occur in areas that at first seemed inaccessible to change (Edelson, 1988; Ford & Urban, 1964). Michel Foucault (1973) has traced these views, usually ascribed in current texts to Freud, back as far as the eighteenth-century reformers who invented asylums as religious–therapeutic institutions to treat the mentally ill.

Originally, psychoanalysis was of short duration, but the process became lengthened by Freud's associates and followers, eventually becoming established as the longest form of treatment. Disputes that broke out among the early psychoanalysts about length turned out to be about content as well, a circumstance that is still the case to this day. The original debate among the psychoanalysts about duration of treatment was temporarily concluded by 1925, when it was declared that psychoanalysis should be "the full reliving of the Oedipus situation in the relation of the patient to the analyst, in order to bring it, with the help of the patient's insight, to a new and more fortunate conclusion" (Strupp & Binder, 1984, p. 8). This kind of ambitious personality and lifestyle overhaul was understood to need extended time.

The 1940s brought renewed interest in reducing the length of psychoanalysis, and by extension psychoanalytically influenced psychotherapies that had begun to emerge. Alexander and French, psychoanalytic leaders and teachers based in Chicago, recognized dangers in overtreatment and took what was then a nontraditional view of what should be the focus of treatment. They veered away from the requirement that there needed to be prolonged work at reconstructing the whole past. They introduced the concept of "corrective emotional experience" to describe the therapeutic relationship and what happened in treatment. Alexander and French's ideas, although initially regarded as too radical for the established profession, eventually became part of the basic taken-for-granted beliefs in the world of psychotherapy.

Brief therapies began to be taken seriously by the mid-1960s. Howard Parad, a social worker, then Dean of the Smith College School of Social Work, emerged on the scene as a key developer of crisis intervention. This approach originated and continued as a multidisciplinary endeavor. Parad and his associates created intense excitement in social work, which was then trying to cope with many concerns, such as the need to establish its effectiveness and to find techniques for changing types of social problems, such as multiproblem families, with increasing demands to take on and solve pressing social problems to which all of society had begun to attend.

Ideas and techniques for crisis intervention began to invigorate the National Traveler's Aid Societies, which had long been the only officially short-term service agency in the social work field. The personnel of that agency became known as innovators and developers with the advent of theories of crisis intervention (Epstein, 1965).

The emergence of crisis intervention created a ferment throughout the psychotherapeutic field, crossed disciplinary lines, and eventually became entrenched, even though conceptually crisis intervention is a hybrid. Its methods are not standardized, and its outcomes are uncertain. Its success is due to the undisputed fact that it serves a practical need to find ways to intervene promptly and relevantly into the myriad emergencies ("crises") that are spawned by the stresses of modern life and the uneven distribution of resources for dealing with them.

Alongside crisis intervention, there began a widespread interest in, development of, and experimentation with planned time-limited treatment. The lead was taken by psychiatrists and psychologists, except for the emergence of the task-centered approach in social work (Reid & Epstein, 1972). That approach was derived from multiple sources: research seeking effective methods, theories and practices of crisis intervention, and the problem-solving concept with origins in the American philosophy of John Dewey's "instrumentalism." That philosophy held that human activity is an instrument for problem solving and that truth is evolutionary and based on experience that can be tested and shared by all who investigate.

Several groups in psychiatry and psychology began to experiment with and develop short-term treatment: The Tavistock group in England began in the 1950s with the work of Michael Balint, later joined by David Malan (Gustafson, 1981). In the United States, short-term anxiety-provoking psychotherapy (STAPP) emerged in 1972 under the leadership of Peter Sifneos of the Harvard Medical School. This work has been kept up-to-date and remains a vigorous player in the brief therapy scene (Sifneos, 1987). James Mann, a Boston psychoanalyst, came out with a model of brief treatment in 1973, and this also has been kept current (Mann, 1981). A group in Montreal, led by Habib Davanloo, spearheaded short-term therapy at Montreal General Hospital (1978). Other groups developed in Europe.

The 1980s saw a new generation of models building on the earlier work and included research in the development, testing, and evaluation of the new versions of brief treatment. Simon H. Budman and Alan S. Gurman (1988) offered an approach that emphasized current developmental issues and the interpersonal and systemic context of problems, paying simultaneous attention to affect, cognition, and behavior, and to how the client interacts with others in everyday life. Budman and Gurman see their approach more as a "primary care or family practice paradigm for internal medicine, than traditional therapeutic models of mental health treatment" (1988, p. x). They may see their clients intermittently over time and do not feel constrained by any narrow theoretical orientation, choosing from what they see as the most beneficial aspects of many different psychotherapy perspectives.

Bauer and Kobos (1987) have pulled together a straightforward, clearly depicted description of methods derived primarily from traditional psychoanalysis. Sol L. Garfield (1989) has produced a readable, well-rounded description of an eclectic approach, grounded in practice, wisdom, and research expertise. Strupp and Binder (1984) offer a sophisticated attempt to devise a generic form of brief treatment. There are now manuals that set forth the techniques of two short-term models: *Cognitive Therapy of Depression* (Beck et al., 1979) and *Interpersonal Psychotherapy of Depression* (Klerman et al., 1984).

THEORETICAL VIEWS AND ASSUMPTIONS

No single, unified theory of causation, development, and treatment exists among the brief treatments, just as none exists among the schools of treatment that are not brief. Today's brief treatment theorists are not hung up on arguments over the correctness of this or that belief about causation and method. Eclecticism is the modal orientation. Rival systems are viewed not as antagonistic but as complementary (Norcross, 1986).

Given the clear eclecticism expressed by developers of various models of brief treatment, it is not possible to assert any authoritative theoretical positions. Rather, one has to look over a diverse field and pull out themes that seem pertinent to one's practice or research needs. There is a tendency in most writings to be atheoretical, or to view theory matter-of-factly, possibly because the practice of brief treatment is informed by many knowledge areas that do not particularly mesh. All seem to have a bit here and a bit there to offer as explanatory frameworks. Brief treatment is above all other things a practice, a way of mediating between the universal and the particular. This means that there are many ways to build the bridge from the general to the specifics of a case, and there are many equally convincing explanations of what transpires in brief treatment. And these explanations run the gamut from essential psychoanalytic theories of unconscious conflict; to theories implicating learned and reinforced behaviors as the responsible agents in problem formation and resolutions; to the ideas of Fisch, Weakland, and Segal (1982) attributing problem formation to ordinary life difficulty and viewing treatment as a process of revising the way people apply solutions.

Some of the modern brief treatment developers remain fully enclosed within the parameters of traditional psychoanalytic or psychodynamic theory. They believe that present behavior is to be understood in terms of the person's life history and the crucial foundations laid down in infancy and early childhood, and that key conflicts are to a large extent unconscious, accessible for change only within the workings of the patient–therapist transference relationship. How then can we account for the decisions of psychodynamic brief treatment developers to depart from long-term historical narration and working through of conflicts? Although this seems a germane question, one searches with little success to find the answer in the writings. The switch from concentration on long-term involvement to focused attention on a sector of the problem, and a sector that is at present an active source of distress, seems to have evolved from the convergence of two observations. First is the observation that the outcomes of long-term therapy are not necessarily superior to those of short-term treatment. Second, experienced therapists have learned that people tend to have the capacity to concentrate on present problem solving and conflict resolution without having regularly to repeat and re-live in depth a painful past, and that working through can be an active and directed process, not necessarily a slow, halting movement. This suggests that, without being specific about it, theorists may have changed their minds as they have changed their practices.

TYPES AND MODELS OF BRIEF TREATMENT

The most comprehensive review done of research on brief therapy (Koss & Butcher, 1986) identified in the literature fifty-three models of brief treatment. Since that review was prepared, new models have appeared. Without trying to minimize the sometimes considerable differences among these models, we can classify them into three basic types: psychodynamic, problem-solving, and mixed-eclectic types. All the models draw from a limited set of frameworks within which modern psychotherapy operates. The appearance of an enormous array of models is misleading. Statements about models tend to bear the individual stamps of their authors, who are often practitioners, reflecting the high degree of individualism that normally exists among practitioners. Some authors emphasize some parts of the general framework differently than others; but the similarity among the models is marked. They overlap, borrow from one another, and follow one another around.

We will distinguish the main thrusts of all psychotherapy models, brief treatment included. The features that distinguish differences among models are how they are distributed along psychodynamic and problem-solving themes. The essential differences are theoretical and stylistic, although these differences may be enshrined in status, prestige, historical, and philosophical considerations that create substantial power to persuade and influence professionals and the public about their various merits.

PSYD (the psychodynamic theme) bases itself on a view of life that assumes people are mostly unaware of their deep or real motives; that they need professional–technical help to interpret the hidden-from-awareness symbols; that childhood experiences and emotions, particularly sexual emotions, are the central features of personal psychology; that culture and the environment are background to the stage where lives are experienced. PSYD practitioners tend to be quiet, thoughtful, listener types, that is, their characteristic style is on the passive side. They are reluctant to advise or be actively interventionist. Their overriding aim is to increase the client's conscious self-awareness and develop insight, which is thought to be the necessary condition for the person's change in consciousness and, consequently, change in behavior. This humanistic view of people and their consciousness is congruent with the deep themes that are valued in modern life.

PRBS (problem solving) is based on a framework derived from modern British and American philosophical pragmatism and from technical science. PRBS tends to develop its theories from cognitive psychology and from behavioral theory and also contains ideas from psychodynamic theories, especially ego psychology. PRBS tends to develop its techniques from research information, if at all possible. It tends to focus on a specific target or related set of targets, to develop ideas of specific goals, and to conduct its work closely according to a recommended structure. PRBS practitioners tend to be active and direct, to teach, advise, and instruct. The problem-solving approaches to practice adopt different types of basic governing concepts. These differences are illustrated by the differing practices found in task-centered, behavior modification, and cognitive therapy approaches, for example. The aim of these problem-solving approaches is to help a client acquire new or altered ways of acting in the environment and with people, and new ways of thinking and feeling about self, others, and the environment. The objective is that the person develop skills with which to satisfactorily negotiate the social context and acquire improved self-image and self-understanding.

This instrumental view of therapy also conforms to sets of philosophical beliefs that are typical of modern society. Thus, both the psychodynamic view and the instrumental or problem-solving view are thoroughly consistent with modern consciousness and reflect deep differences that divide and distress moderns—that is, the seeming conflict between science and transcendental values.

A quick reading of this description of broad-scale differences shows how much the two positions tend to draw together and become alike. For example, psychoanalysis is a highly structured form of treatment, taking years to learn; but psychoanalysis is structured differently, for example, than is task-centered treatment, another highly structured approach, which can be learned in a few months. The psychoanalytic treatment structure necessitates continuous and many-layered individual practitioner judgments because of the complexity of its theories and processes and because it emphasizes a broad range of feelings, thoughts, and behaviors as pertinent to its concerns; its rules are ambiguous, its options numerous. The various problem-solving approaches deliberately narrow their foci and limit the range of their interventions. A good deal of the model development and testing is concerned with writing relatively unambiguous rules, but it is not possible to write a complete set of rules. There always remains ambiguity and the need for professional judgment. The idea, however, is to develop a set of reliable rules.

Psychotherapy has concentrated on developing eclectic treatment protocols, drawing, in varying degrees, on both the PSYD and PRBS sides. There is a marked tendency of practitioners and theorists to adhere to one or the other tendency, that is, to adhere primarily to either the psychodynamic or the problem-solving tendency. Often one side is not well versed in the beliefs and practices of the other, or has distorted views of the other. In the discussion to follow, we will write sometimes as if these differences are more real than we think they probably are. This device is a convenience in exploring the subject.

Table 3.1 helps us visualize the sense of the parameters of the two basic types of approaches, the psychodynamic and the problem-solving. The table outlines the general contents of these two prominent treatment approaches. The general contents are classified according to the usual phases of the treatment/intervention

TABLE 3.1   Structure Compared: Psychodynamic (PSYD) and Problem-Solving (PRBS) Approaches

PSYD	PRBS
1. *Assessment* of individual person, problem, and psychosocial situation	1. *General orientation* to its context
2. *Diagnosis* of psychopathology formulation	2. *Problem defined* and constrained assessment
3. *Treatment process:* in major or significant conflict, both intrapsychic and interpersonal: uncover; re-experience; work through; explore; analyze; interpret defenses, resistance, transference; culminating in insight; supplemented with environmental management	3. *Treatment process:* in mutually selected important problem; at a level that is most accessible to change desired; use of a planned package of problem-solving strategies; based on teaching skills; discussing alternatives and obstacles; evaluating progress and problems; advising; revising; managing environment; providing resources
4. *Goal:* fairly flexible	4. *Goal:* constrained to focus or target

process. The third main tendency among treatment approaches, the eclectic tendency, is composed variously of a diverse selection of the psychodynamic and problem-solving components plus unique additions and rearrangements constructed by particular theorists.

Table 3.2 outlines the references that depict the broad differences in brief therapy between PSYD and PRBS, and the mixed-eclectic models that are heavily tilted toward contemporary cognitive theory although they avail themselves of ideas from the whole spectrum.

TABLE 3.2   Types and Models of Brief Treatment: Selected Examples

PSYD	PRBS	MIXED-ECLECTIC
*Bauer and Kobos (1987)	*Epstein and Brown (this volume)	*Beck et al. (1979)
Davanloo (1978)	Reid and Epstein (1972)	*Budman and Gurman (1988)
Malan (1976)		Cummings (1990)
*Mann (1981)		*Garfield (1989)
*Sifneos (1987)		*Klerman et al. (1984)
		*Parad and Parad (1990)
		*Strupp and Binder (1984)

*The models asterisked (*) are the ten major current models that form the basis for the examination of brief treatment in this book. Detailed information on all models is contained in the basic texts prepared by the developers.

CLASSIFICATION OF BRIEF
TREATMENT TECHNIQUES

As previously stated, despite varying theoretical assumptions and treatment strategies, most brief treatments adhere to many of the same techniques. In fact, they all have more attributes in common than differences. However, it is in the differences that the uniqueness and specialization of the various models are brought to the fore. The differences are what makes one model seem preferable in given instances to another. Table 3.3 outlines these commonalities and differences.

The Common Features of Brief Treatment

Brief treatment has twelve common features, as listed in Table 3.3.

1. *Intervention is introduced promptly.* In crisis intervention, the clinician ought to take advantage of the special window of opportunity offered by the heightened susceptibility of the client at the initiation of treatment (Parad & Parad, 1990, p. 7). This means doing away with waiting lists and trying to arrange for the person who does intake to be the same person who does the treatment.

Research studies have substantiated the probable existence of this "window of opportunity." Some research indicates that early treatment sessions have the

TABLE 3.3   Common and Variable Features of Brief Treatments

COMMON FEATURES	VARIABLE FEATURES
1. Intervention is introduced promptly.	1. Criteria for selection of clients vary considerably.
2. Sequences are timed.	2. Termination plans vary considerably.
3. Problems are defined at the start.	3. Attention is paid to underlying problems.
4. Selected focus is maintained throughout the sequence.	4. Advice and guidance are given.
5. Problem solving proceeds systematically.	5. Treatment protocols differ.
6. Goals are relatively specific.	
7. Interviewing is focused and present-centered.	
8. Interviewing style is direct and active.	
9. Rapid early assessment is the mode.	
10. Practice is flexible.	
11. Ventilation is normally provided.	
12. A positive therapeutic relationship provides treatment leverage.	

maximal impact over the length of time that an individual is in treatment. This advantage found in the early sessions was depicted in Figure 2.1 (p. 60).

There may be a similar opportunity available at the start-up of any brief treatment. However, except for crisis intervention, brief treatment models on the whole are slower to move into treatment, although they move fast. Sifneos (1987) and Mann (1981), for example, rely on a series of interviews before the start of treatment proper, during which assessment is carefully explored. The psychodynamic types of approaches stress a specialized assessment, whereas other approaches emphasize that the assessment and initial treatment be pursued together at the same time. The main reason for setting apart extra time for a special assessment/evaluation is that the models that prescribe the evaluation procedure put a stringent limit on who may be accepted into the particular brief treatment model. Approaches that have more flexible acceptance do not need extra time for particularly focused detailed evaluation and may thus proceed quickly into mixing the treatment with the assessment from the start.

Budman and Gurman (1988) have conceptualized a variety of ways to maximize the leverage obtainable during initial contacts (pp. 46–49):

1. Use initial telephone contact to begin therapy and focusing.
2. Try to identify the present central problem theme.
3. Be active from the beginning, sharing tentative trial formulations.
4. Involve significant others from the start, if possible.
5. Vary the interview schedule, giving more interviews at first and then tapering down.
6. Provide homework or tasks for outside the therapy hour.
7. Project a genuine belief that the client can be helped and in a short time.

2. *Sequences are timed.* What all brief treatment models have in common is that the sequence is timed. How many interviews are provided, over what period of calendar time, how the interviews are spaced over calendar time can all be varied; but they are all timed and the client knows of the time restraints from the beginning.

We do not know at present the optimum time limits. After more research has been done on this subject it probably will turn out that there is more than one distribution of optimum time limits, depending on the type of problem, type of person, setting, and other possible factors. The way time limits are chosen now is basically arbitrary. The limits are derived from some combination of practice experience, cost considerations, practitioner style, commonsense observations, and what goal point along the dose-effect relationship continuum (see Figure 2.1) one wishes to achieve. At present, 5 to 15 interviews are common.

Client objections to setting time limits have been rarely reported (O'Connor & Reid, 1986). There is anecdotal evidence in the occasional instance that clients who raised questions about time constraints had earlier been habituated to long-term supportive relationships that they valued and would have preferred to continue. Minor evidence suggests that some clients would have liked to have had one or two more interviews, and that women clients preferred one or two more interviews. There are anecdotes that tend to suggest that men prefer the business-like arrangements of a few specified interviews, and therefore tend to drop out less. These are straws in the wind; little is known about optimum dose effect, which is what the timed interview structure comes down to when thought of in medical model terms.

The real objection to time limits has arisen among professionals whose basic question has to do with providing service that may be less than optimum, thereby short-changing clients, minimalizing service, essentially rationing service because of cost issues. Under this kind of disguised rationing, the poorest, most distressed, and neediest clients might be shunted into brief treatment, reserving the long-term, supposedly maximizing treatment for the better off. These legitimate concerns are found today in all the medical and service specialties where demand exceeds availability and costs are soaring. The field of psychotherapy has an additional issue, that is, the research suggests that outcomes of psychotherapy are modest and that there is no firm evidence of any sort that more is necessarily better. What has been said here refers particularly to psychotherapy in outpatient psychiatry, or in other types of services that offer clinical treatment of problems such as those seen in outpatient psychiatry.

Data are in short supply comparing outcomes of brief and extended treatment for social work clients who are not voluntary, who need and receive case-management services, referral and linkage to resources, and other practical services combined with supportive relationship counseling. There are questions about adapting short-term treatment to clients whose cases may or may not be suitable for outpatient therapy, but who are not receiving outpatient therapy. We refer to individuals and families receiving an admixture of therapy and environmental services: supportive intervention of all sorts, from child protective services to protective services for the aged, from treatment of children abused to treatment of child abusers, from persons arrested for drunk driving to persons detained for having passed a drug addiction to a fetus while in utero, and so forth. It is reasonably inferred in the task-centered model that brief treatment is adaptable to many cases of intervention with involuntary clients and to those who are treated with supportive-resource-providing methods.

Complicated issues are involved in arriving at a position about what ought to be our stance in such cases. Evidence from reliable research supports long-term supportive attention to certain types of chronically mentally ill persons (Hogarty, 1989). But evidence of success with many of the other deviant persons who are subjects of authoritative social control and enforced treatment is not promising. Other aims are present in such cases of multiproblem, involuntary, deviant clients. Society has responsibility for controlling, correcting, teaching, and providing surveillance to people who are deemed harmful to themselves and others—teenage single mothers and drug abusers, for example. The present climate of opinion seeks to restrain costs. Nevertheless, our society basically believes that it is right to provide decent social services to disadvantaged people. The contradictions inherent in these positions are difficult to work out. It is difficult to arrive at a philosophy of help and treatment that can constrain costs, limit service according to sound technical criteria, and have respect for individual rights, all at the same time (Rooney, 1992; Trotter, 1999).

The research available from the Task-Centered Project (Reid, 1981) and other sources covering a wide range of projects (Brown et al., 1999; Reid & Hanrahan, 1982; Videka-Sherman, 1988; Wood, 1978) suggests the wisdom of following a brief treatment route with many, if not all, of these clients, and seeing how far one can get. If costs and agency policy permit or even require, and if clients wish to and can engage in a continuing type of intervention, it is always possible to extend treatment, to offer intermittent treatment episodes as issues come to a head. Like it or not, cost is dictating brief interventions everywhere, so that it strongly behooves us to take advantage of the present development of brief treatment technology to make the most of what will be brief treatment anyway, and which has a very good chance of being effective in producing wanted behavior change that is meaningful within a short time.

3. *Problems are defined at the start;* and

4. *Selected focus is maintained throughout the sequence.* These two techniques are discussed together because they are inseparable in practice. Problem definition and selected focus are the two main brief treatment procedures upon which all the rest depend. Many who have worked in brief treatment believe that these two procedures make or break the sequence and may be the key determinants of whether or not the outcome will be satisfactory.

Most clinical writing does not distinguish between defining problems and maintaining focus. Problem definition tends to be considered under the rubric of selecting focus. In practice, these two facets of the procedure merge. I prefer to separate this idea into two parts. It is relatively easier to firm up the focus and to maintain it if the target problem has been isolated to a reasonable degree. Defining the problem in terms of its identity, specific features, quality, frequency, and seriousness offers the client and the practitioner an understandable rationale for pointing out what the focus ought to be and the motivation for sticking to it rather than wandering.

Every brief treatment model comes down at the earliest possible moment, many of them in the first interview, to a client–practitioner agreement on the problem that is to be the focus or the target for the whole intervention program. This mutually worked-out agreement on problem and focus is verbalized, clearly formulated as exactly as possible, and then held to by a process of selective attention for the duration. This up-front position for the problem definition, although a universal feature of brief treatment, may be played out with variations, depending on both the viewpoint held by the model developers and the basic practice theory from which a particular brief treatment model is taken.

The procedures for defining the problem require interviews emphasizing acute attention to how the client perceives the problem and the problem situation. In other words, sharp listening, an open mind, and a tentative stance are needed. Combine this with the practitioner's continuous knitting the yarn of the problem as perceived by the client into an assessment system while trying to answer two questions:

1. What is the client really saying, really meaning, and what is the most important part of the problem right now?
2. Out of the general problem situation, what is the nature of the key issue now?

The basic viewpoint of the model being followed will provide the assessment system. Following an eclectic approach necessitates weaving in and out of several theories or frameworks that the practitioner knows—all the while listening attentively.

Maintaining the focus requires the practitioner to check out the relevance of the client's current in interview narrative—that is, the client's statements, responses, and questions, the story the client is telling now. The practitioner has to question themes that do not seem relevant to the target problem. They may be relevant, but the practitioner may not understand and may not know enough about the detailed circumstances to understand.

If the client is asked to explain the relevance of a particular story to the focus, it usually is possible to figure out whether the theme being pursued is relevant or not. If not, the key exploratory lead is to find out whether this present theme is sidetracking or elaborating on the target problem or focus. The practitioner has to find out if there is a credible reason why the treatment should depart from its focus. Usually there is no good reason to do this.

It is most usual and most expected that clients will be discursive. In this therapeutic age, people are socialized at an early age to carry on discursive talk. People who are reserved and laconic, economical in speech, are often thought to be at least odd, if not actually disturbed. It is normal for people to veer away from tough talk and use up time on seemingly important matters that are not crucial. In short-term treatment, however, it is not wise for practitioners to participate very much in the client's discursiveness when off topic. Sensitive interviewing skills must be used to direct the discussion back on topic. (See Chapter 10 for more discussion on interviewing skills.)

5. *Problem solving proceeds systematically.* In contemporary practice, most treatment proceeds relatively systematically because otherwise it would be a questionable professional undertaking. Before the days of third-party payments for therapy, and probably to a degree continuing into the present, there was a tendency for practitioners following a psychodynamic approach to be a bit relaxed in structuring treatment, a bit too laid back perhaps, prone to permit quantities of time to be used to explore and build the relationship. Developing a positive therapeutic relationship is necessary for good results. Although this process does take time, it should be expedited.

Scanning present-day textbooks, one does not find recommendations encouraging diffusion in interviews; rather the written advice of teachers and trainers tends to be strongly in favor of structuring time, whether the treatment encounter is short-term or not. However, it appears that what is at issue is not whether or not treatment should be structured: It is. The question is whether the structure should be tighter or looser. Tighter structure means somewhat less room for the practitioners to make idiosyncratic decisions and somewhat more use of manualized or prescribed processes. Looser structure means more permission to make highly individualized judgments and a high degree of flexibility and improvisation in carrying out treatment.

Systematic techniques in brief treatment usually mean *making clear-cut distinctions between beginnings, middles, and ends.*

1. The beginning is for:
   - problem identification,
   - working-assessment,
   - presentation of a positive client–practitioner working alliance or relationship, and
   - establishment of a working agreement, or contract, containing the mutual understanding of what the treatment work is to be about and how it will be done, including client and practitioner responsibilities, and planning:
     —to generate alternative goals or various solutions
     —to decide on preferred and alternative solutions
     —to schedule, put in priority order, and organize inputs
2. The middle is for:
   - implementing the plan
   - negotiating supports
   - revising the plan as necessary
   - developing actions to take (such as tasks)
   - supporting performance
   - monitoring and verifying progress
3. The end is for:
   - separating
   - arranging for follow-up, check-ups, and booster sessions
   - evaluating results

6. *Goals are relatively specific.* The goals of a particular therapy may be elimination or reduction of a particularly troublesome behavior and change. The goals may be addressed to a particular problem or set of currently interrelated problems; to specific sectors of a general problem condition; or to circumscribed or otherwise defined behaviors, attitudes, and feelings. All these types of goals characterizing brief treatment are distinct from any general wide-ranging change in character, personality, psychic structure, or lifestyle.

7. *Interviewing is focused and present-centered.* Interviews focus on the problem at hand. The interviewing technique is restrained about following or allowing a good deal of wandering in subject matter away from the target problems.

In psychodynamic models that attempt to address a problem which has been perceived to be caused by or strongly associated with a long-standing past pattern, the explorations of the past issues are bounded by their attachment to the focal problem included in the treatment effort.

8. *Interviewing style is direct and active.* Therapist behavior tends to be vigorous and energetic. One relies on such techniques as:

- clarifying
- interpreting
- explaining
- instructing
- initiating
- advising/suggesting
- doing tasks or homework between sessions

The degree of activity is based on practitioner judgment, taking client reactions into account. The degree of activity is also determined by the particular model guidelines.

The basic interview style is characterized by being plainspoken, straightforward, overtly friendly but not effusive. (For further discussion on interviewing, see Chapter 10.)

9. *Rapid early assessment is the mode.* Assessment in brief treatment is characterized by blending the assessment process into the beginning of treatment. Assessment is constrained to the present context, with the exception of some psychodynamically oriented models such as those of Sifneos (1987) and Mann (1981). Techniques for rapid early assessment are provided in detail in Chapter 6.

Robust clinical skills are called for in the area of rapid early assessment. It is in this area that training and experience count for a great deal if one is to avoid mistaken judgment about what is wrong and what can be done effectively.

10. *Practice is flexible.* Brief therapy models of the present day are more structured than traditional open-ended approaches. Brief treatment has restraints of various types, depending on the model. The structure has a tendency to diminish a practitioner's flexibility when following a well-worked-out and thoroughly described model.

Nevertheless, therapeutic flexibility and the freedom to use clinical judgment must be preserved. No model is capable of covering every possible event or impression during the course of a case. Much room exists for the full use of professional judgment and experience, which should be encouraged. Actually, practitioners should be inventing and reinventing the model they are working with all the time; this is the best safeguard for keeping a model from becoming a straitjacket or gimmick.

11. *Ventilation is normally provided.* All major models put value on permitting ventilation for relief of tension. In brief treatment, care must be exercised to keep ventilation within reasonable bounds. If emotional expression and release lead to feelings of being unwell, exhausted, overly stretched out, and the like, the brief therapist may lack the resources for helping a distraught client reintegrate.

12. *A positive therapeutic relationship provides treatment leverage.* All brief treatments consider a positive working alliance to be essential to the proper conduct of the brief treatment process. The techniques for encouraging this type of relationship are similar across models.

The Variable Features of Brief Treatment

Brief treatment has five variable features, as listed in Table 3.3.

1. *Criteria for selection of clients vary considerably, depending on decisions about problem definition and focus.* Selection of clients for the implementation of a particular brief treatment model depends on the terms established by the model developers, and on individual decisions practitioners make when they try to make a fit between a case and the model's principles. Developers define what types of problems are considered appropriate for the model. Defining the problems is generally an integral part of identifying what types of persons are considered appropriate for the model. Usually, the consideration of the person and the problem are two facets of the same assessment process.

Practitioners rarely hew to the developers' line exactly but characteristically adapt, mold, subtract, add, and rearrange the model in the interest of stretching the application to groups of clients not included in the original model trials. From a practical standpoint, all models originate in a selected and accessible problem area or population group of interest to the developers. Practitioners stretch the model because they always need to have better methods for dealing with pressing psychosocial problems.

Developers arrive at their statements about criteria for selection by a process of combining factors according to their judgment. They usually consider (1) judgments of appropriateness of the model derived from clinical experience and research conducted by the developers and their associates; (2) judgments of appropriateness derived from supporting theories, such as behaviorism, psychoanalysis, and cognitive psychology; and (3) where available, research findings comparing outcomes of the model under consideration with competing models.

Most developers' statements about appropriateness are based primarily on clinical experience and theory, augmented by modest amounts of clinical research. This condition is a consequence of the really difficult, lengthy projects and the high expense of good quality comparative research. Only in the National Institute of Mental Health (NIMH) study comparing cognitive behavioral treatment with interpersonal psychotherapy, addressed to outpatients with major depression, and comparing imipramine plus clinical management with placebo plus clinical management, is there for the first time a state-of-the-art comparative research study (Elkin et al., 1989). A decade or more of psychotherapy research has revealed the full range of difficulties of such undertakings and has resulted in valuable accretions of knowledge about methodology and outcomes.

Practice recommendations put forth by model developers about whom to select for a given approach end up as decisions about what problem to treat, that is, problem identification, and what focus to take. In other words, if the problem is appropriate for work with the model, or if the problem is formulated appropriately, and if an appropriate focus can be constructed, then the client can be selected for the model.

Developers normally recommend for the given model whom to treat and what focus to take. If the client can be matched with the developers' views on whom to treat and what to focus on, the model is declared suitable for the client. Extraneous factors play a part in the decision of appropriateness of the model for the client or appropriateness of the client for the model. These factors have to do with the preferences of the practitioner, the style of the agency, the fashion of the times in treatment, the length of waiting lists, decisions about costs, and so forth.

Another way of selecting clients for a model is to take an open position: that is, it can be said within broad limits that any problem in living is appropriate, and it is the practitioner's responsibility to guide the client to formulate the problems and focus so that the techniques can reduce it. This open approach is the one taken in the task-centered model (this volume), and by Garfield (1989).

Table 3.4 summarizes the variations among selected models concerning selection of clients. This table shows the interconnectedness of decisions about problem definitions and focus.

The weight of evidence at present is that brief therapy can be selected as suitable for persons with mild to moderate mental disorders—the types of clients most often seen in outpatient psychiatric clinics or similar agencies. However, brief treatments are being adapted for clients with chronic problems of many sorts. These adaptations are being developed with some research backing, but at present the spread of brief treatment beyond the outpatient psychiatry settings is driven mostly by clinical judgment and experimentation.

2. *Termination plans vary considerably.* Termination is the other side of the coin of time limits. All brief treatments provide that the client will know at the start what the time limits are, or that the therapy will be brief. Thus, the termination is acknowledged and understood from the start. Separation disturbances are minimized. Brief therapists must learn to be firm about enforcing the time limits, using the flexibility features built into most guidelines in such a way as to not allow the treatment to become ongoing and open ended by accident. Table 3.5 indicates the different parameters in some major models to illustrate the type of variety found among models in termination plans.

3. *Attention is paid to underlying problems.* The brief therapist comes up against some deeply held beliefs in the therapy field about the determining influence of problems under the surface of those brought up for help now. Students and clinicians who are undertaking planned, intentional brief therapy are concerned about giving up the extra time that it takes to explore and intuit below the surface to perceive underlying problems. Many believe in the idea that good and durable improvement comes from ultimate knowledge of the cause of a problem. Intervention should thus be addressed to that cause. Otherwise, it is thought that changes

TABLE 3.4 **Summary of Variations in Selection of Clients, According to How Problems Are Defined and Focus Set**

MODEL	PROCEDURE
1. Task-centered model (TC) (Reid & Epstein, 1972)	No inclusionary or exclusionary rules. Define the *target problem,* that is, the problem as it is perceived by the client, for which client wants help, on which client is prepared to work. Maintain this focus, except for clear, credible, necessary change in problem.
2. Crisis intervention (CI) (Parad & Parad, 1990)	No inclusionary or exclusionary rules. Focus attention to crisis configuration, that is, precipitating event, perception of threat, response, and resolution.
3. Time-limited psychotherapy (TLP) (Mann, 1981)	Select clients with intact ego and ability to cope with painful affect. Focus on the central issue (problem) that is the present and chronically endured pain, for example, client feels victimized and has always felt victimized, although in reality this condition, which may once have been the case, is not now the case.
4. Short-term anxiety-provoking psychotherapy (STAPP) (Sifneos, 1987)	Select clients who are able to circumscribe a chief complaint, had a meaningful relationship with another person in early childhood, can relate flexibly and experience and express feelings freely, have above average intelligence and psychological mindedness, and are motivated for change, not symptom relief. Circumscribed chief complaint usually involves problems of anxiety, phobia with obsessive thoughts, grief, mild depression, or interpersonal difficulties.
5. Time-limited dynamic psychotherapy (TLDP) (Strupp & Binder, 1984)	Patient with "sufficient" emotional discomfort, "sufficient" basic trust, willingness to consider conflicts in interpersonal terms, willingness to examine feelings, capacity for mature relationships, and motivation for the treatment offered. Focus on a repetitive, problematic, interpersonal transaction pattern.
6. Brief psychotherapy (BP) (Garfield, 1989)	Focus on conditions in which anxiety or depression are important features, excluding psychoses, addictions, and borderline disorders. Be flexible in choosing.
7. Brief therapy (BT) (Bauer & Kobos, 1987)	Focus on a psychiatric disorder with mild to moderate degree of pathology.

TABLE 3.4   Continued

MODEL	PROCEDURE
8. Brief therapy (BT) (Budman & Gurman, 1988)	Most commonly occurring foci are losses; developmental "dysynchronies" (disequilibriums, or life transitions); and interpersonal conflicts with symptomatic presentation, such as habit disorder, sexual dysfunction, fears, and phobias; severe personality disorders; and substance abuse only if addiction is addressed first.
9. Cognitive behavior therapy of depression (CBT) (Beck et al., 1979)	Major depression in nonpsychotic, nonbipolar clients, with associated symptoms, including appetite disturbance, weight fluctuation, sleep disturbance, psychomotor retardation, energy loss, agitation, thinking and concentration difficulties.
10. Short-term interpersonal psychotherapy for depression (IPT) (Klerman et al., 1984)	Major depressive syndrome: nonpsychotic, nonbipolar depression, exactly as in CBT.

will not endure, that the problem will spring up elsewhere. The term *symptom substitution* is sometimes used to identify this hypothesized phenomenon.

The literature on the subject of symptom substitution has been reviewed by Fisher and Greenberg (in Fisher & Greenberg, 1977). These researchers point out that Freud enunciated that insight is necessary to achieve lasting symptom remission and behavior change and downgraded more direct ways of dealing with symptoms. Thus arose an ongoing debate around the question of whether meaningful changes can be produced without insight. The assumption developed that removing a symptom without treating the underlying cause would result in reappearance of the original symptom or formation of a new one.

There are many problems for therapy scholarship involved in this set of assumptions. The concept appears to be based in part on the theory of the dynamics of hydraulic energy, prominent in the physical sciences during Freud's formative years. The assumption is that the "forces" of human emotions act like hydraulic pressure in, for example, a steam pipe. This is a rather strained analogy in modern science. Modern scholars disagree about the definitions of symptoms and the ultimate or exact causes of human psychosocial transactions. Symptom substitution is probably rare, if it exists at all. Symptom substitution is perhaps a simplified shorthand means of referring to the extensive philosophical literature having to do with understanding the meaning of problematic human events and the intransigence of human acts. Are unwanted behaviors and thoughts symptoms? Where do they come from and where do they go when they go away? In essence, do people change and why do they change and why do they stay the same?

TABLE 3.5 Variations in Termination Plans

MODEL	PROCEDURE
1. Task-centered model (TC) (Reid & Epstein, 1972)	8 to 12 interviews over 3 months; restraint used on making short, planned extensions
2. Crisis intervention (CI) (Parad & Parad, 1990)	Approximately 6–8 weeks, in keeping with the hypothesized crisis state
3. Time-limited psychotherapy (TLP) (Mann, 1981)	1 to 3 pretreatment history-assessment interviews, plus 12 treatment interviews
4. Short-term anxiety-provoking psychotherapy (STAPP) (Sifneos, 1987)	A pretreatment phase (time-limited but time not specified) for history and assessment; treatment phase over a 2- to 3-month period
5. Time-limited dynamic psycho- therapy (TLDP) (Strupp & Binder, 1984)	Up to 40 sessions
6. Brief psychotherapy (BP) (Garfield, 1989)	12 to 25 sessions, weekly, tapering off, decided after session 3 or 4
7. Brief therapy (BT) (Bauer & Kobos, 1987)	Flexible time and number of interviews conforming to a client's natural time frame, as a semester; a school year; or a work, career, or family time frame
8. Brief therapy (BT) (Budman & Gurman, 1988)	Flexibly tailored including intermittent sessions with long breaks between blocks of sessions
9. Cognitive behavior therapy of depression (CBT) (Beck et al., 1979)	1 to 2 sessions weekly, 50 minutes each, over period of 20 weeks; usually 2 per week in first 4 to 5 weeks, tapering off at end
10. Short-term interpersonal psychotherapy for depression (IPT) (Klerman et al., 1984)	Approximately 16 sessions over 4 months; few extra okay if needed

A clinician's wish to influence basic, underlying problems is a relatively straightforward, if unrealistic ideal. In some outpatient psychiatry settings, there may be relative agreement among the staff on diagnosis and treatment. Clients perceiving themselves as mentally ill may share the staff's views on causation and need for insight. Where such consensus occurs, little trouble is created in dealing with how underlying problems should be defined and treated.

However, much practice deals with clients whose problems are located in multiple sectors of their lives, and who experience distressful interpersonal complications and environmental demands. They may be clinically mentally ill. But many clients are not mentally ill; their emotional–cognitive disturbances are more in the nature of social dysfunction than illness. For instance, some lives are dysfunctional in relation to use of drugs and alcohol. Some behave violently toward children and spouses. Some engage in antisocial street warfare. Some are ill with medical–social diseases such as AIDS. Some gamble to excess. Some are so overwhelmed by loneliness and sadness that they cannot perform their social roles. Teenagers have babies they cannot care for adequately. School dropouts lack the education, social, and work skills to find self-supporting work in a technological society.

Brief treatments are the cutting edge of the present trend to focus on currently upfront problems. Nevertheless, different models take different views about the role of underlying problems. The brief treatment models that are closest to the traditional psychoanalytic approaches are those that pay the most attention to underlying problems. The approaches of Mann (1981), Sifneos (1987), and Bauer and Kobos (1987) pay close attention to *underlying problems* as defined in psychoanalytic practice theory. Their treatment protocols provide for a directed focus on those underlying problems in the way they appear at present; thus these models put emphasis on the past of the problem as a means to understand the contemporary form of the problem, keeping both the past and the present in the scene.

Short-term interpersonal psychotherapy for depression (IPT) illustrates the present-centered focus clearly in its attention to problems of impaired interpersonal functioning in which there are issues of grief, interpersonal role disputes, role transitions, and interpersonal deficits. Table 3.4 summarizing variations in defining problems and selecting focus is useful for comparing models in terms of how they target the problems to be the focus of treatment. One can see in Table 3.4 the degree to which the model developers define problems and focus as related to underlying problems compared to here-and-now issues.

4. *Advice and guidance are given.* Under the general rubric of advice can be included such teaching and supportive inputs as:

- instruction
- rehearsals
- didactic information giving
- role-playing practice of new behaviors
- suggestions
- recommendations
- persuasion
- cautioning

There is a general reluctance in clinical practice toward anything but occasional use of these techniques. The task-centered model recommends using these activities in the interest of strongly enabling and supporting the client to recognize, understand, and learn the skills to perform desired behaviors in real life.

This view is essentially that a great deal of the therapy should be teaching the client the social skills needed for negotiating the world.

Other brief treatment models use guidance techniques in terms of mentoring, suggesting, and examining what the patient should think and do. For example, IPT advocates helping the patient manage daily tasks, working around the constraints imposed by the depressive symptoms, helping the patient recognize and avoid depressing situations, and helping the patient recognize and seek out situations in which depressive symptoms are mitigated. CBT helps the patient change thinking about how the problems are perceived. CI practice is highly eclectic in making individualized packages of guidance techniques.

Most models, including those that use advice and guidance, depend mostly on evolving in the interviews a new and clearer understanding in clients of how to perceive the problem situation, how to perceive themselves, how to perceive important interpersonal interactions, and how to understand the nature and influences of the environment.

5. *Treatment protocols differ.* Each model of brief treatment packages its components differently. Many differences appear on the surface to be differences only in rhetoric. However, some of the models are buttressed by being thoroughly worked out, their procedures manualized. They have a body of experience and have been reviewed and revised a number of times. A few have a sturdy research base. Another way of describing the differences in the way protocols are stated is to say that some models are more tightly structured than others. Their procedures are explained clearly and succinctly. A regularized mode for proceeding through the model is prescribed. In some cases, as in CBT and IPT, the procedures are fairly well standardized.

The preceding sections have identified the commonalities and differences among the selected exemplar models. However, it is not possible to devise a straightforward way to depict the variations in the way the procedures are connected, administered, and flexibly joined. To get hold of the internal patterning of each different model, it is necessary to consult the official source of the model. The references to this book provide these sources. Part II of this book describes the general problem-solving approach, exemplified in the task-centered model.

SELECTION OF MODELS

The issue of model selection is a matter of professional judgment, weighing into the decision the following factors:

1. *The practitioner's present repertoire of skills and experience.* All other things being equal, do what you know how to do well. This means that the clinician will be inclined to select the model or models that are closest to the practice habits and beliefs currently accessible.
2. *The model most likely to work, as revealed by the research in its processes and outcomes.* The present state of research offers few strong guidelines that can be

used as reliable predictors of what treatment is best in any given situation. (See Chapter 2.)

3. *The model that seems to make the best fit with the way the client perceives the problem.* There are many possibilities in the outlook of clients about how they define their problems, for example, putting themselves in a "sick role," putting themselves in the position that they need help sorting out and thinking through, needing directive help in figuring out what to do and what resources are available, or seeking ways to influence their environment more advantageously. Various models suggest that they will make a better fit with clients who see their situations certain ways.

Other factors play a part in model selection. At present, due to budgetary considerations, agencies are tending to make administrative decisions about the length of time normally to be used in case processing. In such circumstances, one needs to concentrate on becoming experienced with models that fit the administrative time constraints. Clinicians often have a decided preference for one model or one group of similar models. In that case they will make a personal professional choice for an all-purpose model, to which they will creatively add or rearrange components, borrowing from here and there and making a product which suits them and is adaptable to clients.

Given enough time and research funds, there probably will emerge more hard knowledge about what kinds of models and processes are best with what problems, persons, and situations. However, process and outcome research in psychotherapy is not only immensely expensive, it is difficult because of conceptual and methodological considerations. It will be necessary in the foreseeable future to work with those robust research findings we have and make clinical decisions based on our judgments.

EXTENSIONS AND ADAPTATIONS OF BRIEF TREATMENT

Recently, substantial literature has developed adapting brief therapy methods to circumscribed problem areas, creating in effect *brief treatment specialties*. This literature is of varying quality but is interesting because of the attempt to construct a fit between various brief treatment models and types of treatment situations, problem types, and population groups not contemplated or included in the work leading to the original or basic model.

SUMMARY

The features of brief treatment methods overlap considerably, as has been shown in this chapter. In addition to overlaps, there are significant differences that make for unique combinations of activities in these therapeutic intervention approaches.

The development of models and approaches to brief treatment has mushroomed since the 1960s as has been illustrated. In addition to those methods already discussed, there are now methods specific to client groupings and problem types, such as substance abuse, crises, marital and sexual problems, school behavior problems, family issues, groups, and specific mental disorders. There is a brief treatment method to use with most of the issues raised by clients in any therapeutic context.

CHAPTER FOUR

THE TASK-CENTERED MODEL
The Problem-Solving Paradigm in Action

BACKGROUND OF THE TASK-CENTERED MODEL

The term *task-centered* is today affixed to many different ideas about intervention, but it was just coming into professional usage in 1970 when the Task-Centered Project (hereafter, the Project) was established. The Project was sponsored by the School of Social Service Administration at the University of Chicago, originally through a small start-up grant from a private foundation. The development of the task-centered model was aided by a grant from the Federal Department of Health and Human Services (SRS Grant no. 18–P–57774/5–03). The work began and continued through the collaboration of William J. Reid and Laura Epstein, with valuable support from faculty and administration, and from doctoral and master's students.

The research on the model at the University of Chicago occurred between 1970 and 1978. During those years, the Project enrolled about 125 graduate students. They suffered through the trials of the model, testing and refining the work. Doctoral students were exceptionally helpful in conducting studies, supervising students, and developing the task-centered model in new, ingenious ways. Most of these doctoral students are now teaching in a number of universities. In Chicago, thirteen social agencies collaborated by affording fieldwork placements for the students and research case material to the Project. These agencies included medical and psychiatric hospitals and clinics, school social work departments in public elementary and high schools, child welfare agencies, and others. The Project tests of the task-centered model included approximately 1,300 cases handled by students in Chicago agencies between 1970 and 1977. Of this entire group, a smaller number became the sample for the research on processes and outcomes. The practitioners in the United States were nearly all graduate social work students. A number of studies also were undertaken in England, using experienced practitioners.

The mission of the Task-Centered Project was to develop technologies that could be learned efficiently, increase the effectiveness of direct services, and increase the ability to conduct research on treatment practices. The first three years of the Project, roughly from 1970 to 1973, saw the designing of the basic task-centered model. Its processes and effects were studied in actual case practice. With the publication of *Task-Centered Casework* (Reid & Epstein, 1972), the model attracted interest in agencies throughout the country and abroad. Practitioners and researchers from many settings began to test and develop the model. Specialized literature began to appear. Many of the case examples used in this book came from actual cases handled in the Project. Others are from practice supervised by former doctoral students. All cases have been disguised, and names of the agencies are withheld to prevent improper disclosures.

The technical guidelines described in this book are our attempt to distill and arrange the result of years of model building and practice. Wherever possible, the guidelines are derived from practice research conducted in the Project and from published practice research conducted elsewhere. Since the end of the Project in 1978, personal contacts and published reports have provided new information. A good deal of practice experience and innovation occurs in day-to-day work and is not published. Sometimes, it has been possible to get such information by word of mouth.

The origins of the task-centered model are varied and represent selections and revisions from a host of ideas and practices that preceded it. The experience of the years of research-based practice and its evaluations supports the conclusion that task-centered practice is effective in reducing many of the problems encountered in a range of agencies.

Many of the central ideas of the task-centered model have combined with ideas of practice that have other origins. Put into the stream of practice, the task-centered model has been adapted to coexist within an eclectic practice framework. One of the things that this fourth edition of the book, first published in 1980, does is add material about how the task-centered approach can be used flexibly and in more settings than originally conceived.

TASK-CENTERED PRACTICE
AS A SET OF PROCEDURES

Task-centered practice is a technology for alleviating specific *target problems* perceived by clients, that is, particular problems clients recognize, understand, acknowledge, and want to attend to. Important other people who care about the clients or put pressure on them influence and shape the target problems. Sometimes authorities require clients to work on problems; in other words, some problems are mandated.

Task-centered practice has a particular way of unfolding. It consists of a start-up and four sequential but overlapping steps. (See Figure 4.1.) The regularity of the steps is important because orderly, systematic processes are most likely to result in good outcomes. Under the pressure of problem solving, these steps tend to occur out of sequence; nonetheless, the practitioner should return to the normal procedure as soon as possible.

The steps in the task-centered approach are methodical and systematic. To the extent that practice is systematized, it tends to be as thorough as circumstances

FIGURE 4.1   Detailed Map of the Task-Centered Model

| Start-up

Chapter 5	*Client referred by an agency source*	*Client applies, independently and voluntarily*
	FIND OUT ■ Source's goals **NEGOTIATE** ■ Source's specific goals ■ Source's resources to achieve goals	Not needed

| Step 1

Chapter 6	*Client target problems identified*
	FIND OUT ■ Problems defined by client ■ Client priorities (hold to three) ■ Referral source priorities (mandated problems) ■ Preliminary, rapid early assessment

| Step 2

Chapter 7	*Contract*
	COVER ■ Priority target problems (three maximum) ■ Client's specific goals (accepted by practitioner) ■ Client's general tasks ■ Practitioner's general tasks ■ Duration of intervention sequence (time limits) ■ Schedule for interviews ■ Schedule for interventions ■ Parties to be included

(continued)

FIGURE 4.1   Continued

Step 3	*Problem solving, task achievement, problem reduction* *Select as needed*
Chapter 8	

DEFINE AND SPECIFY TARGET PROBLEM (THREE MAXIMUM)
- Restate and name the problem (the particular conditions and behaviors to be changed)

Specify
- Target problem
  How often it occurs (frequency)
  Where it occurs (site)
  With whom (participants)
  What immediate antecedents (forerunners)
  What consequences (effects)
  What meaning (importance)

Assess
- Social context (social conditions precipitating and maintaining the problem)
  Work–school circumstances
  Economic status
  Family organization
  Peer group organization
  Housing state
  Cultural/ethnic background
- Cognitive-affective circumstances
  Client characteristics
  Mode of functioning
  Personal resources
  Other assessments

GENERATE ALTERNATIVES
- Find out and identify a feasible range of possible problem-solving strategies

NEGOTIATE SUPPORTIVE AND COLLABORATIVE ACTIONS OF OTHER PERSONS AND AGENCIES

DECISION MAKING (confirm goals, select what will be done, and design details of the intervention strategy)
- Re-affirm contract and goals
- Determine basic interventions
- Plan timing and sequence
- Select participants
- Get client agreement and understanding (informed consent)
- Get agreement and understanding of others

IMPLEMENT (carry out strategy)
Develop tasks
- Formulate tasks
- Get client understanding and agreement to tasks
- Get client understanding of rationale and incentives for tasks
- Summarize tasks
- Review expected difficulties

FIGURE 4.1   Continued

Step 3
 	
Chapter 8
(continued)
	Develop tasks (continued)
	■ Devise plans for client task performance
	■ Summarize tasks
	■ Devise plans for client task performance
	Support task performance
	■ Review number of sessions outstanding
	■ Obtain and use resources
	■ Find out obstacles to resource provision
	■ Give instruction
	■ Give guidance
	■ Do simulations
	■ Do role plays and guided practice
	■ Accompany client for modeling and/or advocacy
	■ Other
	■ Find out obstacles to task performance
	   In the social environment: lack of resources, stress, discrimination,
	      structural problems
	   In the interpersonal transactions: deficit and conflict, lack of cooperation
	   In the psychological state: fears, suspicions, lack of knowledge
	■ Plan actions to remove, reduce, or alter obstacles
	■ Remedy practical barriers to task performance, for example, lack of skills,
	   lack of cooperation and support from others, and lack of resources
	■ Alleviate cognitive barriers to task performance: discuss fears, suspicions,
	   lack of knowledge, adverse beliefs
	■ Plan and state practitioner tasks: inform client of practitioner tasks, review
	   implementation of practitioner tasks, review problem state
	Verify (check, test, confirm, substantiate probable effects of interventions) and
	Monitor (record problem status regularly—use structured notations, charts,
	        graphs, plus brief, succinct narrative comments)
	Revise contract, or some parts of it, if:
	■ Progress unsatisfactory
	■ Progress exceeds expectations
	■ New problems emerge
	■ Problem takes on different characteristics
	■ Tasks not performed, or poorly performed
	■ Supports and resources ineffective
	■ Practitioner tasks ineffective or not feasible

Step 4 Chapter 9	*Termination* **END** **EXTEND** on evidence of client commitment **MONITOR** when mandated by law, court order, or formal agency requirements

permit. Being systematic can protect clients and practitioners from extremes of bewilderment, frustration, and irrelevancy. Systematic practice minimizes waste of time, effort, and money and encourages effective practice. The influence of structured practice on good outcomes has been demonstrated in studies that cut across various fields of practice and various helping occupations (Brown et al., 1999; Reid & Epstein, 1972; Reid & Hanrahan, 1982; Rubin, 1985). (See Chapter 2.) Task-centered practice will take a lot of weight and still produce reasonable results. Take a look at Lester's case, which reflects one type of task-centered practice.

CASE 4.1

LESTER

Lester is 30. Family, friends, residential care personnel, and social workers say, "He looks mentally retarded." Pushed to explain what such a look is, they say he is thin, has buck teeth, squints often, and has a silly grin. We often rely on such stereotypes to form a commonsense appraisal of others, but it is deplorable if such stereotypes are exalted as "diagnosis."

Lester comes from an average family with a complicated life. His father is a truck driver. His mother died when he was 15. The father was left with Lester, his twin brother, and a small child of 4 years with cerebral palsy. As children, both twins seemed "stupid." Shortly after their mother died, their father married a divorced woman who had custody of her two young children.

The stepmother could not care for the teenaged twins as well as for the handicapped son and her own children. Looking for a way to take care of the twins, the father and stepmother had them evaluated at the local psychiatric clinic. Tests showed that both had IQs in the 50s. They were committed to a state residential facility for the mentally retarded; that is, they were sequestered in a place where they could be educated and cared for.

As such places go, the institution was good. The twins attended school. They were to be prepared for "independent living"—meaning self-support. They received vocational training in ceramics, sawmill work, and dairy farming in a western state with lots of tourists (who might buy ceramics), lots of trees (which can be sawed in mills), and lots of cows (for milking). The cost of this care and training for fifteen years was substantial. What did Lester and his brother get out of it? A 20-point jump in IQ. The twins learned a lot of the things tested on IQ examinations, and that is obviously all to the good. With IQs raised to the 70s, they were no longer so "stupid."

When the twins entered the institution, their state had not yet implemented a deinstitutionalization program. But in the first wave of deinstitutionalization programs that began in the 1970s, Lester's brother was released first. He fared satisfactorily. Lester stayed inside for another two years. Then, fifteen years after his admission, Lester was sent to his father, and this started a huge contretemps. The other twin was supporting himself on odd jobs and living in a rooming house, where his father visited him occasionally. But Lester was home, just sitting around, a strange, helpless, 30-year-old man—in the way, scary, disrupting the home. His father and stepmother were in a panic, furious, and overwhelmed. They demanded that the local welfare office take Lester off their hands—at once!

But should an agency intervene and in what way? Parents are supposed to like and want their children and to offer them care and protection. When the parents came to the welfare office to be interviewed, they defined two and only two target problems: They did not want Lester at home, and they could not afford to pay his rent elsewhere and feed and clothe him.

Could Lester's parents accept counseling to think about how to adjust their style and habits with Lester at home? To think about how they could make him self-supporting? No. The father's income was too high for him to be eligible for counseling at no cost; he would have to pay a fee. Lester's father was of no mind to receive counseling, let alone pay for it.

What did Lester think was his problem? He had no job, and he did not know his way around the city to look for one. The regulations of that state prohibited cash benefits to able-bodied, single men (Lester was "ineligible"), and Lester's IQ was now too high to qualify him for disability benefits, one category of an income-maintenance program.

What was the practitioner's judgment? There were all kinds of possibilities. It could be stated that the father was a narrow-minded bully or a selfish, opinionated, passive-aggressive personality; that the stepmother was a rigid, obsessive personality; and so forth. Taking such positions would box the practitioner into a corner. As soon as these labels are attached to persons and problems, current logic often holds that counseling is needed to alter the personalities, attitudes, and behaviors involved. In this case, that change would probably mean that the people would need to change part of their personal make-up in a way to achieve their adaptation to the new person in the home; after all, he was their son.

This particular practitioner suggested that work be done to decrease the problems targeted by the parents and son, using about eight interviews with the son. Lester was eligible for free counseling because he had no income, and the agency was responsible by administrative regulations for counseling those recently deinstitutionalized. The father would be consulted by telephone (to get around the fee charge). Lester's father said this sounded good: "We'll do what you want; you're the boss."

At the end of that first and only in-person interview with the parents, the father added another target problem: Lester's worrisome conduct. He was lethargic and unhelpful around the house. He had been home one month, had not gone out, and had not lifted a finger (*target problem specification*). Operating on the general assumption that people do what they know how to do and avoid what they do not know how to do (i.e., they have or lack particular cognitive and/or social skills), the practitioner advised the parents to teach Lester how to do things in the home, as long as he was there, and to treat him as if he had a reasonable amount of skills. At the same time, Lester was advised to come for a series of eight interviews, once weekly.

Meanwhile, the practitioner took on her own tasks. She phoned a halfway house to find out if that agency could provide Lester job-finding services. The agency was willing but, as it turned out, not able to find him a low-skilled job. The practitioner phoned the vocational rehabilitation office. It was willing to accept Lester for job training but could not accomplish anything because he was erratic about workshop attendance. The practitioner consulted a public psychological testing service for a retest for Lester. If his IQ were lower on a retest, he might be eligible for financial support. This idea was dropped. In truth, Lester's was not a problem of low intelligence anymore. His problem was lack of knowledge about the city map, streets, and how to talk to ordinary people about the ordinary things people talk about daily.

No one rescued the practitioner. Other agencies were reasonable but ineffective. Each had a particular work focus and style; they all did what they thought they were supposed to do and what they could. The practitioner should have understood this but did not. She thought the official job-placement services ought to take over and do whatever was necessary to get Lester placed. Her expertise was not in finding jobs for clients but in general counseling and in making and monitoring appropriate referrals for specialized services.

Feeling stymied, she nevertheless did what needed to be done, but she felt let down by the other agencies. In interviews with Lester, the practitioner worked out tasks designed to get him a job and a room in a boarding house. The start-up tasks were to make a list of possible places where he might ask for work and to make a list of possible rooming houses where he might live. These are ordinary and unexciting things, yet for Lester they made the difference between knowing and not knowing, doing and sitting around, having tolerable circumstances and intolerable circumstances. Self-actualization and fulfillment of one's potentialities come down to tolerable versus intolerable circumstances. When solving problems, no neon signs light up; no cymbals clash. Problems get solved and life looks better after a hundred ordinary and unexciting details are taken care of.

To help Lester get his tasks done, the practitioner sat down with him and looked over the want ads and notices from the public employment service about vacancies as well as the rent ads and lists from real estate firms. She taught Lester first how to make the lists, then how to approach a businessman and a landlord: what to say, what to expect, what to do, think, feel. Interview after interview Lester tried, and his results were nil at first. The worker and Lester drudged on.

Meanwhile, at home the parents were teaching Lester to use the dishwasher and vacuum, to make his bed, and so forth. They made the effort to talk straight to him and have reasonable expectations. From time to time they felt defeated (depressed), afraid, and enraged. They called up the practitioner and complained loudly. She suggested things they could do and described how they could do them.

SCOPE OF THE TASK-CENTERED MODEL: WHERE SHOULD IT BE USED?

The task-centered model can be used with a variety of personal, interpersonal, and situational problems and with many different types of clients and settings. Published reports concerning use of the model have come from those who work with the aging (Cormican, 1977; Dierking, Brown, & Fortune, 1980; Rathbone-McCuan, 1985); with families and groups (Fortune, 1985b; Garvin, 1974; Reid, 1981, 1985; Reid & Epstein, 1977); with children in foster care (Rooney, 1981; Rzepnicki, 1985); with children and adults (Fortune, 1979; Reid, 1978; Reid & Epstein, 1977); with clients in corrections (Goldberg, Gibbons, & Sinclair, 1984; Larsen & Mitchell, 1980; Marshall, 1987); and with mental health, health, and medical patients (Reid & Epstein, 1977; Gibbons, Bow, Butler, & Powell, 1978; Goldberg, Gibbons, & Sinclair, 1984); schools (Bailey-Dempsey, 1993; Reid & Bailey-Dempsey, 1995; Reid et al., 1994); with elderly (Naleppa, 1995; Naleppa & Reid, 1998); with sex offenders (Kilgore, 1995); in mediation (Donohue, 1996); with surgical patients (Moriarty, 1990; Chapter 12 this volume); with HIV/AIDS hospice patients (Parsseghian, 1993; Chapter 13 this volume); and with the homeless (Brown et al., 1999; Chapter 14 this volume).

The task-centered model can be used with difficult cases, easy cases, and all the cases that fall between those two categories. Obviously, the most important problems and the most involved conditions will probably need the most complex applications of the model.

Most troubles have two components: The person lacks resources for alleviating a problem, and the person lacks skills for alleviating a problem. By configuring for these two problem sections, the practitioner should be able to plan workable interventions.

BASIC PROCEDURES: IN BRIEF AND IN GENERAL

Ordinarily, a client has a target problem; that is, there is a state of distress, uneasiness, upset, turbulence, malfunction, handicap, or perplexity, or the client perceives a threat to goals and expectations; he knows or believes that a particular event or occurrence is the center of the trouble. The target problem is what the client thinks is the problem, what he thinks should be alleviated, and what he thinks should be worked on. The client can generally make a coherent statement defining, or at least describing, the target problem. When he cannot do so, the practitioner can help in various ways to develop a target problem statement. The practitioner can sometimes usefully consult important other people to identify the problem. In task-centered practice, everything begins and may end with the client's target problem.

The target problem is embedded in a *target problem context*, that is, the real conditions shaping the problem. These include important interpersonal relations, role performance difficulties, economic and financial difficulties, and other features of the social environment. Influential other people, including professionals, agencies, or other social institutions, may also have opinions about the client's situation.

In the task-centered model, the target problem becomes operational only upon the explicit willingness of the practitioner to focus on that defined problem. If the practitioner judges that the client's selected target problem is wrong, or that it is not feasible to work on that problem, then she is obligated and is responsible for giving her professional opinion and helping the client explore other options. (Chapters 1 and 6 discuss working with target problem definitions and focusing in greater detail.)

Task-centered intervention combines a set of procedures for alleviating the specific target problem decided upon for the focus of the work. (See Figure 4.2.) When people are referred to or obliged to use a service, that is, when they are *involuntary clients,* a start-up sequence draws out the client's problems and draws out the problems identified by the referral agencies. To alleviate target problems, we depend on problem-solving processes. Goals are as specific and tangible as possible. Stretching out a client's motivation is normally not necessary and rarely

FIGURE 4.2   Basic Steps

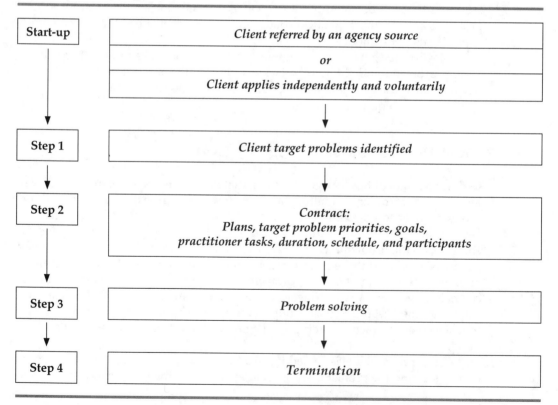

succeeds. What is necessary is that the client obtain the resources and skills for problem-solving work.

Case Planning

The general strategy for a case plan consists of assessment and a problem-reducing program of action. The focus is on client target problems. The assessment is elaborate about the details of the problem occurrences in the present, and is narrowed to the boundaries of the target problem and its immediate context.

The practitioner constructs a program by making judgments about what changes can be expected to reduce the problem. To make this judgment, he considers the substance and direction of action the client is willing to undertake, the available formal information (i.e., published, reported in official channels, or communicated in official supervision and consultation) indicating actions expected to have greatest impact on the problem, and the resources and rules of the particular agency responsible for the case.

Implementation

A *contract* is made to shape and organize the problem-solving work. *Tasks* state exactly what the client and practitioner are to do. To overcome obstacles to the client's task performance, the practitioner concentrates on providing clients with the resources for getting the tasks done. The client is also instructed in the skills needed for accomplishing the stipulated tasks. Goals, problems, and tasks are set firmly but with reserve flexibility. The practitioner's responsibility is to create a favorable climate for task performance. The practitioner procures resources; instructs the client in relevant social skills; negotiates resources and favorable attitudes (with other agencies and with the family, peers, and important others); reviews progress on problem alleviation; and arranges to terminate, extend, or follow up (monitor) the original contract.

Tasks

Tasks state what the client or practitioner is to do. A task may state a general direction for the client's action, but general tasks are broken down into more detailed task specifications. Tasks change form and content as intervention proceeds. Some tasks are dropped; others are added. Target problems sometimes change. The practitioner's tasks are actions to be taken on the client's behalf.

Assessment

In the initial phase (the first two sessions with a client), the practitioner makes a rapid early assessment. (See Chapter 6.) However, throughout the case, she continues to obtain information and refine her assessment. (See Chapter 8.) Assessment consists of finding out the problems (also called exploration), as well as classifying and specifying the problems. The practitioner also identifies the influential conditions in the environment—the problem context—and should note the client's special traits, talents, abilities, and problem behaviors. Assessment is confined to the logical boundaries of the target problems. A target problem can be classified according to its best fit into a typology that defines the scope of the assessment (Chapter 7). Assessment does not extend beyond problems that can be subsumed under the target problem classification or the logic of the target problem. Reassessment occurs if and when the target problem has to be changed; the practitioner may decide to alter the treatment plan and strategy in those circumstances.

Psychiatric Classifications and Assessment.   The task-centered model does not usually require the therapist to formulate a psychiatric diagnosis of the client. However, that information, if available, may add a useful dimension to the assessment. The psychiatric classification is always made if the client is in treatment in a psychiatric hospital or clinic. The psychiatric classification is useful in other settings, but may not be essential. It is an additional way to describe clients and to aid in understanding their traits and abilities.

The standard guidelines for making a psychiatric classification may be found in the *Diagnostic and Statistical Manual of Mental Disorders* (fourth edition), known as the *DSM IV* (American Psychiatric Association, 1994). The *DSM IV* guidelines attempt to provide clear descriptions of diagnostic categories to enable clinicians and investigators to diagnose, communicate about, study, and treat various mental disorders. The psychiatric classification is never adequate for prescribing treatment; it is an initial step. Practitioners need specialized training to use the *DSM IV* competently. Persons without this training should work under the supervision of or in collaboration with a professional trained in the use of the system.

The *DSM IV* classification is required in psychiatric treatment facilities because they are under the hegemony of the medical profession and governmental regulations. The classification is one way of controlling quality of care, and it also provides necessary statistical information. In other types of helping organizations, these classification processes are optional and their use depends on custom and agency styles. There is no conflict between use of the *DSM IV* classifications and the task-centered model, although the model needs to be adapted to fit into the usual clinic setting. Regardless of the setting, the psychiatric classification is invariably useful when the target problem is, or is affected in important ways by, a physical or neurological disease; when drugs or other biological interventions are being administered; or when the client is suffering from delusions, hallucinations, or thought disorders.

Life History, Problem History, and Assessment.   In normal task-centered work, it is not useful to obtain extensive life-history data. Such information can reveal a good deal about how a person is thought to have developed and how his character seems to have evolved. However, personal histories seldom need to be used in interventions to reduce the client's target problem. In fact, accumulating substantial past history is inefficient and may mislead the client about the intentions of the practitioner; that is, the client may infer that he is to be an unwilling participant in a "deep" psychotherapy process. Long duration of a problem may or may not color its meaning in the present. Although information about a problem's duration and how it has changed or remained constant over time is sometimes an aid to clear understanding, identifying minimal demographic and historical characteristics is usually enough. Research evidence suggests that such minimal data are surprisingly powerful in describing clinical situations and helping therapists make predictive judgments (Sundberg, 1977, p. 107). These facts pin down and clarify the problem, especially if attention is given to the immediate personal and social context, and to what the problem means in the present time. However, past history may be explored if the emphasis on the present does not shed enough light on the assessment.

Personality and Behavior Theories and Assessment.   Personality and behavior theories deal with the characteristics and tendencies believed to determine a person's thoughts, feelings, and actions (Maddi, 1980). A practitioner trying to assess a client and her situation will find that an understanding of personality and behavior factors is valuable. There are many theories, and each has its adherents, but at this stage in the development of psychology, it is not known what theory is best. Efforts to create some unifying framework have proved elusive. Each of the important theoretical positions is informative and often helpful.

The framework of the task-centered model primarily offers guidelines for problem-solving actions, but task-centered intervention calls for practical eclecticism so far as personality and behavior theory are concerned. Practitioners, of course, bring to practice their own beliefs and preferences in the area of personality theory. The flexibility built into the model generally allows it to accommodate different opinions about personality and behavior functioning, although it is a poor fit with personality and behavior theories addressed to deep intrapsychic characteristics and the assessment and treatment of widespread psychological dysfunctions thought to reside primarily inside a person's mind. The task-centered approach *is* adaptable to theories that attend to interpersonal transactions and transactions between the person and environment and to theories that view thought, feeling, and action as a linked pattern of being. The task-centered model is compatible with explanatory theories of behavior derived from ecological, cognitive, behavioral, and psychodynamic approaches. Let's revisit the Joseph and Rita case from Chapter 1.

CASE 4.2

JOSEPH AND RITA

Joseph is 11; his sister Rita is 8. They are black children living in a deteriorated neighborhood. Before Joseph and Rita were born, this neighborhood was crowded. Two main business streets were heavily trafficked and noisy. There were lots of shops. The merchandise was overpriced. Bright, ugly signs grabbed you. The "El" train ran on top of one of the main streets. Every block had some variant of tavern, gyp joint, greasy spoon, welfare office, bank, gambling and drug joint, or mental health clinic. Gangs fought. For ten years the neighborhood burned; today, empty lots are cluttered with bricks. Buildings are shells; here and there a block or a building stands in the rubble. The streets are dangerous. The two main streets are deserted. Urban renewal high-rises and town houses show up strangely. The real estate speculators are there. The urban renewal experts are there. The school attended by Joseph and Rita used to be a loud, teeming place. Now it has empty rooms and lots of special education classes.

Joseph and Rita live in an apartment with their 31-year-old mother and two younger sisters. Their mother is on welfare. She came to this northern city from the South twelve years ago. She has never had any paid employment; she has been on welfare during most of her years in the city.

Joseph and Rita were referred to the school social worker because they were dirty. This is a mandated problem but of relatively low power: that is, no one is likely to be deprived of liberty or subjected to police action for poor body hygiene. But this problem raises potentially more important ones: the mother might be labeled "neglectful" and become subject to investigatory procedures; the children and mother might be pressured by school officials, reported to the welfare department, and so forth. Because cleanliness is a high priority in our society, it is sometimes believed that a parent who fails to keep children clean may be doing worse things, may be guilty of neglect, even abuse, for instance.

The teacher who referred Joseph and Rita for a dirtiness problem had both children in her room, an ungraded learning disability (LD) class. The two children were first interviewed by a social worker. Joseph was a spontaneous, lively, talkative child; Rita was his follower, quiet, shy, and depending on big brother to talk for her and fight for her. When Rita wanted to add something or change something Joseph was telling the social worker, the girl would gesture to Joseph and whisper.

The social worker told the children the reason for the referral. They denied the accusation. They were only dirty from being on the playground. They had different woes (target problems): the teacher was unfair to them, singling them out for criticism when they acted no differently from the other children; they did not know why they had been put in an LD class; and they did not know what to do to get out of the class.

The children agreed that the social worker visit their mother. She did and found the apartment clean, the laundry facilities adequate, the quantity of clothing adequate. The mother showed the social worker her things to defend herself against the false accusation of uncleanliness. The mother's target problems were that she had never been informed her children were to be placed in an LD class (a violation of law in that state, if true) and that the white teacher was prejudiced against black kids.

The practitioner's judgment was that Joseph and Rita were, in her experience, average in cleanliness and in their mother's attention to cleanliness. What came through was the family's distress and indignation at the children's being labeled *LD*—that is, dumb. The family blamed the school officials; they thought the teacher was prejudiced and generally unfair.

DISCUSSION: THE CASE OF JOSEPH AND RITA

Start-up and Steps 1 and 2, Combined

The information just summarized in the case of Joseph and Rita came out in the first two interviews, one with the children in school and the other with the mother in her home. No case is "perfect." This one is no exception. The good points are that the social worker involved the mother immediately and obtained her opinions; she observed the children's home to get a direct impression; and she paid attention to concentrating on the problem as viewed by the clients. Unfortunately, she did not confer and negotiate with the referral source (teacher) to find out how often, when, and to what degree the children were dirty; why they were in an LD classroom; what their learning disabilities were; what they could be expected to learn, how fast, with what educational program; what the teacher wanted to change and why; and what the teacher could do to help change along.

In the case of Rita and Joseph, then, the start-up step was bypassed. Steps 1 and 2 were done simultaneously, and Step 3 was begun all in the first two interviews. (And yet, in real practice the steps tend to run into one another in just this way and the task-centered model is adapted to fit real-world circumstances. However, in combining steps, the practitioner should nonetheless not overlook the necessary parts of the steps even though he adjusts their order and priority.)

The content from Steps 1 through 3 was that the target problems were identified and general tasks were stated as follows:

1. Joseph and Rita were to obtain an understanding of why they were in an LD class.
2. Joseph and Rita were to get along better with the teacher.
3. Intervention was to last six weeks; the children were to be seen twice a week for thirty-minute sessions, together or separately.
4. Their mother was to be seen as needed, alone or with the children.

Step 2: Contract

This contract is on the right track but lacks enough specifics to move things along. The errors follow:

1. *Target problems not sufficiently congruent with clients' viewpoints.* The target problems have been given a practitioner's twist, or bias, altering the way the children and mother want to go. The clients want information and redress of grievances. They could be expected to have high motivation to get action on those problems. However, when the practitioner influences the children to think about ways to cut down on conflict with the teacher, the children's motivation will not be high. The children are too powerless to put themselves in the position the practitioner is suggesting.
2. *Mother's participation not sufficiently structured into the work plan.* Work with the mother, who has certainly been interested, exists somewhere out on the sidelines. The contract is really only with the children. The practitioner

should have pinned down how often the mother would be seen and for what, and whether the children would be seen separately or together. The most efficient way to get action may well have been to see all three together.

3. *Practitioner tasks not developed on time.* From the start, there should have been practitioner tasks to find out from the school officials why the children were in an LD class, whether their rights had been violated, what the teacher recommended regarding uncleanliness and school program, what the teacher could do to get the desired changes, and if the charges of unfairness and prejudice had any observable basis.

Step 3: Problem Solving

Interviews three through twelve took place over five weeks. These interviews were with the children together and with their mother by phone. There was virtually no assessment. The practitioner developed one client task only and with the children only: The children were to ask their teacher why they were in an LD class. This task was steady and unchanged in interviews three through eight, six 30-minute sessions. The children did not do the task.

The immediate obstacle was that the children did not know what to say to the teacher. This obstacle was worked at by discussion, instruction, simulation, and role playing. They did not do it anyway. The children said that on some days they had no opportunity because the teacher was absent due to illness. On other days—all the days she was in school—she was in a bad mood.

The problem context was fuzzy. The children acted as if they liked the sessions. They recited for the practitioner what the task was and rehearsed repeatedly, but they never did it in real life. The practitioner urged them on, mentioning that the sessions had a time limit. Also, during the sessions the children became lively when talking spontaneously about their "Dad," but information they gave about their father or about problems related to him was not recorded, if it was obtained—not even who he was. Possibly the practitioner was trying not to be intrusive; but it would seem that if the children talked about this man spontaneously, they would not object to having the practitioner ask a relevant question or two. Perhaps they were even inviting the inquiry. At the end of the eighth session, the practitioner decided to take on the tasks of conferring with school officials and involving the mother with school officials to work on the target problems.

Why were these errors made? It seems that the practitioner made a judgment: to give the children maximum independence in solving their own problems. This judgment has a certain moral attractiveness but is unrealistic for an 11- and 8-year-old in these circumstances. These children and their mother do not have enough clout and self-assertiveness to take on successfully a formal bureaucracy such as a school system. They need a mediator and possibly an advocate. Those are the roles the practitioner should have taken on at once.

Because of the slow start of focused work, the bulk of the interventions were bunched together at the end of the sequence. By interviews nine and ten the children were telling the practitioner that they felt smarter than kids in the regular classrooms, that they did their work conscientiously, and that no one had explained to them or their mother why they were in an LD classroom. The target problem surfaced again. The practitioner-imposed task is not even being attempted by the children. Belatedly, the practitioner hears. She contracts herself for several tasks: to arrange for an appointment for Joseph and Rita with the teacher; to accompany the children to that appointment; to request a staff meeting with appropriate school officials to explain to the children and their mother what the LD placement is all about; and to obtain exact and detailed information about the laws and regulations dealing with LD placement procedures and rights of the parents and children.

The staff meeting took place. Present with the family and practitioner were the teacher, the adjustment teacher, and the principal. The school people produced from their files a signed form showing that a parent gave permission for LD placement. At first the mother did not recognize the signature. It then came out that the children had been taken for psychological tests (the basis of the LD placement) by the mother's boyfriend (the "Dad") and he had signed the papers. The civil rights mystery was solved. The staff recommended that Joseph be provided with a typewriter so he could practice fine motor skills at home, that he keep a notebook to identify words he did not know, and that he be relieved of a baby-sitting job (it was just now discovered that he had one) that kept him up every night until midnight. Rita (the follower) was not mentioned in the staffing, an important oversight, probably due to time pressure and insufficient planning for the conduct of the conference.

Step 4: Terminating

By session thirteen the target problem disappeared. Everyone now knew why the children were in an LD classroom. The children and their mother were satisfied. Joseph and Rita agreed the teacher was not so bad. Joseph was going to move into a regular classroom soon. Rita would be left behind. The mother was to pay special attention to Rita.

CONCLUSION

What was done in sessions nine through thirteen could have been done in sessions one through four. A plan for Rita should not have been overlooked. Such a plan could have been worked into the intervention if so much time had not elapsed before the practitioner corrected the strategy. The focus would have been more correct if the problem context had been assessed and if the logic of the client's target problem had been more painstakingly adhered to.

There are many loose ends to this case. It should be said at once, however, that every case does *not* have to finish in a state of neat completeness, because life does not allow such a nirvana. But certain loose ends really stand out here. For example, what accounts for the wide difference in interpretation between the practitioner and the teacher as to whether or not the children were dirty? It seems likely that the teacher's reason for referral was more complicated than a simple concern about surface cleanliness. Again, what exactly were the extent and types of learning problems that had originally caused the school to call in the psychological testers and what exactly did those tests reveal?

There should have been a more robust recommendation about these children's learning needs besides the somewhat unrealistic advice to buy Joseph a typewriter and teach him to type. Who was going to buy the typewriter and do the teaching? What should he type? Maybe a computer would be better! And maybe the school would have one.

How can we account for *everyone's* almost complete disregard of Rita? What might that portend? And was it the job of the practitioner to explore the family composition to find out if that disregard was a problem and if it could be helped? There was enough room in this timed sequence to look into these problems if the case had been better planned and focused. Furthermore if focused exploration suggested an extension of time, and if the clients and referral source wanted it, there is no barrier in the model for maximizing service if the time and effort are used productively and by mutual agreement.

SUMMARY

Task-centered practice is a set of articulated actions designed to be put into effect in an organized and planned manner for the purpose of alleviating client target problems. The heart of the task-centered model is close congruence between the practitioner and the client on the problem that is to be the focus of work, the *target problem*. The model provides for an agreed-upon plan in the form of a contract that describes the nature of the actions to be embarked upon with the client's informed consent and provides for a time plan to mark off the duration of the intervention sequence. The model can be used in dealing with a variety of personal, interpersonal, and situational problems, and with many different types of clients and settings.

The basic procedures of the model concentrate on case planning addressed to the specific features of the target problem and aimed at its alleviation. Implementation of the model concentrates on achieving performance of a variety of specific tasks designed to reduce the problem. Assessment is important to define and describe the problem to be addressed, to sketch in the social context, and to evaluate the personal, interpersonal, and environmental resources and deficits that will influence what can and should be done. Assessments should be for immediate use in planning and restricted to understanding the target problem in detail in its present form and in obtaining an overview of the client's personality, family, work or school circumstances, health, finances, and ethnic and cultural background.

PART II

GUIDELINES FOR BRIEF TREATMENT

In Part I, we set forth the fundamentals of brief treatment. Chapters 1 through 4 discussed the position of brief treatments within the context of psychotherapy and other types of clinical work, the characteristics of treatment in general, the special characteristics of brief treatment, and the features of the task-centered model, a general approach to brief treatment applicable to a wide variety of clinical situations where problem solving is called for. The task-centered model is the problem-solving paradigm in action and serves as the basis of our study of how to put brief treatment into action in practice. Problem-solving practices are augmented by discussion of brief treatment techniques from a variety of psychosocial viewpoints. A special section (Chapter 10) highlights interviewing techniques particularly pertinent to the task-centered model and useful in other approaches also. The concluding chapters discuss flexibility in brief treatment, adaptations of the task-centered model, and three new studies of task-centered treatment with client populations: medically ill, HIV/AIDS hospice patients, and the homeless.

CHAPTER FIVE

STARTING UP
Receiving Referrals and Applications

REFERRALS AND BRIEF TREATMENT

Referrals take on special characteristics in the context of brief treatment. Some of these characteristics are particular to agency rules and practices. Others are particular to a given case.

The agency-related features may occur when there are divergent opinions and expectations of the use of brief treatment between the referring and the receiving agency. As discussed in the following section, both parties to a referral have implicit expectations that result in interagency conflict, necessitating negotiations. The way the client reacts to the referral complicates the interagency relations. There may be differences between the agencies about the appropriateness of brief treatment in a particular case, or the appropriateness of a given model.

A good deal of the potential difficulty between receiving and referring agencies may be related to issues concerning the way the problem is to be defined, setting the focus that will determine how the case will be handled. In this chapter, we review the nature of referrals and the practice issues resulting from brief treatment techniques of problem definition. Suggestions will be made of ways to negotiate conflicts of this sort.

What Is a Referral?

A *referral* is the sending or dispatching of a client from one agency to another in search of or to obtain concrete resources, counseling, therapy, or any other type of welfare or social service. In complex, multidepartmental and multidisciplinary staffs, one department may make referrals to another department within the same agency. Issues arising in interdepartmental and interagency referrals are similar. In the following discussion, the parties to a referral will be called *agencies*, but it should be understood that the parties may in fact be departments within agencies.

Arranging to transfer a case from one agency to another or to collaborate on a case with another agency may be done by letter, phone call, or conference. (See Figure 5.1.) In other words, practitioners may link a client to the other agency by making an appointment for the client, identifying the person the client needs to see, discovering any special requirements of the receiving agency, and doing whatever else is indicated to make the referral "stick." If possible, the referral should make a bond between the person and the resource (Weissman, 1979). The practitioner can enhance the effectiveness of the referral by following up with the agency and the client to check on progress and problems and intervening when necessary to make the linkage work.

The client can sometimes be *steered* or sent to another agency without prior arrangement. This usually, but not necessarily, has less certain results. Steering may be appropriate if an agency has rules against accepting cases without the client's having shown an initiative in seeking the referral and the ability to act on her own. Steering may be used to save time or to pass the buck.

A referral is also an exchange. One agency exchanges the client with another. Although clients may obtain resources through referrals, they may also receive the runaround. When agencies accept, reject, or lose referrals, their supply of resources is affected. Their funds, staff, time, and position in the social welfare system are diminished or augmented, depending on whether resources are used, used well, used up, or wasted (Kirk & Greenley, 1974).

The fates of clients referred to an agency vary. Weissman (1979) estimated that about one-third of those referred will not follow through and contact the

FIGURE 5.1 **Map Detail**

Start-up	*Client referred by an agency source*	*Client applies, independently and voluntarily*
	FIND OUT • Source's goals **NEGOTIATE** • Source's specific goals • Source's resources to achieve goals	Not needed

agency. They will give up, change their minds, forget the matter, or get help from informal channels or alternative services that do not report into official statistical data banks. Two-thirds of those referred will make contact with the agency, but about a third of those will subsequently drop out.

In any year, it is likely that hundreds of thousands of persons pass in and out of the referral mechanisms. No one knows exactly the frequency and scope of referrals or why about half fail to receive service. Attrition has been attributed to various causes, including the practitioner's lack of skill and lack of total resources in a community.

Organizational processes, however, affect the rate of acceptance of clients. A client can be an asset or a liability to an agency. Clients are assets if they commit their time and effort and pay a fee or if the agency is reimbursed by the referring agency or receives grants from funding agencies to support the services. Clients are a liability if they consume staff time, occupy room in a scarce facility, fail to change in the desired ways, expand the caseload to an extent that lowers staff morale, or affect the agency's public reputation in a negative manner.

An agency's organizational objective to accept clients who for the most part are assets cannot usually be fully attained. Human service agencies may be obliged by law or custom to accept referrals from authoritative agencies such as the courts or police. Thus, clients and agencies may be involuntary participants in intervention programs imposed on them by third parties.

Agencies develop traffic patterns to stabilize and regulate the flow of clients within certain networks of the welfare system. These networks evolve over time as a result of habit, preferences, legal mandates, and reimbursement or purchase of care arrangements. For example, contracts may provide that one agency pays another to perform certain services for a client who is shared between them.

Barriers to the flow of referrals are created by budget allocations among agencies. For instance, problems defined as "mental health" tend to be referred to a department of mental health; those defined as "child abuse" tend to go to a department of child welfare; "financial support" problems go to a department of public aid; and so forth. Referrals may be blocked if agencies differ about how to define the case: Is it a child abuse case for child welfare service, or a mental health case for the department of mental health? Such disputes are not only time-consuming but are also the reason why some cases fall through the cracks.

Why Referrals Are Made

Referrals, or exchanges, are made for many practical reasons, including:

- An agency may be short of staff and may attempt to refer a client elsewhere to cut down on internal pressure and still get the client to some needed service.
- An agency's staff may lack necessary skills and believe the client will be more appropriately served elsewhere.
- Clients or their problems may be outside the normal and usual mission or function of the agency.

- Another agency is presumed to have some quality or quantity of service that would make a better fit with the client's application.
- Another agency is believed to be vested with responsibility for certain classes of clients and problems.

For example, when Lester (see Chapter 4) was referred for vocational training, his practitioner attempted to exchange his case. The practitioner lacked time and expertise in vocational assessment and knowledge of the labor market. The initiating agency had no job training program, but another agency was funded to develop and provide those resources. The first referral did not stick; the other agency did not seem to be able to get the client to commit himself to following its procedures and fitting into its pattern of service. The referring practitioner had to stretch herself to do the work.

Divisions of Labor.   A division of labor and responsibility among agencies exists in every community. Figure 5.2 demonstrates this division of labor in a general way. Fields of service are often highly stable. A particular agency or a sector of a field may have a tradition of providing certain services. It may be sanctioned by law and custom to monopolize a particular service, or it may be funded to provide a particular service. Supplementing or substituting for earned income, for example, is exclusively the domain of public welfare agencies. Other agencies give very little cash to clients except small amounts, amounting to petty cash, for the most extreme emergencies.

FIGURE 5.2   Fields of Service

Private sector ◄————————————————————————► Public sector

Interconnection

Grants
Subsidies
Purchase of care contracts
Agreements and understandings

Fields of service
Child welfare
Corrections
Physical health
Mental health
Community development
Family services
Income supplements
Institutions
Job training and placement
Schools
Others

However, some subdivisions of fields of service are less stable or highly unstable. Ever-changing funding patterns, trends of public attention, and innovations in practice create flux. It is difficult to keep up with new and defunct agencies and new programs. In this fluctuating domain, traditional agency boundaries meet, cross over, solidify, and liquefy again.

Agencies initiating a referral are often uncertain how that referral will be received. For this reason, agencies that make many referrals often work out interagency agreements to guide the staff decisions made case by case. Agencies receiving referrals are ordinarily not prepared to give a quick response, especially if there is no definite, detailed agreement about what they will accept and under what conditions. The referral has to be evaluated by the receiving agency, that is, judged in terms of the current position of the agency. The way the problem is defined often influences how a referral will be made or received.

Problem Definition and Referrals.   Behind a referral lies an implicit or explicit problem definition and specification. As discussed in Chapter 1, the problem definition explains the problematic issues at hand by describing the problem briefly and succinctly, formulating its scope and limits, specifying it by sharply pinpointing the focus, and naming the problem to improve communication about it. The problem specification is the concrete individualized problem definition that individually characterizes the problem, such as "The couple fights six hours in the evening almost every night about what bills to pay, what purchases to make, and who will control the money."

Problem definition and specification practices vary according to the prevailing style of an agency. Practices also vary according to the particular practitioner's or agency's style and beliefs. Whether the process of defining is explicit or implicit, soundly based or vague, a referral agency will have made its problem definition. Its referral assumes that the receiving agency can or should alleviate the problem it has identified.

NEGOTIATING REFERRALS

Negotiations are carefully planned and conducted discussions that aim at determining who will do or give what to whom and in return for what. If a referring agency is going to purchase the service for a client, there is little difference between negotiating to use the service and negotiating to purchase an airline ticket. Ordinarily, however, agencies conducting negotiations must also deal with issues of function, prestige, and rank. In other words, human service agencies, being customarily nonprofit, find many intangible rewards by being recognized for doing good jobs in worthwhile work, being well regarded in the professional community, and commanding a high position as a result of public approval.

Negotiating Inter- and Intra-Agency Understandings

When negotiations are conducted with a referral source or an agency being requested to accept a client, a plain, straightforward approach controls the potential for producing anxiety. Straightforward negotiations increase the confidence of the referral source and the receiving agency in each other because expectations are practical and realistic.

Practitioners, however, need to follow up on a good initial negotiation with reports to the referral source and to collaborate with that source as new conditions emerge. The expected payoff from ongoing contact between agency representatives is worth the time even when it means letting some other things go (Rooney, 1978).

Problems in negotiating inevitably arise, and some are not easy to solve. The agency making the referral often seems to require the receiving agency to make massive changes in the client's lifestyle, culture, basic personality, or intellect. A reasonable explanation of practical limitations can reduce this kind of demand, but it is not unknown for a referring agency to set up unreasonable or impossible goals. A practitioner may need to bear this conflict stoically, but it is better to have upper-level agency administrators work out a compromise with which all parties can live.

In follow-up conferences (by phone or letter, or perhaps in person), the practitioner may need to negotiate one additional area, that is, the client's own target problem—the center of intervention. A referral source may have a long list of problems, and the client a short list. The referral source may emphasize a focus for intervention that contradicts the client's focus. The receiving agency has to deal with this disagreement by negotiating a compromise. The referring agency will very likely respond to the practical value of such a compromise, especially in order to create the conditions for the best outcome.

Negotiating Conflicts with Other Agencies and Departments

It would be ideal if the social agencies in a community all had reliable knowledge about what is best and what works best, but as discussed in Chapter 2, they do not. Furthermore, the individual histories of agencies, along with their aspirations, community relationships, and the caliber of their staffs, make for different viewpoints and interagency conflict. Nevertheless, because service components are distributed unevenly among agencies, coordination is necessary for clients to receive needed packages of service.

The typical interagency discord that requires negotiating occurs when

- A case is referred with a specific service request (often really a recommendation)
- The client's target problem is not consistent with what the referring agency wants
- The receiving agency disagrees with the referral source, or at least is not ready to agree or disagree definitely

For example, a teacher refers a child who is underachieving, fearful, passive, and often in conflict with parents and siblings. The child's target problem is singular: poor grades in math and social studies. The parents' target problem is singular: poor grades in math and social studies. If the grades do not improve, they want to transfer the child to another school. The negotiating strategy called for here is to persuade the referral source that the child's and family's position is reasonable and that the clients are probably capable of good achievement on problems of high importance to them (learning math and social studies, in this case). Reasonably regular reports to the referral source normally alleviate this kind of dissonance. If this process is repeated several times with the same referral source, and if they see some satisfactory results, conflict tends to disappear or be cut to a low level.

Negotiating Strategies

In general, a negotiating strategy can be conducted along a continuum from

1. Explanation to referral source
2. Explanation, plus mutually agreed participation of referral source in its services and actions
3. Explanation, plus solid position statement
4. Explanation and solid position, plus plan for available backup and alternatives.

Specific strategies recommended here have been adapted from Fisher and Ury's study of negotiation processes (1981).

- *Don't bargain over position.* Instead, discuss problem-solving alternatives on a principled basis. For example, the wrong thing to say is, "I'm calling to get temporary shelter for a couple of weeks." The right thing to say is, "I'm calling about a child who needs shelter. I'd like to discuss how your agency might help."
- *Confront the problem, not the person.* For example, a good response to a refusal might be, "Your program is full? Hm . . . I really think your service would be best for this particular child. I wonder what might be worked out?" Put yourself in the other practitioner's shoes; don't blame him for your problem. Discuss each other's perceptions, and have the other practitioner participate in the process. Help the other practitioner save face. Allow him to let off steam and don't react to emotional outbursts. Listen actively and acknowledge what is being said. Speak clearly and to the point.
- *Keep the focus on the interests of both agencies and talk about those interests.* Do not stray from the particular purpose of the discussion, except for personal pleasantries.
- *Introduce options for mutual gain.* Present many tentative ideas; one may catch on.
- *Frame each issue as a joint search for objective criteria.* Always converse from an assumption that the other practitioner is a collaborator of goodwill, not an adversary.
- *If the other practitioner has more muscle than you do, stand on principle.* Bring all your knowledge to bear on the subject. Take your time; don't be rushed. Use your wits.

- *If the other person turns you down cold, avoid a confrontation.* Start reconsidering terms.
- *If you feel you have been deceived and pressured, don't be a victim.* Be polite and make your principles clear.

Task-Centered Approach to Negotiating

In the task-centered model, it is necessary for the receiving agency to pin down the problem defined and identified by the referral agency and the goals it seeks in order to collaborate with a client on the client's target problem. The client, the referring agency, and the receiving agency have to negotiate any incongruence among their target problem identifications and goals. They must also negotiate—and, if possible, contract—the resources offered by the referral source that can or should be supplied to the client. These resources can be tangible (goods and services) or intangible (attitudes and skills).

Some problem identifications passed on to a receiving agency from a referral source are nonnegotiable. These are mandated problems. The receiving agency dealing with involuntary clients (i.e., clients required to apply or appear) secures these referrals usually by a letter or by written order from a court. Sometimes such referrals are made on the phone or result from a case conference.

The crucial first step is to find out the referring agency's reason for the referral, that is, its particular reason, not only its general reason.

Negotiating Goals in Referrals

Implicit assumptions about the goals are attached to every referral. But if the goals are only implicit and are not concrete and particular, they are often excessively ambiguous. Ambiguous goals hinder systematic intervention procedures and create dissonance between the agencies and the client that can impede the making or receiving of referrals. In the task-centered model, goals should be negotiated at the referral point so they can be stated as explicitly as possible.

CASE 5.1

RON

A public child guidance clinic received a referral from a teacher and the school social worker in a conference. The teacher said that Ron, 11 years old and overweight, was well behaved and compliant. His problem was wanting other children to praise him for being good and making himself obnoxious by soiling his pants in school. The social worker said that Ron was clinging and "bizarre." He believed the mother was the chief problem and thought the mother should be helped to focus on her own problems and learn how to allow Ron to be independent. Analyzing this referral, one can make a chart like the one shown in Table 5.1.

TABLE 5.1 Ron's Problems Identified by Source and Goals

SOURCE	IDENTIFIED PROBLEM	GOAL
Teacher	Ron wants praise for good behavior.	Not stated
	Ron soils himself.	Not stated
Social worker	Ron is clinging.	Not stated
	Ron is bizarre.	Not stated
	His mother has personal problems.	Not stated
	His mother keeps Ron dependent.	Not stated

In this case, the absence of specific goals stated by the referral sources necessitates an analysis of the possible implicit goals. Without pinning down, or specifying, the concrete goals of the referral source, a practitioner could get the idea that the goals were to deliver Ron in two to three months as an independent, nice 11-year-old who would be self-confident, modest, neat, and clean and whose placid, comfortable mother would take joy from having an independent son. Undoubtedly, the referral sources are not so foolish, but without specific understanding of the objectives and an evaluation of their feasibility, who is to know?

Once goals have been put in feasible terms, a referral source should be able to provide the results of their observations and other information to describe Ron's praise-seeking, soiling, clinging, and bizarreness; his mother's problems and what she does to keep him dependent; any medical cause of his soiling problem; medical care; and assessment of Ron's capabilities.

The troublesome gaps between assumed goals and actual feasible goals are depicted in Table 5.2, which states what may have been the assumed goals in Ron's

TABLE 5.2 Analysis of Assumptions about Goals for Ron

ASSUMED GOAL	ANALYSIS AND QUESTIONS
Reduce Ron's praise seeking.	How much reduction does the teacher want? In what explicit praise-seeking actions? What exactly are the praise-seeking actions that are considered obnoxious? Because most of us enjoy and seek praise, why should such an ordinary characteristic be eliminated? What would be the result? Might the teacher be misstating what is obnoxious? Does she mean that Ron lacks appropriate self-esteem? What specific behaviors does the teacher want changed?
Stop Ron's soiling.	First, are there any medical problems? Exactly what are his toilet habits? Is there a history of previously competent toilet behavior? Any evidence of upset or trauma that interfered with competent behavior?

case and what kinds of questions still must be answered before the goals can become explicit.

Ron's case illustrates the unnecessary technical complexity caused by failure to clarify the referral source's goals. Ambiguous assumptions about what was wanted opened the door to unrealistic and fictive goals.

CASE 5.2

MYRA

Some interagency discord is very complex. More actors or highly charged ambitions are involved.

A prestigious, private psychiatric institution for residential treatment of children referred Myra, a teenaged girl, for placement. It named a long-term residential treatment institution as its preferred placement. The referring institution's policy was to provide care for no longer than three months—a period of time needed, in their opinion, to do a diagnostic work-up and also in keeping with the time limit in many hospitalization insurance policies.

The analysis in Table 5.3 shows the situation of each of the actors.

THE REFERRAL AGENCY'S OBJECTIVE

The referral agency wanted to place Myra in a long-term institution of its choice on the grounds that psychotherapy was needed for a borderline psychotic condition.

RESPONSE OF THE RECEIVING AGENCY

1. Would consider Myra if referred by public agency on purchase of care contract, but had no immediate vacancy.
2. Not sure if it had the resources to provide treatment.

TABLE 5.3   **Target Problems in Myra's Case**

MYRA'S TARGET PROBLEMS	HER MOTHER'S TARGET PROBLEMS
1. Mother antagonistic to her	1. Afraid of her daughter
2. Cannot live with mother	2. Distress about her own personal circumstances (nature of distress obscure)
3. Will not agree to further institutional placement	3. Heavy indebtedness (reason obscure, because income from employment average for working-class woman)

PUBLIC CHILD WELFARE AGENCY (THE AGENCY WITH CENTRAL RESPONSIBILITY—MYRA'S LEGAL GUARDIAN)

1. The policy is to place in institutions as a last resort.
2. The agency is not convinced that the girl is psychotic.
3. This diagnosis was not confirmed by a public mental health consultant.
4. The agency knows that a maternal aunt is interested in having the girl live in her home with the aim of eventual return to the mother.
5. The agency is willing to consider foster home placement.

NEGOTIATING STRATEGY

The public agency has a firm opinion. Therefore, it must be prepared to take a solid position against institutionalization and for placement with the aunt or foster home care. It must offer counseling services to the girl to help her learn to cope with her distress about being rejected by her mother. It must be prepared with a backup plan for institutional psychotherapy in case the diagnosis of the referral agency proves accurate.

Myra's case illustrates the extreme complexity of deciding on goals when there are many actors in the referral. The greater the number of actors, the greater the likelihood for conflict among agencies in setting agreed-on goals. In Ron's case, there were only two referral sources, working in tandem: the teacher and the school social worker. In Myra's case, there were three powerful agencies, one of which was the child's legal guardian; each of the other agencies had at least one service worker, a supervisor, and a consultant—all together at least nine actors in the referral process. The large number of participants and their power created a pronounced conflict over the objectives for the case and the intervention strategy. The presence of that many actors tends to overpower the client's own personal focus unless care is taken to preserve the client's rights.

The case of Sally Roscoe (Case 5.3) illustrates another type of referral issue, the difference in focus between agencies about who is the identified client.

CASE 5.3

SALLY ROSCOE

Sally, an 8-year-old, was referred to a multiservice community agency by a school teacher who thought the child was underachieving in her school work. Sally seemed agitated and was not clean. Following normal procedure, a practitioner briefly interviewed Sally. He explained his reason for the referral. Sally acknowledged doing poorly in school and was willing to work on improving her grades. She did not speak of any other problems. She gave permission for the practitioner to talk with her mother, a necessary step required by the school.

The practitioner made an appointment to visit the mother at home. On the first home visit, the practitioner found a timid young mother. Sally's mother, Mrs. Roscoe, was tense and worried, troubled about her child's school problem. She knew no details of the school problem and had not conferred with the school. She thought it likely that Sally was not doing her homework but had done nothing to schedule homework time for Sally. The mother showed concern but no interest in taking any action. If the practitioner wanted to get Sally some extra help at school, that was all right.

Because of the mother's weak response to her daughter's school problem, the practitioner asked Mrs. Roscoe if there was something she wanted help with. That question caused a flood of problems to emerge. The father, Mr. Roscoe, had failed to pay the rent for three months. After several weeks of threats, the landlord had now obtained a court order permitting the authorities to evict the family. There was no money to rent another apartment. Mr. Roscoe was not looking for another apartment. He became enraged when Mrs. Roscoe said she would look. In addition to Sally, Mrs. Roscoe had a 3-month-old infant to care for. Mr. Roscoe was bringing in food, but no rent money and no moving money. Desperately and strongly, Mrs. Roscoe asked for help with her target problem—eviction.

Exploration of how this problem came about brought out the story. Mr. Roscoe was a painter whose work was seasonal and erratic. Sometimes he made good money and sometimes he made nothing. Before the infant was born, Mrs. Roscoe worked on an electrical parts assembly job. Her steady income took up the slack when her husband was not employed. She was no longer able to work because of the young child's care. She could not afford a baby sitter. Her relatives were in another state; her husband's relatives were not friendly. There was just no one to care for the child. Mr. Roscoe did not want her to work anyhow.

Mr. Roscoe was at home while this discussion was taking place. Asked to join, he refused although he was obviously listening at the doorway. Lowering her voice to keep him from hearing, his wife explained that he was sick and so was she. He had no company group medical insurance. Her insurance lapsed when she quit her job. They could not afford medical care.

To Mrs. Roscoe's relief, the practitioner contracted with her on the target problem of eviction. The goal was to prevent the eviction, if possible, or to help her find, rent, and move into another apartment. The other target problems—the parents' ill health and Sally's school situation—were put into a pending status, to be activated or not, depending on the outcome of the eviction problem.

DISCUSSION

Sally did indeed have a serious school problem and had shown a low but definite interest in working on that problem. The referral source expected action to reverse

Sally's underachievement. With tutoring, Sally had a reasonable chance of improving her grades.

However, here was a mother who could not participate in the reduction of Sally's problem because of a real and imminent threat to her and her family's survival. Mrs. Roscoe could work on solving her problem and would have to let Sally's problem go.

It has been said, "When the house is burning down, do not stop to wash the curtains." Figuratively the Roscoes' house was burning down. The referral source, the school, had no difficulty in agreeing to a delay in taking up Sally's problems so that time could be spent with the mother on safeguarding the home.

Frequently, a referral deals with a peripheral problem. Interviewing the identified client and the other significant persons, the practitioner often comes upon a problem condition that is closer to the client's interests than the problem identified and defined by the referral source.

In Sally's case, Sally's school problem was attended to in a second contract, much later, after the family's housing crisis was solved; after public assistance was obtained, including medical care for the parents; after Mr. Roscoe joined in the effort; and after the family settled in another apartment. There were fourteen interviews in all over four months. To have worked with Sally on her schoolwork while her family life was a shambles would have been ineffective. To have ignored Mrs. Roscoe's plight would have been cruel.

APPLICATIONS

Applications are distinguished from referrals, because in applications there is no obvious intermediary. Applicants come to an agency on their own. In a referral, the arrival has been prearranged, recommended, strongly recommended, or imposed by an authority with warnings or penalties in case of noncompliance. Most practitioners and many agencies prefer the voluntary client to the involuntary one because there is an inherent dissonance in conducting treatment under duress. For this reason, agencies often attempt to transform the involuntary client into a voluntary client. However, even when there has not been any official or authoritative intermediary, applicants learn about various treatments through relatives and friends; the media; courses they take; and suggestions made by employers, teachers, ministers, physicians, and other respected sources. What people know about treatment is often inaccurate, and their expectations may be unrealistic. One task-centered client wanted help in deciding what kind of treatment would be best for his family; he was interested in the various methods available and their relative effectiveness before he decided where to go to get the pre-selected treatment approach.

The publicity given to treatment can be misleading and create false expectations. For all these reasons, the voluntary client is also likely to have reservations, reluctance, and resistance more commonly associated with involuntary clients but present also in varying degrees with the voluntary applicant.

Task-Centered Approach to Applications

The task-centered approach to applications emphasizes finding out both what the problems are as defined by the client, what the client's priorities are, and making a rapid early assessment. This process logically determines whether or not the client fits the rules of eligibility of the agency, whether the receiving agency is the one that can serve the client, or whether another agency should be suggested instead.

Normally, the answer to whether or not the agency can bring effective resources to bear on a problem is a straightforward "yes" or "no." Sometimes, however, the answer is not obvious and the decision is "maybe." In such instances, the practitioner should clearly explain to the client what is uncertain and make a contract to explore possibilities. These processes are the subject of Chapter 7.

SUMMARY

A referral is sending or dispatching a client from one agency to another or from one department to another in search of and to obtain resources, including concrete resources, counseling, therapy, or any other type of welfare or social service. Referrals may be made because of staff shortages or lack of skill in an agency for dealing with a particular problem or type of client. The request may be outside the agency's function; another agency may have some quality or quantity of service that would better fit the client's situation; or another agency may have undertaken responsibility for the class of clients and problems involved in the case. Underlying each referral is an implicit or explicit problem definition and specification.

There is considerable chance that disagreements and ambiguities will arise when making and receiving referrals. To work efficiently and to preserve the client's active participation, it is advisable to conduct planned negotiations with referral sources. These negotiating discussions should mediate conflict and promote understanding about what the client is seeking and can do, what resources can be provided, and what goals are feasible and realistic.

The essential actions in responding to a referral are to find out as neatly, specifically, and concretely as possible what the source's goals are; to negotiate with the source directly to reach an agreement on feasible goals and on what resources, if any, the source will provide to get these goals in place; to make explicit to the source what resources the receiving agency can apply; and to negotiate the strongest possible support for reducing the client's target problem.

When a referral is received, the receiving agency or staff member may feel obliged to do that which the referrer is asking. What the referring agency or staff wants represents its best judgment at the moment. Referring agencies are within their rights to ask for service in whatever way they deem best, particularly if they have an appropriate rationale. Given that differences of opinion are likely to exist about how a referral should be handled, the receiving agency can surreptitiously pursue its own opinion and wait for a conflict of interests to emerge. Or the receiving agency can impose the referral agency's opinion and wait for an impasse to take place with the client. The best action is to explain, interpret, and reach agreement with the referring agency.

The position of the task-centered approach is that being able to work unimpeded on the client's target problem is the necessary condition to using the guidelines properly and to conducting the case in the best possible way to obtain good results. The first aim, therefore, is to negotiate with the referral source to achieve understanding and agreement on the target problem. The second aim is to conduct planned negotiations with referral sources to obtain the resources that are expected to support problem solving, also in the interests of obtaining good results.

FIRST STEP: PROBLEM IDENTIFICATION

This chapter describes how to identify a target or focal problem; how to define the problem through the processes of describing, specifying, and naming it; and how to decide on a problem focus. Frequent practice issues of targeting a problem and deciding on focus will be discussed, and guidelines for dealing with them will be suggested. Among the practice issues of most concern are deciding on problem focus; handling mandated problems; facilitating client's participation in target problem identification, both expanding and drawing boundaries around problems; preventing trivializing problems; handling long-standing and deep problems, problems that appear to be constantly changing, and crises; establishing priorities; conducting a rapid early assessment; and managing the relationship. (See Figure 6.1.)

OVERLAP OF STEPS

The next several chapters are divided up into the normal steps of a treatment sequence. Chapters 6, 7, and 8 deal with the steps of problem identification, contracting, problem solving and goal achievement, and termination, in that order. This sequence is the same as the consensual order that is widely applied to the unfolding of human events: beginning, middle, and end. Applied to the therapy process, this order assumes that treatment will not be a well-intentioned and empathic muddle, but will be goal-oriented and will show a demonstrable progression from start to finish.

However, a treatment sequence is first and foremost a human encounter occurring on several planes of interaction at the same time and over time. Not everything can be known and understood about such interactions, and not everything can be neatly classified and understood. Therefore, the division of the sequence into a beginning, middle, and end will be neither sharp nor neat. There will be processes of going back and forth over the steps, of changing their order, of repeating and reorganizing the steps. This is expected and should be no surprise. Of what use, therefore, is this classification of steps or stages? The use is that without a vision of the orderliness of the procedure, the danger is great for the whole process to become a muddle, to be driven helter-skelter this way and that by the winds of feeling and interest that blow through the process. The concept of steps proceeding in a systematic way over time is meant to be held as a standard. The changing events of the treatment need to be put into perspective against the order and effort made to return the process to the order as soon as possible.

FIGURE 6.1   Map Detail

Step 1	*Client target problems identified*
	FIND OUT • Problems defined by client • Client priorities (hold to three) • Referral source priorities (mandated problems) • Preliminary rapid early assessment

DECIDING ON PROBLEM FOCUS

Problems Defined by Clients

Analyzing a problem situation to pick out a focus is a crucial step in brief treatment. Given the amount of uncertainty and inexactness in the social sciences about defining *problems* as a concept, it is little wonder that there is confusion about how to pin down or operationalize this concept in professional practice (see Chapter 1).

Dealing with Our Own Assumptions

In approaching the process of determining the problem as defined by clients, we tend to start with traditional assumptions.

The Assumption of Universal Criteria.   It is often assumed that there are universally known and accepted criteria for defining problems. In fact, as we have seen, a problem to one person may be no problem to another. The definition depends on the interests of each and on how aware the person is of her own interests. How problems are stated and what priority is given to them rests on changeable methods, theories, values, and societal norms and expectations.

To guard against undue influence on the client, the practitioner should always keep in mind what tendencies and inclinations dispose us to adopt a particular mode of problem definition and simultaneously attend to the exact and precise form the client gives to the problem definition. In that way, a problem definition may be worked out mutually and openly with the client to legitimate the client's perception and to give the practitioner an appropriate opportunity to influence how the client makes this choice.

The Assumption of Total Coverage.   Another assumption is that a problem defined should turn into a problem solved. Human services, almost universally recognized as problem-solving enterprises, often behave as if they are obliged to act upon whatever appears dysfunctional. That thrust often fails to consider the likelihood that some things may be better left alone, that no intervention or minimal intervention, in some instances, may be better than maximal interventions. More is not necessarily better. Another way of putting this is that a problem identified is not necessarily a problem to be worked on now.

It is not feasible to provide total coverage of the whole array of problems in a person's life. The techniques of professional helping are indeed of modest power and availability. To deal with the assumption that total coverage is the way to go, it is necessary to discriminate among problems on the basis of what problems need priority attention to make an important difference in the present situation.

Assumptions About Self-Actualization.   Some practitioners believe that helping clients to become self-actualized, to grow, to potentiate themselves, to be involved "in new and possibly more productive ways of reasoning about his or her problem . . . [is] the most vital aspect of the helping experience" (Goldstein, 1986, p. 355). These expressions refer to influencing personal beliefs, attitudes, feelings, and capabilities and creating in the client good feeling, personal satisfaction, and control over his circumstances.

Self-actualization is an attractive viewpoint. Many people are making reasonable or better salaries. They have leisure to contemplate art and architecture and to decorate themselves and their homes. They have time and money to have fun, to travel, and to study. Self-actualization seems a reasonable preoccupation in the context of today's highly ambitious consumer society and contrasts with the frustrations of real limits on achievement; high prices; strangling red tape; and the dangers of fire, theft, mugging, catastrophic illness, old age, desertion, terror, nuclear accidents, and waste of people.

It is commonly acknowledged that frightening social forces in modern society are turning people's attention inward. But believers in self-actualization are also problem solvers. They may prefer the language of feelings (that is, emotions, sentiment, attitudes, and other subjective states), but they help their clients alleviate crises; overcome depressions; and get public aid, medical care, better housing, jobs, or childcare. They help clients repair the thousand mean, destructive slings and arrows of outrageous fortune that real people face, the so-called "problems in living."

In dealing with our own preferences for self-actualization goals, it is advisable to refrain from imposing on clients any problem definitions that are restricted only to the emotional and cognitive realm. Clients, as do all of us, usually prefer to deal in the realm of tangible practicalities as well as in the realm of feelings. Reducing tangible problems or increasing tangible resources goes far in improving a problem situation.

Assumptions About Client Reluctance-Resistance as Pathology.   An inherent tension may exist between *problems* as defined by clients and *problems* as defined by helping practitioners. Professional definitions are the product of specialized training and occupational socialization. Client definitions are the product of ordinary living and commonsense experience. Experts tend to define the client's problems in terms that fit their expert views. Clients tend to define problems in terms that make sense to them, preserve their competence and dignity, and are consistent with their knowledge of the world and their world views.

These two viewpoints—the practitioner's and the client's—come out of different worlds of personal experience, culture, and class. They are the same to the extent that the life experiences of the client and practitioner have been similar. Differences *may* be caused by resistance; pathological processes of thought and personality *may* be at work to maintain the status quo and avoid the change needed for progress. On the other hand, the differences may be mostly due to the client's strong interests in her own aspirations, reluctance to undertake what the practitioner wants, lack of understanding and know-how, fear, or differences in cultural, moral, ethical, or normative views.

A practitioner using the task-centered model should be in touch with the problem as it is perceived and defined by the client, understanding it as much as possible in the client's terms and sensing how it is relevant for the client. The client is thus responsible for describing and explaining the situation, for participating in how the problems are defined, and for being a real partner in determining the solution.

Assumptions About History as Destiny.   All accounts of one's own life (autobiography) or of another's life (biography) are arranged selections chosen at the time of telling, in the present. These narratives explain and make sense of what happened. When clients tell us of their lives and when we practitioners inquire about their history, we are following deeply embedded, old traditions that require a story or narrative to have a beginning, middle, and end (Whan, 1979).

Many theories explain present problems in terms of the past. On the whole these theories, or the uses to which they are put, are reductionist in their effect. Too often simplistic and linear reasoning results in conclusions about the causal effects of previous experience, particularly of hypothesized phases, stages, or patterns that supposedly predetermine a person's life.

Systematic studies have questioned the extent to which the course of life can be understood as an ordered and predictable developmental sequence. A person may make sense of his life by continually reconstructing his view of it, that is, by telling his story in changing ways while we hear and interpret it according to our own views at a given time. Cohler (1982) suggests that life seems to be characterized by often abrupt transformations determined both by expected and eruptive life events and by intrinsic, but not necessarily continuous, developmental factors. The shift from early to middle childhood and the transformation to middle age and then to old age are particularly conducive to disruption and subsequent revision of the personal narrative. Lives are much less ordered and predictable than some deterministic hypotheses suggest. Our changing social context has much influence on what happens to us and how we interpret ourselves.

To avoid undue attribution of the causes of present problems to hypothesized past events or an interpretation of those events, the task-centered approach recommends that practitioners accumulate and use past history cautiously. The history of a problem can be explored for practical clues as to what the problem means currently and for previous problem-solving activities, but the practitioner's primary effort should be in understanding the problem in its contemporary setting and form.

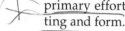

GENERAL ORIENTATION TO
THE ELEMENTS OF A PROBLEM

To get a problem into focus, we need a general orientation. We need to perceive the problem in relation to the persons involved, the environment in which the problem is occurring, and the knowledge available to describe and explain the problem.

Four perspectives—needs, personal deficiencies, lack of social skills, and classification or boundaries—used by practitioners and clients alike represent ways to become acquainted with and arrange the terrain of the problem.

These perspectives are not mutually exclusive, but adopting one or another as a major approach to a problem tends to shape what problem will be emphasized and what will be the content of the intervention.

The Needs Orientation

The needs viewpoint makes the basic assumption that a person's needs result from deficits in social and personal resources. The client is perceived to need certain material goods, skills, personal attitudes, relationships, or services. For example, consider these statements:

- "Mrs. A needs daycare." This means Mrs. A does not have the resources to care for and teach her children during the day, does not know where to get daycare, and probably does not have funds to purchase daycare.
- "Mr. B needs a psychiatric evaluation." This means Mr. B is thought to lack normative interpersonal skills and the knowledge, will, and funds to procure an expert opinion from a mental health professional.
- "John needs treatment." This means John is thought to lack normative interpersonal skills and lacks the knowledge, will, and funds to procure advice and guidance from a mental health professional. This statement assumes that treatment can improve his interpersonal skills and well-being.

A needs viewpoint may be the result of reliable information about a client's concrete deficits. Examples of presumably reliable information that show the existence of needs deficits are intelligence test results, measurement of degree and type of malnutrition, economic status above or below a poverty line, number and quality of rooms in an apartment, sufficiency of a welfare grant, stability of the home environment, health, and so forth. Perceived needs may also be consensually held beliefs about what it is good for people to have, for example, loving and caring parents and spouses, personal self-sufficiency, fulfilling work, the ability to give love and to care, flexible attitudes and responses to other people, and so forth.

Needs can be converted to social welfare service categories such as daycare, protection, health service, family planning, or foster care. Needs are an indirect way of stating a problem. Although subject to inaccuracy, they also have a commonsense basis.

A needs viewpoint is both a moral and rational accompaniment to understanding the social context of a client's target problem. Identifying perceived needs helps a practitioner be specific about the particular resources and social skills in which the client and her situation are deficient and about the presence of disordered emotional states, mental illness, ill health, employment and vocational problems, and other complex personal troubles. However, the needs viewpoint must be tailored to match a client's particular target problem; otherwise, it may do harm to aggressively fulfill some "need" that is not real to that client. For example, a practitioner or agency may impose professional or personal standards about what the client should have or should do and disregard the client's self-appraisal of what she should have or do. Imposing actions on a client can cause harm by introducing pressures that cannot be handled under all the circumstances. The case of Mr. and Mrs. Chris illustrates how a needs viewpoint shapes the problem definition.

CASE 6.1

MR. AND MRS. CHRIS

Mr. and Mrs. Chris, both in their eighties, were brought by the police to the emergency room of a local hospital. They were weak and incoherent, their bodies and clothes covered with coal dust.

Their weakness was diagnosed as malnutrition. The coal dust was accounted for by their living in a basement amidst the furnace and coal bins. A social worker attached to the psychiatry department was called in, but Mr. and Mrs. Chris were so incoherent that he could not find out what the situation was and what had happened to them. The couple were hospitalized, bathed, and fed.

The next day Mr. and Mrs. Chris were coherent. It was learned that the malnutrition was the result of their trying to live on the husband's meager social security. They did not know they were eligible for a supplementary public assistance grant. A neighbor who used to give them food had recently moved away, and so they were hungrier than they used to be. They had lived in the basement for fifteen years, rent free, because they watched the coal. The landlord was—he thought and they thought—befriending them. The couple had no children. They were very attached to one another. They were old and their lives were restricted.

The social worker perceived their problem as "needs protective housing because of age." He offered to locate a nursing home and help them be admitted to it. The couple blew up. They eagerly accepted intervention to get them a supplement to their social security and help them apply for public aid. But they would only return to their accustomed living quarters—the coal bin! No place else.

The question of whether this couple did or did not need housing has no single or simple answer. More than an obvious need for better housing was involved and had to be taken into account.

 ## The Personal Deficiencies Orientation

Deviant behavior is objective in the sense that it can be observed and verified if adequate criteria for identification exist. It is subjective in the sense that judgments about what constitutes deviance are often based on unverifiable inferences and a variety of moral judgments. Deviant behavior has conflicting definitions in the sociological literature as well as in the popular literature and the media.

It is conventional to think that a client's or a family's specific problem consists of the deviant behavior of individuals, and that the deviance is revealed by the part of their conduct that departs from consensual norms (Chapter 1; Thio, 1978). It is more difficult to understand how particular social and economic conditions interact with specific personal situations to extrude problems.

The personal deficiency framework is useful in the task-centered approach but should be combined with an assessment of the social context. The practitioner needs to evaluate personal deficiencies to see if and how altering the environment, providing resources, making some changes in how significant people relate to one another, or increasing the client's store of social skills through education, advice, and guidance can ameliorate the focal problem.

If practitioners manage only to isolate certain personal deficiencies and place them in the central focus, they may ignore real difficulties in the physical and social environment. They may overlook the extreme difficulty of altering some personal deficiencies without also—or instead—altering crucial environmental conditions. They may overlook the opportunity of making relatively simple and direct change in the socio-physical environment which might improve the situation promptly and efficiently.

The Lack of Social Skills Orientation

Ordinarily, the social skills needed for carrying out a reasonable lifestyle include

- Providing childcare (minimum basic parenting skills)
- Maintaining reasonable personal hygiene
- Maintaining a home
- Learning subject matter from school or special training courses
- Perceiving relatively accurately the intentions and expectations of other people, especially parents, close friends, siblings, spouses, authorities, and peers
- Communicating understandably to other people, especially parents, close friends, siblings, spouses, authorities, and peers
- Earning a living, especially finding and doing a job, getting along with fellow workers and employers, and getting the rewards of work
- Planning problem-solving steps
- Taking problem-solving actions

Identifying deficits in social skills is another way of organizing thought about needs and personal deficiencies. There are, however, potentially important differences among these three ways of formulating a viewpoint about problem definition. The logic of the needs approach is to provide what is missing as directly as possible, for example, a clean home, a father figure, a mutually satisfying marital relationship, psychotherapy, medical treatment, and so forth. The logic of the personal deficiency approach is to provide therapy that is intended to develop a mature (or more mature) person. The logic of the lack of social skills approach is to educate, teach, and train a person how to do things that are necessary for day-to-day living.

Because of the different tilt of each of these viewpoints, it is possible that each one could lead to a unique way of identifying the problem and designing the treatment. In actual practice, however, all these viewpoints tend to merge; in fact, it is possible to argue convincingly that all of these orientations to problems are different facets of the same thing or that the nature of problems is so complex and changeable that the problems appear in different guises at different times.

CLASSIFICATION OF PROBLEMS

A broad classification of problems affixes a name or label to social problems that are collective, aggregated troubles judged to be afflictions of sizable groups of individuals. Examples are delinquency, crime, illegitimacy, academic underachievement, unemployment, single-parent families, child abuse, and child neglect. Such labeling organizes information about conditions in social life and serves as an important use for categorizing issues of public and professional concern. Labels or categories guide scholars in organizing information and knowledge so as to enable us to think, reorder, rearrange, plan, and otherwise work with the ideas and observations that are represented by the labels. However, broad labels are useless as guides to understanding individuals or particular social situations. They give information usable in social planning on a broad scale; but they are nearly useless for planning interventions on a case-by-case basis.

A more useful problem typology is one that can capture features of problem conditions and behaviors illuminating the individual problem of concern at the moment. This kind of a problem typology does not exist in the area of individual psychosocial problems because of the immense variation among problems, the difficulty of arriving at consensus among professionals in the field, and the essential uncertainty about the best way to classify psychosocial problems. The *DSM IV* (American Psychiatric Association, 1994) is the accepted way to classify problems definable as *psychopathology*, but that leaves out the myriad problems of psychosocial difficulty and environmental issues that beset hosts of clients in the real world.

The task-centered model developed a problem typology that was thought potentially to be capable of helping to assess problems, decide on focus, and create boundaries to help keep the focus. This typology has not met with general acceptance and has not been used much. It is given here for heuristic purposes in the event it should be of value to practitioners who want to experiment with a technique that might have the ability to put boundaries around a problem.

Task-Centered Problem Typology

The task-centered model suggests a rough typology useful for putting systematic boundaries around target problems (Reid, 1978). It helps to visualize the classification as a fence that contains the content of the assessment, the interviews, the treatment plan, and the implementation. The task-centered approach classifies problems as follows:

1. *Interpersonal conflict.* Overt conflict (such as marital conflict, parent–child conflict) between two or more persons who agree that the problem exists.
2. *Dissatisfaction in social relations.* Deficiencies or excesses that the client perceives as problems in interactions with others, such as dissatisfaction in a marriage, with a child or parent, or with peers.
3. *Problems with formal organizations.* Problems occurring between the client and an organization, such as a school, a court, or a welfare department.
4. *Difficulties in role performance.* Problems in carrying out a particular social role such as that of spouse, parent, student, employee, or patient.
5. *Decision problems.* Problems of uncertainty, such as what to do in a particular situation.
6. *Reactive emotional distress.* Conditions in which the client's major concern is with feelings, such as anxiety and depression, rather than with the situation that may have given rise to them.
7. *Inadequate resources.* Lack of tangible resources such as money, housing, food, transportation, childcare, or job.
8. *Other.* Any problem not classifiable.

MANDATED PROBLEMS AND SERVICES WITH INVOLUNTARY CLIENTS

In many instances, a problem is mandated by an authority. The consequences of ignoring that mandate may result in severe losses to the client's interests and well-being. Agencies cannot ignore mandated problems, for instance, those ordered by courts or required by law, without jeopardizing their public sanctions and funding. Therefore, the agency is obliged to insist that certain mandated problems be part of the work. Normally, mandated problems are agreed to by clients on the basis that the client's own target problems are accepted by the practitioner. Few clients are so foolish as to completely flout authority by refusing any kind of participation. Clients may not state a mandated problem in the same way as an agency, or they may take a different or opposite view from the agency, but they will nevertheless be expected to select the same area for attention.

FACILITATING CLIENT PROBLEM IDENTIFICATION

The Problems Arrayed

The practitioner's first activity in the first step of the task-centered model is to elicit the client's views on the problems in the present situation as she sees them now.

This array of problems will undergo change and be organized and reorganized as the first step proceeds. But the problem array is the building block of all that comes later to shape the problem definition and problem-solving work. It is common to put this list of problems in writing and to use the written document, which may be pencilled notes, as a guide to grouping problems. Once grouped, these problems become a basis for discussion that ends up with a description and eventually a name that symbolizes the centerpiece of the work.

Target Problem Preeminence

The task-centered approach puts the client's expression of the target problem in the central position. This position is practical because it mobilizes as much power as possible from the client's own individual particular motivation. Concentrating on the client's target problems is the most direct route to tapping the reservoir of problem-solving effort in the client. It eliminates endless struggles to influence the client to want and do things she does not care about. At the same time, it concentrates the client's effort to tackle important problems he wants to work on.

This single-minded concentration on the client's target problems is consistent with the observation that intervention is usually more effective when client and practitioner agree on problem focus. To minimize dropout and increase the probability of good results, the practitioner needs to put and keep the focus of intervention on a problem that both she and the client define in the same or a similar way.

The task-centered approach concentrates primarily on those problems explicitly acknowledged and stated by the client, spontaneously or as a result of client–practitioner discussion. The target problem emphasis is a way to get a general orientation to a problem that may include needs, deficiencies, or lack of social skill.

Clients Who Cannot State Their Target Problems

Sometimes clients are unable or seem unable to come forth with target problems. Such clients tend to be extremely fearful or confused. Extreme fears are the result of experience. A client may have learned that it is too risky to reveal oneself to a representative of an agency. Relatives or friends may have told the client of negative consequences brought about by too frank statements to persons in authority, or the client may have experienced negative consequences firsthand. Some clients have learned to transfer fears of teachers, police, physicians, or other officials to all or most helping persons. Clients may have suffered punishments or reprisals from unsympathetic relatives and peers. It is difficult, perhaps impossible, to risk exposure with a strange practitioner when a client's experience suggests caution.

Internal fears are probably also learned from experience, but they seem to have become a permanent part of an individual's character. Some people are afraid and suspicious even when the evidence shows that no harm will come to them in reality. They have become so habituated to being suspicious that almost no amount of checking out will convince them to come out of their protective shells.

Some fearful people can take the risk of stating a target problem with a reasonable amount of encouragement, but they require a steadfast and trustworthy practitioner with patience and persistence. It ought to be expected that these clients will remain tentative in their trust, which is as it should be in view of the known realities that caused their distrust in the first place.

Confused Persons.   Some people may also evince an inability to clearly identify their target problems; they may blur their thoughts, mix their ideas in illogical ways, and make important mistakes in the way they think. They may lack experience in sizing up situations. Young children may misperceive an offer of help because of limited experience in deciphering the intentions behind the offer. Some people, both adults and children, may be handicapped because of low intelligence or disordered thought processes.

Experience with the task-centered model used with elementary school children reveals that, with rare exceptions, children of school age can develop clear and cogent target problems (Epstein, 1977). Many mentally handicapped and ill persons make relevant statements of their problems (Brown, 1977; Newcome, 1985). Although it is not to be expected that all confused people can be straightened out, it is important not to assume serious pathology in situations that may be only passing, superficial, or temporary.

Suggesting and Recommending Target Problems

The practitioner working with fearful or confused persons can make suggestions or recommendations, and/or institute a problem search process. These suggestions allow the client to select the one he views as the most appropriate, thereby enhancing his motivation to work on change efforts. These remedies go together and will often be carried out together or interwoven.

The practitioner will normally form an assessment impression and as a result may have some tentative ideas about possible and relevant focuses. These can be put before the client for consideration as suggestions, or more strongly, as recommendations. In either case, the practitioner should state and explain the suggested or recommended target problem as fully as necessary to be clear and should provide ample opportunity for the client to question, react, and consider.

The Problem Search Process

The problem search is a one- or two-interview special phase designed specifically to assist the practitioner in helping a client establish a target problem in circumstances where there is little if any spontaneity. Problem search can be initiated in the start-up phase or in Step 2 and is used with clients of two types: those who are referred by an authoritative agency but acknowledge no problem, and those who apply to an agency for a specific service but who seem to need broader or different service. The agency, or the practitioner, would like the client to expand the request.

The agency possesses other services and believes them to be equally appropriate, and the practitioner wants to interest (engage) the client. The problem search, or an adaptation, also may be useful in other circumstances. A practitioner may use this process at any time when there is an impasse about establishing practical and relevant problems for work.

The essential ingredient of the problem search is that the client be informed exactly what the subject of the interview is: namely, to come up with a notion of her problem from her viewpoint. The practitioner then leads a discussion to explain what the contact is for, how it will be done, what the client can expect from participation, why she stands to benefit, and what the alternatives are. To the extent the client will cooperate, she should be afforded ample opportunity to examine all these questions and give whatever responses she will.

Clients who get involved in this process can be expected to develop for themselves and for their practitioners background and contextual information that helps get hold of an understanding of their predicaments. If this effort is not successful or sufficiently successful to start intervention, the case can be terminated. On the other hand, it is often neither wise nor practical to terminate. It may be necessary to monitor the situation, to confer with the referral sources and the client's close relatives to help them affect the problem. It may also be possible, and often is, for the practitioner to reach agreement with the client upon some problem of seemingly secondary or peripheral importance that may or may not lead to more significant contact. When there is a mandate, however, that is, when a client is obliged to participate, it may be necessary to invoke the practitioner's authority and make insistent demands.

Rationale for the Problem Search.   The rationale for the problem search is that it provides a structured, purposeful opportunity for the practitioner to concentrate on assisting a client with the process of developing his own ideas about what problems should be attended to and what he is willing and motivated to attend to. Many clients find this a novel opportunity. It can have much importance because it clearly is respectful of the client by providing him with a chance to dig into issues and decide matters that are often decided for him.

Problem Search in Mandated Cases.   Practitioners are faced with an obligation and a responsibility when problems are mandated, despite a client's lack of acknowledgment of problems. Typical circumstances that suggest a problem search when the client has no self-formulated problem include a child referred for misconduct or underachievement in school, a mother referred for correction of child management practices as a condition of having her children returned from foster care, and parents referred for correction of child abuse.

A practitioner has two options under these and similar circumstances. First, the practitioner can insist on attending to the mandated problem. The legitimacy of such insistence is the authority vested in the practitioner. Second, the client can be offered an extra two-session problem search. If the client does not come up with a personally perceived target problem in two interviews, further attempts will probably not be useful. The first option then becomes the operating procedure, that is, the practitioner will have to set the agenda authoritatively.

Under normal conditions, clients authoritatively referred because of serious, incapacitating, threatening problems do state problems of their own accord, related logically to the mandate. If nothing else, the pressure placed on them by the authorities is aversive. They want to be rid of an implied or overt threat, such as not graduating, going to jail, or having children placed in foster care. Sometimes the problem comes down to "getting that agency, teacher, judge, doctor off my back." It is often sufficient to deal with a mandated problem in terms of what the client has to do to reduce the pressure of the authorities.

Dilemmas of the Problem Search

The problem search is a way to try to draw out specific client target problems under an adverse condition, one in which the client is either a nonparticipant or a reluctant participant. The client has not revealed what she is concerned about or will not share her concerns with the agency. It can be argued with conviction that a practitioner ought to refrain from intruding into aspects of the client's life that the client has closed off. In fact, the value position of the task-centered model supports a nonintrusive posture. However, when an agency has the legal responsibility for investigating wrongdoing, as in the case of child abuse, it is obligated to intrude into family matters to the limit permitted and required by law and administrative regulations.

Problem search procedures have been devised from practical experience. They are plausible procedures if an agency has the responsibility to try to influence and convince a client to use services maximally or in the way the agency thinks best and if the agency has the resources for providing more services.

The problem search is a way to deal with clients who appear to need time to accustom themselves to the idea that intervention may take time and may require their commitment in a way they had not previously contemplated. The problem search is an adaptation of outreach, common in many sections of practice, that is based on assuming responsibility to extend maximum services, with the hope that those services can support problem solving and contribute to a client's well-being. However, there has never been any firm evaluation that supports the success of outreach (Fischer, 1976; Mullen et al., 1972).

Many clients will view the problem search and its implication of outreach as intrusion and be reluctant to participate. Although its effectiveness is unproven, outreach will be done, because it offers a way to make services more widely available, to expand services. In many instances, it is an ethical practice to extend service even in the face of client reluctance. However, it is advisable that the intrusiveness be limited, constrained to problems clearly and explicitly stated, and offered in a climate respecting the client's right to refuse.

Depending on the kind of agency, every practitioner has two parts to his job function. One part is his helping function, but the other is his social control function. The nature of our agency roles and our legislated function determines how much of each accurately describes our work. A private practitioner has, perhaps, the most potential helping function with the least potential social control function, depending on who is paying his fees. Probation and child protective services may have the highest potential level of social control functions and varying degrees of the helping functions. As long as we try to influence the behavior of others, we have a social control influence. The more the client's work is voluntary and desired (our helping function), the more we may assume that clients will change in ways that are beneficial to them.

Dealing with Fear and Confusion.   If it appears that the client is not able to focus because of fears, the practitioner should try to learn just what she is afraid of. Common fears have to do with the client's believing she will not be believed or respected, believing the meaning of the situation will be distorted, or thinking she will be jeopardized in some way. Provided that the situation is not really unfair, exploitative, or manipulative, the client in actuality has little to fear; it is often possible to convince her by means of careful and painstaking discussion. Above all, a fearful client can learn the truth about these fears by observing the actual behavior of the practitioner and the agency.

The client whose fears have become internalized may not be accessible to a logical discussion; nevertheless, the practitioner should attempt to discuss unfounded fears. It may not be possible to accomplish much by way of fear reduction, in such instances; but it may be possible for the practitioner to avoid behavior that will trigger a client's deep fears.

The confused state of some clients may be temporary and due to crisis emotions, stress, illness, or shock. In such instances, just waiting a bit probably will abate the confusion. On the other hand, the confusion may be the result of some permanent or almost permanent state of mind and health. If the client is severely handicapped, the problem-solving work has to be limited to those areas where the client is functioning, and the work must be supplemented by involving family and the available social network. In other words, the task-centered approach and all other treatment approaches require, as a basic condition, a functioning social person with verbal capacity. If the major client lacks those abilities, the practitioner must work with the persons responsible for the client.

Dealing with Laconic, Taciturn Clients.   From time to time practitioners encounter laconic clients who use a minimum of words and are concise to the point of seeming rude or mysterious. Persons who present themselves in this way are often taciturn, that is, temperamentally disinclined to talk. On the whole, this is an inconsequential personality trait. Nontalkative people do what they think is important with an economy of expression that contrasts with the conventional emphasis in our society on communication and talking things out. Sometimes, however, the laconic client is deeply afraid and protects himself by underinvolvement. There is no unique technique known to dissolve either the character trait or the fear.

If fear is stopping the client from communicating, it will take some convincing experience to convey to her that it is safe and possibly helpful to communicate.

If the client is unskilled in communication, it may be desirable to confirm this lack of skill and, with the client's agreement, provide her with relevant skill training.

Resolving an Impasse in Stating a Target Problem.   What we call an impasse is the deadlock that occurs when there is strong, important disagreement between practitioner and client on what the target problem is and should be. Unresolved, this situation produces the prototypical incongruence between client and practitioner associated with poor outcomes.

The client's persistent and enduring disinterest and refusal to accede to professional opinion calls up the explanation of client resistance, a condition often not subject to much, if any, change. The client may not be able to deal with the recognition of the problem. The practitioner may be overly invested in certain stereotyped explanations of problems because of preference and adherence to a given occupational viewpoint.

When such a deadlock arises, it is advisable to be flexible and to accept the client's way of thinking about the problems, at least tentatively, in order to see where that leads. In other words, this deadlock situation is the acid test of the practice of the task-centered approach. It should not be assumed that confused or unskillful people do not know their trouble and cannot state it. Most clients know, or can develop in a discussion, what their problems are.

Skillful, flexible practice with the task-centered approach often results in a serious effort to accomplish what it is the client wants and what it is he will give a lot of effort to. Often this effort pays off with good results. The attempt to pursue the client's aims may produce failure as predicted by the practitioner, but if it does, the client has the actual experience of finding out what the difficulty is for himself. Now the client is in a better position to deal with the practitioner's suggestions and recommendations either at this time or in the future.

Voluntary clients nearly always produce reasonable, relevant target problem statements. An impasse often arises when a practitioner is reluctant to deal in the client's terms. The most common difference is that the client believes the problem lies in the environment or in the attitudes and behaviors of other persons and that she is only tangentially responsible. The client often tends to target the problem in a narrow area and in a relatively specific manner.

On the other hand, the practitioner may be inclined, by preference, experience, and training, to assume that the problem is broad, that the client is the important actor causing and maintaining the problem, and that the client is the one who must do the changing. Furthermore, unless the case is being handled as a family matter, with important others participating, the practitioner usually has no leverage with which to affect the behavior of someone who is not part of the treatment transaction.

Practitioners worry about what to do if a client should propose a target problem that is unrealistic or trivial, or that involves illegal or immoral activities. It is obvious that the practitioner should not participate in anything that is trivial, unethical, immoral, or illegal. However, it is exceedingly rare for such situations to occur. What may happen is that the client proposes work on problems that in the practitioner's judgment are wrong or bad target problems. It is usually possible to discuss changes and influence the client's view so he can accept a formulation considered reasonable by the practitioner.

Expanding the Scope of the Target Problem.   A practitioner may believe that the mandated problem or the problem selected by the client is embedded in a host of other problems. Many human behavior theories assert the existence of underlying problems that require attention in order to make effective changes. A practitioner has a right and an obligation to explain this or any other professional reasoning to a client. The obligation is especially pertinent if resources exist and are accessible for reducing other suspected problems. To persuade the client to open up other problem areas, the practitioner can propose the problem search.

In the absence of a mandated problem, the practitioner's professional judgment may still suggest that the client ought to consider other problems and that resources exist for their solution. The practitioner may believe there should be an attempt to broaden the problem scope from a specific concrete problem identified by the client to other areas. For example,

- A discharged mental patient, receiving posthospitalization follow-up, finds that the boardinghouse landlord is failing to provide services for which payment has been made.
- A mother, trying to live up to child and home management standards required by the court, is in jeopardy because the public aid department has inexplicably cut off her grant for homemaker service.
- A married couple, both employed, are threatened with loss of income due to garnishment of wages, or wage assignments, from bill collectors.

Most human service practitioners would feel obligated to suggest exploration beyond the concrete remedies implied in the target problems. For the examples just discussed, the practitioner might attempt to have some authority put pressure on the landlord to provide the service, put pressure on the public aid department to resume homemaker service, and get legal counsel to stop the bill collectors from harassing the couple. It is often correctly assumed that problems such as these are embedded in a web of circumstances that ought to be dealt with and probably can be dealt with successfully.

To proceed with a problem search to broaden the client's target problem, the following steps could be taken:

1. *Provide an explanation of the rationale for a broader examination of the problem.*   For example, "I suggest that you and I discuss whether this boardinghouse is the right place for you to be living. I can probably help you find and move into a better place to live and also help you deal with your landlord so you won't have to worry about him all the time. It seems to me that the whole atmosphere of this house is upsetting and that you ought to have a more pleasing home base from which to rebuild your life out of the hospital."

2. *Inquire about how the client perceives the relevance of an extension of exploration to these other areas.* For example, "What would you think about discussing your housing and its effect on you? It seems to me that there are quite a lot of problems you might be having there. No? Why would you prefer not to discuss this with me?"

3. *Recommend a problem search and plan on two interviews for that purpose.* For example, "Because you think that maybe you could benefit from more discussions, let's set up one or two interviews to see if we can hit on the problems it would pay you to work on." Or, "I strongly urge that you come to see me once or twice more before you decide against doing nothing about the hospital's child abuse report. The police and the department of child welfare may find that your child is in danger and may place your child in foster care. I could help you."

4. *Suggest no more than three problems and fully inform the client why these three are chosen.* For example, "I suggest we review your medication in case it is giving you trouble. We need to find out what is causing your lethargy. We can also review your landlord's actions to ensure he is not taking advantage of you. If we work just on these three problems, we can accomplish a lot in a short time. Then if there are other issues of concern to you we can target those for work."

5. *Follow the regular procedures for exploring and specifying the target problem with a problem search.*

The difference between this approach to problem targeting and the normal task-centered approach is that the focus is initiated and largely determined by the practitioner who must be highly active and talkative, ask questions, reflect verbally on responses, and make explorations and suggestions. The research on task-centered intervention suggests that the results of practitioner-initiated target problems are not likely to be as satisfactory as those defined by the client. To promote the likelihood of a good outcome, the practitioner should provide the client with ample opportunity to consider the relevance of her suggestions, to become interested in them, and to formulate a rationale for not acting on them. The client can be expected to spin off on his own into a problem formulation more befitting his situation. If this does not happen, then the practitioner's obligation is fulfilled and the problem search is ended.

Drawing Boundaries Around Problems.   In the task-centered model, problems must be limited by boundaries to minimize loose, diffuse, and rambling work. Boundaries permit specifying the locus of the problem, its substance or content, and its scope and range. In other words, boundaries help set the focus so that the client and practitioner can concentrate effort on specified sectors of a problem situation. Depicting a clearly bounded problem area starts the process of structuring, or systematic planning, essential to efficiency and good outcomes (see Chapter 1).

Boundaries are readily devised if the target problems are assigned to the best fit within the task-centered target problem typology discussed earlier in this chapter. Using a specific classification focuses only on those problems that can be logically subsumed under the classification. Classifying the target problems according to the typology provides a relatively simple way to separate problems to be addressed from those to be put aside. However, many practitioners find that referring to the typology is not a comfortable process for them. Because the problem types are not discrete and tend to overlap, a decision to classify the problem must be made. Many practitioners lack confidence in drawing boundaries in a live case and would prefer to depend on practice wisdom to judge what is within and what is outside the boundary. This is a weakness of the typology, but it is still a useful tool in putting necessary constraints on a process that easily gets overly expanded. Problem boundaries can be set by a practical, commonsense process of grouping together those boundaries immediately related to the target problem.

Excessive Number of Problems.   The task-centered model is capable of embracing two or three problems within its normal eight-session sequence. (Time limits and duration techniques are discussed in Chapter 7.)

The need to limit the number of problems comes up if the client perceives complex and interwoven problems covering a wide scope and lists a long array of problems of various types. Sometimes referring agencies may also infer or observe a long array of problems. It is the practitioner's immediate task to help the client select the two or three most significant problems on which to concentrate her energies.

Cases where the sheer number of perceived and defined problems are large have been labeled in various ways over the past three decades: problem families; multiproblem families; hard-to-reach, crisis-ridden, difficult, urban girls; single mothers; child abusers; the chronically mentally ill; substance abusers; and, lately, the underclass. These labels are not well-defined and researched entities. Rather, they are temporary and convenient code words that generally have a short life in both the professional literature and the media. Problem definitions that encompass the breadth of deficits and disadvantages suggested by these terms are not useful.

The guide to constructing target problems in overloaded circumstances is to adhere to the preeminence of the target problem as perceived and selected by the client, modified to the minimum judged necessary by the practitioner, and in mandated, involuntary cases, adhering to the essentials of the mandated problem in the form in which it is negotiated so as to be feasible.

Other problems, beyond the two or three that can be accommodated in the six- to eight-session time frame, need to be put aside. They may be taken up at a later time if doing so proves necessary or possible. It is naive to imagine that we could take up and resolve every stated problem, or that clients, supervisors, and the public actually expect us to do that. In real life, problem solving seems to be accomplished through the creation of improved conditions that have some spillover effect. Reducing some problems puts others in a new light, making it possible to reduce those with less effort, or making it possible to live with them.

Trivializing Problems.   In the interests of formulating problem definitions in a specific and bounded way, it is possible to become mechanical. This process is observed when problems are broken down into minuscule pieces, each piece being dignified as a central focus. This results in problems being taken up that are of little worth or importance, trifling, too simple, and in the end meaningless.

Constantly Changing Target Problems.   It is common in practice with the task-centered model to see some clients, from interview to interview, for the whole sequence, changing the form of the target problem by adding on, subtracting, and expressing uncertainty about whether the focus is right. This phenomenon is so common that it should be expected. It does not necessarily mean that the practitioner has erred in conducting the process of problem definition, although that possibility exists and should be checked; it also does not necessarily mean that the client is fickle, impulsive, or erratic, although that may be and should also be considered.

Usually what these constant changes mean is that problems in general are not finite entities but are perceptions, viewpoints, and tentative explanations. (See Chapter 1.) Normally, the "new" problem is the problem already targeted but seen in a new light because the client and the practitioner are undergoing new experiences and consequently revising their perceptions.

When such constant changes seem to be a problem the practitioner's judgment on boundaries to be observed in the treatment becomes useful. As long as the new facet or new problem can be logically included within the boundary, relatively small alterations in the problem mean a change in the rhetoric. If the problem really does take large swings, it will be necessary to reformulate the problem to get at a more stable formulation. Unless changes are real and substantial, they should be incorporated in a somewhat altered phrasing of the originally defined problem.

Long-Standing and Deep Problems.   Old problems that hang on and appear to take on new life and new forms as time goes on are what is usually meant by "deep." *Deep* may also refer to problems that are recondite, obscure, grave in nature or effect, and pervasive.

Many old problems are relieved by correcting present conditions. To the greatest extent possible, the most feasible way to deal with old problems is to rearrange the present to minimize their impact on the present. The problem of old wounds and hurts, and entrenched, habitual ways of responding may be intractable; people often learn to manage without necessarily obtaining basic change in long-standing patterns and problems.

Should wounds from the past defeat efforts to ameliorate the present, the practitioner can ascertain whether other treatments are available and if the client can use them. These treatments may be those customarily planned to take long periods of time, or they may be family-oriented or group treatments that aim for a broader scope than that offered by the task-centered model.

Crisis Problems

The term *crisis problem* is used so indiscriminately and is so dramatic that it has come to be practically indistinguishable from the term *problem*. The term *crisis* is often reserved for *a stressful problem due to an emotional upset touched off by a disruption* such as

- a substantial *change in the environment* (moving, disaster, flood, fire, war)
- temporary or permanent *loss of physical function* (accident, sudden onset of severe illness)
- *onset of maturational development points* (starting school, leaving school, starting new job, getting fired, being forcibly retired)
- *loss of important interpersonal supports and personal identity* (rape, battering, abuse, death, separation, abandonment)

When applying the task-centered model to crisis problems, the practitioner should confine the problem definition to the boundaries of the crisis. In the past, some theories suggested that intervening in a crisis was a good way to enter into a client's deeper problems, which are aroused by the emotions surrounding the crisis. Indeed, one often observes people who are very upset (say after a fire has destroyed their home) easily talking about old and painful problems. However, it has not been established that treatment occurring in a crisis is a real route to uncovering and pursuing deep problems. It may also be asked whether or not it is ethical to take advantage of the emotions of a very upset person to dig around in the past.

An extensive literature about crisis intervention in specialized problem areas, such as rape, battering, and other forms of interpersonal violence has developed, but it is too specialized to include in this discussion. The interested reader is advised to seek it out when needed (Dixon, 1987; Golan, 1978).

THE ROLE AND RESPONSIBILITY OF THE PRACTITIONER IN DECIDING ON TARGET PROBLEMS

The role of the practitioner in arriving at the target problem as perceived by the client is to elicit fully and in detail what the client sees as the problem; to aid the client in trying to understand what that problem means to her; to form an independent professional judgment (assessment) on what an appropriate and feasible problem definition should be; and to arrive at a mutual formulation with a minimum of difficulty and a maximum of cooperation.

THE ESSENCE OF TARGETING PROBLEMS

Principles

1. A practitioner is obliged to define and identify problems. The whole sense of the human service enterprise is to solve or abate problems.
2. The way to reach a practical focus is to start with and stay with the particular client's definition.

3. It is practical to state a problem definition that is congruent with the client's sense of the situation.

4. Staying with the client's definition clarifies the issue of motivation. Task-centered practice gives priority to the areas in which the client is motivated.

5. It is unlikely that a client's motivation can be readily enhanced, or that he can be maneuvered into a genuine commitment for a personal change not wanted, not sought, and not accepted.

6. Clients seek and value help that makes sense to them, is useful in their daily lives, and gets or keeps them out of trouble. The whole purpose of the task-centered model's emphasis on target problems identified by clients is to take maximum advantage of the existing client motivation.

7. The client's statement of the target problem puts necessary boundaries around the exploration and intervention.

8. Assessment begins as the target problem becomes relatively definite, and is carried out more fully in Step 2 (contracting and planning), proceeding to be more developed in Step 3 (problem solving).

9. The client's target problem determines the focus.

Basic Actions

1. *Specify the problem.* Normally, with a little encouragement, the client states and at least partially describes the nature and location of the problems as she defines them. The client establishes the actual presence of a problem. The practitioner helps the client name and state what the problem is explicitly and in detail. The practitioner must phrase the problem in a definite and specific way so that it can be developed into a statement of what is to be changed. The phrasing of the problem is important in the same way that a label is important. It formulates the problem in a distinctive way and is an aid to focus.

There are right and wrong ways to phrase target problems. The right way gives information that leads to plans for change, that is, to specific tasks. The wrong way contains insufficient information to lead to ideas about what can be changed. A wrong formulation may not do any harm; it just blurs the process, impairing the direction and efficiency of the work. A few examples of target problem specifications clarify the differences between correct and incorrect phrasings.

Right: Arthur fights too much with his foster father.

Wrong: Conflict in the foster home.

Right: Ben hits his mother every day. He broke windows in the apartment three times in a fit of rage. Mrs. C believes her son is too interested in sex.

Wrong: Mrs. C cannot control Ben.

Right: Mr. and Mrs. D quarrel too much.

Wrong: Marital conflict.

Right: They leave the children alone.

Wrong: Inadequate parenting.

The "wrong" statements may be accurate, and they may be useful shorthand statements, but they are wrong as target problem statements because they convey both too much and too little information. They are abstractions. A target problem statement must be a concrete, individualized description of the condition to be changed. "Arthur fights too much with his foster father" means that a goal will probably be reduction in the frequency of these particular fights. "Conflict in the foster home" has no boundaries and no specificity. This wording can refer to matters all the way from leaving the cap off the toothpaste to a vague, general climate of unease and resentment among the family members.

2. *Specify the conditions or behaviors to be changed.* What is to change is implicit in the target problem. "Arthur fights too much with his foster father" implies that the change desired is reducing the frequency of those fights. To be particular and explicit about the conditions to be changed is to be sure that the problem is consistent with the goal. If practitioner and client do not specify conditions to be changed, it is easy to disconnect the problem from the goal. This disconnection can be illustrated with the case of Ben. Take the target problem "Ben hits his mother every day." This problem implies that the goal will probably be to eliminate Ben's hitting his mother. Suppose, however, we did not specify that the condition to be changed is Ben's physical aggression. We could easily transform our goal from stopping Ben's aggression to improving the mother–son interactions. Making that transformation could lose the mother's attention, open up an area too broad for Ben to handle, stretch the boundaries of the target problem too much, and possibly overtax our ability to intervene with good results. If broadening the problem is indicated and acceptable, the broader problem should be specified *in detail.*

3. *Make tentative goal statements.* Tentative goal statements are preliminary *working goals* that are needed to help make problem definitions that are practical and worthwhile because they will lead to something attainable, desired, and significant. These tentative goals may very well be honed later. They are needed from the start, however, to frame the problem definition. The obvious reason for having a tentative and realistic goal in mind as background for developing the target problem is to prevent wishful thinking from driving the decision on the target problem.

Goal statements confirm what the end product of the sequence is supposed to be. If a goal statement is not concrete, there is no way to find out if it was attained or how much was attained. A diffuse goal statement prevents achievement or lack of achievement from being recognized.

Goals are not limited, nor are they ultimate or stretchable. Mr. and Mrs. D, who "quarrel too much" and "leave the children alone," acknowledge those problems and want to do something about them. The only logical goal for the first target problem is to cut down on the quarreling. There are two alternatives for the second problem: making safe child care arrangements when they are gone or staying home. (See Chapter 7 for more discussion of goals when pulling together the contract.)

4. *Explore the target problems.* Defining target problems involves discussion. Sometimes the problem seems to change as the interview or series of interviews

proceeds. Although the practitioner should try to get hold of firm statements, he should explore the issue further if the target problem is uncertain or is starting to appear uncertain after being stated.

   Exploration means a systematic search and examination. In the task-centered model, the exploration concentrates on scrutinizing the target problems and their social context and discerning the client characteristics that shed light on the problem. This information is of immediate use for getting a first assessment impression. The first impression pushes the process along. Later on, this impression will also be honed. Increased accuracy and relevance of the assessment information may help select what interventions are going to be most effective with this client in this situation at this time. Exploration and assessment occur together. In Step 1, making the target problem identification, the purpose of exploration is to be clear and quick in settling on target problems so that intervention can start as soon as possible.

Exploring the Social Context.   The social context consists of housing and neighborhood conditions, work and school conditions, socioeconomic status and financial constraints, health conditions and health care provisions, family and peer relationships, and cultural and ethnic background. The social context is a primary source of information on which to base assessment of the meaning of the problem. Conditions in the social context and the client's transactions with elements in the social context will provide clues to stresses and dysfunctions that cause, contribute to, and maintain the problem. Environmental alterations may be feasible and may make a significant difference in the client's well-being.

   Normally, a client spontaneously provides a good deal of information about the social context during the process of problem specification. Noting this information and expanding it with a few questions provides the practitioner with essential facts about who clients are in their particular circumstances. It is not necessary to go into obscure, hidden, and old information. The gross exploration outlines the circumstances in which the problem exists.

   A gross exploration of this type is likely to identify important deficits or exploitative and oppressive conditions. The practitioner should secure enough information to show how much these conditions are responsible for the problem. His observations and inquiry should attempt to identify the source of the stresses that are precipitating and maintaining the client's problem. Attention should be held to present environmental stress. A long history of environmental stress has a cumulative effect and may give a strong coloration to the client's situation. However, some of the undesirable effects of long stress are reversible if the stress is lifted. There are various theories about the debilitating effect of stress (Golan, 1978). From the point of view of the practitioner handling a case, common sense and experience are good guides to pinpointing grave stress in the environment.

   Among those conditions likely to produce excessive stress are separation from and loss of close relatives and friends; status changes; unemployment; tedious, demeaning, and poorly paid work; hostile authorities; unsanitary, ugly, and unsafe housing and working conditions; poor health; discrimination; and poverty. Some problems are closely associated with socioeconomic status, particularly the condition of the poor and those at the low end of the income scale. The social context of poverty gives a rough gauge of what opportunities exist for problem solving.

Exploring Client Characteristics and Mode of Functioning.   A practitioner can acquire a great deal of the necessary information about a person by simply observing her during the interview. A practitioner can size up whether a client is timid or aggressive, suspicious or trusting, angry or calm, reasonable or unreasonable, logical or illogical, lethargic or active. See Brown and Levitt (1979) for details of specifying problems.

Sometimes, if a client is upset or confused, the practitioner must confer with other people who know the person. Information about intellectual and psychiatric status is sometimes important, particularly if the client is hard to understand. Information obtained from others, however, can be misleading. Judgment always has to be made about how much credence should be given to secondhand information. Having a firm grasp of a client's target problem will keep the practitioner from making unnecessary explorations and help him make a decision on the appropriateness of the views of other informants.

Clients' Cultural Beliefs and Human Diversity Factors.   Exploring clients' belief systems is an essential component of our work with them throughout the intervention process. The many ways in which people develop and hold dear their world views determine what they will and will not do to change their problems in living. The ease with which clients engage and enter into work with us is partly (if not mostly) determined by how well we understand their views and belief systems. Many clients become discouraged from seeking and using our help when we inadvertently act insensitively toward them. Such can be avoided by learning about clients from clients.

It is axiomatic that each person is a unique individual. However, how many of us meet an American Indian, a person with a disability, a lesbian, or a Latino American and assume we know something about that person simply because we know some facts or information reported about the group of which they are part? General descriptions about a culture or group (standardized or stereotypical information) will not help us know any one person. We have to assume each person is unique and understand and appreciate that uniqueness (Brown & Alley, 1999a & 1999b). The following statement to a client is a good way to accomplish this therapeutic task: "I have some expertise in problem solving and helping people. However, you are the expert about you. I need you to teach me what I need to know about you so our work together can be successful."

Exploring Previous Problem-Solving Efforts. Finding out about previous problem-solving efforts, particularly recent past efforts around the same target problem, can be enlightening. These past experiences offer analogies that can be drawn on for good ideas about actions to repeat, change, or avoid.

Determining Priorities

The types of problems handled in human service programs are characterized by lack of resources and lack of social skills. The resource deficit may be extreme or minor, obvious or inferred. People perceive resource deficits as serious restrictions on their freedom and well-being. Deficits in social skills may vary from being simply awkward to life-threatening.

Resource deficits are both tangible and intangible. The basic tangible resources are those essential minimums that sustain and maintain body and subsistence: food, clothing, and shelter. Beyond the basic minimums are other tangible resources also considered in modern societies to be necessities: furniture, utilities, laundry equipment, pots and pans, heating and cooling equipment, telephones, medical care, and educational opportunities.

Social skill deficits are always intangible. Social skills are a developed and acquired power to perform physical and cognitive acts and to use knowledge effectively and proficiently in the performance of particular and necessary acts. Deficits in social skills vary from the inability to talk to abrasive garrulousness; from the inability to concentrate to a rigid obsessive fixation on a single idea; from the inability to learn to the inability to play; from the obsessive concentration on one's own internal state to total ignorance of one's own feelings, attitudes, and beliefs; from an absolute insensitivity to others to offensive attention to others; from the inability to be alone to complete withdrawal into one's private self.

Most social skills deficits include a lack of problem-solving skills. Persons referred to social agencies as well as those who seek help voluntarily often come with a long laundry list of problems to be cleaned out. Being deluged with problems is one sure way for a person to become overwhelmed and immobilized or frantic. To restrain this tendency to immobilization ("I don't know what to do: I can't do anything!") or frenzy ("These things have to be all done at once or else!"), a person must establish realistic priorities.

The practitioner and client can establish these priorities according to several criteria, including the characteristics of the method being used to address the problem in question, mandates from authorities, and the client's viewpoints. All three of these criteria play a part in all decisions on priorities. However, which viewpoint is the most powerful determinant of priorities makes an important difference in how the priorities are structured within an intervention strategy.

Methods Priorities.   Methods priorities come from a style of thinking. Ideological preferences and beliefs, theoretical concepts, and values combine to explain a problem. The particular method may favor certain explanations of how problems are caused, although ordinarily beliefs about causation are incomplete and variable. The method may favor certain interventions thought to be best.

Practitioners learn and agencies support actions called for or consistent with a method. The key action in carrying out a methods priority is that the practitioner's decision about priorities is thought to be an application of the method. There is a tendency to reify methods. Emphasizing their assumed priorities may result in distorted treatment strategies. For example, priority may be accorded a client's compliance with the method, attending sessions regularly, achieving insight, facing problems, forming a good relationship, and so on.

Mandated Priorities.   Mandated priorities can be set according to an authoritative directive from a powerful institution, usually the referral source. Mandated target problems, as discussed earlier, originate with a legal or social authority, whether or not the client is in agreement. Such target problems can be ranked according to the power of their source. Mandates to act in a certain manner imply that the client and agency are obliged to change a situation, sometimes in a predetermined way, by restraining, curbing, or requiring identified action, for example, being drug-free or giving a child regular medical home care.

Sources of mandated problems can be classified into the following broad categories that vary in power according to their degree of influence and jurisdiction.

Legislation.   Some legislation requires that agencies or clients act according to the provisions of specific statutes. The client's problems are governed by rights and restraints set forth in the applicable statutes, for example, legal prohibitions of assault and theft.

Police and Court Orders.   When problems of the client are public, the client may be ordered to act differently, for example, in the case of a police arrest and a court order.

Impending Police and Court Orders.   When problems of the client are public or in danger of becoming public, there may be a threat of police or court order, for example, in case of a complaint of child abuse by a legally designated authority.

Professional Opinion.   If problems are identified because of professional opinion, for example, an opinion registered by a school official or mental health professional recommending foster care for a child, the client may feel pressure to conform but can avoid changing behavior fairly easily.

Public Opinion.   Problems of the client may be identified because of a complaint about the client's behavior from a person in the community: a relative, neighbor, acquaintance, newspaper reporter, or government official.

How Powerful Are Mandates?   Only legislation and police and court orders have real power to create consequences of the highest seriousness for the client: deprivation of liberty, coercive removal of children, or coercive commitment to correctional institutions. Threats of police or court orders, if real, have almost the same power.

Professional and community opinion are ambiguous. Professional opinion is likely to be more powerful to other professionals than to clients who dislike or reject the opinion. Community opinion, because it may express the wishes of prestigious or significant persons on whose goodwill the agency depends, may, like professional opinion, exert much pressure on an agency. Staff may easily feel compelled to maneuver the client, if possible, into submitting to the wishes and expectations of other professionals and influential community people. Professional and public opinion is, at times, capable of acquiring such general acceptance or prestige that new laws evolve that become high-order mandates on agency clients.

Practitioners in agencies have authority, as legally sanctioned agents, to inform the client and explain exactly what consequences are to be expected if they ignore mandated problems. A list of specified actions the client will have to take to avoid negative consequences should be drawn up. The client should be helped to avoid those consequences by making the change specified.

When it comes to clients who ignore professional and public opinion, that is another matter. Clients have the right to make a voluntary choice about the propriety of opinions held about them by others. Professional helping people sometimes have an inclination to give out opinions with more authority than is warranted by the state of their knowledge. The ability of professional opinion to predict harmful acts is low. This is not meant to suggest that professional opinion should be ignored at will. But experts frequently disagree about psychosocial diagnosis, treatment of choice, and predicted consequences. There are degrees of expertness; in the helping disciplines it is sometimes hard to know who is and who is not really an expert. Public opinion about a client is capable of being genuinely altruistic but may also be spiteful, prejudiced, and exploitative.

It is difficult to motivate, influence, and induce unwilling people to agree to recommendations and commands of referring professionals and community people. However, it is common for clients referred, if given the opportunity, to target a problem differently from the referral source. They may or may not include an item from the referral source's list of problems.

When the involuntarily referred client is under a low-power mandate, the practitioner should accept the client's target problem choice and begin work on it. However, if the mandated problem is identified by a source with real and legal power, capable of imposing important negative sanctions for disobedience, two parallel sets of target problems can be established: one mandated and the other identified by the client. It is likely that these two sets will be related and may merge.

Legislative mandates do not ordinarily identify, specify, or command the focus of cases directly. Legislative mandates are direct for persons charged with crimes: homicide, theft, sale of prohibited drugs, and so forth. Even for persons who are so charged, the court and welfare systems mediate and interpret the application of the law to individuals. Legislation establishes rules for conducting the affairs of society and enforces them by punishment or threat of punishment. Legislation reflects history, social conflict, and social change, but there are always ambiguities in what the law is and how it should be applied in individual instances.

Court orders provide a way to transform laws from general rules to specific rules to govern the management of a particular case. Because violation of a court order can have disastrous consequences for a client, a problem identified in a court order is a high-power mandate commanding great attention and the highest concentration. Police powers result in high-power mandates because they contain the possibility, sometimes the probability, that ignoring the police will result in the client's being arrested. When the police refer a case to a welfare agency, their problem identification cannot be ignored.

Administrative regulations are a source of many mandated problems. Agencies are established, sanctioned, and funded to effect types of outcomes or results with certain classes of persons identified as deviants. Partly to carry out their mission as they perceive it and partly to continue to receive public sanction and funds, agencies develop complex regulations, some highly specific; for instance, a person is ineligible if her income exceeds a stated ceiling (a means test). A variant of the means test is fixing a sliding-fee scale for applicants above a stated income ceiling.

Beyond the means test, agencies develop regulations about various circumstances in which they will or will not provide goods and services. Most of these regulations contain large amounts of discretionary power and are interpreted variously case by case. Usually supervisors and higher-echelon staff exercise the formal power. But in the daily routine of practice, the regular practitioner is powerful.

Mandated problems with involuntary or semivoluntary clients pose a major source of difficulty in practice. The prevailing intervention custom is for direct service provision (resources) and social treatment (skill training or therapy) to be lumped together in one inseparable package. On the one hand, the ethics of social treatment support client voluntarism. On the other hand, the expectation that agencies will exercise benign social control is always present. The dissonance between voluntarism and social control is immense. The reality of much practice often makes the separation of voluntary engagement and social control impossible: it is often *not* possible to fuse treatment and social control. Therefore, it is advisable to deal with them separately, even though both are present. This means confronting ourselves and our clients with the opportunities and requirements of both social treatment and social control and using the authority we have been given by legislation and collaboration (as with courts and police).

Because clients understand the source of authority very well, open admission of it is no surprise to them. Covert disguise of authority as treatment gets the distrust it deserves.

Problems mandated by professional opinion probably cause practitioners more distress than more powerful mandates. Professional opinion sets our internal standards for ethical and appropriate practice. However, we have no right to impose our views by using our authority over vulnerable clients who may see their world differently.

Client Priorities. Client priorities can be selected from the client's statements of how the problem is perceived in particular circumstances. Client statements are prioritized by asking a leading question, namely, which three problems—if fixed—would make the most difference to you? The most effective way to set priorities is to

1. Establish the client's priorities among the target problems. The three problems most important to the client make up the priority list.
2. Include the mandated priority (if any) as one of the three.
3. Recommend to the client, if necessary, a preferable priority list. It is unlikely that the client will work on any but her own priorities. However, many clients are receptive to professional advice about a preferable priority list when it can be shown that another order will achieve more.

To establish client priorities, *start* with the client's list. This produces the array of problems. Next, *introduce* the practitioner's recommendations, if any; include any mandated problems, stating the degree of authority they carry. Then *classify* the problems according to logical combinations. The task-centered problem classification assists in making such combinations. Alternative ways to classify problems are according to their similarity in behavioral or situational characteristics or according to their expected consequences.

Name, state, and review each problem as specified. *Make an independent judgment* about which elements in a multiple-problem list are most important. Judging importance means considering which problems weigh most heavily on the client's situation, have the most negative consequences, would have the most positive consequences if corrected, interest the client most, and are most amenable to change. *Engage* the client in making a judgment about importance. Finally, *put aside* prioritized problems that exceed the rule of three. They will be activated later if there is a time and if it is necessary. The *rule of three* refers to constraining the sequence to three prioritized problems.

EXAMPLE 6.1

SPECIFYING CLIENT TARGET PROBLEMS

Ron (Chapter 5), in interviews 1 and 2, acknowledged two target problems, specified the behavior to be changed, and stated his target problem and goals as follows:

1. *He is too fat.* He has been fat for the past four years. His peers humiliate him because he is fat. They call him insulting names. His mother and sister are overweight. In addition to three full meals, Ron eats snacks four times each day—leftovers, pie, potato chips. He would like to lose weight. He would like to be normal size. Ron's goal is to lose 40 pounds.

2. *He soils his pants.* At home after he wakes up and before he leaves for school, Ron has one to three loose bowel movements. In the past seven days he had such bowel movements on six days, every day of the week except Sunday. After he gets to school, he has loose bowels again. He is embarrassed about leaving the room to go to the toilet so often and so he soils his pants. Ron thinks his eating so much food and so much junk causes the loose bowels and soiling. The teacher says he

soils on four out of five school days. Ron says he has had this problem since he started school and that he used to soil at home before he started school. Ron's goal is to stop soiling.

REVIEWING THE SOCIAL CONTEXT
AND PAST PROBLEM-SOLVING EFFORTS

Information was obtained from the first two interviews with Ron and from two separate interviews, one with the mother and one with the teacher. Items are listed separately to emphasize their distinctions.

Social Context and Specifications of the Problem

1. Ron is twelve years old.
2. He has an unkempt appearance.
3. He is worried about his problems.
4. Peers avoid him.
5. He is interested in a girl who is friendly to him, but
6. He fears he will lose her.
7. He is inactive.
8. Mostly he watches TV
9. And eats.
10. He plays basketball occasionally.
11. He would like to bike,
12. But his bike is always broken.
13. He thinks of food all the time.
14. His three basic meals are heavy on fats and carbohydrates.
15. His demeanor is friendly.
16. He acts as if he would like to be close to people and less lonely.
17. His attention span is short.
18. He does not sit or stand still, jiggling around most of the time.
19. He lives with his mother and 9-year-old sister.
20. His parents were divorced seven years ago.
21. His father died less than a year ago.
22. He does not want to discuss his family.
23. He has to be pushed to give basic information.
24. He says that the family is supported by social security benefits.
25. The mother is generous with food and toys.
26. She prefers the children to stay in the house or close by.
27. The mother is overweight.
28. Ron's mother said that he was a colicky infant who did not sleep soundly.
29. He was given enemas.
30. He had surgery at four years for undescended testicles.
31. The surgery scared him.
32. That was when he started soiling.
33. He refused to use the potty.
34. The mother is intelligent and conscientious.

35. She pays lots of attention to Ron, but she is critical of him.
36. For the past year, the mother has been dating a man about whom she seems to be serious, and they are thinking about getting married.

Past Problem Solving

1. Medical information contains no known physical basis for Ron's incontinence. A report from the physician and a psychiatrist concluded that Ron has a moderately severe behavior problem.
2. As a result of getting medical and psychiatric reports, the mother enrolled Ron as a patient in a child guidance clinic.
3. He did not change, and so
4. He was sent to a residential treatment center.
5. After the insurance ran out, Ron was sent to a special education school, where he is at present.
6. He takes three prescribed medicines: one for diarrhea, one for hyperactivity, and one for depression.

Working Explanation

The several therapeutic agencies that Ron has attended have been in agreement about the presumed causes of his problems: a strong fear reaction to his surgery years ago and an anxiety about his mother's serious consideration of remarriage. The present agency has a different view:

1. Whatever conditions led to Ron's undesired behavior in the past, at present Ron wants to lose weight and stop soiling.
2. These problems cause him to be seriously unhappy as he enters his teen years.
3. He knows how unattractive these problems are and he wants to become a more normally behaving teenager.
4. Overeating and soiling have become bad habits he has acquired to get some control over his inner feelings of emptiness and his desire for attention from his mother, teacher, therapists, and the like.

MANDATES

The referral source, the teacher and the school social worker, thought Ron's problem was an obscure, deep-seated conflict involving his mother in some way. The school personnel were determined that something substantial be done to relieve Ron of his problems and also to relieve the school. In the negotiating discussion with the referral sources, it was found that the teacher and social worker were willing to focus on Ron's selected target problems (being fat and soiling).

The teacher was willing to schedule trips to the bathroom as an aid in forestalling soiling. There were no powerful mandates with drastic consequences. No destructive acts were being committed or needed to be controlled.

RAPID EARLY ASSESSMENT

Assessment Defined

The assessment is a professional formulation, a systematized statement. It is produced by combining the information acquired and developed from interviews, observation, supervision and consultation, thoughtful professional consideration, and other sources. It is a set of interpretations, judgments, and hypotheses that provide a working explanation of the person or persons, the problems of present concern, and the situation or social context in which the problems are found. In some practice theories, the assessment attempts to identify the etiology, origins, and development of the problem. Historicity of this type has limited use in the task-centered approach. There is, however, no bar to exploring history if there is some appropriate use for the information in the present problem-solving effort.

The assessment formulation outlines the nature and major characteristics of the problem; the persons most closely associated with it; the major circumstances; and an estimate of the problem's seriousness, that is, its intensity, frequency, and duration. It tells what is going on, where, with what consequences, with what frequency, over what period of time, and involving what people.

A practitioner forms impressions and images of each client, defines the client's problem, and makes a judgment about its seriousness. From these impressions, images, and judgments, he makes a tentative explanation (hypothesis) regarding the nature of the problem, the people, and the situations involved. These impressions and his explanations constitute the assessment, leading to the intervention plan. He assumes the assessment will suggest what actions are needed and what actions can be expected to correct the problem.

The process of problem definition, as described in this chapter, is the basis of the assessment. As the problem definition is developed, it produces information about the problem, the client's characteristics, social context, and past problem-solving practices, and suggests a working explanation of the problem. In the course of the interviews in which the problem-defining process is conducted, the practitioner will have many opportunities to observe the client's behavior and personality, to receive reports about significant other people and personal relationships, and to learn about relevant socioeconomic factors.

Thus, the processes of problem definition in the first step of the task-centered model and observations made in the course of the interviews together provide the information that makes up the rapid early assessment. Defining the problem and attempting to understand the people and their social situations lead to an idea of what needs to be changed, restored, or enhanced. A practitioner can make a judgment about how much change is necessary, desirable, and feasible. Resources can be examined to judge their availability and usefulness.

Focus and Assessment

The assessment is the practitioner's way to define the problem in professional terms, in accordance with the set of theories to which she subscribes and any pertinent rules and regulations of the agency and profession. The assessment stabilizes the treatment processes to the extent that it provides a degree of certainty about what is wrong and what should be done. The assessment is a guide to the possibilities and constraints on treatment planning, which must take into consideration the limits and opportunities suggested by the assessment. Thus, the focus of the case activity comes about by extracting from the assessment what point or area is thought likely to be the most effective concentration.

Rapid Early Assessment Described

It is customary to think of assessment as a long, thorough process because of the importance attached to it as a determinant of treatment. However in real practice conditions, assessment conclusions have to be reached rapidly. Treatment is brief by plan. Or, the person is in crisis, and the only humane and ethical approach is to take useful action right away or as soon as possible. Or, there is strong pressure from the community to do something at once. These conditions indicate the need for rapid assessment, at least of a tentative type. More complex and comprehensive assessments may have to be made in complex and obscure situations or when required by regulations. Comprehensive assessments take time and, if needed, may be conducted subsequently.

Keys to Rapid Early Assessment

1. *Provide an appropriate interviewing atmosphere.* Adopting a straightforward, moderately assertive, friendly, cordial, and generous manner lowers the client's defensiveness and encourages confidence. This atmosphere, together with a commitment to legitimate the target problems as perceived by the client, provides the best opportunity to obtain needed information.

2. *Depend on the immediate interviewing situation for the data from which to generate significant assessment hypotheses.*
   - Collect information constrained to the target problems and the present time.
   - Explore selectively areas of strength and weakness in personal traits, immediate environment, culture and ethnicity, family and peer relationships, and work and school situations.
   - Draw full value of immediately available interviewing data from observing interview behavior, relationship with practitioner, and communication patterns, and from information elicited regarding problems and social context.

3. *Exploration should be parsimonious.* Extensive explorations are conducted on the assumption that the fullest accumulation of information will be a hedge against error. The flip side of this belief is that we cannot profitably make use of excess information. Explorations should not exceed what is needed to form a commonsense understanding of the target problem and its most immediate area. Uncertainty can be checked against available professional literature and with supervisors, colleagues, and consultants.

Assessment Data Available in the Immediate Interviewing Situation

1. *The practitioner develops a broad sense of personality traits and typical behaviors of the client under stress.* This means making gross observations, without special attention to detail. The purpose is to get hold of a working image of the other persons. These gross observations are interpreted according to professional and personal experience and practical common sense, augmented by behavior theories espoused by the practitioner.

Gross observations focus on physical appearance, bodily demeanor, facial expressions, vocabulary, and manner of speaking and expressing oneself. These characteristics portray a person's self-image, something about his expectations, interpersonal demands, personality traits, and manner of relating to others, and some idea of his income level. Ways of dealing with stress are revealed in the way the person makes requests, whether in a fearful, anxious, unreasonable, overly reasonable, submissive, suspicious, manipulative, controlled, or disciplined manner.

How the client deals with an interviewer—a person in authority, either a man or a woman—can usually tell a good deal about the person's customary pattern of relating with men and women in authority. One can infer how it is likely the person is now dealing with other figures in real life, such as spouse, children, and employer.

2. *Observations should be put into a tentative pattern, configuration, or diagram based on behavior theory and practical experience that explains who the client is, what her background is, and what is the matter at present.* This pattern is constrained to explain only the problem situation related to the problem definition. Information supplied by the client that is not related to the target problems can suggest areas about which the client is concerned and possibly confused or upset; however, including a wide range of problem areas defeats focused attention and decreases the probability of successfully intervening to accomplish some problem reduction.

3. *Impressions of a person form very quickly.* Considerable evidence from research studies suggests assessment is formulated impressionistically in the first few minutes of a contact and that the rest of the time allotted is used for checking and verifying. The final assessment is most likely to be the same or similar to that created in the very first impressions (Kendell, 1975; Sundberg, 1977).

Because this is so, the question arises: Why do more? First, in order to work effectively with a person in his situation, the practitioner needs to understand more than the name or label to give to the problem. He needs to have a feel for the human being with whom he will be working, for his qualities and characteristics, and for a sense of how he lives and what he suffers. That kind of feeling for the person and situation takes more than a few minutes of technical appraisal.

Some situations are harder than others to assess. Less difficult situations are those that have been extensively studied and described and for which assessment and intervention have been somewhat standardized, for example, adjustment disorders with depressed mood; the straightforward depressive reaction consisting of depressed mood, tearfulness, and hopelessness; or the clear-cut, uncontradictable evidence of violent assault on a child.

However, few situations are truly clear cut. Even those that seem clear cut in a general way show much variation from individual to individual. Hence, it is important to try to avoid imposing mechanical stereotypes and allowing them to pass as assessments that may have an important effect on a person's life. It is a delicate matter to balance between the tendency toward extensive data accumulation to be on the safe side—while postponing interventions—and acting on a rapid assessment.

The balance is best achieved by starting intervention as soon as possible, based on the rapid early assessment. Meanwhile, one should be scrutinizing what happens in order to alter the assessment and alter the plan when the evidence turns up to indicate error. There is no such thing as an error-free assessment. But there are varying degrees of rigidity that become installed in a case process, making people continue on a less than useful path and feel embarrassed about changing course. Flexibility should be the byword. Flexibility does not mean whimsical changing, but rather, disciplined alterations based on new information and new insights.

RELATIONSHIP MANAGEMENT

Despite much research on the characteristics and dynamics of the therapeutic relationship, the subject remains elusive. The therapeutic relationship is some combination of communication and social interactions occurring between practitioners and clients as influenced and shaped by their backgrounds and the present environments including the helping organization involved.

Social interactions are among the most difficult phenomena to study because researchers and practitioners are totally immersed in the subject being studied. Scientific objectivity is hard to come by in these circumstances. Furthermore, the subject of client–practitioner relationships is encumbered by our feelings that something supernatural or supranatural is involved, something that partakes of human essence or soul, that makes the subject mysterious.

As if this were not enough, relationships are powerful. We all need and want to possess, enjoy, manipulate, and exploit relationships because we all need and want the good things obtainable from intimate relationships; from good relationships with people in power; and from soothing, compassionate, and loving relationships with parents, mates, friends, and others.

The helping relationship has become idealized and virtually enthroned as a necessary and almost sufficient condition for successful treatment. The helping relationship is often conceived of as something ephemeral, distinct from its empirical moorings that are influence, attraction, confidence, inspiration, and communication of support, warmth, and respect. Something about the client–practitioner relationship is very powerful, if not magical. A good relationship matters, but is not sufficient in and of itself.

Suggested Practitioner Behaviors for Creating Good Relationship Conditions

In the task-centered model, and particularly in its beginning phase, a few suggestions are worth following to create the right atmosphere for helping clients to participate fully in targeting problems and providing enough self-disclosure to enable the practitioner to form a reliable rapid early assessment.

1. Use a manner that is plain, straightforward, and overtly friendly, but not effusive.
2. Verbalize understanding of major feelings and attitudes of the client: that is, say you understand and, especially, what you understand.
3. Verbalize awareness of overall stress and dominant mood or dilemma: that is, say you are aware and, especially, of what you are aware.
4. Foster identification between yourself and the client.
5. Assume an assuring and supportive posture and demeanor.
6. Discuss and clarify, realistically, what you and the client mean to one another.

SUMMARY

Identifying target problems is the first step in the task-centered model. It is a distinguishing mark of this model that the problems identified by the client are placed in the center of attention. It is the responsibility of the professional practitioner to discuss openly with the client what difficulties there may be in attempting to implement a program of intervention focused on problems as perceived by the client and to offer suggestions and recommendations to change the client's view if necessary. However, in case of impasse or strong reluctance on the part of the client, the client's view will prevail. In real practice, a respectful handling of these discussions is likely to produce a mutually satisfactory conclusion.

The basic actions for targeting a problem are establishing the actual presence of a problem, describing the problem, formulating the tentative assessment, determining the conditions or behaviors to be changed, stating the tentative goals, getting information about the social context, and getting relevant information about the social context of the problem. Clients who have difficulty in formulating target problems on their own can be assisted by a problem-search process. When involuntary clients are required by an authority to participate in making changes they do not themselves seek, practitioners must be sure that clients know the exact consequences of avoiding the mandated problem and also that clients are assured that problems of particular concern to them will be attended to.

Rapid early assessment develops from the process of targeting the problems and becomes the basis for treatment planning. A supportive, friendly, but not effusive, relationship posture on the part of the practitioner is most likely to encourage the desired self-disclosure and confidence needed to move rapidly into assessment and intervention.

How to Specify Target Problems: Summarized

Purpose

1. To name, state, and describe the target problem(s)—not to exceed three
2. To establish the center—the *focus*—of intervention activity
3. To organize the treatment efforts so that they are efficiently directed to reducing the problem(s)

Basic Actions (Order Is Approximate)

1. Establish the actual presence of a problem acknowledged by the client.
2. Describe and name each problem specifically.
3. Formulate the tentative rapid early assessment.
4. Determine conditions or behaviors to be changed.
5. State tentative goals, that is, what the desired changes are to be.
6. Get information about the client's social and physical environments (social context) and the client's characteristics and mode of functioning.
7. Get information about the necessary history and development of the problem to the degree the information is usable in conducting the present interventions.

CHAPTER SEVEN

SECOND STEP: CONTRACTING
Plans, Goals, Tasks, Time Limits, and Other Agreements

CONTRACTS AS CASE PLANS

A contract is a contemporary form of the conventional client–worker agreement, a basic ingredient of intervention. The assumption underlying an agreement is self-determination. The assumption underlying a contract (a formal agreement) is a commitment to work. A *contract* in direct service work is an agreement to work toward the reduction or alleviation of stated personal problems. See Figure 7.1.

The contemporary professional climate values the client's right to exercise maximal choice in connection with decisions and acts that will seriously affect the quality of her life. The client's participation in such choices is thought to be right in and of itself. In addition, client participation is thought to have a strong payoff in terms of better outcomes. Practitioners can make bad decisions. The client's knowledge of what is to be done and why can help avert such mistakes. A client who

FIGURE 7.1   Map Detail

Step 2	*Contract*
	COVER • Priority target problems (three maximum) • Client's specific goals (accepted by practitioner) • Client's general tasks • Practitioner's general tasks • Duration of intervention sequence (time limits) • Schedule for interviews • Schedule for interventions • Parties to be included

understands the risks and benefits of intervention and the alternatives to treatment is likely to be more cooperative than one who is a passive recipient of authoritative actions from "on high." Information about purpose, forms, and structure helps demystify intervention and strengthens realistic client–practitioner relations and expectations of treatment (Lidz, Meisel, Zerubavel, Carter, Sestak, & Roth, 1984).

Planning treatment or intervention is necessary for the practitioner to handle cases purposefully and intentionally. Formalizing the plan in a written or oral contract makes the matter explicit. Rosen, Proctor, and Livne (1985), in developing the concept of planning in direct practice, describe the plan as a map of the "components of intervention, that is, determining which problems will be addressed, which outcomes will be sought, which interventions will be employed, and the order and sequencing of these components" (p. 165).

To the extent possible, the practitioner should select intervention activities deliberately on the basis of available knowledge about types of social situations, problems, persons, and evaluative information about probable outcomes. In developing the treatment plan, he chooses from a range of alternative treatment components available. Planning requires judgment; therefore, treatment plans will vary with the preferences of the practitioner and the client, the style and requirements of the agency, and the obstacles, unforeseen events, and improvements that occur as treatment proceeds. Systematic work necessitates that planning be emphasized and formalized early in the process, but because of all the variations that occur in an actual case, planning takes place, in different forms, in all phases of the sequence.

THE ROLE OF ASSESSMENT IN PLANNING

The assessment acts as an instrument in decision making about the contents of the plan. It suggests the probable limits and capabilities of the persons, the situation, and the resources. It also suggests the practical limits so that the plan adheres to the constraints as well as to the possibilities of the realistic situation. It is usually possible to derive the goals of the intervention sequence from the assessment; that is, in view of the limitations and capabilities identified, the assessment suggests what is necessary to achieve in the intervention program.

Assessment goes on for the life of the case. The practitioner is always noting information, scrutinizing the situation, and evaluating what is going on. However, it is the essence of professional responsibility that a decision to act is made at certain key points.

The first key point is in the first step of the task-centered process, that is, at the point of target problem identification and definition. The rapid early assessment data are influential in helping the practitioner decide on a target problem. (See Chapter 6.) By the time contracting and treatment planning are about to occur, the practitioner and client may have had one or more additional interviews, and possibly some information from collateral sources, that is, family members, other professionals, home visits, and the like.

Regardless of how much or how little additional information has come in, some time has elapsed and the practitioner has reviewed the situation in her mind. She might want to change some of the conclusions she made in the rapid early assessment—or she may not. Either way, the initial assessment should be reviewed at this point and put into as clear a form as possible given the natural limitations of the data. It is this second-stage assessment, in which the rapid early assessment is evaluated, that now comprises the working assessment.

The assessment process can become a barrier to helping people. It can be a costly ritual, contributing little to the efficacy or efficiency of treatment. Garfield (1986) points out that "prediction of therapeutic outcome on the basis of pre-therapy appraisals is disappointingly low with the average correlation ranging from 0.10 to 0.20" (p. 140). The rapid early assessment and its review should ordinarily suffice for making the treatment plan. An exception occurs when circumstances are obscure or baffling or when potentially critical issues require considerable study, consultation, and evaluation to be understood. In those exceptional instances, case planning and contracting may be delayed as necessary, and the task-centered model should be applied flexibly to conform to the real-life circumstances. Exceptions should be kept to a minimum and not be confused with the usual and expectable difficulties of case handling.

WRITTEN AND ORAL CONTRACTS: ADVANTAGES AND DISADVANTAGES

Both written and oral contracts are used in practice. The written contract has an advantage if a high degree of explicitness is wanted, usually with intention to exercise control. The technical aim of the written contract in the task-centered approach is to make mutual agreement open and explicit. The aim may be to control quality so that the process conforms to standards and can be more readily monitored.

The aim may be to control the client by suggesting the possibility or probability of sanctions should he fail to abide by the terms of the contract. The aim may be to control the behaviors of staff by holding them accountable for performance on the contract.

Written contracts are common in agencies that have many involuntary clients and reluctant participants. The control exercised by contracts under those circumstances is not necessarily negative. For the client, the written contract may be a useful means for getting specific information about what the agency wants or intends, what it will do, who will do it, how it will be done, and with what expectations for final outcomes. For the agency, the contract can be a way of monitoring performance—the client's, the practitioner's, and even the agency's own performance.

Although using the contract as a control is understandable, it poses ethical dilemmas. The contract mixes treatment, social control, and quality control. It opens avenues for manipulating the provisions of the contract to increase the appearance of good performance without actually achieving it.

Making a contract is a significant way to achieve clarity between client and practitioner. If well done, the client is an informed participant, in a good position to act independently on her own behalf, and a competent partner in the treatment enterprise. A client who has gone through careful discussion and planning should have a better understanding about what she has to do to reduce her problem effectively. Both client and worker will think twice about committing themselves to something that is not reasonable, not specific, and not feasible. The written contract is a barrier to a client's being misled about what she can expect; becoming confused, untrusting, or irate; and not getting available and appropriate services.

Although oral contracts should and can be specific, written contracts have a clear advantage in accountability (Maluccio & Marlow, 1974). Anyone can determine what actions were agreed to, and finding out whether those actions did or did not occur is potentially straightforward. A written document, with the participants' signatures, provides an easy referencing for keeping track of what is supposed to be done and who is responsible. Clients, staff, supervisors, administrators, and consultants can use the written contract to make judgments about performance. When staff turnover is high, the written contract gives important information quickly to staff new to a case.

Written contracts have been used only within the last few decades. Although only a small amount of information has been gathered about the extent of the written contract's use and its effectiveness, the idea has caught hold in the field. What little evidence exists is positive. Clients have reported liking the specificity (Salmon, 1977). One study found that clients' willingness to develop and sign a contract was a good indicator of effective action to return children home from foster care (Stein, Gambrill, & Wiltse 1977). In juvenile delinquency cases and in foster care custody adjudications, judges have used written contracts to inform people of their decisions (Hofstad, 1977; Rooney, 1978).

Written contracts present a number of problems. For one thing, there has been no test of their legal status. We do not know if a client could sue a practitioner or an agency for failure to perform on a contract. We do not know if a contract is legally binding on a client and what, if any, sanctions can be applied legally if the client fails to perform. Furthermore, there may develop a trend toward evaluating performance of practitioners, deciding whether or not to promote someone, and deciding whether or not to raise salaries according to the results of goal attainment (McCarty, 1978).

The problem with basing personnel decisions on clients' performance of contracts is that there is always uncertainty about the cause–effect relationship. Clients' failure to perform, as well as clients' success, can be related to uncontrollable personal and situational conditions. Although the basic idea of connecting client and worker performance is logical, making those connections probably exceeds our present technical capacity; that is, these connections probably cannot be made reliably.

As computerized management information systems continue to develop, contract items will be tracked. Interesting data, now largely unavailable, may then be obtained. However, the accuracy and meaning of such data depend on its quality: How good is the information in terms of appropriateness, relevancy, and accuracy? For instance, if staff members believe they will be judged by the quantity of performance, they will become skillful at contracting for easy, simple actions that can be readily performed and so produce a good performance "score." Staff workers may find themselves given poor performance ratings for failing to act because they did not know how and were not provided the training and resources.

It is conceivable that an agency performing maximally on all the easy, simple actions might provide many badly needed services. On the other hand, overemphasizing easy actions could lead to concentrating on trivia and avoiding serious problems that require risk taking. Because the reasons for poor performance on a contract are hard to discern and identify, contracts are not the only, or necessarily the best, data from which to judge performance. They are one source of data.

Involuntary clients cause concern about contracts being misused. Involuntary clients tend to be vulnerable and powerless. They may agree to a contract that is not realistic for them and find themselves punished for failure: not getting their children returned to their custody, for example, when the resources for putting their situation in order were not available or not provided. Clients who are highly vulnerable—extremely ill, confused, very young, or imprisoned, for example—may lack the ability and the resources for making contracts on their own. Having contracts made for them by caretakers would be one solution. On the other hand, caretakers may be unwilling or may enter into contracts with reservations.

Despite the problems of administering them, written contracts have merit. They can and should be used in the bulk of ordinary practice. However, written contracts should not be viewed as a remedy for all difficulties or as rigid machinery for pushing a case toward some hard and fast end. If a contract has been agreed upon and put into writing, it represents a degree of commitment to an arrangement worked out between the client and practitioner—a promising basis for positive movement. However, the contract is not permanent and could be altered at any time. It exists and remains in force at the discretion of the parties to it. The contract is a help to conducting a case process to a hopefully desirable result. But it has to be backed up by continuous work toward goal attainment. Although the contract is a technique for structuring the treatment process, it does not have a mechanical effect. Without mutual agreement and continuous work, the contract has little force for change.

Rothery (1980) has succinctly cautioned against mechanical agreements and ulterior agreements. The latter are hidden agendas created by unstated and possibly unperceived aims. Either the client or the practitioner may initiate a hidden agenda and cause it to be reflected in the contract. Or, it can be the case that both participants agree to provisions appearing appropriate on the surface but that are really pretenses. Such underlying assumptions may represent attempts to maneuver or manipulate the situation in the interests of one of the participants. This kind of practice is misleading and may spoil the honest working relationship.

An oral contract can be thought of as a gentlemen's agreement, a binding understanding between people who trust each other and have some real basis for that trust. An oral contract is a flexible agreement but lacks the sense of commitment if not negotiated as explicitly as a written contract is (or should be). The same discussions should precede the formulation of the oral contract as precede the written one. The fact is, however, that oral contracting allows both parties to evade dealing with the content, purpose, and consequences of treatment, and hence may not be as straightforward as the written contract. Of course we can speak in a straightforward manner if we choose. In the end, whether a written or an oral contract is used, the choice is a matter of preference.

Oral contracts are more flexible and adaptable, and are easier to handle than written contracts. Oral contracts are really semiwritten. In normal agency practice, their substance should be written into the agency record, shown to the client, and at least initialed by the client and practitioner. The record of an oral contract can also serve for administrative control purposes, that is, for case accountability and client and staff performance measurement. Oral contracts, when written into the record, are about the same as written contracts, with the same advantages and disadvantages. What they lack is the appearance of firmness that is present in a written contract document.

MAKING UP THE CONTRACT

Contents of the Contract

The nine subjects to cover in the contract include:

1. Major priority problems—three at most
2. Specific goals
3. Client tasks: activities the client will undertake

4. Practitioner tasks: activities the practitioner will undertake
5. Scheduling of interventions
6. Scheduling of interviews
7. Duration of intervention: approximately how long the process is to last, or the time limits
8. Participants: who will take part
9. Location: where the sessions will occur

These nine items can be thought of as the basic structure of the intervention plan. It is the aggregate of the elements of the plan and shows a planned relationship among the parts.

Interviewing Technique during Contracting

Interviewing during the contracting should be conducted in a manner that achieves (Epstein, 1985) the following:

- as much participation as possible from the client in making suggestions for the contract
- complete and detailed explanations from the practitioner about his suggestions and recommendations
- adequate opportunity for the client to raise questions, give reactions, and ask for and receive clarification

Contract discussion begins discursively. There is circling around the subject, exploring what the client thinks and believes the priority target problems should be, what would help most, what should be done first, and what should follow.

The practitioner shares her opinion with the client. If the practitioner thinks the client's formulation is mistaken, she should try to convince the client to make a change. That is done through discussion, exploration, explanation, and clarification. Many clients adopt a practitioner's recommendations to a greater or lesser degree because they respect the professional's qualifications as an expert. The practitioner's attempts to influence the client may fail, however, if the client considers the practitioner's opinion to be wrong or if the professional opinion contradicts strongly held beliefs and values of the client.

Should the client be strongly opposed to the practitioner's opinion and should he not be convinced by an ordinary amount of back-and-forth exchange of views, an impasse will occur. The task-centered approach recommends that the practitioner accede to the client's choices unless those choices are (extremely rarely) unethical, immoral, illegal, or so clearly impossible that she must refuse to go along with them. The idea is to achieve some gains, even modest ones, for the client. Most people do not easily change their minds about what they want. If the practitioner is unable to convince the client to follow a recommendation, she can still concentrate on developing a program of work that is congruent with the client's stated concerns.

If the practitioner feels unable to comply with a request, he should tell the client the reason, that it is not out of unwillingness to help but because he knows there is no way to do what the client asks. In addition, the practitioner should thoroughly "walk through" the specific circumstances in order to show what cannot be done, why, and what would be the probable consequences of pursuing the client's idea. The practitioner should fully state and explain his reservations. The major communication to facilitate reaching an agreement on what to do is this: *What acts, if done first, will help most?*

Stating Priority Target Problems

The contract should state at least one and no more than three target problems. This can be done after the array of problems has already been elicited in the first step of the task-centered process. Problem statements should be prioritized, preferably by the client. The practitioner helps the client decide on priorities and may discuss the appropriateness of the client's selection or recommend priorities if necessary. The farther away one gets from the client's own real interests, the more difficulties may arise. If there is a mandated problem from a powerful source, this problem should be among the priorities.

Guidelines for Selecting Priorities

First Action.   In Step 1, the initial problem-defining phase, the discussion should have elicited from the client an array of problems as perceived by the client. Taking up that array, the first action is to *group the problems into classes or categories to depict the problem as an umbrella for a group of subproblems.*

Second Action.   Proceed to select priorities as follows:

1. *Assign priority to the problem that the client asserts is of the highest interest, that most needs to be taken care of, and that will make the most difference to improve the situation.* This choice has a high probability of success because it is congruent with client motivation.
2. *Assign priority to the problem according to a judgment made mutually between client and practitioner.* This choice is not as likely to produce as good results as the client's spontaneous selection; nevertheless, it is likely to produce satisfactory results if the client has been genuinely involved in arriving at the decision.
3. *Setting priorities may be postponed for a short or a long time, during which the participants explore questions from a number of perspectives.* This tentative posture on priorities is appropriate when an issue is obscure. The client's commitment may be ambiguous, or the client may be perceived as needing more time to become secure in the helping situation. By postponing the selection of priorities, however, the impetus for work is almost certain to be slowed, causing the helping process to become inefficient. This option should be used sparingly and reserved only for the most obscure situations.

Guidelines for Stating Problems in a Contract

1. *Grammar of statement*

SUBJECT	**ACTIVE VERB**	**OBJECT**
Client	*is having*	*stated deficit, excess, conflict or dissonance.*

Mrs. A ⟶ is lacking ⟶ adequate child care.

John ⟶ is fighting ⟶ too much with his mother.

Mr. and Mrs. B ⟶ are ⟶ in continuous and serious discord about his jealousy of her.

Mr. and Mrs. C ⟶ are clashing ⟶ seriously over the budgeting of their income.

Sample Shortened Contract Statements
- Mrs. A lacks adequate child care.
- John fights too much with his mother.
- Mr. and Mrs. B are in conflict about his jealousy.
- Mr. and Mrs. C are in conflict over budgeting.

2. *Parsimony of statement.* Avoid long phrases that purport to explain the problem. Explanations are not necessary in the contract.

Stating Target Problems in a Multiple-Person Case.   When more than one participant is involved, it is possible to state the three problems from the viewpoint of each person. Normally the viewpoints of the different participants will be related. When several people in multiple-person cases participate, the firmer the formulation of the target problems of each, the better. For example, when dealing with a whole family or a part of a family, it is preferable to interview each person alone to elicit each one's views about the target problems. When the group meets together later, the separate statements are made to the group. Differences of opinion can be aired at that time and negotiated to the extent possible before the contract is set. Because of lack of time or because of other logistics such as distance to be traveled to come together, it is not always feasible to conduct separate interviews with each participant. In that case, the practitioner needs to spend time and give all individuals as much leeway as possible to give their viewpoints when the group meets.

Not infrequently individuals or family members may place blame for their problems on others, that is, one will blame another. These "blame" statements give an accurate view of the aggrieved family member's view of the problem and are acceptable in the task-centered approach. If all blame another family member, it will be helpful to find some problem statement that all agree on, such as "We are in conflict" or "We are in disagreement with each other." These general summarizing statements may then be targeted as the main family problem. The blame statements become the specifications of the overall problem. Each person contributes to defining the family issue to be resolved. Each person's view of the problem is accepted as a valid place to start.

It is to be expected that there will be differences when the target problems of the individuals become public in the group. These differences are to be negotiated in the group session. Some differences seem so extreme that they become, for all practical purposes, nonnegotiable. Some members may state problems that seem unrelated to those that the others have brought up. Some differences that seem unrelated are not. Rather, they are mirror images; that is, the problem statements of two persons in conflict are opposite, but the connection is that they are about the same condition. The disjunction is that the different clients seek different solutions.

Reducing a Long Array of Problems in a Multiple-Person Case.   To reduce the problems stated in a multiple-person case to three, the practitioner has three options:

1. *Settle on the three problems about which there is the most agreement.* These are three problems for all participants together. Hold the remainder for later consideration, after work has begun on the three agreed-on problems.
2. *Settle on up to three problems, with or without agreement among the participants.* All participants will have separate lists (as seen later in this chapter in Example 7.3, which describes the case of Rick and his mother) that will be interrelated but not identical. This option makes for a complex situation because time has to be allotted to give proper consideration to each participant's work, often by interspersing individual sessions between group sessions. This second option reflects the most common practice in multiple-person client sequences.
3. *In case of extreme disagreement, settle on up to three problems to be dealt with in group sessions, and provide additional individual or subgroup sessions.* This option can be used alone or together with the other options.

Stating Goals

Three guidelines are important to remember in stating goals:

1. *The contract should state the goals of the intervention from the client's standpoint, not the agency's or the practitioner's standpoints.* This would normally legitimate the client's motivation and serve as a criterion statement against which to evaluate results.
2. *The number of goal statements should be few and should address the priority target problems.* It should be possible to show a direct connection between the problem and the goal.
3. *If the agency has use for recording its own goals, distinct from those of the client, these should be labeled as agency goals or agency service objectives and recorded separately.* Caution is called for to avoid imposing agency goals on clients. Agencies will often want to keep tabs on their own organizational goals in a given case to evaluate themselves and to conform to requirements of legislative and funding bodies.

Here are some examples of right and wrong goal statements.

Right: Temporary foster care home is to be available on a 24-hour notice in case Mrs. A needs to enter the hospital.

Wrong: Family assessment.

Right: Cut down the frequency of John's fights with his foster father 50 percent.

Wrong: John is to report for counseling.

Planning and Stating Interventions

In the same way that goals are made explicit, the planning of interventions is part of the contracting process. The practitioner has the most responsibility in this process, because planning, selecting, and organizing interventions need professional expertise. The practitioner has access to professional knowledge about useful interventions that meet the problem circumstances in the case. The practitioner should state, describe, and explain the rationale for the interventions, being sure the client understands them, and taking care that the client has adequate opportunity to raise questions and to contribute toward the planning.

Planning and Stating Tasks: Client and Practitioner

Tasks are particular kinds of problem-solving actions, planned by and agreed on between practitioner and client, and capable of being worked on by the client and the practitioner outside, as well as inside, the interview. *Client tasks* are actions clients intend to take that are expected to reduce the target problem. *Practitioner tasks* are actions practitioners take on the client's behalf to reduce the same problem.

The way tasks fit into the problem-solving paradigm can be diagrammed in the following manner:

PROBLEM-SOLVING PARADIGM	TASK-CENTERED MODEL
General orientation	Problem explored
Generation of alternatives	Task possibilities developed
Testing and implementation	Tasks tried out
Verification (evaluation)	Results tallied

Types of Tasks.   There are two broad types of tasks—general and operational (Reid & Epstein, 1972; Reid, 1978)—and numerous types of subtasks. These classifications are heuristic and help in thinking about how to formulate actions. They have no particular virtues or purposes other than as planning aids. One should not worry about how to classify tasks, only that tasks should be sensible and capable of being put into action with help as needed.

General Tasks.   *General tasks* state the direction of an action but do not spell out exactly what is to be done. General tasks always imply the client goals. Often a general client task and a client goal are the same. They refer to two aspects of the same phenomenon. The general task says what is to be done, and the goal says what the condition ought to be when the task is done. They may converge. It is necessary to state and understand both the goal and the task. For example,

Right: Ray is to enroll in the Adjustment Training Center. (specific)

Wrong: Job training (broad, complex, not specific)

Right: Ray is to find and maintain living arrangements near the center. (specific)

Wrong: Independent living (broad, complex, not specific)

A general task consists of a package of separate or separable actions that together form a whole action recognizable as a unified thing, for example, "To obtain medical care." The definite separate sections of the general task can be thought of as subtasks. For instance,

Mrs. A will phone the doctor tomorrow.

She will get an early appointment.

She will explain her health problem to her children before her next medical appointment.

Subtasks come and go as client and practitioner work to achieve the general tasks. The contract should not be encumbered with listing subtasks that are part of the regular give-and-take between practitioner and client as they work together to accomplish something. If significant, subtasks can be mentioned in the running record or log.

Operational Tasks.   *Operational tasks* state the specific actions the client is to undertake. They are a type of subtask because they contain information about definite actions. Operational tasks are often broken down further into subtasks. For example,

Right: Fill out and submit an application to the center.
Visit the center.
Keep an appointment for psychological tests.
Have an interview with a public information officer to get an advertisement placed in the newspaper to locate a boarding home.
Visit boarding homes.

Wrong: Come for regular counseling.
Obtain psychological and social assessment.

Note that the wrong statements are too complex, broad, and vague.

Other Types of Tasks.   For purposes of analysis, we can classify subtypes of general tasks. In real practice, these types are fluid, become combined with one another, and drop in and drop out as practical. Classifying tasks has no particular operating use and is of value only for thinking carefully about the processes. Some classifications include:

1. *Unique tasks.* Planned for a one-time effort, for example, "Mrs. A is to see the foster home finder Tuesday."
2. *Recurrent tasks.* Planned for repetitive action, for example, "Mrs. A is to talk to her children each day to explain how she feels and what she is doing to regain her health."
3. *Unitary tasks.* A single action requiring a number of steps: "Mrs. A is to arrange for her hospitalization."
4. *Complex tasks.* Two or more discrete actions that are closely related, for example, "To discuss with her physician the several possible types and effects of surgery and consider what each would do to her ability to work and to care for her home and her children."
5. *Individual tasks.* To be carried out by one person.
6. *Reciprocal tasks.* Separate but related tasks to be worked on by two or more persons; usually exchanges (e.g., "Mrs. B will refrain from yelling at Arthur and Arthur will tell his mother what worries him instead of running out of the house").
7. *Shared tasks.* Two or more persons doing the same thing (e.g., "Mrs. B and Arthur will talk to the psychiatrist together").
8. *Cognitive tasks.* Mental activities, for example, "Mrs. E is to think about what exactly she likes, dislikes, and is uncertain about in her marriage." Care must be used that cognitive tasks do not degenerate into unproductive ruminations that have no references to present problems. At the same time, being aware of and understanding what she wants, needs, and deserves can clarify the client's priorities and help her make choices and decisions (Ewalt, 1977).

Interrelations Between Task Types.   Ordinarily, operational tasks flow from general tasks. They are a prominent part of Step 3 task achievement. (See Chapter 8.) Operational tasks are started as a result of making the contract. However, they do not need to be written into a formal contract because they change frequently. Operational tasks usually begin as an immediate result of the contract. They continue as a major activity into the problem-solving, task-achievement stage to be discussed in Chapter 8.

How to Plan Tasks.   Task planning starts after target problem specification. It consists of generating alternative tasks in discussion and crystallizing a plan of action or a strategy. Tasks are agreed on, and task implementation is planned. The whole strategy is summarized.

Task planning starts with the contract. It continues into the next steps as often as necessary, that is, any time the client or practitioner is uncertain or lacks information about what to do next. However, to keep up momentum, tasks should be planned to take care of major actions. Minor or peripheral matters should be handled in a commonsense, helpful way without subjecting them to a full-scale process. In other words, the idea of the sequence is to help the client along, and the steps of the process are to be used for that purpose. Overplanning and over-mechanizing the process will simply clutter the works.

"Piecemeal" Planning.   A task plan may be made in one session, following the problem specification, but it is more usual for tasks to emerge piecemeal, during several phases of a single interview or over two or more interviews. Whereas target problems tend to remain stable over the life of the case, tasks change often. Tasks change because they are done, are not done, cannot be done, or are determined not to be necessary. Completed tasks are dropped. Tasks not done are analyzed to obtain information about the barriers to task achievement. They are then revised or dropped.

Sources of Information for Task Planning.   The sources of information about reasonable tasks to reduce a problem include the following:

1. *The clients' own experience (the basic source).* The first step in planning a task is to find out from clients what they think they could do to cut down their target problems. Most clients have sound ideas on this subject once they are convinced that it is safe to state their own ideas and that their ideas will be respected. The practitioner is responsible for clarifying and molding clients' suggestions and introducing tasks for consideration to clients who do not readily generate their own ideas.
2. *Brainstorming is a useful activity for developing tasks.* Sometimes clients are at a loss for a task idea. By coming up with a range of options, the client may then be able to select the best task in his view. Suggesting one is helpful, but selecting encourages clients to learn how to develop tasks for problem solving. Early work on problem solving found that psychiatric clients and those without psychiatric problems varied on their problemsolving skills in their abilities to generate problem-solving strategies and actions (Spivack, Platt, & Shure, 1976). Clients needing help would, we assume, be unable right then to solve their problems in living on their own. Learning or increasing their problem-solving skills may be beneficial in the future (Brown, 1980).
3. *Expert knowledge about reliable or reasonable problem-solving actions.* It has been common for service workers to depend on familiarity with a few general treatment methods for knowledge to use in their cases. Selective information from general reading and conferences and advice from supervisors and consultants are used. It would be preferable for a practitioner to have access to knowledge that is directly related to particular case problems, but getting that information is often difficult and time-consuming. The literature is spread out in university libraries; rarely do agencies have sufficiently complete and up-to-date libraries that can provide practitioners with quick access to the latest and best quality information. Because practitioners do not have time to run down this knowledge for themselves, resource people on the staff, cooperating specialized agencies, and consultants must secure this information for them.

The time is here and now that much information is available via computerized information systems and is organized in practitioner-friendly systems. Although not a perfect source, the Internet can now be used to find information and resources related to solving certain kinds of problems.

4. *The practitioner's own experience.* Practitioners should not hesitate to draw on their own practice and personal experience to suggest client tasks. If we have had a similar experience ourselves, we have ideas about actions that failed or succeeded. A collection of previous practice experiences with similar situations is especially pertinent.

Formalizing Tasks.   After task alternatives have been generated with a client, the next step is to reach an explicit agreement about which ones will be undertaken. Then details of implementation should be discussed. This means client and practitioner agree on what is to be done, when, with whom, where, under what specific conditions (if any), and how. The client should emerge with a clear idea, a blueprint to help her accomplish the tasks.

The client and practitioner should know how each task is to be started up and pursued. The client needs only to have a brief review of the expected actions for tasks that involve familiar actions. Tasks involving novel actions for the client require detailed step-by-step discussion, including alternative actions in case of unexpected developments. All task agreements should be briefly summarized at the end of a session.

Review: How to Plan Client Tasks

1. Generate alternatives.
2. Agree with client on tasks.
3. Plan details of implementation.
4. Summarize.

Practitioner Tasks.   Practitioner tasks are actions that the practitioner is committed to do on the client's behalf between sessions. Practitioner tasks supplement the client's actions and should facilitate the client's work. Negotiating and conferring are the practitioner's chief tasks.

Negotiating and conferring include working with agency and community officials and with client collaterals such as neighbors, friends, and family. Negotiations are conducted to transfer resources, services, and goodwill from the organization to the client; to package or design the resources, services, and goodwill in a way to reduce the client's target problems; and to satisfy the official terms and conditions as well as powerful mandates held by the organization. Conferring resembles negotiating but emphasizes transferring helpful or needed information and personal relations.

Guidelines for Negotiating with Agency and Community Officials

1. Identify the terms and conditions the agency requires the client to meet.
2. Specify what persons must or should participate.

3. Specify what documents must be produced, by whom, and where they are to be delivered.

4. Specify the authority for the requirements or expectation, that is, what legal, judicial, professional, or customary authority exists to justify the expectations.

5. Elicit a clear and concrete understanding of an agency's or official's intentions and plans.

6. Secure information possessed by the agency or official about the problem.

7. Secure information about the agency's special knowledge concerning a client and a problem area.

8. Secure information about what agency resources are available to the client.

9. Reach agreement on resources and services to be supplied by the agency or official.

10. Influence the agency to take a positive attitude toward the client to ease his entry into its system and to encourage his participation.

11. Request that the agency or official report, confirming or revising agreements.

Example 7.1 shows the guidelines put into action on a specific case.

EXAMPLE 7.1

SAMPLE MEMORANDUM RECORDING FOR THE FILE OF THE RESULTS OF A NEGOTIATING SESSION WITH OTHER AGENCY OFFICIALS*

(1) Required terms and conditions

(4) Authority

(5) Agency intentions and plans

Met with 24-year-old Mark Jones' probation officer and his supervisor. The judge ordered Mark to report for psychiatric counseling while on one year's probation. The probation department referred him to our clinic. The probation department staff thinks it is probable that Mark's repeated traffic offenses (driving without a license, speeding, failure to pay parking violation tickets) are due to psychological problems for which he should be treated. They see Mark as an intelligent and agreeable person who could benefit from treatment that would "straighten him out." By this they mean clearing up his troubled relationship with his girlfriend, with whom he has a child, getting regular employment, paying regular child support, and getting married. Along with such improvement in the organization of his life, the court wants him to get driver training and a license. The court does not want to sentence this man to imprisonment and hopes for a better outcome through therapy.

*Numbers within parentheses refer to Guidelines for Negotiating on pages 178–179 and are shown only for reference.

(6) Securing information

Mark's history contained problems. He was thought to have been physically abused by his parents when he was a young child. As a result of the investigation at that time, Mark was placed in a foster home for several years. He ran away several times and associated with youth known to be involved in theft and drugs. But Mark himself seemed to behave within the law. He graduated from high school and is now employed irregularly as a garage mechanic. For four years he has been living with his girlfriend. She is a secretary whose mother provides child care for the couple's son. When they are together Mark and his girlfriend fight continually, and sometimes there are drinking bouts. Mark can give no coherent explanation of what they fight about or what the source of their difficulties is.

(2) Required participants

The court requires only Mark to be in treatment. The court staff would like to involve Mark's girlfriend but realize that her participation must be voluntary, even though they know the couple have much conflict.

(8) Available agency resources

The probation officer will see Mark once per month for a checkup interview. This is expected to remind Mark that the court has authority over him and that he could go to jail if he fails to cooperate.

(9) Agreement on resources and services

We agreed on the probation plan previously stated (monthly checkup by probation officer).

(10) Influencing the agency

We agreed that the probation officer will be receptive to Mark's complaints and distress about being required to go into treatment and that the officer will take a supportive and clarifying attitude toward the treatment. For ourselves, we did not think we could predict how Mark would react to treatment. The probation personnel indicated that they were realists and expected only that we try our best.

(11) Reporting

We confirmed that this summary represents the sense of our interagency understanding of each other's roles, but that we would check with each other at the end of each month to see how we each were doing with Mark and determine if our understanding still held or needed revision.

Not applicable:

(3) Documents

(7) Agency special knowledge

Conferring with Collaterals. Conferences may be held with the client's family, friends, teachers, physicians, a state's attorney, and so forth. The major purpose of these conferences is to win these other interested parties over to take one or more actions to reward, legitimize, respect, teach, or help the client. Actions taken by collaterals should fit the plan for task achievement and be specific. Conferences often give the practitioner an opportunity to solicit information that will be of help in assessing the situation and weighing alternatives for intervention. (See Example 7.2.)

EXAMPLE 7.2

SAMPLE RECORD NOTE ON CONFERENCE WITH MARK'S EMPLOYER

I met with J. Battleman, with Mark's agreement, and after he had discussed with Mr. B that I would call and got his okay. Told Mr. B that I knew that he was aware of Mark's problems and that Mark had been unreliable in his work. I was there frankly to intercede for Mark who saw the handwriting on the wall and understood he was finally going to be fired. I said I understood Mr. B's frustration and also that Mark was an expense at present and that Mr. B was not getting his money's worth out of Mark. Mr. B was quite resentful about my interceding for Mark and let me know he thought it was pretty outrageous. Standing my ground, I explained that I thought and the judge thought that Mark could straighten out but needed time. That was all I wanted—some time. Both Mark and I were ready to work to get him to work regularly and on time. Mr. B said that was the problem. Mark got him into all kinds of trouble with customers by not showing up, showing up late or drunk, or both. And that crazy business about Mark's driving his car without a license! In the end, Mr. B agreed to a one-month probation, to give Mark and me enough time to get started on a treatment program.

Providing Resources.   The contract should state what resources are planned for inclusion in the service to the client and describe the general means for their procurement. These resources may be tangible and material, for example, cash, food stamps, medical care, clothing, housing, or education; or they may be counseling services, for example, psychotherapy or interpersonal skill training. The resources provided may be controlled by the agency or may need to be procured from another agency through prior agreements about division of services, referral, advocacy, or purchase of care.

Selecting and Scheduling Interventions

Selecting tasks and selecting interventions are intertwined. Professional usage does not clearly distinguish between these two terms; both are relatively new, nontraditional, technical terms whose meanings are still evolving.

The term *intervention* is used to describe something that occurs and comes between various interests in a discordant situation, for example, interference with or mediation of conflicting interests. Intervention usually refers to some preassembled group of techniques that have been conceptualized in a coordinated manner and have achieved recognition in publication or another official medium. Tasks are small units of intervention that are individualized and not permanent features of the sequence of intervention or treatment. Intervention has come to be a synonym for treatment and is used by practitioners and theoreticians who prefer not to associate themselves closely with the implication of medical practice that is implied by the term *treatment*.

A feature of contemporary practice is that new and revised intervention programs are constantly being designed and disseminated. In addition, it is characteristic of practice that individual practitioners continually invent interventions out of their own experience and as a product of their interaction with particular clients and settings. It is not possible to be up-to-date on all the sources of information about intervention. However, the most efficient sources are

- computerized data banks, provided that they can screen and analyze the detailed information that is provided
- professional journals
- conferences, workshops, continued education, in-service training
- formal university-based professional education
- synthesized and summarized literature reviews
- supervision and consultation

Selecting interventions tends to be more art than science and depends on habit and preference. To increase the realism and objectivity of the process, certain guidelines make sense (Gambrill, 1983; Thomas, 1984).

Guidelines for Selecting Interventions.   Interventions selected should

1. Have a credible record of success in similar cases
2. Be acceptable to all participants
3. Be efficient and capable of being implemented with reasonable cost and time
4. Be as nonintrusive as possible, minimizing the amount of change needed to put the intervention in place, thus probably decreasing the risk of negative side effects
5. Have a positive orientation
6. Be likely to generalize and be maintained, and enhance problem-solving skills (see Chapter 9)
7. Be individualized, taking account of unique situational and individual differences that necessitate adapting recognized interventions to fit the present case

Interventions should be scheduled in an organized way rather than depend on momentary flashes of insight to show the way. This is not to say that if some very good idea emerges out of the blue we should not catch it and run with it—we should—but we cannot rely on such luck to see us through the hard work of planning and implementing problem solving. Some programmed intervention packages recommend the order of the interventions. Some suggest stages that clients can go through and suggest stopping at the stage that accomplishes the desired results. Most intervention scheduling is flexible and follows the conventional logic of beginning, middle, and end. The most important guideline for scheduling is this: *The plan should provide and the contract should include a decision reached with the client and any other important participants about what interventions will start the process, what effects are expected to follow, and approximately when the intervention will end.*

Taking the target problem priorities as a guide, the schedule of interventions should start with itemizing what is to be done first, second, and third, roughly at the beginning, middle, and end. Interventions have a way of losing specificity and order as they progress. The chain of events they start is not capable of being fully anticipated. Many actors and actions get involved that influence the interventions.

Intervention schedules should be definite. However, they should be changed readily in the face of obvious need. Their purpose is to push and to get movement in the intervention program.

Scheduling Interviews

The preferred way to schedule interviews is to establish specifically how often they will occur, where and when they will be held, and how long they will last. These specifics can be changed later if they prove to be inconvenient. However, to start off without a systematic schedule is to invite uncertainty, inattention, and misunderstanding. A fluid and diffuse mode of scheduling time invites drift.

Setting Duration or Time Limits

A review of current literature reveals considerable variation and disagreement among authors about what time limits to set for interventions. Absence of research evidence only adds to the lack of consensus. A recent exploratory study concluded that criteria for planning duration of treatment were primarily idiosyncratic (Fortune, 1985a). Other writers have attempted to develop theoretical positions about the appropriateness of time limits (Kanter, 1983). Given this state of affairs, the guidelines in the task-centered approach should be construed as practice-based information to be used in a flexible and commonsense fashion until robust information is generated. Four general rules can guide practice in defining time limits for a particular case:

1. Task-centered intervention should be planned to take place in eight to twelve in-person interviews with the clients, spaced out in a regular schedule over a two- to three-month period.
2. Negotiations and collateral conferences in any number can be included or excluded, depending on need.

3. The planned number of interviews should be noted in the contract, together with the planned dates and times.
4. The number of interviews may be reduced or extended to fit any natural time limits inherent in the problem situation; for example, if Mrs. A is to be incapacitated for only four weeks, the time limit for the intervention could be one month.

There has been no research to study what time limits are "best" for any particular problem, age group, or personality type. (See Chapter 2.) Agencies develop practice styles about how they apportion time and set time limits on the basis of their judgments. Some agencies set numbers of interviews on the basis of an administrative decision. Available staff time may also determine time limits. Experience develops practice knowledge about what time allotments seem appropriate. Where third-party payments are made, it is customary to set the limit to equal the amount of service that will be paid for or reimbursed by another agency or an insurance company.

Rule of Thumb.   The experience of the research projects on which the task-centered approach is based suggests a "rule of thumb"—eight client interviews, plus any number of agency negotiations and collateral contacts, over a two- to three-month span. The contract for an eight-interview sequence can be shortened or extended.

Reasons for Time Limits.   Time limits appear to mobilize effort. As with any deadline, they set an objective towards which clients and practitioners can organize energy and expectations. Time limits create a push to get things done.

Rarely do clients object to time limits. Those who do object often have been habituated to an open-ended style as a result of previous treatment experience. Or they may have adopted the view that long-term treatment is a status symbol or an interpersonal security situation. Occasionally, clients seem to pick up nonverbal cues from practitioners who feel anxious about using time limits. No deleterious effects from time limits have been reported except the occasional verbal anecdote about a client who develops a severe separation anxiety that a practitioner new to short-term treatment attributes to time limits. (Actually, the client's anxiety might have been induced by any number of other causes.) In fact, there appears to be a significant decrease in dropouts when explicit, time-limited sequences are compared to open-ended sequences. Time limits also put the client–practitioner relationship on a work basis, cutting down on the development of the client's unnecessary personal dependence on the practitioner (Tolson & Brown, 1981).

Special Conditions for Time Limits.   There are a number of conditions where special time limit conditions pertain: children and adults in foster care, chronic care, or long-term care; children or adults in legal custody or under court-ordered treatment; children or adults receiving medical or mental health treatment; young children in direct treatment; or parents learning new child care skills.

1. *Clients in foster care, chronic care, or long-term care.* In foster care or chronic care, living arrangements are provided that are separable from counseling. The counseling should follow the usual rules for task-centered intervention addressed to specific target problems and should include time limits. The contract for living arrangements is distinct. The living arrangement contract can be open ended if that arrangement is intended to be permanent or indefinite. If this is not intended, the plan should specify the expected duration of the living arrangement, the discharge plan, and the alternative plan. While the particular living arrangement exists, there may be a series of separate task-centered sequences. Critical points in settings that would normally call for such sequences are admission, personal crises, changes in living plan, and discharge.

2. *Children or adults in legal custody with court-ordered requirements.* Typical incidences of legal custody with court-ordered requirements include children who are wards of the court and ordered to be in foster care, children or adults on probation or parole, and persons legally declared incompetent who have a court-appointed guardian. The terms of the court order may exceed the task-centered model's normal time limits. The contract for intervention in such cases should follow the normal task-centered time limits. Thereafter, additional sequences can be contracted for, if advisable, or the situation can be placed in a monitoring status.

3. *Children or adults receiving medical or mental health treatment.* Clinics vary a great deal in their expectation that medically supervised or medically oriented treatment will be open ended or time limited. Because of side effects and legal requirements, the provision of medication almost always requires continuing medical supervision. Medical and psychiatric care may involve some regular checkup or monitoring to observe the development of a chronic health condition. When the medical or mental health agency opts for extended time and the social welfare agency agrees, the intervention plan proceeds according to the medical recommendations. Interventions concerning the problems in living, however, can be restricted to one or more task-centered sequences.

4. *Young children in direct treatment.* Young children have relatively short attention spans that need to be considered when planning the eight-session interviewing schedule. Young children may be interviewed in short segments of time, with two short segments counted as one for purposes of the interview scheduling.

5. *Parents being re-educated in child care skills.* Evidence suggests that parent education is an effective activity to reduce parent–child conflict problems and modify child-rearing practices (Levenstein, Kochman, & Roth, 1973; Pinkston, Friedman, & Polster, 1981). There is also some evidence that frequent contact and service beyond the usual two to three months characteristic of task-centered intervention—up to one year—enhances effectiveness in dealing with these types of problems (Sherman, Neuman, & Shyne, 1973). In view of this evidence, it would be appropriate to contract for extended duration if doing so accords with the practitioner's judgment and the client's

interest in particular circumstances. The extremely important proviso is that cases be kept open *only* when definite plans and implementation are actually desired by clients who also show credible evidence of improvement and *only* if appropriate services actually exist and can be provided.

Extensions.   When convincing evidence exists, there should be no artificial barrier to extending time limits. But lacking that concrete evidence, extending a contract on some general belief that more is better has no known value. It would be better to conclude with the completion of the planned brief intervention sequence. There should be no bar to reopen cases if requested to do so or if an involuntary client is referred again.

The reasons some cases continue for long or very long periods of time are varied. There are economic advantages to providers of long-term interventions. Some types of medically supervised interventions are established to continue over long periods of time, partly because of habit and style, or partly because of what is known or believed about stages of development in diseases. Interventions that involve large investments in re-education of children and adults may justify long-term intervention. The fact is that the state of knowledge does not justify any hard and fast conclusions about the conditions under which long-term intervention is or is not justified.

The present tendency is to curtail the length of time used in interventions. Especially when cost is important and when effectiveness is doubtful, long-term interventions are not justifiable. The number of people who benefit from brief, focused interventions is large and potentially larger.

Deciding on Participants

The universe of persons who can be involved in an intervention sequence is closed. Only certain categories of parties may be included: family members, peers, nonfamily persons in the household, a relevant group (interest group, age group, neighborhood or civic group, for example), or immediately influential authorities (teachers, doctors, caregivers, for example). If possible and if feasible, those who are an immediate part of the problem and its solution should be included in the contract, but only if they are available and have expressed a willingness and ability to participate.

Some people, such as parents of minor children, can be included because their social role commands their involvement. Persons can be deemed an immediate part of the problem and its solution if they are in a continuing, current relationship with the central client and if they occupy a position that seems to precipitate, exacerbate, maintain, or restrain the problem. Persons whose social role commands their involvement are those who exercise direct care of and give financial support to the central client.

In deciding which parties to include in the contract, the crucial factor is their willingness. Rarely do persons of potential value to the success of an intervention agree to total involvement. They have their own agendas, which come first. It is not uncommon, however, for a married couple or parents and children to agree to joint interviews. It is sometimes the case that whole families will come together for interviews or that men and women friends will attend together. Mostly, however, persons other than the central client will take a lesser degree of responsibility. They can contract for moderate or minimal inclusion. They may be prepared to attend once or only occasionally, or they may participate by telephone. The degree of involvement of persons close to the client is not crucial. What is crucial is that there be discussion with them to find out what they are ready to do and to commit them to specific actions.

Location of Interviews

Where interviews are to be held is a matter of custom, convenience, and expediency. Interviews in the client's home offer observations and interactions with real living conditions and excellent opportunities for assessment. However, they may be subject to interruptions, lack privacy, and in certain circumstances, such as high crime neighborhoods, pose security problems. Office interviews are most convenient for practitioners and are also less costly than home interviews, but some clients are much less comfortable in the ageney's office than in their own homes and neighborhoods. Interviews are sometimes held on the street and in public buildings depending on the purpose and on what is practical and prudent. The important thing for making a contract is to plan for the place to hold interviews and to schedule the interviews and collateral contacts.

EXAMPLE 7.3

EXAMPLE OF A CONTRACT

Rick is a 15-year-old black youth in foster care. He is an only child being reared by his mother who was deserted by his father when Rick was only 4 years old. He came into foster care one month ago with his mother's reluctant approval after having been picked up by the police twelve times within the past year for running away, fighting, and belonging to a gang. The practitioner is employed in the state child welfare agency and regards both the mother and Rick as clients.

CONTRACT TOPIC	SPECIFICATION
1. Major priority problems	*Rick*
	■ Too many people are trying to raise me.
	■ My mother pays too much attention to my aunt's advice.
	Mother
	■ Rick does not go to school.

CONTRACT TOPIC	SPECIFICATION
	■ He stays out too late at night.
	■ He keeps bad company.
	Mandated
	■ By court: Minor in need of supervision.
	■ By agency opinion: Mother too strict.
2. Goals	*Rick*
	■ To be discharged from foster care.
	■ To return home and enroll in school.
	Rick and Mother
	■ To set up a curfew plan.
	■ To stop aunt's interference.
3. Client tasks	*Rick*
	■ To decide what vocational training Rick wants.
	Mother
	■ To decide on latest possible curfew time.
	in exchange
	Rick
	■ To advise mother of a plan for reporting lateness to her.
	Mother
	■ To put limits on aunt's interference.
4. Practitioner tasks	■ To arrange vocational testing for Rick.
	■ To get and deliver to Rick and mother all available information about work training programs.
	■ To confer with aunt about her role in mother–son conflict.
	■ To prepare recommendations for court about plan for Rick's discharge from foster care.
	■ To negotiate Rick's re-enrollment with school official.
5. Duration	■ Two months
6. Intervention schedule	*Sessions 1, 2, 3*
	■ Decrease aunt's interference.
	■ Start decrease in Rick's performance problems in school and gang membership.
	Sessions 4, 5, 6
	■ Prepare return home, re-enrollment in school, how mother and son are to

CONTRACT TOPIC	SPECIFICATION
	interact regarding curfew, friends, and other interests of Rick.
	Sessions 7, 8
	■ Review, evaluate, plan forward.
7. Interview schedule	■ October 6, 13, 20, 27; November 3, 10, 17, 24.
	■ 4 P.M.
	■ Two months.
8. Participants	■ Rick, mother, aunt, foster parents.
9. Location	■ Agency office.

REVISING THE CONTRACT

The written contract tends to become solidified, and amending it seems difficult. However, a written contract should be amended when it becomes more or less irrelevant. Revisions are needed when a good deal of change has taken place or when understanding of the situation has changed in some major way. Amendments can be made easily if the contract sticks to major items rather than great amounts of detail. For example, a contract should state that "Lester is to look for and rent housing," rather than "Lester is to read the housing advertisements in the *Daily Express* on Monday, Wednesday, and Friday, at 8 o'clock after breakfast." It is unnecessary, artificial, and burdensome to revise contracts for details.

OTHER CONTRACTUAL ACTIVITIES

In view of the endless possibilities that arise in real life, it is always necessary to take into account activities that need to be done but are not included in the basic contract recommendations of this book. The contract is a living document that is only useful to help organize, plan, and monitor the ongoing interventions. Many activities not specified here may need to be and should be included.

SUMMARY

The contract is an agreement to work toward the reduction or alleviation of stated personal problems. Rapid early assessment can be used to make a practical working identification of the problem and the probable and feasible alternatives that could be expected to alleviate it. Contracts may be written or verbal, according to preference, although the written contract makes for a tighter planning process.

The contract covers major priority problems, goals, tasks, duration, schedules for interventions and interviews, participants, and location. The major communication to facilitate reaching an agreement with clients on what is to be done and thus included in the plan is: *What acts, if done first, will help most?*

There are numerous types of tasks. Their selection is a matter of individualization plus information about successful interventions from various professional sources and experience. Successful tasks tend to be those to which the client has a great deal of commitment and in which he has been as fully involved as possible in selecting and planning. Practitioner tasks are those the practitioner is committed to perform on the client's behalf. Client and practitioner tasks are stated in the contract.

Tasks should have a credible record of success in similar cases, be acceptable to all participants, and be as efficient and as nonintrusive as possible. There should be a likelihood that the improvement obtained from task performance be generalizable and maintainable.

Task-centered sequences should be planned with time limits of two to three months. The number of interviews can be revised if necessary. Extensions should be made not whimsically but based on evidence of need and evidence that results can be reasonably anticipated.

CHAPTER EIGHT

THIRD STEP: IMPLEMENTATION

Problem Solving, Assessment, Task Achievement, and Problem Reduction

IMPLEMENTING THE TASK-CENTERED MODEL

This chapter sets out ways to put into effect a reasonable amount of problem solving, or problem reduction. Figure 8.1 shows the steps covered in problem solving. Most experts believe that corrective experiences during treatment enhance problem-solving skills

FIGURE 8.1   Map Detail

Step 3	*Problem solving, task achievement, problem reduction* *Select as needed*

DEFINE AND SPECIFY TARGET PROBLEM (THREE MAXIMUM)
- **Restate and name the problem:** the particular conditions and behaviors to be changed
- **Specify**
  Target problem:
  How often it occurs (frequency)
  With whom (participants)
  Where it occurs (site)
  What immediate antecedents (forerunners)
  What consequences (effects)
  What meaning (importance)
- **Assess**
  Social context (social conditions precipitating and maintaining the problem):
  Work-school circumstances
  Health care circumstances
  Economic status
  Family organization
  Peer group organization
  Housing state
  Cultural/ethnic background
- **Cognitive-affective circumstances**
  Client characteristics
  Mode of functioning
  Personal resources
- **Other assessments**

GENERATE ALTERNATIVES
- Find out and identify a feasible range of possible problem-solving strategies

NEGOTIATE SUPPORTIVE AND COLLABORATIVE ACTIONS OF OTHER PERSONS AND AGENCIES

DECISION MAKING   (confirm goals, select what will be done, and design details of the intervention strategy)
- Reaffirm contract and goals
- Determine basic interventions
- Plan timing and sequence
- Select participants
- Get client agreement and understanding (informed consent)
- Get agreement and understanding of others

IMPLEMENT   (carry out strategy)

Develop tasks
- Formulate tasks
- Get client understanding and agreement to tasks
- Get client understanding of rationale and incentives for tasks
- Summarize tasks

FIGURE 8.1   Continued

Develop tasks (continued)
■ Review expected difficulties
■ Devise plans for client task performance
■ Summarize tasks
■ Devise plans for client task performance
Support task performance
■ Review number of sessions outstanding
■ Obtain and use resources
■ Find out obstacles to resource provision
■ Give instruction
■ Give guidance
■ Do simulations
■ Do role plays and guided practice
■ Accompany client for modeling and/or advocacy
■ Other
■ Find out obstacles to task performance
In the social environment: lack of resources, stress, discrimination,
structural problems
In the interpersonal transactions: deficit and conflict, lack of cooperation
In the psychological state: fears, suspicions, lack of knowledge
■ Plan actions to remove, reduce, or alter obstacles
■ Remedy practical barriers to task performance, e.g., lack of skills, lack of
cooperation and support from others, and lack of resources
■ Alleviate cognitive barriers to task performance: discuss fears, suspicions,
lack of knowledge, adverse beliefs
■ Plan and state practitioner tasks: inform client of practitioner tasks, review
implementation of practitioner tasks, review problem state
Verify (check, test, confirm, substantiate probable effects of interventions) and
Monitor (record problem status regularly—use structured notations, charts,
graphs, plus brief, succinct narrative comments)
Revise contract, or some parts of it, if:
■ Progress unsatisfactory
■ Progress exceeds expectations
■ New problems emerge
■ Problem takes on different characteristics
■ Tasks not performed, or poorly performed
■ Supports and resources, if ineffective
■ Practitioner tasks ineffective or not feasible

(Brown, 1980). Spivack et al. (1976) suggested that Jahoda (1953) made the earliest
statement in the contemporary professional literature about the probable relationship between problem-solving thinking and personal adjustment.

It is widely assumed that intervention in human problems is problem solving. The idea of problem solving as the theme of intervention is not only useful

but has achieved almost universal consensus. The task-centered model can be interpreted as comprising a set of problem-solving techniques. The term *problem solving* is a neat way of capturing the theme of intervention. *Problem solving*, as used in this book, means a process of decreasing the frequency, quantity, and intensity of problems, that is, problem-reduction or alleviation.

Problem solving should always take into account that increasing the material or social resources activates and perpetuates problem solving, and, except in the most unusual circumstances, increases well-being. A single-minded concentration on psychological conditions in isolation or divorced from the social context is always inappropriate. The reverse, that is the single focus on the environmental and social context, is also wrong but is an error only infrequently made. It is wrong to attend only or primarily to what a client feels about a problem unless at the same time we find out and say what the problem is in the real world. It is wrong to lead a client into talking that does not connect to problems and does not result in some burdens lifted, some straightening out of lifelines, or benefit of some kind.

Objectives of the Task-Centered Model

The overall objective of the task-centered model is to focus effort on those problems likely to be influenced by presently known methods. With the best will in the world, many human problems evade reduction. We do not know the answer to many problems. At our present level of knowledge, some problems are intractable.

In the task-centered model, the implementation phase (Step 3) takes up most of the available time. Typically, implementation occurs during interviews two through seven, assuming an eight-interview sequence. In a longer or shorter sequence, the implementation phase is the middle of the time planned for the case. The major objective of implementation is to help clients achieve tasks. Problems are usually reduced and alleviated as tasks are achieved.

REFINING THE PROBLEM STATUS

Implementation often starts with refining the problem definition and specification. This process is most likely to occur at the start of Step 3 and may be taken up periodically if the problem becomes vague or confused for either the practitioner or the client. Refining attempts to improve the target problem definition and specification by pruning and polishing, introducing subtleties and distinctions. Refining serves to confirm what has already been decided. Care should be taken to confine exploration of the problem only to the extent that it will clarify exactly what problem is being worked on. If the matter is already sufficiently clear, more exploration is unnecessary. These continual specifications of the problem make measuring, documenting, and/or knowing the extent of problem change simpler.

ASSESSMENT IN THE THIRD STEP

Characteristics

Previously, we have discussed rapid early assessment in the first step (Chapter 6) and working assessment for contracting in the second step (Chapter 7). These assessments are sufficient to launch the case and may be sufficient to anchor the third implementation step. Nevertheless, in complex, natural circumstances, certain aspects of a case may appear enigmatic, equivocal, or obscure. Rather than engage in extensive exploration, it is preferable to conduct a planned and bounded exploration constrained to the present problems for which the interventions are to occur.

Reassessment

The refining of the original assessment is similar to what is meant by reassessment. This is a process of building on the original, correcting it, adjusting it, "fine-tuning." In brief treatment, the reassessment is normally confined to the problem area that is the focus of the treatment and forgoes interest in large-scale, historical assessment or in assessments of areas not clearly having an impact on the focal problem.

Assessment and Diagnosis Compared

Assessment is a judgment of use to practitioners and may have considerable effect on clients. It may result in a more knowledgeable and expert professional understanding that will help a practitioner design productive interventions. Assessment can be a positive experience for a client by sifting out and clarifying what are the parts of the problem situation and how that situation exerts its influence on her. Assessment that is overly concentrated on just one aspect of a situation, ignoring other potentially important aspects, will be distorted.

The assessment is a type of problem definition that is cast in professional terms and according to a professionally determined pattern that is derived from practice, behavioral, and personality theories. Unless modified by other considerations, such as client interests and social context, the assessment strongly influences how the target problem will be defined.

Assessment is a judgment, an opinion, or an appraisal of the problem made to understand and interpret it. Diagnosis may include the same information, but it is primarily concerned with recognizing a disease by its symptoms. In many practice settings, we are not dealing with disease, but rather with routine to extreme problems in living. Illness may or may not be present, and it may or may not be a focus of intervention. Present-day culture tends toward belief in psychic determination, interpreting problems in living as symptoms of disease and identifying those problems as mental illness, developmental arrests, deficits, disorganization, emotional turbulence, or disorder. The concepts of assessment and diagnosis overlap. Their differential use is related to whether or not we view problems in living as medical issues, or the degree to which we "medicalize" social deviance and disadvantage. Both the assessment intent and the diagnosis intent are present at the same time in many case situations.

Ordinarily, neither an assessment nor a clinical diagnosis will indicate what the treatment or intervention should be. Clinical diagnosis of psychopathology does not prescribe treatment. It defines and describes disease. Both assessment and clinical diagnosis provide some explanations of the problem and imply some or a range of interventions that may be appropriate and others that may be irrelevant or contraindicated.

Target Problem Assessment

Some regularly recurring circumstances suggest elaborating assessment in Step 3. The target problem may seem to slip or slide out of place in the focus. The details may become vague, contradictory, inconsistent, or not properly connected to the intervention plan and tasks. There may develop an uncertainty about how to proceed with the problem and/or situation. The problem may be defined as mental illness or social dysfunction and become subject to mental health intervention or medical diagnosis and classification. Given any or all of these circumstances, a prudent judgment would be to conduct limited and focused elaboration of the existing assessment with concentration on tightening up the details, meaning, and ramifications of the target problem. The kind of assessment that has been useful for understanding the client's problem in task-centered practice answers the following questions:

- *What is the target problem?* The problem identification, description, specification, name
- *What is the frequency?* How often does the target problem occur? When does it occur?
- *With whom?* Who are the participants?
- *Where?* What is the site?
- *With what antecedents or consequences?* What happens before and afterward?
- *In what context?* What are the significant conditions?
- *In what cognitive-affective situation?* What is the mental state of the person?

The process of specifying problems is described in detail by Brown and Levitt (1979). The next section shows two examples of assessment.

EXAMPLES OF ASSESSMENT AND PROBLEM SPECIFICATION

MRS. F

Mrs. F found a lump in her breast four weeks ago. She became afraid she might have cancer and need surgery. She worried constantly and could not rest or sleep well, regardless of who was with her or where she was. She became fatigued, overwhelmed, confused, and anxious. She procrastinated for two weeks, trying unsuccessfully to ignore the matter. She finally saw a doctor who confirmed her worst fears. While not definitely making the diagnosis of cancer, the doctor recommended that Mrs. F enter the hospital for a biopsy.

Mrs. F is a single mother who supports two young children and herself doing low-skilled sales work in a local grocery. The work is physically exhausting with long hours and compels her to make precarious child care arrangements that are too costly for her meager income. She has been so tired and chronically overwhelmed that she has no personal life or social life to speak of, having little to do even with her mother and sisters who live in the same city but at quite a distance. Her affections are totally directed to her two children and she is an excellent mother. She attends church but is not involved in activities; she has made a few acquaintances but no friends. The coworkers at the store are her real support group, but her relations with them are confined to the workplace and do not extend into her personal or home life.

Mrs. F is a hardworking, decent person with limited education and narrow interests. She is a sturdy problem solver in ordinary mundane matters. She was deserted by an alcoholic, brutal husband three years ago and picked herself up, found a job of sorts, and has made do. Faced with the terror of a life-threatening cancer and a significant bodily mutilation, she has become thoroughly disorganized and depressed.

MRS. G

Mrs. G is worried and resentful that her only son Arthur, 12, hits her in the stomach and on the face. In the past year, he has done this about six times, always when they are at home alone. The last time was a week ago. Arthur hit his mother right after she yelled at him to stop being so curious about a girl. She ran into her bedroom and slammed the door after this last incident, and Arthur ran out of the house. Mrs. G is excitable, speaks in a loud, frenetic tone of voice, and is probably given to exaggeration. She says, for example, that Arthur is "always" and "constantly" hitting her when in fact these attacks are infrequent but very disturbing.

Mrs. G is extremely perturbed about Arthur developing a strong interest in girls and regards this as a bad sign. Her husband vanished years ago. She has no relatives locally and is estranged from her siblings in a distant city. She is not a churchgoer. She receives support from the welfare department, has no skills, does not work, and has never worked. She seems to have no interests except Arthur, but she is very worried about him.

Arthur does poorly in school and is inattentive, but he plays satisfactorily with the other boys his own age in the neighborhood. Lately, he has become sullen and constantly alert to girls, making lewd remarks about them, and Mrs. G has no idea where this behavior comes from. She is really frantic about what to do with Arthur.

Baselining and Assessment

Baselining helps to understand the problem in detail and to design relevant interventions. The techniques of baselining, developed in the field of behavior modification, are thoroughly explained in its literature such as the text by Gambrill (1983). A baseline ensures an accurate account of the frequency, intensity, and characteristics of the problem. A baseline can answer many assessment questions. A baseline is necessary for empirical evaluation of progress or change.

Ordinarily, baseline information is obtained after the problems have been decided on and the contract has been made. The baseline may be the first implementation act. However, a baseline can be taken earlier if it will help make the target problem more specific. Baselines may be current or retrospective. For a current baseline to be concrete and useful, it should give accurate information about how things are.

The common ways of getting current baselines are direct observation and logging. *Direct observation* requires the practitioner to be present when and where the problem occurs and to systematically keep a record of observations. If it is possible for another reliable person to make observations, the objectivity of the information may increase. *Logging* involves the practitioner, client, or outside observer keeping a record. Logging one's own situation can shed light on a problem and often leads a client to generate a change strategy quickly.

To generate a retrospective baseline, the practitioner leads a client to think back in time and to offer examples from memory about frequency, site, antecedents, consequences, and meaning of the problem. A retrospective baseline imposes some form on the assessment and at times may be the only information available. People are not necessarily accurate informants about details of their problems. Their information is influenced by lapses and distortions of memory, their moods, and their beliefs about the kind of information a practitioner and agency think is acceptable. Retrospective baselines may be improved by collateral information from other sources. Although those sources may be biased and inaccurate, a retrospective baseline is probably better than none at all. The next example illustrates a baseline in a natural setting.

BASELINE IN A NATURAL SETTING

TINA

Tina, a 22-year-old woman, has two children, ages 4 and 6. She has no husband and is on welfare. The agency provided her with training as a typist. For two months she has been employed in a large firm as a clerk–typist, her first job. The agency secured daycare for the 4-year-old. Tina's mother provides after-school baby sitting in her own home for both children.

Tina gets up at 5 A.M. to do housework, prepare meals, and take one child to the daycare center and the other to her mother's. Then she travels forty-five minutes to work. She is already frazzled when she gets there. After work she picks up the children, eats, puts on the TV, and collapses.

Tina's supervisor reported to the job program office that Tina is in danger of being fired. The work she does is satisfactory, but she is not energetic and she causes trouble. Called in by the counselor, Tina disposes of the lack of energy problem; there is nothing she can do about it because she is legitimately exhausted by her schedule. Tina does not want to be fired. She admits that she cannot restrain herself from insulting her supervisor and fellow employees. This is the trouble she causes. She admits she is "too mouthy," and she would like to cut that out. The goal of the contract is to reduce the frequency of her insults to her supervisor and the others.

Initial exploration and retrospective baseline information result in complications. Tina says that her boss and the others treat her as if she were "invisible," meaning unworthy. Meanwhile, she observes other employees making mistakes and goofing off. That gets her goat because she tries so hard. Her boss does not like Tina because she fails to "con" her with compliments and gratitude the way the others do. Tina does not think her boss has very good judgment.

She suspects her boss holds her job because of friendship with "bigwigs" in the company. Tina is always so tired and so offended that she constantly blurts out insults to all of them. She rages inside about their disrespect toward her.

At the start of Step 3, Tina agreed to keep a daily log for ten-minute intervals at critical times in the day's work flow from 8:30 to 8:40, from 10:15 to 10:25, from 1:30 to 1:40, and from 4:00 to 4:10. (See Table 8.1.)

Tina's log showed that she insulted two people and did not insult two. Each insulting statement was preceded by a need to work on someone else's papers. With this assessment, the problem was cut down to size. Being "too mouthy" became "mouthing off at certain people who usually give me bad work to follow up."

TABLE 8.1   Tina's Log (Simplified)

TIME	WHAT I SAID	TO WHOM	WHERE	WHAT HAPPENED
8:30–8:40	Your papers are illegible.	Corinne	Corinne's desk	She cried and complained to other workers.
10:15–10:25	Talked about TV show.	Betty	Coffee room	She was nice.
1:30–1:40	Bad food at lunch.	Betty	My desk	She sympathized.
4:00–4:10	Corinne and Helen don't fill out forms right.	Supervisor	Supervisor's desk	She glared; said I should mind my own business.

Usefulness of Baseline Information.   A baseline gives an estimate of the frequency, magnitude, duration, antecedents, and consequences of specified events and behaviors. It reveals whether or not a problem is sufficiently important to warrant intervention, and what is important about it. A baseline provides data from which to measure change or nonchange.

Baselining in Complex Problem Conditions.   A baseline can be obtained when the target problem is a person's behavior, for example, insulting the boss, or fighting with other children or a spouse. There are, however, no techniques for baselining a many-faceted problem condition. Many target problems are bad social conditions; for example, a mother does not have custody of her children; an elderly person does not have an adequate home; someone has been refused care at a mental health clinic; or a parent has been refused privileges to visit the children. These conditions call for accurate identification of the problem condition, that is, the negative combination of circumstances or state of affairs.

Efforts to deal with these issues help to provide a baseline of activities that are relevant to the problems. For example, not having a job can only be specified as client does not have a job. It is more useful in such cases to specify the activities that a client has done. For not having a job, one might determine that a client has read the job notices in the daily newspaper each day for a week and has called two places about openings. Keeping track of client activities related to such problems is more useful for specifying the nature of what needs to change to accomplish the ultimate goal of having a job.

Some complex conditions containing many parts and many persons acting in relation to one another can be baselined by selection. If some crucial behavior can be isolated and if changing this behavior can alter the situation, then a baseline can be taken. If the condition is too complex for taking a baseline of distinct behaviors, exact information should be obtained about the important facets of the condition.

Assessment of Social Context

The social context is comprised of the physical environment, the social network; the socioeconomic condition, culture, ethnicity, neighborhood, and community; and macrosystems such as the national economy and the driving priorities of the politics of the time. All these elements should be considered together in relation to what impact they have on the client; how they influence what the client thinks, believes, values, and wants; and what opportunities and deprivations are the client's lot because of her particular niche in the social system.

Many unsolved technical problems seriously impede the ability of the helping professions to adequately incorporate assessment of social context into a practical and useful assessment. The variables seem too numerous and too diverse; there are too many varying definitions of concepts and development of theory is uneven. However, particular segments of the social context can be judged to be precipitating and maintaining problems. If these influences can be identified and understood, they can then pinpoint an area or areas of the social context amenable to change that can improve the client's situation directly. A gross appraisal of the social context often suggests a relevant selection from among all the conditions and actors. Only those sectors that are judged most relevant to the problem should be selected for a focused exploration.

The following list briefly characterizes the conditions that are important in analyzing the social context of a client's immediate problem. A full exposition of meaning and issues involved in the social context is beyond the scope of this book, and the reader is well advised to consult specialized works usually classified under the field of "human behavior and the social environment" (Ashford, LeCroy, & Lortie, 1997; Green & Ephross, 1991; Longres, 1995).

1. *Work–school circumstances*. Work is central in the lives of most adults because it provides economic independence, status, family stability, and the opportunity to interact with other people in the most basic activity of society. Unemployment restricts or eliminates work opportunities, and dissatisfying work incurs severe negative repercussions in individual lives and in the social order. School plays the same role for children and youth as work does for adults. If school is repugnant, frightening, uninteresting, and unattractive, school problems will emerge and do a good deal of damage.

2. *Health care circumstances*. Ill health and inadequate health care undermine the well-being of many people. Illness itself creates immense problems that are compounded for those who may not have access to good care or who may not know how to negotiate their way through a cumbersome system for locating and funding health care.

3. *Economic status*. Educational attainment, occupational pursuit, family income, and occupational background of parents combine to depict economic status or, more properly, socioeconomic status. An individual's place in society cannot be characterized adequately by reference to any one single feature of this group of conditions. Nevertheless, lower levels of socioeconomic status are often closely associated with individuals having less control over their environments and living conditions, and give rise to disaffection and an absence of well-being.

4. *Family organization*. It is widely believed that individual problems can be understood in relation to the nature and organization of the family system in which the individual is embedded. It is frequently possible to note and intervene in dysfunctional family relations that maintain a problem. Indicators of trouble in the family can be located by observing or becoming informed about power arrangements, hierarchies, communication patterns, exploitative and abusive patterns, dependence and independence, financial arrangements, handling of conflicts and crises, and problem-solving patterns.

5. *Peer group organization*. A person's circle of friends provides support and nurture, help and intimacy, and closeness and comfort. An individual's social circle can also be an embarrassment, a source for envy and jealousy, for

undermining one's strength and ambition, or for acquiring destructive modes of living such as excessive use of drugs and credit cards.

6. *Housing state.* Decent housing is a source of comfort and strength. Living in unsanitary conditions, in ugly or overcrowded surroundings, or in unsafe and unsavory neighborhoods is an inducement to poor mental health.

7. *Cultural/ethnic background.* A client's cultural and ethnic background is a major determinant of her values, norms, expectations, and reactions to everyday living, crises, and other problems. Substantial personal, interpersonal, and political turbulence today stems from varying culturally determined beliefs, from differential access to wealth and power, from unemployment, and from lack of opportunity. These areas are sources of considerable maladjustment in personal lives. (See Chapter 1.) Cultural traits, however, can significantly help in problem-solving efforts, for these are the client's strengths (Alley & Brown, in press).

Starting from the gross exploration of the social context, the assessment of social context attempts to judge what factors in the environment and in the problem situation are precipitating and maintaining the problem. However, the social context is a source of strength and help as well as often a source of trouble. The positive elements should be identified as carefully as the negative ones. A comfortable apartment or house, moderately understanding relatives and friends, interested teachers and authorities, moderately good health, basically adequate income with health insurance, access to credit, individual talents and interests, a reasonable degree of security about acceptance, and respect of one's cultural characteristics— all these add up to opportunities that can be called on to aid problem solving.

Proceeding from the original exploration of the gross features of the social context, assessment at the start of Step 3 helps make a more specific judgment and is thus an aid to intervention. The practitioner may conclude that some feature of the social context is precipitating or perpetuating the problem. This assessment leads to the development of an intervention strategy that will concentrate on influencing and changing the conditions of the social context. Having such a social context assessment gives the practitioner the ability to give advice and make recommendations about actions to the client, referral sources, family members, and other agencies. On the other hand, an assessment of the social context can lead to the conclusion that the social context factors cannot be changed. That judgment is also the basis for advising the client and attempting an alternative strategy.

Gil and Brown (1985) point out that problem definitions, hence also assessments, are culturally determined to a large extent (p. 95). One must be careful not to assess a situation as problematic if the behavior or condition is considered appropriate within the client's own culture. Different groups have their own beliefs about what social agencies should do and how they should do it. These beliefs may be at variance with what the American-reared and trained practitioner regards as appropriate. Many non-American cultures place a high regard on individual and family privacy and are averse to disclosing intimate information to outsiders. It is difficult to provide firm guidelines for conducting a culturally sensitive assessment because the whole experience of helping across cultures is new on the contemporary scene. It will take time and effort to work out and test guidelines. For the present, it is advisable to be alert to the variations among groups in how they regard the place of the individual, the family, and the helping services, and to make sensitive professional judgments about what adaptations to make in the normal guidelines to assessment and intervention (Alley & Brown, in press; Brown, 1997; Brown & Alley, 1999a, b; Devore & Schlesinger, 1996).

Assessment of Cognitive–Affective Circumstances: Client Characteristics and Mode of Functioning

The client's personal resources and cognitive–affective traits are summed up and revealed in his presentation of himself to others and his perception of himself within the privacy of his own mind. These characteristics make the statement about who he is and where he came from. A client's personality and modes of functioning are shaped by his biological equipment; upbringing and education; habits; and expectations and views of himself, other people, and social institutions arising from his ethnic background, culture, social class, personal traits, values, and circumstances. Personal resources and traits reveal themselves in such attributes as mood, intelligence, affective life, and modes of thought.

An assessment of the client and her functioning can be organized by using the observations made about the client during the initial exploration (Step 1, Chapter 6) and adding other relevant information. The practitioner draws a conclusion and makes a judgment about the client's talents and capabilities, personal inadequacies, and style or pattern of conduct. This assessment gives a practitioner some clues to understanding what the client may do to precipitate or exacerbate the problem and what potentials and limits there are for personal change, that is, change in the client's characteristics, traits, lifestyle, patterns of interpersonal relating, problem solving, and cognition.

The personal assessment process lends itself to overuse of psychiatric examinations and psychological tests. Such examinations and tests are required in many settings and may produce informative, valuable, and useful information. The criterion for referral for specialized diagnosis is that the client's actions are extremely odd or not understandable, or show sensational contrasts or striking incongruities. Such clients may be helped or protected by being directed into the psychiatric treatment stream of intervention. If there is a real possibility clients will be helped or adequately protected, such resources should be used. A clinical diagnosis may help the practitioner design an intervention strategy. The service delivery system may require extensive use of psychological and psychiatric assessment procedures because of the increasing tendency for treatment resources to be concentrated in the mental health stream of services.

Other Possible Assessments

Other areas, in individual instances, may be helpful in rounding out an assessment.

Causal Explanations.   In our science-oriented society, we seek causal explanations. Real knowledge about causation of social and behavioral events is weak. Various theories try to identify causation, but ordinarily these theories are difficult to apply to problem-solving undertakings. The American Psychiatric Association's *Diagnostic and Statistical Manual of Mental Disorders* (*DSM IV*), for instance, explains that it adopts a descriptive rather than an etiological approach to describing diagnostic entities because for most disorders the cause is unknown.

Nevertheless, people often want explanations of the origin or fundamental basis of their problems to obtain a cognitive map of their lives, to provide boundaries, to simplify a condition, and to reduce the problems to manageable proportions. A working explanation of causation can be obtained from the client's reflections and from the practitioner's and agency's knowledge and experiences. Although underlying problems are sometimes apparent or discernible, they are often obscure, and explanations are based on ideological grounds. An explanation of problems based on common sense, experience, or up-to-date research, if available, provides usable explanations. What is needed is a rough working explanation. People who want greater self-understanding should locate practitioners rigorously trained in the art of developing self-understanding: psychoanalysts, advanced social workers or other therapists with special expertise, philosophers, or wise religious people.

Past Problem-Solving Explanations.   A moderate amount of information about what the client has recently done to try to solve the problem can be helpful, provided that history taking of too broad scope is avoided. Recent past problem solving provides information about possible tasks to do and to avoid. If a target problem is chronic, the past three to six months provide adequate information on which to make an assessment.

History.   The history of how the problem developed may be limited to broad information about prior occurrences, duration, and fluctuations in its course. Ordinarily the history of a problem is of interest in explaining a problem but does not contribute much to organizing present problem-solving tasks. That the problem is old does not by itself predict the difficulty of present problem solving. However, an old and obdurate problem will have established habits in the client, in her social network, and among social agencies that may be hard to change.

GENERATING ALTERNATIVES

As we buckle down to serious, focused work on reducing the problems, we need to find out and identify a reasonable range of feasible problem-solving actions. The sources of alternative actions or tasks are the client's own experience, the practitioner's personal and professional experience, professional and technical literature, and other expert information.

The client and the practitioner develop alternative strategies for problem solving. To begin with, brainstorming might be used to generate a range of strategies. As discussion proceeds about the relative costs and benefits of each alternative, the range of probable strategies or solutions is narrowed considerably by the following two questions:

> The first question is addressed to the client: *What kinds of things could you do to tackle this problem?*
>
> The second question is addressed to the practitioner: *What can I do to help the client tackle this problem?*

The practitioner has to clarify and shape these alternatives into understandable form. Important persons and officials in the client's social network should also be asked what actions they should, can, and will take. As far as possible, what these other persons and agencies suggest should be pinned down and discussed with the client.

NEGOTIATING SUPPORTIVE AND COLLABORATIVE ACTIONS OF OTHER PERSONS AND AGENCIES

In discussing the start-up phase, Chapter 5 recommended a negotiating strategy for achieving consensus among collaborating agencies. In the implementation phase of the task-centered model, there may be need to renegotiate with agencies because the original agreement may have deteriorated or because new developments may have recast the situation. The implementation phase may also require the practitioner to actively negotiate with private individuals who seem to be in a position to help the client perform tasks through instruction, direction, modeling, encouragement, clarification of situations, and innumerable other types of support. Individuals in potentially supportive positions include relatives, friends, neighbors, teachers, physicians, ministers, landlords, and employers.

It is not easy to construct supportive networks among others who are busy and preoccupied with their own lives or who are fearful of getting involved because of potential deleterious effects. On the other hand, their friendship, advice, encouragement, and relief of pressures may be valuable to the client. This is particularly the case if one or several of these persons are the source of pressure being felt by the client who needs and may deserve relief. The direct intervention of the practitioner may have beneficial effects beyond what the client can do for herself.

Practitioners can consult in person with those involved in conflicts related to the target problems. This interaction may successfully decrease pressures, particularly by locating what it is about the client that is precipitating and maintaining the interpersonal problem. If a process of reciprocity can be started, and if the significant other persons can perceive a potential personal benefit to accrue from helping the client, it may be possible to negotiate a series of exchanges in which the client makes certain desired concessions in return for what he can get from the other. The reverse process may also occur; the client may give in certain areas in order to get the obvious benefits from the other person.

DECISION MAKING: GOALS AND INTERVENTIONS

The preliminary decision making will have been done already in the making of the contract. (See Chapter 7.) At this stage, those understandings should be confirmed and changes made if necessary. Discussion of the preliminary decisions often will produce commitment on some aspects of the contract. In some areas, however, new and revised goals and actions may be considered and approved. Out of the alternatives generated, choices should be made. The choices are the result of considering what is known to be an effective or reasonable program to reduce the target problem, what is within the resources of the client and agency, and what is perceived by the client to be most suitable. The ability to identify the most promising interventions is the result of professional study, practical experience, supervision, and consultation.

The assessment information indicates what is within the client's social and personal resources. Agency rules, regulations, expectations, and norms outline what resources the agency has or can readily acquire. What the client perceives as actions in her interest for which she is willing to work is known already from the Step 1 and Step 2 discussions, that is, from the initial targeting of the problems and the initial contracting.

Substantial clarity is needed to ascertain that the goal is feasible, meaning capable of being done or carried out. The goal should follow the results of assessment in being within the client's abilities and resources and within the agency's ability, mission, and style. There must be a body of practice knowledge that explains and directs intervention. At the same time, care must be taken not to select trivial goals because they are thought to be easy, or mechanical goals, because they are thought to lend themselves to concreteness. Goals have to be significant for affecting the client's situation in thoroughly meaningful ways.

The product of these choices is the intervention strategy, which consists of a list of actions to be taken, when they should be taken, in what order, and by whom. It is of the highest importance that the client know and understand the strategy. It is equally significant that important others be well informed in order to neutralize their reluctance and obtain their support.

INFORMED CONSENT

The doctrine of informed consent holds that practitioners of the helping disciplines should disclose to the client information about the content and probable consequences of interventions as a matter of right, as an ethical act, and as a means for promoting individual autonomy and encouraging rational decision making. Research evidence suggests that well-informed clients who participate maximally in decisions about their treatment are likely to be those who make the most effective use of treatment.

In the practice of medicine, the doctrine of informed consent is so established that clients can sometimes sue and collect damages if the procedures for informed consent have not been appropriately followed. In the practices of helping professionals who are not physicians, the legal implications are not definite. However, the nonmedical professions are attracted to the doctrine of informed consent on ethical grounds and because of its value in motivating genuine client participation. The process of pursuing informed consent consists of

- providing the client with ample and adequate information about what will be done and why
- providing ample opportunity for the client to ask questions, get answers, and discuss concerns in a serious and responsible atmosphere
- repeating, amplifying, or correcting the information as needed

Lidz et al. (1984) found that staff communicated information not so much to ensure that clients were well informed but rather to gain their compliance with decisions that were already determined by the nature of the service delivery system and the particular training of the professional groups involved. The research also revealed that patients were not inclined to be the primary decision makers in these circumstances.

The work reported by Lidz et al. (1984) shows that there are many issues about the processes of securing informed consent. Abstract and obscure expectations routinely signed by clients without clear notions of their practicality and the means of their achievement probably represent the form but not the substance of informed consent. Clearly, more attention needs to be paid to this subject by the professions and agencies. The values involved are fundamental ones that have important consequences for achieving successful intervention.

OVERLAP OF PROCESSES

Step 3 overlaps with Step 1 (target problem identification) and with Step 2 (contracting and planning). Studies of the processes of task-centered practice reveal that practitioners do in fact overlap these steps through a process of repeating the initial exploration (Basso, 1986; Reid, 1978; Rzepnicki, 1985). For the sake of efficiency, the overlap of processes should be minimized, but not at the expense of clearing up important questions. There should be no hesitation about overlap if needed to clear up uncertainties.

IMPLEMENTING THE INTERVENTION STRATEGY

Developing Tasks

The basic rules for planning tasks were explained in Chapter 7 in connection with the initial statement of general tasks for the contract. During the middle phase, implementation, new tasks can be expected to be developed as movement or its absence occurs. In evolving and expanding tasks, the basic rules in Chapter 7 continue to apply. In addition, further work is done so that the client gets as much help as possible in carrying out his tasks. The object is to develop tasks that have a reasonable possibility of being performed. Make sure that beginning tasks are easily achievable. This better ensures that a client will be motivated to try more difficult tasks later.

Supporting Task Performance

A great deal of the implementation is devoted to supporting task performance, that is, to obtaining and using resources; showing the client how to accomplish the tasks; finding out what obstacles are barriers to good performance; removing, reducing, or altering those obstacles; finding remedies for practical barriers to task performance; alleviating cognitive barriers; and judiciously using practitioner tasks to move the activity along. Guidelines for increasing the probability that a client will carry out tasks include

1. *Ensure client understanding.* Enough discussion time needs to be allowed to ensure that the client understands and agrees to the tasks. Tasks should not be selected without a discussion that obtains genuine, or at least tentative, consent. It is common for the practitioner to suggest alternatives from which the client chooses tasks; however, good client performance can be expected only if the client is committed to the actions. Clients can be directed when they ask what to do, and clients do ask this question often. If the practitioner knows what the clients should do, she may say, for example, "What I suggest is...." Clients can be expected to change or contradict these suggestions.

2. *Identify incentives.* Establish incentives for task completion. The client needs to believe that the effort is worthwhile and that it will alleviate the problem. For example, "Talking to the children about your health problem will be stressful, but it will calm their imaginary fears."

3. *Identify rationales.* Establish the rationales for the task work. There must be an understanding of a compelling reason why the difficulties of task work should even be attempted. For example, "I have to do these things in order to live through the distress of my illness and be in a position to resume some kind of normal life later, even if I am left handicapped and disfigured."

4. *Anticipate expectable difficulties.* Raise, discuss, and elicit the client's fears about obstacles that he will encounter while working on tasks. Sift out what may or may not be real. Reassure the client maximally but do not mislead him.

5. *Summarize tasks.* At regular intervals, particularly at the conclusion of an important discussion or at the end of an interview, summarize briefly and concisely what exactly is going to be done in the next immediate time period. This process seems to be beneficial in pinning the tasks down in memory and attention.

6. *Devise concrete tasks for client performance.* Discuss plans in a manner as detailed as necessary to make concrete outlines of what the client needs to do, when, where, and with whom. With some clients and some tasks, the client's own capability and initiative will make it possible to be brief about this step. However, when the client lacks information and is fearful and inexperienced, this step may need to go into exhaustive detail.

Providing Resources.   Weissman's (1976) research on linkage technology offers a methodology for linking clients with resources. This methodology can be outlined as follows.

Locate and Select the Appropriate Community Resources.   To accomplish this activity, an agency must have extensive up-to-date lists of available resources. Knowledge of the caliber of those services is also needed. The practitioner needs to be able to describe and explain to the client the characteristics of the resources and how the particular agencies operate. She should also provide the client with an evaluation of the quality of the resources. The client is then in a position to make an informed choice among the possible resources and to have some idea of what can reasonably be expected. Weighing the advantages and disadvantages of either course, the client may also opt for not using the resources. Most often, the client will seek and should be given the practitioner's opinion of the usefulness and drawbacks to using each resource.

Connect Client to Resources Firmly.   Obtaining a good connection between client and resource is where many such efforts fail (Kirk & Greenley, 1974). It is often assumed that there is or should be a fit between what the client needs and what the resource can do. This assumption, however, is often illusory. Various connection techniques have been described.

1. *Giving simple directions.* Directing means writing out the name and address of the resource, how to get an appointment, transportation directions, and basic expectations about what the resource can be expected to provide. Simple direction appears to effect a connection when clients already know what they need but have not known how to locate the resource.
2. *Giving directions plus a name.* This technique adds to the directions the name of a person to contact.
3. *Providing a letter of introduction.* The practitioner can add a brief written statement, read and approved by the client, describing the problem and what the client would like done.
4. *Facilitating with phone calls.* In addition to or as a substitute for the foregoing, the client makes the phone call to contact the resource from the referring practitioner's office. The practitioner assists, if necessary, by making the call and turning it over to the client.
5. *Facilitating in-person contacts.* The practitioner may accompany the client to the other agency or may request a relative or friend to go with the client.

6. *Cementing the connection*. These are techniques for assuring that the connection will get results:

- *Check-back*. The client reports back to the practitioner on the effects of contact with the resource immediately after the initial connection.
- *Persisting*. The practitioner contacts the client at frequent intervals to find out what is taking place.
- *Interspersing*. The referring practitioner has an in-person contact with the client both before and after interviews with the resource.
- *Monitoring*. The referring practitioner monitors the resource provision at interviews scheduled for that purpose or during regularly scheduled interviews.

Weissman's (1976) preliminary findings in his study of the effectiveness of these techniques suggests that most referrals in the setting studied (industrial social work) were successful. The simpler techniques were effective when the target problems involved obtaining legal, financial, and health resources. Complex social-environmental and mental health problems required the most elaborate of the techniques.

Find Out Obstacles to Providing Resources.   Some resources are in short supply and cannot be easily obtained. Slowness of resource procurement and meagerness of resources can create substantial obstacles to task performance. The best substitute available will have to be used. Clients sometimes need advice, instruction, and guidance in how best to use resources, once obtained.

Show Clients How to Do Tasks through Instruction, Simulation, and Guided Practice.   The practitioner should inform the client about conditions the client does not know about or understand, the people he will be dealing with, the expectations of others, the location and structure of places he will be encountering, and the normative behaviors that will be expected by other people.

Instruction of various types is the main technique for showing clients how to perform tasks and includes imparting information, giving training in skills, and furnishing direction. *Didactic instruction* is systematic imparting of information a client needs to act in the most effective manner. For example,

> I can see from what has already happened that you need a lot of information about how to deal with your husband's anger. We have decided already that you will start a conversation with him as soon as he comes home in the evening. The conversation will be about what was good and bad in his day at the shop. Let me go over the kinds of things you could say and what would be important to him. You already know that there is a lot of talk about the plant closing down or moving South. That worry is on his mind all the time. You could start out with, "I'm glad you're home. What's the news today about what they are going to do with the plant? Any new gossip?" Because it will be a novelty for your husband to hear that from you, you could expect a grumpy response.

This kind of instruction will be interspersed with the client's reactions and further instructions to handle those reactions.

Role playing and simulation provide another type of instruction. The practitioner can set up a stage where the client rehearses actions to carry out the tasks. The practitioner, for example, can act the husband while the wife tries out the tasks. Role playing provides a vivid means to learn skills and also to find out obstacles to task performance. Role playing is easy with children. With adults it is possible but should be avoided if either the client or practitioner is embarrassed.

Guided practice can occur in an interview where the problem is played out in the session. Practitioners can guide the client by modeling, for example, preferred behavior toward a child, spouse, or relative. Family quarrels often occur in an interview. The practitioner can intervene with suggestions and create discussions to clear up misunderstandings and wrongdoing. Practitioners can accompany clients to see landlords, lawyers, judges, and relatives to show and teach clients how to handle troublesome affairs. Guidance of this kind should be partial; that is, it should concentrate on a few key actions. Clients should not be held back from following their own bent and style, nor should their confidence be undermined. They should never be denied available advice.

Accompanying the client. When necessary the practitioner can accompany the client and directly help her in performances that are difficult or where the practitioner has expert knowledge that can come immediately to the client's aid.

Other Ways to Support Task Performance

1. *Work toward task achievement in increments.* Break tasks down into parts and attend to the easiest first and the more difficult ones later. Care should be taken not to underestimate the client. However, it is easier to raise the demand from simple to more complex so as to generate success than to go backward after failure.

2. *Devise any necessary plans to help clients perform tasks.* Plans can be detailed or simple, entirely depending on what the client needs. If a client's fear, inexperience, or lack of knowledge is substantial, plans should be as detailed as needed.

3. *Summarize the plans for task performance often,* especially whenever there is a new phase.

4. *Review task performance regularly in a systematic way.* Keep understandable and simple notes on task performance. Agency resources can be developed to keep uniform records (measurements) of task performance. Task review begins with an inquiry about what the client has been able or unable to do since the last session. Credit and then set aside complete, substantial, or satisfactory performance. Then proceed to the circumstances that stood in the way of performance and the identification and analysis of barriers.

5. *Review time limits and number of sessions remaining.* Such review is a simple, straightforward matter that causes difficulties only if not done.

6. *What to do in an unexpected difficulty.* Strongly advise the client how to slow down, stay cool, temporize, procrastinate, evade, and avoid unexpected difficulties. Advise him to take time to think, and to consult the practitioner or others. Persuade him that if he feels relatively sure, he can and should act.

Obstacles to Task Performance

An obstacle to task performance is anything that gets in the way of task performance. There may be many diverse kinds of obstacles with many possible sources. Much of the time patient scrutiny of the situation and the circumstances will suggest some relatively straightforward, commonsense analysis of what is standing in the way. It is highly advisable to work on the basis of the simplest and most straightforward and obvious identification, or the most parsimonious explanation of the obstacle, rather than reach for a complex, hidden, or obscure obstacle. Thus it is more feasible, for example, to try out an explanation of lack of resources or lack of skill as the cause of an obstacle, rather than go at once for identifying the obstacle as repression, neurosis, or repetition compulsion.

What To Do If Tasks Do Not Get Done. The first assumption might be that the task planning was bad. One task-centered practitioner is always the first to say "My planning with you was obviously wrong. I'm supposed to make sure this does not happen" (Alley, 1999).

There is no way to ensure that all clients will work on all tasks and be successful. It is, however, reasonable to expect that most clients will work and that most, but not all, will be successful. There is enough evidence in the numerous trials of the task-centered model to be optimistic about outcomes. Generally, satisfactory performance on tasks is correlated with satisfactory problem alleviation, although this relationship is not perfect. Obstacles to task performance arise in three overlapping areas:

1. *In the social environment.* Obstacles in the social environment will appear as lack of resources, stress precipitated by external pressures (such as sudden illness, job loss, failure at some undertaking, loss of loved one, attack); pervasive discrimination; or dysfunctional structural problems in the social environment (such as epidemic, failures of the economic system to provide employment, poor schools, and the like).
2. *In interpersonal transactions.* Personal relationships may lack necessary intimacy, security, reinforcements, and cooperation. There may be not only deficits in these necessary relationships but also substantial conflict among the persons most important to the client.
3. *In the psychological state.* Obstacles to task performance may reside within the mind or reflect the inner psychological state of the individual. Prominent among such obstacles are unwarranted fears and suspicions of others that nevertheless have a strong influence on how the client perceives himself in the world.

Reasons for a Good Deal of Low Task Performance

1. *The client lacks concrete resources to facilitate task work.* Examples of necessary sustaining resources are money, medical and psychiatric care, adequate housing, adequate work and school, or adequate child care provided by relatives, homemakers, or daycare.

2. *The client lacks necessary reinforcements from other persons such as family members, peers, or authorities.* Those other important persons may be estranged, uncaring, hostile, oppressive, or exploitative, or they may be unable to help the client because of their own problems.

3. *The client lacks skills, and does not know how to do the task work.* She may be painfully awkward or may have only enough skill to perform incompletely or erratically.

4. *The client has adverse beliefs.* His beliefs may lead him to thinking that the tasks have little value or will have negative consequences. He may be afraid of taking the task actions.

5. *The client lacks capacity for task performance.* There may be some incapacity to make attempts. She may misunderstand the task.

6. *The practitioner may be biased and unskilled.*

Guidelines for Overcoming Obstacles

Removing, reducing, or altering obstacles demands that a systematic plan be developed to remedy the practical barriers to task performance, e.g., lack of skills, lack of cooperation and support from others, or lack of resources. The plan should include alleviating cognitive barriers to task performance through discussion and counseling regarding fears, suspicions, lack of knowledge, and adverse beliefs.

Listed here are some specific explanations for clients' low task performance as well as some specific guidelines that are frequently applicable for alleviating these obstacles to performance. The practitioner will need to exercise judgment in particular circumstances.

Lack of Concrete Resources.   The practitioner procures the resources at once by ordering them, if that is possible, or by using the referral techniques discussed earlier. If necessary resources are not immediately available or accessible, the client should be instructed to withstand delay. Alternative resources should also be developed. At worst, the client should be helped, as best one can, to tolerate and relinquish expectation of the resource. However, if a genuinely necessary resource is totally unavailable and if no satisfactory substitute can be made, then task performance is not within the control of the client and probably will not occur.

Lack of Reinforcements.   The practitioner discusses and guides the client, showing him how to communicate and behave toward important other people, shows others how to respond, communicates what actions others should take, and lets others know that what they do will be reciprocated. The practitioner can undertake facilitating tasks to approach the important other people (teacher, supervisor, spouse, parent, child, relative, etc.). The practitioner should interpret the client's actions; learn what the other persons could do to help the client; discuss what the others might gain; and plan a program with them. The practitioner can confer, refer, request, instruct, negotiate, or accompany the client, and, if necessary, advocate on the client's behalf.

Lack of Skill.   In the sessions, the practitioner carries out work with the client to help her acquire skills. The techniques of instruction have already been described. The practitioner can refer the client to available experts to augment this learning of social skills.

Adverse Beliefs.   The client's own experience may have induced beliefs, convictions, or opinions that hamper or inhibit task performance. Examples of inhibitors are low self-esteem; awareness of cultural and economic oppression and discrimination; well-established ideas that others view him as lowly; and a genuine disregard and disapproval of dominant customs, folkways, ethics, or social conventions. Unrealistically low self-evaluations are learned attitudes; they decrease with factual, realistic discussion of their inappropriateness. This is particularly so if these discussions are supported by real experience with some others who like, respect, and appreciate the client. Few people cling to low self-esteem if it can be transformed into a more satisfying self-appraisal. Some people might not be able to make this switch, but they are few indeed.

Beliefs based on a negative attitude toward dominant customs, on the other hand, may be intransigent. Possibly an appeal to basic self-interest and an open discussion of the pros and cons of a particular view may succeed in changing the person's opinion or may not. In any case, the client can at least understand how to be protected from clashes with convention.

Lack of Capacity.   First, caution is called for to avoid underestimating clients, be they young, antagonistic, old, or mentally handicapped. Obviously, children too young to have developed sophisticated verbal and cognitive skills and persons seriously deteriorated and ill probably lack capacity for many acts. Those clients should be cared for and protected. However, the actions usually called for are to scale down the tasks to be within the person's capacity and to involve others in doing the tasks for and with the client.

Practitioner Bias and Lack of Skills.   Practitioners should restrain their biases. Ideally, lack of skills should be remedied by in-service training and professional education. However, experience is a masterful teacher. Experience and access to a library or a good resource person are excellent ways to improve skills.

Checklist for Overcoming Obstacles.   If tasks do not get done, here is a checklist of what to look at.

1. Are you working on a problem of high interest to the client?
2. If working on a mandated problem, does the client understand the consequences of ignoring, avoiding, or failing to change?

3. Does the client understand the tasks? Has she been shown how to do them and given help in getting them done?
4. Is the goal specific?
5. Have you reviewed the target problems and task sufficiently, and adjusted the tasks often enough to fit the client and the situation?
6. Have all the available resources been fully provided?

Planning and Stating Practitioner Tasks

Practitioner tasks are actions to be taken by the practitioner on behalf of the client and between the in-person sessions. These actions are intended to support the client's task performance. There are three types of practitioner tasks.

1. Getting information the client needs in order to perform tasks.
2. Conferring with other agencies to interpret the client's needs, develop a positive attitude toward the client, and arrange for commitments to deliver services.
3. Conferring with relatives, friends, and officials to negotiate actions they will take on the client's behalf.

Practitioners are obligated to report to clients what they did, what they found, and, when they fail to accomplish a specific task, the reason for nonperformance.

VERIFICATION AND MONITORING: CHECKING ON PROGRESS OR DIFFICULTIES

To verify their effectiveness in a simple manner, the interventions and their results should be monitored regularly to test, confirm, and substantiate the effects of the intervention. Such monitoring is not the same as scientific research into effectiveness, which requires a methodology to show that the intervention being tested was in fact responsible for the changes occurring in the clients and/or the situation. Scientific methodology takes into consideration that change may be due to factors other than the interventions, for example, passage of time; luck, chance, or accident; and developmental, economic, or social events. On a case-by-case basis, however, periodic verification as part of practice is both common sense and makes for accountable practice, that is, practice that can be justified, substantiated, and made clear and credible to client, peers, and authorities, and which is cost effective.

Monitoring Guidelines.   At each interview, check the following:

- Task performance
- Problem status and change
- New or revised problems

Caution.   Do not expect spectacular improvements. Do not be surprised by no movement. Do not be surprised by real or supposed new or revised problems.

These are all ordinary happenings in the intervals between contacts. Monitoring problem status leads to clear pictures of alterations in problems.

There are many ways to track or monitor cases. Some methods need sophisticated research techniques and are practical only if an agency provides staff with the necessary training, time, and consultation. Simple monitoring devices can be used, however, and although they will not satisfy the demands of research, they will satisfy minimum accountability demands. They will provide concrete information to guide practice in particular cases toward productive efforts.

Figure 8.2 shows an example of a simple monitoring chart. Case circumstances and the preferences of the practitioner and agency will influence what kinds of records are used to pin down the facts uncovered in a verification process. Many types of structured notations, charts, graphs, and brief narratives are used (Epstein, 1985).

FIGURE 8.2 Example of a Simple Monitoring Chart

INSTRUCTION: Put check mark indicating the rating

1. Task performance	Complete	Substantial	Partial	Minimal	No opportunity
T_1	☐	☐	☐	☐	☐
T_2	☐	☐	☐	☐	☐
T_3	☐	☐	☐	☐	☐

2. Problem status	No longer present	Considerably alleviated	Slightly alleviated	No change	Worse
P_1	☐	☐	☐	☐	☐
P_2	☐	☐	☐	☐	☐
P_3	☐	☐	☐	☐	☐

3. Problem altered	Explain
P_1	
P_2	
P_3	

What to Do with the Verification Checks.   When monitoring task performance, complete or substantial achievement is an excellent result. Partial or minimal achievement is a signal to study what obstacles are in the way. Obstacles can often be resolved by following the guidelines already given. Another way is to revise the tasks. Study of task-centered practice suggests that if a task has not been completed after three attempts, that task should be changed. Observing that the client had no opportunity to carry out the tasks provides information to interpret failure objectively.

Interpreting Performance Ratings.   When monitoring problem status, making a rating of "considerably alleviated" indicates a success. Under adverse conditions, "slightly alleviated" is not a failure. However, when ratings are in the "slightly alleviated" or the "no change" categories, the intervention strategy may need revision. Ratings of "worse" might or might not mean that the interventions are responsible; such ratings might also be the result of stresses in the environment. In any case, "worse" signals a need for thorough reevaluation starting with the client's health; deterioration in the environment; hostile actions from relatives, friends, and authorities; and adverse effects of an agency program. At the very least, any conditions that jeopardize the client should be attended to. It is always possible that we cannot find out or understand the cause of deterioration. It stands to reason, however, that if a client's problem becomes worse, more of the same interventions are not called for. At present, not much is known about the cause of deterioration in the course of intervention.

Single-Subject Research Designs

The basic strategy for assessing treatment in *individual cases* is the group of procedures known as single-subject research designs. These are sets of information collected over time about an individual (or group) under different conditions. Data collected under a certain condition are compared to data collected under other conditions. For instance, information may be obtained to compare the client's behavior, thoughts, feelings, and circumstances before treatment—the baseline—and at stated times after treatment began. Similar comparisons may be made at the end of treatment and at planned times selected for follow-up (Barlow & Hersen, 1984; Bloom, Fischer, & Orma, 1999; Levy, 1983; Thomas, 1983).

Corcoran and Fischer (1987, pp. 6–9) explain the basic components of single-system designs:

1. *Specification of the problem* (see Chapter 6). The problem the practitioner and client agree needs to be worked on—a problem that can be formulated in terms of behavior, cognition, or affect—is specified.
2. *Selection of a way to measure the problem.* There is a large variety of ways to measure problems:
   - *Behavioral observation,* that is, observations made of the frequency, duration, and/or interval measures, meaning whether or not the behavior of interest occurs during a stated time interval.

- *Logs,* that is, brief journals kept by the clients of events considered relevant to the problem.
- *Self-anchored and rating scales,* that is, individually constructed paper-and-pencil scales that ask how the client perceives the problem, the degree or extent to which the client experiences some feeling, thought, or condition. A rating scale is similar except that the client does not rate himself. Instead, someone else uses the scale to rate the client.
- *Unobtrusive measures,* that is, data collected from a source other than direct face-to-face involvement of the client, such as data from case records or from one-way mirror observations.
- *Standardized measures,* that is, short, paper-and-pencil questionnaires that have been tested and standardized. An excellent guide to the availability and use of such measures is found in Corcoran and Fischer (1987).

3. *Implementation of the design,* that is, information about the problem is systematically and regularly collected.

These comparisons are typically charted on a graph for ease of visual inspection. This is the simplest way to accomplish a quick and ready estimate of what kind of movement is occurring in the problem while the client is receiving treatment and at follow-up. A review of all the information will provide data from which to make a clinical judgment as to the success or degree of success in attaining the desired goal. (See Chapters 12, 13, and 14 for examples.)

There are more complicated procedures to follow if one wishes to determine the relationship between the intervention and the change in the client's problems. These procedures require specialized training that is beyond the scope of the present book.

Self-Assessment: A Means to Evaluate One's Own Practice

Self-assessment practices are defined as single-subject designs that have the purpose of studying the work of only one practitioner and that use both quantitative and qualitative approaches to collect and analyze information (Alter & Evens, 1990). Teaching-learning aids exist to help acquaint oneself with a range of designs, based on and adapted from the single-study method. These materials are accessible and can be perused by practitioners to locate those that appear feasible in the practice setting, with the types of clients one has, and with one's own personal style.

Detailed explication of the various designs available to evaluate one's own work can be found in Bloom et al. (1999) and Corcoran and Fischer (1987).

REVISING THE INTERVENTION STRATEGY

During intervention, a problem can change its appearance enough to warrant redefinition of the problem and a revised contract. Contract revision should follow the monitoring checkup if progress is unsatisfactory or exceeds what was expected, if new problems emerge, or if old problems take on different characteristics.

The contract can be revised at any time during the established time limits. Revisions do not necessarily call for an extension of the time limits. The new contract can facilitate the achievement of goals already set. Any time an extension is justified, it should be provided. Without necessitating formal revision, whenever task performance is poor, the contract should be revised. If the support services already in place do not work or if the resources supplied are ineffective, remedial planning should take place. This means that the negotiations with other agencies should be reviewed and changes made. Understandings arrived at earlier with relatives and officials should be revised. When it turns out that the practitioner-supported tasks are not feasible or are ineffective, they should be revised.

The whole purpose of verifying the effects of the intervention is to make midcourse corrections while the case is active. These corrections will temporarily destabilize the structure of the task-centered model. However, as soon as a revised intervention strategy is decided on, the regular procedures can be put back into place.

EXAMPLES OF TASK-CENTERED INTERVENTION

ELEANOR

PRIOR TO TASK-CENTERED INTERVENTION

Eleanor, a 15-year-old African American girl, was referred by the juvenile court for foster home placement. She had been living since early childhood with her widowed grandmother, a recipient of social security. Her grandmother had complained to the police that Eleanor was out of control. Eleanor was pregnant, refused to attend school, and was argumentative and disobedient. The grandmother feared that Eleanor's future was in jeopardy and wanted her to be "straightened out." The police took Eleanor to the detention home with her grandmother's consent.

Eleanor was in good health with no evidence of mental handicap or disturbance. Her grandmother was elderly, infirm, and poor; a decent, caring person, worried and concerned about Eleanor's bad conduct. The grandmother's home was plain and comfortable, located in an insecure public housing high-rise.

Eleanor's father left when she was an infant. She was an only child. Her mother was an excitable woman given to bouts of public drunkenness, lonely, often receiving public aid, and sometimes working as a day housecleaner.

Eleanor had been given over to her maternal grandmother to be reared. For short periods, she lived with her mother to give her grandmother a respite. Eleanor and her mother fought because the mother was excessively demanding that Eleanor be perfect.

The grandmother cooperated fully in planning Eleanor's placement. The court's reason for placement was to see Eleanor through her pregnancy, arrange for child care for the baby and continued schooling for Eleanor, and provide supervision to control her sexual behavior and argumentativeness.

Eleanor stayed in the foster home two years with her baby girl. She attended school erratically and eventually dropped out altogether. Infant care was left to the foster mother. The infant was healthy and normal. Eleanor fought with her foster mother. She continued to be argumentative, disobedient, and undisciplined. Then she ran away and left her baby in the foster home.

Months later, Eleanor reappeared and went to live with her grandmother again. She came back with a second baby girl. The father was a 22-year-old unemployed youth who was also the father of the first child. Their relationship was a continuing one. He was the only boy Eleanor dated. Both her grandmother and her foster mother disapproved of him because they thought he was a "layabout" without prospects. When Eleanor became pregnant for the second time, her boyfriend took her to his relatives in the South until after the baby was born. Eleanor's grandmother had been stretching her social security to provide for herself, Eleanor, and the second baby.

TASK-CENTERED INTERVENTION

Application

Eleanor applied to the agency for return of her first child.

Client Target Problems

1. Eleanor does not have custody of her child.
2. Eleanor is herself still a ward of the court.
3. Eleanor does not know what the agency requires of her in order to be freed of their control.

Mandated Problems

1. *Court:* Eleanor and her first child are both minors in need of supervision (legal mandate).
2. *Agency:* Eleanor lacks adequate parenting skills, education for becoming self-supporting, and income for self-care, and she is probably emotionally disturbed (professional opinion).

Client Priorities

1. Get custody of her first child.
2. Find out the law and agency requirements preventing her from getting her child back.

Negotiating Strategy

1. Intra-agency conferences to support work on the client's priorities.
2. Conferences with the court to provide evidence of Eleanor's ability to care for her child.

Assessment

Eleanor became a ward of the court because of having become pregnant out of marriage and because of her own family's lack of resources and skills to cope with this problem. She did not behave maternally toward her first child because of youth and inexperience. Her anger was due to being kept away from her stable relationship with her boyfriend and her feeling of being denied satisfactory work and life opportunities. Now only a few months away from being 18 years old and automatically freed of court supervision, Eleanor wants to be independent and get what belongs to her—the child in foster care. Eleanor is capable even though she lacks social skills. She has a basically good relationship with her mother, grandmother, and boyfriend. She lacks confidence in herself and is fearful of the power of the court and agency.

Contract

Target Problems	*Goals and General Tasks*
1. Lack of child custody.	1. Obtain child custody.
2. Lack of skills and resources for independent living.	2. Enroll in continuation school.
Time Limit: 8 weeks	3. Obtain public assistance grant.

Major Interventions

1. Eleanor was fully informed about legal and administrative requirements to explain her status as ward of the court and her child's status.
2. Specific tasks were planned to help her acquire basic child care information, to follow procedures for re-enrolling in school and obtaining public assistance, to share household duties with her grandmother.

Client's Response

Eleanor became extremely agitated when she found that she could not be freed of court supervision unless she changed her child care behavior. Once this was clear, Eleanor was committed to doing what was required in order to win her independence.

Practitioner Tasks

1. Teaching basic child care in interviews
2. Mediating with grandmother about housework planning and implementation

3. Instructing Eleanor in legal and agency administrative requirements
4. Negotiating on Eleanor's behalf with the agency, court, public assistance, and school

Obstacles to Task Achievement and Interventions

1. Eleanor's rage at authorities. The rules of the agency were explained. Their rationale was discussed. What seemed unfair was openly confronted.
2. Eleanor's inconsiderateness of her grandmother. Joint sessions with the grandmother were held. Reciprocal tasks were developed so that the grandmother could get some benefit from keeping Eleanor.
3. Foster mother's resentment of plan to return child to Eleanor. The practitioner taught Eleanor how to refrain from provoking the foster mother on visits to her child. She was not to visit in the home but to take the child out and return her clean, cared for, and comfortable. The foster mother was offered an opportunity to express her opinion through agency channels and in court. She did not do so.
4. Eleanor's delayed contact with school for re-enrollment. The practitioner gave repeated drill in how to talk to school officials so as to diminish Eleanor's fear of them. It had been that fear that made her delay contacts.

OUTCOME

Eleanor became adept at feeding and clothing both children, keeping them clean, and responding to them. The grandmother helped generously. Eleanor completed all steps to obtain public assistance for herself. Last, she finally completed re-enrollment procedures for school. The court was pleased but cautious. Hence, although they ordered the child in placement to be returned, they set up a 6-month continuance for the agency to monitor and help maintain Eleanor's gains.

ELAINE

REFERRAL

Elaine, a 5-year-old white child, was referred by a public assistance worker because of "bizarre" behavior.

Social Context

Elaine lived with her widowed maternal grandmother (age 73) and her maternal unmarried uncle (age 45). She could not be cared for by her parents. Her mother most of the time was either in the state hospital or under its supervision in semi-independent living. Her father lived alone in bachelor housing. He was a seasonal farm laborer with meager earnings. The grandmother reported to the public assistance worker that Elaine stayed in bed under the covers in cold weather. She had tantrums, could not talk in sentences, and could not be toilet-trained. The grandmother feared Elaine would be "mad" like her mother. The grandmother and uncle were both illiterate. Both were responsible and concerned persons, kept a clean home, and were decent and considerate to neighbors and authorities. They were supported by public assistance.

Target Problems

Grandmother: (1) She was unable to provide proper developmental conditions for Elaine. (2) She was afraid Elaine is "crazy."

Mandated Problems

Mental Health Agency, Public Health Agency, Community Services Agency: All agree Elaine is "developmentally disturbed." The mental health agency diagnosis is mental retardation; their recommendation is special education.

Client Priorities

Grandmother: Proper training resources for Elaine.

Negotiating Strategy

Questions were raised in the interagency conferences about the propriety of this grandmother, at 73, being the chief person responsible for Elaine's rearing. Because she might be short-lived and become infirm, some agency officials thought that Elaine should be placed in an institution. Consensus was achieved that the agencies would respect the caring qualities in the grandmother's home and her cooperativeness. This meant that for the time being no plans for placement away from the grandmother would be made.

TASK-CENTERED INTERVENTION

Assessment

Elaine is a mentally retarded child being reared by relatives of limited intellectual capacity. Elaine's eccentric behavior is due to lack of training in speech and social skills. The home climate is excellent.

Contract

Target Problem: Lack of child training resources
Goal and General Task: Secure child training
Time Limit: 8 weeks

Major Interventions

1. Psychological and psychiatric evaluations were secured.
2. The results of these evaluations were explained to the grandmother and uncle.

3. The grandmother agreed to apply for Elaine's admittance to a local daycare facility. Transportation was arranged for the grandmother to attend parent education sessions.
4. Resources were obtained as follows:
    a. The daycare center officials were influenced to admit Elaine for alternate half-days despite her developmental deficits. The primary agency assured the daycare center that services would be provided to augment the regular daycare program.
    b. Individual speech therapy was obtained in a clinic located in another city. Transportation for several times each week was arranged.
    c. Elaine's admittance to a local special education class in the public school was secured for alternate half-days. She was to learn motor coordination. Transportation was arranged.
    d. A schedule for Elaine's attendance at all these resources was made up. The schedule was distributed to all agencies and explained fully to the grandmother and uncle.
    e. Regular reporting and coordinating conferences were set up between all the involved agencies.
    f. It was arranged for the grandmother to join and participate in a parent group at the daycare center.

Client Response

Positive

Practitioner Tasks

1. Arranging for evaluations
2. Locating and developing child training resources in a sparsely populated rural area

Obstacles to Task Achievement and Intervention

1. Some of the local agencies opposed Elaine's remaining with her aged and limited grandmother. This was resolved through numerous conference discussions.
2. There was a lack of readily available resources for child training in the locality. The practitioner organized and packaged the resource by combining various existing services.
3. The grandmother was sometimes late to pick up Elaine from the various places she was attending. This was overcome by planned, regular reminders.

OUTCOME

The "crazy" behaviors stopped. Elaine began learning to talk and play with others. She liked music and water play. She started to use scissors, modeling clay, and cookie cutters. She was clearly a happier child.

JOHN

PRIOR TO TASK-CENTERED INTERVENTION

John, 15, a black teenager, lived with his grandparents who were his legal guardians. At age 13, he began running away. He was finally made a ward of the court and was referred to the agency for supervision. After two more runaways, John was placed in detention and thereafter in a foster home.

TASK-CENTERED INTERVENTION

Client Target Problems

Grandparents: (1) John does not want to go to school. (2) He stays out too late at night.
John: (1) Too many people are trying to raise me. (2) My grandmother pays too much attention to my aunts' advice.

Mandated Problems

Court: John is a minor in need of supervision (legal mandate).
Agency: His grandparents are too strict (professional opinion).
Foster Mother: Too many people are involved in supervising John (individual opinion).

Client Priorities

Grandparents and John: John should return home.

Negotiating Strategy

Intra-agency conferences reached agreement on goals; conferences with the court provided information about what evidence was needed to order John returned to his grandparents' home.

Social Context

John was friendly and willing to talk. He had a realistic appraisal of the bad consequences of not attending school. He stated that his truancy, staying out late, and running away were a "disease." The grandmother was cooperative but anxious. The grandfather left all decisions up to his wife. The housing is a single dwelling in an old and rundown public housing project. There was no evidence of health or psychiatric problems. The natural parents were not in the picture. The father had been absent for years. The mother was in a state hospital. The grandparents were on social security.

According to John, the grandmother discussed every bit of his behavior with his aunts. The aunts were "all over him" and his grandmother, telling him and his grandmother what he must do. John frequently stayed away from home overnight.

This is the runaway behavior. He went to a friend's house. He did not call home because he was afraid his grandmother would holler. He did not have any safe way to get home late at night. So he stayed overnight with whatever friend he was visiting. John ditched school because that was more "fun" than staying at school. John and his friends were not into drugs or any other antisocial behavior. They "played around" with girls. This worries the grandparents.

Assessment

This problem is one of unskillful handling by anxious grandparents and an expectable rebellious attitude in a normal teenager.

Contract

Target Problems	*Goals and General Tasks*
1. Separation of family.	1. Reunite the family.
2. John's staying out late.	2. Arrange for safe transportation and phone calls home to cut down staying out late.
3. John's not attending school.	3. Cut down truancy from school.
	4. Stop the aunts' interference.
	Time Limit: 8 weeks

Major Interventions

1. Negotiations with the school resulted in their agreement to readmit John.
2. Negotiated agreements between John and his grandmother set rules for his staying out and getting transportation home.
3. Negotiated rules with the aunts regulated their contacts. They are to talk directly to John, rather than go through the grandmother.
4. John went home on a trial basis.

Client Response

Moderately positive, with reservations.

Practitioner Tasks

1. Explored possibilities of the school to accept John and of alternative schools
2. Interpreted situation to court

Obstacles to Task Achievement and Interventions

1. The grandmother was afraid to tackle the aunts about their interference. Rehearsal and guided practice were repeated several times. The practitioner conferred with the aunts.

2. John could not tolerate going back to school. The problem was retargeted to lack of job training. Referrals were made to explore job training opportunities for teenagers.
3. John was erratic in following the rules of staying out late. There was review and repetition of the contract, explaining the effect of nonperformance on the court: The court would be reluctant to let John go home.

OUTCOME

John agreed to the necessity for seeking job training instead of re-enrolling in school. The plan to stop the aunts' interference was fully performed. Staying out late was cut down 80 percent. The court released John to his grandparents.

SUMMARY OF BASIC ACTIONS

The basic essential actions to implement the task-centered approach are as follows:

1. Define and specify target problems to a maximum of three.
2. Assess the target problem, the social context, and the cognitive–affective circumstances of the problem(s).
3. Generate alternatives.
4. Negotiate supportive and collaborative actions of other persons and agencies.
5. Confirm goals, select what will be done, and design the details of the intervention strategy (decision making).
6. Carry out the strategy, relying upon developing tasks; supporting task performance; finding out obstacles to task performance; planning actions to remove, reduce, or alter obstacles; remedying practical barriers; alleviating cognitive barriers; and planning and stating practitioner tasks.
7. Verify and monitor progress.
8. Revise plan as needed.*

*Adapted from D'Zurilla and Goldfried (1971) and Brown (1980).

CHAPTER NINE

FOURTH STEP: TERMINATION

Discontinuance, Extension, and Monitoring

TERMINATING BY PLAN

The subject of termination of treatment has not undergone much study. It has been thought of as part of the whole process of intervention and thus is hard to consider separately. In practice, the criteria for termination are judgments about clients' mental states and predictions about their future actions.

Practitioners vary considerably in their ideas of the exact criteria that indicate treatment is completed. It is admittedly difficult to accurately predict what a person can and will do in the future. Despite these difficulties, for practical reasons, we make these predictions all the time, based in part on empirical information and in part on intuition and experience to supplement or substitute for hard information.

Rules in some agencies put a limit on length of service so that the termination time is prescribed by agency policy or established practice. These rules are laid down to economize on resources, to hold down waiting lists, to make use of the motivating pressure of deadlines or cutoff dates, and to conform to the reimbursement policies of third-party payers or insurance companies.

A consensus in the field of practice maintains that terminations should not just be stumbled into but should be planned (Levinson, 1977; Siporin, 1975). Yet the little empirical evidence that exists suggests considerable diversity among practitioners in how they go about planning and implementing termination (Fortune, 1985a). There is also increasing attention to the built-in termination planning in brief treatment because of its being technologically advanced in its specificity, differentiation, and evaluation of results (Pardes & Pincus, 1981). (See Figure 9.1.)

Terminating because goals have been met is one of the common criteria suggested for ending treatment. The practice problem with this criterion is the uncertainty about whether the practitioner's or the client's goals drive the decision to terminate and whether the goals are feasible under all the circumstances. In the task-centered model it is expected that goals will be reasonably definite, reasonably specific and concrete, and hence capable of being identified and measured when they have been achieved. Many clients will approximate rather than completely achieve goals.

Time limits set within the first few interviews provide structure for setting an end to the treatment sequence. Time limits enable clients to exercise control over their participation. It is a rare client indeed who truly becomes unhappy or is set adrift when termination occurs. Practitioners tend to overestimate the value they have for a client's well-being. The rewards of termination to a client are great: more money in the pocket (if the client is paying a fee), more time, freedom from the practitioner's influence and surveillance, and greater independence.

A practitioner may provoke a client's unhappiness about termination if she has overvalued the relationship and if she has communicated that belief to the client by word or deed.

The duration of the sequence will have been established in the contract. (See Chapter 7.) In order to effect an orderly and appropriate termination, the following guidelines are suggested:

1. *Reminders.* At each interview there should be a reminder to the client about which interview is being currently conducted. The fact that the next-to-last or last interview is occurring should not come as a surprise or a shock to either the practitioner or the client.
2. *End at next-to-last interview.* The next-to-last interview is the last in which actual work on the problem is handled.

FIGURE 9.1   Detail of Map

Step 4	*Termination*
	END
	EXTEND on evidence of client commitment
	MONITOR when mandated by law, court order, or formal agency requirements

3. *Reviewing and pointing to the future.* The last interview, the termination interview, should be a review of what has taken place. The purpose is to fix events in mind so they may be recalled to guide future problem solving.

There are five communications in a termination interview:

- "This is what we accomplished."
- "This is what we did not accomplish."
- "This is what you did."
- "This is what I did."
- "Come back if you need to."

A number of problems have been noted in terminations, but it is difficult to know how frequently these problems occur or how important they are. A pervasive professional folklore views termination problems as potentially difficult and defeating to the treatment aims. Hence, many practitioners are reluctant to adhere to termination decisions made in a contract, fearing that the termination will adversely affect the gains made.

Observations of practice within the task-centered approach have shown that some clients do not show up for the final or termination interview. The explanation for this finding is not known, but it is possible that some clients perceive the work to be over and have no interest in a summary; a few may develop separation anxiety and feel upset by the ending, preferring to avoid it. Practitioners may feel distress over ending a sequence of interviews; on the one hand they may criticize themselves for things they now wish they had done differently; or they may have become genuinely fond of certain clients and hate to see them go. Sometimes a practitioner is proud of a client's accomplishments and of his own work and does not want the experience to end.

Other termination problems have been perceived and described generally by Levinson (1977). Those problems are summarized here:

1. The client may cling to the treatment experience and to the relationship with the practitioner.
2. The practitioner who sees termination as traumatic may unintentionally postpone the termination or support the unrealistic wishes of the client to hold onto the experience.
3. The problems may suddenly emerge all over again or in an aggravated form.
4. Entirely new problems may emerge in the last interview.
5. The client may make rushed efforts to create intimate friends to substitute for the practitioner.
6. The client may react defensively toward the feelings aroused by termination: she may be unmoved by the ending, begin complaining, become critical, or act out (for example, become angry or miss appointments).
7. If the practitioner reacts defensively, the client may become convinced that he cannot get along without the practitioner, setting off an angry, threatened,

fatigued reaction in the practitioner and starting a set of circular behaviors in which the client and practitioner reinforce each other's problems.

It is wise not to anticipate that these complicated problems will necessarily occur in implementing a planned termination. Their likelihood is diminished by the relative brevity of the time used in task-centered intervention, by the business-like arrangements resulting from the explicitness of the contract, and by the congruence between practitioner and client on target problem focus, goals, and priorities.

However, should untoward difficulties arise, it is necessary to analyze and reorganize the client's thoughts and attitudes toward a practitioner to whom the client has become emotionally attached. This is time consuming, but only in extreme circumstances should an extension be given to work through these feelings. Rather, the time for such work should be obtained by putting aside any planned discussion about the problems and concentrating on the feelings aroused by the termination. That process often involves intimate discussions about feelings. It is better to place a businesslike constraint on the working relationship than to face the separation troubles accompanying the loss of a practitioner who has become too important to a client.

Many clients experience a normal and natural degree of dependency. The practitioner may in reality be a vital source of resources, advice, and affection. There is nothing at all wrong with clients being dependent when they lack resources in themselves or in the environment. Practitioners should make sure that clients are fully informed about alternative resources and rewards and grasp the fact that they have managed and can manage on their own. Clients can also touch base with the agency and the practitioner from time to time if they really need to, including returning for the same or another problem. If the provision of service was businesslike in the first place, termination will probably be the same.

UNPLANNED DISCONTINUANCE

Clients who drop out of treatment without a termination plan or contrary to the termination plan pose other problems. For one, substantial irregularity in appointment keeping causes expensive problems in scheduling staff and is a real waste of agency resources. The only way an agency can protect itself from substantial loss of resources from no-shows is to overbook, which causes other problems.

It is assumed that if the client were to continue treatment, she would receive benefits that would be lost if she were to drop out. On the other hand, evidence suggests that clients often discontinue treatment because they have received the help they want and need at the moment. Some clients may be dissatisfied with the terms, conditions, and content of the help they are being offered.

It has been suggested that unplanned discontinuance may be minimized by congruence between practitioner and client on target problems, contract agreements, and keeping the contact short (Parad & Parad, 1990; Reid & Shyne, 1969; Tolson & Brown, 1981).

EXTENSIONS BY PLAN

The issue of extending the sequence comes up when the client is dissatisfied with termination, when the practitioner wishes for more time to increase the effectiveness of the treatment, or when there are some known conditions or events forthcoming in the immediate future that can be helped by continuing the contact. Extensions should be mutually agreed to by practitioner and client with the number of additional interviews made definite in a revised contract.

Extending when the original contract has failed to meet expectations on the assumption that the practitioner and the client will try a little harder is unwise. Some problems are intractable because of client characteristics, excess deficits in the environment, lack of knowledge in the field, agency limitations, and lack of practitioner skill. Most social and personal problems are long-lived and recur repeatedly. Expectations of "big cures" are unrealistic. If everything possible has been done and has failed, extending treatment makes no sense. After a lapse of time, if the client returns and the case is reopened, the outcome may be better.

Studies in the task-centered model show that most clients appeared satisfied with the amount of time in brief treatment but some would have liked more contact, meaning one or two more interviews. Other research in brief treatment has shown similar results. Women want additional contact more often than men. A recent study of these issues concludes that clients who react negatively to termination do so because their expected goals have not been attained, or because they have developed a dependency upon the practitioner that may not be resolved (O'Connor & Reid, 1986). Because both these reactions are legitimate, it might be appropriate under particular circumstances to extend to the extent necessary to clarify expectations, substantially revise the treatment plan if possible, and work through the treatment-induced dependency.

Extensions are warranted if the target problem is self-limiting (that is, if the target problem will dissipate in the near future) and the client can use additional help to complete tasks. For example, a marital separation will occur in a few days or weeks, a discharge from a hospital is scheduled, or a move from one apartment to another is scheduled for a few weeks in the future. Extensions are also warranted when the client asks for an extension and can state what work is to be done. An example might be when a family has moved and is settled in a new apartment and the parents want to work on a parent–child conflict.

UNPLANNED EXTENSIONS

The practitioner should be vigilant about the tendency to drift into long-term, open-ended treatment (driven perhaps by desires to attain elusive goals) without a clear contract. These could be called unplanned extensions and are full of problems. For instance, the interpersonal practitioner–client relationship can become overly important. Clients may be misled into expecting results that are not likely to occur. Caseloads become filled with cases that show little or no movement. All the while, waiting lists may accumulate, and new clients may go without help because there is not enough room for them in the caseload.

MONITORING

Monitoring takes place because the practitioner and the agency initiate it. Clients do not initiate this process. Monitoring means to watch, observe, or check for a particular purpose and to keep track, regulate, or control. The circumstances that call for monitoring in social welfare are of two types: those required by court orders and those advocated for professional reasons.

In numerous instances, a court orders supervision, for example, foster care, probation and parole, or legal protective guardianship. This type of monitoring can be structured by clearly and accurately informing the client of the legal requirements and establishing a schedule for episodic client reporting or practitioner visits.

Monitoring for professional reasons, mainly to enable the practitioner to check regularly on maintenance or deterioration of gains, requires discussion with the client. The intention of professional monitoring is to detect early problems and to provide early interventions. This type of monitoring ought to be set up only if the client is willing. There should be some reason to believe that early detection can actually be performed, and that if performed, a remedy is known and available. Most professional monitoring tends to become surveillance.

In some settings, oversight of clients is standard procedure. Effective preventive interventions on an individual case basis are needed and wanted, but our understanding of early warning signs of problems is limited. Ideas about early warning signals are heavily weighted by ideology and intuitions. It would seem more efficient to avoid cluttering up caseloads with long-term, inactive cases by reserving monitoring for cases where surveillance or supervision is court-ordered or where eligibility has to be reviewed due to legal or administrative requirements. Short-term monitoring is reasonable if it has a clear-cut objective. Ordinarily, ongoing monitoring in the absence of a mandate should be avoided. Instead, clients should be encouraged to return when and if they need further service.

MAINTAINING GAINS

A great deal remains to be understood about how best to maintain gains that occur in treatment. Behavior modification practitioners and researchers have given the most attention to this subject (Gambrill, 1983). The following guidelines, suggested by Gambrill, have merit for assisting in maintaining gains:

1. Ensure that significant other persons provide ongoing support for new behaviors.
2. Ensure that the improvements are continuously useful and are perceived by the client as useful; otherwise, they will not be continued.

3. Substitute natural reinforcers in the real environment for reinforcers used during the treatment experience such as therapist approval, token points, and so forth.
4. Ensure that reinforcement is on an intermittent, real-life schedule to replace the planned, regularized reinforcement provided in treatment sessions.
5. Help clients learn to perform actions they can carry out independently after the sequence is finished.
6. Help clients attribute their gains to their own effort and perceive themselves to be in control.
7. Help clients understand the rationale for maintaining change.
8. Help clients anticipate and recover from relapses.
9. Provide plans for booster sessions with the therapist.
10. Arrange follow-up contacts, with the client's agreement, to check on progress and problems.

Rzepnicki (1991) has constructed a set of strategies for maintaining intervention gains. These strategies have empirical support in the research literature:

1. Create similarity between the intervention situation and the client's natural environment:
   - Select a setting that resembles the one in which the problem occurs.
   - Select as a change agent someone who can intervene in the client's own environment.
   - Fade out the incentives for the change so the client learns to go it alone.
2. Increase environmental support for improved client functioning:
   - Select behaviors that are likely to be supported in the natural environment.
   - Elicit support from relevant collaterals.
   - Refer client to self-help or support group.
   - Use booster sessions.
   - Arrange for the receipt of ongoing resources.
3. Provide opportunities for thorough learning of new behavior:
   - Use several change agents or settings.
   - Teach problem-solving skills.
   - Attribute positive change to client's own efforts.
   - Anticipate and plan for obstacles to problem resolutions.
   - Gradually increase the interval between sessions.

REOPENINGS

Reopening a case at the client's request is often frowned upon as an undesirable "revolving door." Yet it should be noted that something of interest keeps a client returning to a place where there may be reluctance to work again on the same problem. This kind of a situation is difficult to understand but is worth the effort if time can be made available. Reopenings have productive possibilities in that they can provide the client with another chance to make improvements. Most important, reopenings provide the setting for "booster shots" that can be of very short duration but may make a difference in helping a client who has temporarily lost ground to regain it and to avoid further relapse or deterioration.

CRISES, EMERGENCIES, AND ULTIMATUMS

Cases on a monitoring status are often subject to crises, emergencies, and ultimatums. A *crisis* is a particular state of affairs that is life-threatening or threatens basic habits of conducting oneself. Crises are believed to occur when there is a severe threat, loss, or challenge (Dixon, 1987; Golan, 1978). Crises are sudden discontinuities in the life arrangements, for example, the sudden death of someone close to the client, the onset of a critical illness, extreme or mutilating surgery, being criminally assaulted or burglarized, becoming burned out, and so forth.

Emergencies are situations where prompt action will remove or retard a threatening crisis: for example, making a phone call to stave off an eviction, influencing a school to stop or slow up a suspension, calling the police to stop an assault, finding temporary accommodations to keep a person from living on the street, or getting clothing to help a person who has none.

Ultimatums occur when there is pressure on an agency to act. There may be pressure to get a patient out of the hospital immediately, for example, or to remove a child from his home immediately. Ultimatums result from a variety of complex pressures on a delivery system. They are rarely true emergencies, although they may produce a crisis state for clients unless they are buffered.

Because crises, emergencies, and ultimatums may occur while a case is being monitored, practitioners must allow leeway in their schedules to meet urgent problems. These unexpected events should be managed by rapid problem specification, high practitioner activity to arrange for stress abatement, termination of the episode, and return to the planned work as soon as possible.

SUMMARY OF BASIC ACTIONS

We have seen that termination involves five basic actions:

1. A plan should be made for termination from the inception of the case. The plan should be put into effect by regular reminders of the number of interviews left and reserving the last interview for a review of progress and a look to the future.
2. Unplanned discontinuance can be variously understood. It may be that the client has actually received what he needed, or it may be that the client is dissatisfied in some important way.

3. Cases may be extended by contract when there is a clear and mutually understood and agreed-upon purpose. Unplanned extensions should be scrupulously avoided.
4. Monitoring may occur as a result of a court order or a professional interest.
5. Maintaining gains should be planned for by attempting to construct reinforcers in the natural environment and influencing the client's thinking so he perceives changes as continuously useful.

INTERVIEWING TECHNIQUES FOR BRIEF TREATMENT

Interviewing techniques cannot be readily separated from models, approaches, or viewpoints. The particular way in which an interview unfolds is shaped by the characters and traits of the practitioner and the client, as well as by the style and mission of the agency or practice. Interviewing techniques generally are of two types: (1) the practitioner's conduct, that is, behavior, demeanor, and speech; and (2) the practitioner's intentions. These two—conduct and intentions—join and are transmuted into communication directed toward accomplishing some improvement in the client's personal life. The model, approach, or guidelines contain explicit and implicit information about how the practitioner should conduct himself and what his general deportment and thought patterns should be. The model also tells, in a general way, the recommended goals to be accomplished.

Techniques are named and described differently by different authors. Nevertheless, there is remarkable similarity in the general conduct of interviews. There is sometimes a startling difference among authors in the rhetoric, the descriptive labels, and the explanations ascribed to techniques. But one ought not be misled by the wording or the name of technique. Examination of the actual substance will often reveal its similarity to a technique going by another name.

A book such as this is not the place for a general tract on interviewing. For that purpose, we suggest several readings of particular merit (Hersen & Turner, 1985; Kadushin, 1990; Othmer & Othmer, 1989). This chapter highlights techniques that are common to the general interviewing process while being particularly useful and necessary to carrying out the processes of brief treatment. These techniques mainly cover focusing and maintaining focus, and concentrating on goal achievement.

Othmer and Othmer (1989, p. 4) analyze interviewing styles of two main types: the insight-oriented (psychodynamic) type and the descriptive, problem-oriented type. This distinction is the same one made in Chapter 2 between the psychodynamic and the problem-solving approaches.

1. *Interviewing led by the psychodynamic approach* is conducted.
    ■ to reveal the details of the present problem, crisis, or impasse
    ■ to lead the client through discussions aimed at making deliberate altera-
      tions in behavior
    ■ to secure and use needed resources
    ■ to acquire enough understanding of self to be self-supportive.
2. *Interviewing led by the problem-solving approach* is conducted
    ■ to uncover decisive past experience
    ■ to lead the client through discussions that induce understanding, clarifica-
      tion, and insight
    ■ to change the unwanted behavior
    ■ to reduce the client's unhappiness.
3. *Interviewing that combines the psychodynamic approach with the problem-solving
    approach* is conducted
    ■ to reveal the details of the present problem
    ■ to induce an efficient degree of self-understanding and awareness of past
      decisive issues
    ■ to aim at making deliberate alterations in behavior
    ■ to get for the client enough clarification and insight to understand and
      support herself emotionally.

BRIEF TREATMENT INTERVIEWING
IN PERSPECTIVE

Brief treatment interviewing has two main aspects.

1. *The general pattern of interviewing consists of forms of somewhat ritualized, some-
    what standardized communications.* Ideas are transmitted from one person to another through language, including gestures and nonverbal signals—body language. The messages are received, processed, and decoded in a back-and-forth, turn-taking, transactional manner, shaped by the social and physical context as well as by the meanings of the message senders. Interview communications are understood by a complex process of inferring meaning on a multidimensional scale. Patterns of language used in interviews have become more or less standardized over time as they have been written down in texts, produced in teaching videotapes and audiotapes, and acted out in films and on the stage. In fact, there has developed a kind of ritual-ized therapy-speak in our society that can be heard at all levels in many places.

2. *A positive working relationship is considered essential in all forms of interviewing.* The positive working relationship, as it exists throughout the entire treatment process, is an interpersonal relationship concerned with the business of the therapy. The features of the relationship are revealed in the interview communications. It is characteristic of good, positive treatment relationships that the practitioner communicates respect, liking, acceptance, and empathy; and that the client evidences an attitude of trust.

This working relationship has acquired connotations of complexity and a fascination that go all the way back to Freud's original formulations of the transference. Over time, the popular press has taken up the idea of this special relationship and spread it everywhere. Among serious literary writers, on the stage, and in the cinema, there has developed a large body of written, photographed, and spoken art that has observed, examined, analyzed, and pronounced judgment on the therapeutic relationship. It is little wonder that this aspect of therapy has become a cultural icon, an object of devotion and interest to many intellectuals and to the public at large who view and read academic and popular works embodying ideas of the therapeutic relationship.

Regardless of the uses made today of the concept of the therapeutic relationship, there is ample evidence of its high value in therapy as an enabler of useful work in treatment and as a helpful transaction. In most problem-solving modes of brief treatment, the management of the interview relationship is not overly complex and is confined to fostering a sense of partnership with the client in an important piece of work that has strong meaning for the client and is, therefore, special. In psychodynamic brief treatment, the handling of the relationship is more complex because of the stress that is built into the psychodynamic models by the emphasis on the transferential aspects of the relationship. In the psychodynamic models, the expression of the interview relationship is thought to be a means of observing the underlying problems and of working through the problems thus revealed in order to develop the requisite insight or self-understanding.

3. *There are basic communication categories that are commonly found to exist in virtually all types of interviewing in all types of models.* Although different authors put somewhat different labels on these categories, by and large when they are defined there are strong similarities among most of them. Fortune (1981) extracted a listing of categories and their basic definitions from two of the best known typologies. Table 10.1 is essentially Fortune's listing with a few changes of our own.

The generalized communication categories in Table 10.1 will be used differentially, depending on what phase of the treatment one is in. Some are more relevant to the early phases, and some appear more reasonable for use in the middle phase. The tightness or looseness of focus will dispose practitioners to emphasize techniques that result in a greater or lesser degree of control of the direction of the interview. Brief treatment, with its heightened emphasis on focus, will emphasize techniques of structuring, direct influencing, and understanding of current conditions. Other techniques should be used as appropriate to enhance a client's ability to take hold of and create movement within the problem situation.

TABLE 10.1   **Basic Communication Categories**

CATEGORY	DESCRIPTION OF CATEGORY
Reassurance or sustainment	Expressions of understanding, concern, encouragement, appreciation of client's abilities and qualities.
Advice or direct influence	Suggestions and recommendations to influence client's decisions and behavior in specific directions.
Exploration	Examining and searching client's narrative telling of circumstances concerning the environment, social context, and the client's relationship to the environment and social context, and examining and searching to know and understand the client's own behavior, feelings, attitudes, beliefs, etc.
Identifying specific reactions, or person–situation reflection	Expressions intended to enhance awareness of the nature and meaning of specific incidents. *Includes confrontation,* a sharply focused assistance to enhance awareness of the nature and meaning of behavior, attitudes, and feelings about functioning in the treatment situation and in family and other interpersonal roles, about one's own personality and personal history. *Includes logical discussion* to enhance understanding by identification of an evaluation of beliefs, attitudes, and interpretations, and back-and-forth discussions of what these are, what they mean, if they work for the person, and so forth.
Clarifying current intrapsychic antecedents	Enhancement of client's understanding of own intrapsychic patterns.
Clarifying developmental causation, or early-life reflections	Enhancement of understanding of developmental origins of patterns of behavior.
Structuring the treatment	Explanations of treatment, securing informed consent, agreement, etc.

ANALYSIS OF TECHNIQUES

The techniques named in the maps that follow are described in this section in the ideal chronological order. This order actually exists in interviews, but not to the degree suggested by the structured order. The real order is flexible and is changed according to the professional judgment of the practitioner, and according to the manner in which the client responds. The interviewer may select from the techniques, omitting those that are not necessary for the present purposes, and also rearranging the order as necessary, as well as integrating these techniques into a whole communication experience by buttressing these techniques with general interviewing techniques as suggested in Table 10.1.

Decisions on the specific timing of techniques are formed from a combination of observations, conclusions, and hunches, often made on a split-second basis.

These decisions are informed by communication processes that arise from many channels and produce the practitioner's sense of what the client is saying, feeling, and expressing. Each phase of the interview and techniques involved are described in the following sections.

Starting Up

The starting-up phase shown in the three boxes is the phase in which the initial encounter (or the beginning of a renewed encounter) takes place. The participants begin to define the situation and assess one another.

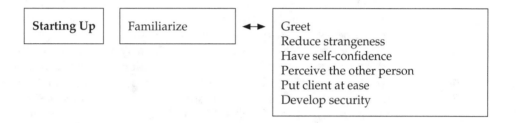

Starting Up	Familiarize	◄─►	Greet Reduce strangeness Have self-confidence Perceive the other person Put client at ease Develop security

Familiarize.   The familiarizing technique is used at point zero, that is, the absolute start of the interaction. The client and practitioner meet for the first time, never before having set eyes on one another.

This point is fraught with tension. The client may be a supplicant, asking, pleading, or perhaps imploring the practitioner for life supplies—money, caring, or surcease of pain. Full of pride and resentment, the client may pour out entreaties that sound like demands, commands, threats, or complaints. Having learned to disguise pain and need, the applicant may exhort the practitioner humbly. A really scared or shy client may just be numb. A more sophisticated client may adopt a demeanor of rationality, which is the preferred demeanor in our culture. A street-wise client may size up the interviewer and put on an ingratiating attitude. The client is likely to be in the down position. The practitioner is in an up position; he has professional status and the backing of a powerful organization. The organization often has a monopoly on the services the client is seeking. Sometimes there are no available services on the market for a fee. Sometimes the fees in the marketplace are beyond the ability of poor and middle-class clients to pay.

The quality of strangeness encountered in interviewing stems from a perception that the interview experience deviates from other usual or expected experiences. Confrontation with strangeness may be surprising and disarming. We may take protective cover if we interpret a strange event as peculiar or bizarre. Fear of the stranger and the strange context is a common denominator that afflicts both client and practitioner in these circumstances. The practitioner's knowledge, experience, and supports should help to control fear and enhance personal security.

Conventional social communications reduce the client's tension, which results from the strangeness, and put the client at ease. Techniques for helping a client to be more at ease are greeting, or extending a welcome; reducing strangeness by demonstrating basic knowledge of the problem of concern; and sitting at ease and expressing or displaying warmth, empathy, and genuineness. Table 10.2 provides examples of dialogue to put the client at ease.

Greeting and welcoming activities include:

1. *Hosting.* Ask the client to come in and be seated comfortably, and express pleasure at meeting her; extend other greetings.
2. *Physical arrangements,* or *proxemics.* Make reasonably comfortable arrangements for seating with a moderate distance between client and practitioner. Coffee, ashtrays, and decent ventilation should be provided if possible. These arrangements convey that the client is welcome.
3. *Straightforward, businesslike, and friendly demeanor.* Having the proper demeanor is necessary for most client–practitioner relationships. Keep facial expressions appropriate; try to take turns smoothly; keep the body relaxed; maintain an interested tone. This attitude ordinarily allows a proper degree of empathy to start to flow. However, if a barrier becomes evident between practitioner and client, the practitioner should try to determine if his attitude is biased, or if he expects too much or too little from the client, or if the client and practitioner have brought distorted attitudes to the interview that should be studied so that a normal relationship can emerge, or if the client and practitioner are focusing on different matters.

TABLE 10.2   Techniques for Familiarizing and Example Dialogue

TECHNIQUES	EXAMPLES
Greet	Hello. Good day. Come in, please.
Extend greeting	Please sit down. You can put your coat there. Are you cold? Shall I shut the window? The weather is fierce.
Reduce strangeness	The intake department says you need daycare for your daughter. I understand you are a single mother and have just started work.
Perceive the other person	Yes? Okay, then would you describe the kind of arrangements you are looking for?
Put client at ease: Developing security by having client explain her situation in her way.	No? I haven't got it right? Tell me about it, please.

To reduce strangeness and enhance security and self-confidence, it is advisable for a practitioner to acquire basic knowledge about the major characteristics of the client group that will be seen. Practitioners can reduce strangeness by demonstrating knowledge of the problem of concern.

Human services organizations tend to specialize in a sector of the population. The organization usually has access to experts who are knowledgeable about that category of the population. Literature and short courses offered as in-service training and continuing education help to familiarize a practitioner with the special group of persons that constitutes the clientele. The practitioner needs to know the socioeconomic conditions ordinarily found in the population group, the characteristics of the general range of problems usually identified, and the estimated value of the several major types of interventions thought to be effective with those problems.

Warmth, genuineness, and empathy are ordinarily shown by maintaining a serious demeanor and close attentiveness when listening. The client thereby perceives that there is a commitment to her. Understanding can be shown by a moderate amount of eye contact and by leaning toward the client without getting too close. Encouraging remarks help the client express her ideas and attitudes. Practitioners should maintain a natural spontaneity to reduce alienation that may be the result of the practitioner's status and power (Pope, 1979).

First Phase

The first phase (shown in the three boxes) proceeds in increments to assess the situation, to define it in more detail, and to propose priorities, goals, and contracts. At the start, there is a tacit agreement about purpose and goals; it becomes more explicit as the phase proceeds and merges with the middle phase.

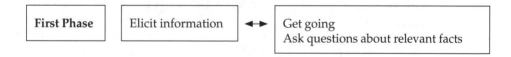

| **First Phase** | Elicit information | ↔ | Get going
Ask questions about relevant facts |

Elicit Information.   Information is elicited directly and indirectly. The only way to get information directly is to ask questions. Practitioners need not have inhibitions about asking clients questions as long as they are germane and well intentioned. However, they should try not to ask clients "why" questions. "What" questions should be asked instead. "Why" questions might be answered with "I don't know" or with some unfounded hypothesis from television psychology. The resulting discussion might sound like the script of a play and have limited value in an assessment or intervention effort.

"What" questions tend to produce useful information that describes and may even explain a piece of the problem. Table 10.3 shows a typical interchange to elicit information.

TABLE 10.3   Information Derived from Questions and Answers

QUESTION	ANSWER
"Why did you feel that way?"	"I really don't know." (*Silence*)
"What did you do there?"	"I started to be very down."
"What happens to you when you are down?"	"My guts get in a boil."
"Then what?"	"I had to go to eat something. Some people can't eat when they are blue. I gorge myself and get overweight...."

Sometimes practitioners fear that their questions will hurt or anger clients. This is sometimes the case, although not frequently. If it is anticipated that a question will be hurtful, a verbal explanation should be given about the question's purpose. The practitioner should say that he is *not* asking the question in order to criticize, scold, invade the client's privacy, or satisfy idle curiosity. He should stress that questions are a way for client information to be transferred to the practitioner and that this information can then be used by the practitioner to understand, think, and plan how to help intelligently. If the question is too hurtful, the practitioner should express regret and perhaps apologize. For example, the practitioner should say, "I am sorry that question hurt you," or "I did not realize how painful that was. I am sorry. Tell me how I made you feel."

Another reason to avoid "why" questions is that they are often perceived as scolding. "Why did you do that?" is often used in social conversation as a prelude to criticism. It means not "why" but "you should not have done that." People in our society place a high value on being in control and understanding why they behave as they do, often without realizing how little is known about causality in human behavior. Even when reasonable inferences can be made about causality, they are often of little practical use. It is far better in the usual practice situation for the practitioner to know details of specific events so that she can pick out what should and could be changed and make practical plans to change it.

Even when confining themselves to "what" questions, practitioners still need a framework to understand which questions are relevant. There is no universal guideline for judging relevance. Common sense should be respected as a good guide in defining information that will assist in making sense out of a problem. The best rule is this: If you do not understand what the client says or means, or there is any ambiguity, ask him.

Intervention methods are derived from models of practice that, among other things, recommend guidelines for assessment (see Chapter 2). These assessment guidelines identify relevant content for circumstances often encountered in practice. To enhance the relevance of questions, it is advisable to consult current assessment models in a particular field of human service work. In general, most assessment models advise that relevant questions are those that

- obtain basic identifying information
- produce a clear and understandable picture of the present problem
- elicit a general picture of the client's social context and a reasonably specific notion of client capabilities, resources, supports, and liabilities
- give a reasonably clear idea of what the client wants to happen and what the client can do to make it happen.

Example questions to elicit information follow:

- "It would help me to know where you work and what you do."
- "I am trying to see why you can't get any rest at home. What is your apartment like?"
- "What kinds of things do you like to do?"
- "Are you strapped for money?"
- "Does anyone help you out?"
- "What kinds of things get in your way?"

Indirect means for eliciting information include certain kinds of statements and observations. Reliance on direct questions exclusively is perceived by most people as cross-examination; it may seem as if the practitioner has the client in a witness box. That type of relationship is fearful or potentially fearful for the client and should understandably be avoided. However, the direct question in an interview can be used any time there is a need for starting the flow of information, moving a topic along, or getting something pinned down, especially if there is little time.

Statements that substitute for questions keep the discourse flowing without undue leading of the client. The practitioner should avoid strong leading because he needs to know what is on the client's mind, not how much his mind can influence the client's. Statements that are question substitutes are of several types. We can say that we would like to know more about a topic. This allows the client to select what she is going to say in a way that makes sense to her. We can also comment on what the client has just said: for example, "That remark your mother-in-law made must have cut you to the quick," or "That must have been awful." Such comments not only elicit information but also support the client.

As important as verbal communications are, information can also be elicited nonverbally by observing the client. The practitioner can observe the client's face and posture for emotions that seem to be associated with certain topics. Information can be gained from clarity or unclarity of speech and from the amount of reality orientation the client has. Body motions, head motions, speech patterns, and spatial arrangements convey information about tenseness, openness, anger, and other attitudes. A client sitting on the edge of his seat, ready to flee, gives the practitioner an indication of his fear. Settling comfortably into a chair suggests being ready to work.

Nodding vigorously suggests agreement. Looking grim suggests fear or anger. Failing to speak intelligently or talking too fast suggests tension and confusion.

Explain Roles.   It is unwise to assume that a client knows what a human service consists of or what a practitioner does. Therefore, it is necessary to communicate information that explicitly conveys what the practitioner intends to do and can do. The technique of explaining roles is briefly illustrated in the boxes that follow.

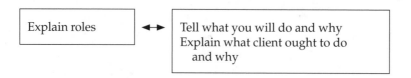

Most clients are under a great deal of stress. The functions of various social programs are often incompletely presented in the media. Common knowledge of programs, passed on verbally from person to person, is affected by group influences. A picture may be painted that is distorted, out-of-date, and confused. Many occupations are represented among the personnel of the human services agencies. Each occupation has a particular style, background, status, and type of education. Clients may not understand these differences.

Clients need to understand what will be attempted or done from an ethical standpoint, because under normal circumstances they have a right to give or withhold informed consent to the arrangements. Only in special circumstances, in which a practitioner operates from a strong authoritative position to stop or prevent harm, can the necessity of informed consent be avoided. Furthermore, only a consenting person can behave cooperatively.

Clients have expectations that affect how they perform their roles. They may be resource seekers, trying to obtain such things as employment or job training, funds, child care, care of aged parents, medical care, or schooling for children. Clients may be seeking information and skills to manage their personal affairs, emotional reactions, close relationships, and uncertainties. Clients may be seeking relief from extreme hardships such as poverty, discrimination, serious illness, or dangerous social hazards.

A client's hopes and expectations are affected by whether or not he perceives that the practitioner can, at least in part, provide what is wanted. Incongruence between practitioner and client expectations is a major source of strain (Blizinsky & Reid, 1980; Pope, 1979, p. 324). To bring expectations into congruence it is advisable to elicit information from the client about who did the referral and what the client knows about the agency and its activities. Is the client optimistic, pessimistic, or uncertain about his reception? How long has he had to wait?

It might also be necessary for the practitioner to comment on the correctness or incorrectness of the client's understanding of what the agency does, to express regrets for tensions that may have been caused by wrong information or insensitive handling, to explain what the agency can and cannot do in relation to the problem, to detail the agency's resources and staff availability, and to clarify agency limitations as well as possibilities. It is necessary to tell the client what work will be done, where it will be done, how often the practitioner will be seen, what the client will be expected to do, and about how long all this will take.

Most clients understand clear explanations of these matters. However, such explanations need to be repeated if understanding seems to be uncertain in later interviews. Time used to speak about these role descriptions is well spent and contributes to good outcomes.

Explain the Problem Circumstances.   In the first phase of the interview, explaining the problem circumstances is an integral part of the assessment process. The process of defining the situation proceeds and is elaborated on along with the process of clarifying images that the participants develop about one another. From these processes are made agreements on focus, usually in increments.

These explanations involve getting and understanding information about the client's problems, personal characteristics, and social context, as illustrated in the boxes. In many intervention models, these discussions are called *exploration*. In order to search out information in the interview, the practitioner's major activities should be asking questions, observing nonverbal behaviors, suggesting explanations to the client to see how they fit, and discussing with the client what has emerged and what needs to be thought about in the future.

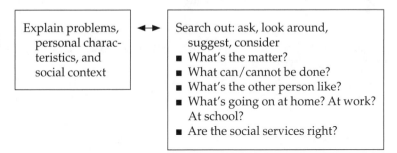

The inquiry, which is made up of questions, statements that substitute for questions, suggestions, and content for consideration, is determined by general questions or lines of investigation. There are many variations on the question, *"What is the matter?"* For example:

- What is wrong as you understand it?
- What trouble is the problem causing?
- How important is that trouble?
- Is it dangerous? Occasionally? Always? Is it only a nuisance?
- To what degree is it a problem?
- When does it happen?

- What seems to bring it on?
- What happens afterward?
- What other people get involved in the problem?
- What are they like?
- What do they think about you?
- What do they do to you, for you, or with you?
- What kinds of things go on at home, at work, or at school that set your mood, help you out, hurt you, or deprive and hamper you?
- What do you think can be done or ought to be done?
- Are the services you have already received satisfactory? In what way "yes"; in what way "no"?

The answers to these questions have easily understood meaning on paper. However, nearly all responses are further colored by the client's personal characteristics, whether she is intelligent, moody, pessimistic, timid, easily frightened, extremely fearful, clear-thinking, lacking in self-confidence, anxious, suspicious, excitable, withdrawn, or lacking in affect.

The interviewer gets impressions of these traits from observations in the interview, from nonverbal cues, and sometimes from other people who get involved in the intervention program. It is also possible to get such information from personality inventories, although for ordinary purposes the interview observations suffice.

In cases in which the client is hard to understand, it may be useful to collaborate with experts who can shed light on what obscure personality traits mean, especially traits that might indicate the existence of mental illness.

Identify and Specify Problems.   Identifying and specifying problems in the first phase allow practitioner and client to get closer to agreement on priorities, goals, and a contract, as illustrated in the boxes. These communications begin to pave the way for the intervention program. Later these communications serve to evaluate progress and show what revisions have to be made in an intervention plan.

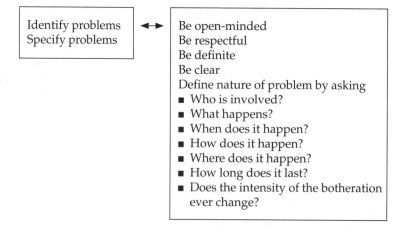

From explanation-seeking discourse the interview moves to identifying and specifying. Time may not permit going this far in a first interview. Such discussions may carry over into the second interview and come up repeatedly thereafter.

Explaining is making a problem plain and intelligible. *Identifying* is an exposition of the essential character of a problem, or its objective reality. *Specifying* a problem means naming it and stating it explicitly and in detail. For problem-solving purposes, the specification is what counts most, because it names what the practitioner can and should intervene on. Human thinking tends to be roundabout, so it is rare to get right to a specification. People go through phases or stages to get to specifics. The pattern of discourse becomes complex and involved. Usually we return to the explanation again after the specification is made and find that we now have a better explanation, that is, one that fits the known facts more closely.

CASE 10.1

EXAMPLE OF IDENTIFYING AND SPECIFYING

Mr. S. is a 35-year-old man, overly tied to his mother. He has just been laid off his steelworker's job. In the interview, he emphasizes that he has been rejected by his girlfriend, Ms. O. He acts unconcerned about being unemployed. He does not want to discuss job prospects. He says he wants help to improve his relationship with Ms. O.

Mr. S. is a union steward and is an expert on the employment situation in his trade. The stress of his unemployment has brought him forcibly to confront the fact that at 35 he ought to emancipate himself from his mother and get married. He cannot understand why his girlfriend has lost faith in him and become cool and distant. He has increased his attention to her without the desired results. The problem is identified as conflict with the girlfriend. Mr. S. specifies the problem as Ms. O.'s drawing away from him, not accepting dates, and refusing to talk about marriage.

Ms. O. seems to be drawing away from involvement with a jobless man. Mr. S. may have been keeping up his courage by making light of the unemployment problem. He might want her closer so she can help him keep up his courage. The practitioner wants to carefully examine whether Mr. S. ought to consider his joblessness as a problem.

In going from an explaining discussion, as illustrated in Case 10.1, to the identifying and specifying discourse, the questions and statements take on certain different qualities. We go from questions such as, "What is the matter?" to questions about naming, stating, and describing in detail what is bothersome, painful, or destructive. The practitioner needs to create an unpressured climate that respects a view of circumstances as the client sees them.

The possible communication lines between the practitioner and Mr. S. in Case 10.1 might be:

- So you see the problem as your needing help with your girlfriend's coldness.
- Tell me the details about how she shows this coldness.
- How is her attitude different now from earlier?
- What is she doing all this for, do you suppose?

The practitioner's statements have to be definite and clear in order to encourage the client to be specific:

- Am I hearing you right?
- Is your job situation under control?
- You know what to do?
- But your girlfriend is a mystery to you?
- Give me an example.
- Another example, please?
- What did she say?
- What did you say?
- Then what happened?
- How did that make you feel?
- Can you put yourself in her place?
- How might she have felt?
- What do you suppose she is afraid of?
- Have you discussed all this with your mother?
- What does she tell you?

Defining the problem is fixing its context and essentials:

- So—the essential thing is that you want to get married, and she wants to have less to do with you?
- Until you lost your job, she was interested in you as a date, but she never allowed you to get really close? Now she is more distant?
- Because you are worried about your job future, you would like very much to have the support of closeness with her? And she says "No"?

Discuss Priorities, Goals, and Contracts.   To make any helping process work it is necessary to establish priorities, goals, and a contract, which is an agreement on what is to be done and how to do it. This process is illustrated in the next set of boxes.

There are several ways to decide on priorities. Each way has values and drawbacks:

1. *Priority may be assigned to the problem that is identified by the client as being of highest interest.* This choice contains a high probability of success because it is congruent with client motivation. However, it is possible that the client's

decision is peripheral, which poses questions about the appropriateness of proceeding.

2. *Priority may be assigned to the problem as it is identified by professional judgment.* This judgment is more or less significant depending on the strength of the knowledge it is based on. Professional recommendation is especially needed in cases in which the client is unable to develop appropriate and feasible ideas about priorities. Professional recommendation may be needed where legal or police authorities require that the client work on a particular problem. Without some degree of client agreement, however, it is not likely that much progress can be made. The client may consider the issue raised by the practitioner as a potential obstacle to resolving the problem she selected herself. If the worker sees his issue as interfering with work on the client-selected problem, then the issue is dealt with as an obstacle to be overcome in some fashion. This way, attention is given to the client's problem, and the issue raised by the worker received the attention it deserves as needed.

3. *Setting priorities may be postponed for a short or long time, during which the participants explore questions from a number of different perspectives.* A tentative posture on priorities is appropriate when an issue is obscure. The client's commitment may be ambiguous, or the client may be perceived as needing more time to become secure in the helping situation. The difficulty of this position is that the impetus for work may be slowed, causing the helping process to become inefficient.

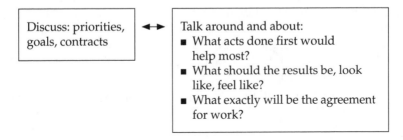

The guidelines of the helping model that are being used can assist in decision making. This phase begins with discursive discussion. We may circle around the subject to start with, exploring what the client thinks and believes would help most, what he thinks should be done first, and what should follow. The intervention model the practitioner follows and her own experience and knowledge about similar problems indicate what should be done.

The practitioner shares her opinion with the client. If the practitioner thinks the client's formulation is mistaken, she should try to convince the client to make a change. That is done through discussion, exploration, explanation, and clarification. The practitioner's attempts to influence the client may fail if the client considers the practitioner's opinion to be wrong or if the professional opinion contradicts strongly held beliefs and values of the client.

Some intervention models may view the client's reluctance to be influenced by the practitioner as resistance. Considerable discussion and interaction would be required to unearth the hypothetical causes of client inability to accept the professional person's view. Starting up such a discussion prolongs the time needed to reach a working agreement. A more rapid accommodation of views may be achieved by accepting the client's formulation after a reasonable amount of discussion, provided that the client's view does not contain any unethical components. The idea is to achieve some gains for the client, even if they are modest.

Most people do not easily change their minds about what they want. However, good results are still obtainable. If the practitioner is unable to convince the client to follow a recommendation, he can concentrate on developing a program of work that is congruent with the client's stated concerns.

The major communication to facilitate reaching an agreement on what is to be done is this: What acts, if done first, will help most? In Mr. S.'s case he wanted two priorities, arranged in this order:

1. The practitioner should talk to Ms. O. to appeal to her to change her attitude.
2. The practitioner should show Mr. S. how to talk and behave to have more influence with Ms. O.

This is an example of a common occurrence when priorities are discussed. The first priority (that the practitioner should talk to Ms. O.) is impossible for the practitioner to do. The second priority is possible, but the practitioner disagrees with it because the idea is too narrow and oversimplified. This means that the practitioner has to take issue with the client, knowing that the client may be distressed by that disagreement.

To put the refusal in a positive light, the practitioner ought to say: "You and I could talk with Ms. O. together, provided she is willing to come here for such a conference."

The client should be told the reason for the practitioner's inability to comply with the request: It is not out of unwillingness to help but out of the practitioner's knowledge that there is no way to call in Ms. O. for a talk without being extremely rude. It is fairly certain that she will respond negatively to such a call, making things worse for Mr. S. However, if he wants to ask Ms. O. to come and she agrees, the practitioner will discuss the interpersonal problems they have.

How Mr. S. should go about asking her to come can then be rehearsed. Mr. S. and the practitioner can rehearse when and where to broach the subject, what should be said, what attitude should be projected, what should be done if she says "No," and what should be done if she perhaps says "Yes." If all this seems too difficult for Mr. S., the practitioner should propose that the second priority—helping

Mr. S. learn some interpersonal skills that might be more effective—should be made first priority.

The practitioner may choose to explain that he has reservations about both these priorities. The problem is composed of more complicated factors that are not directly touched on by Mr. S.'s suggestions. It is not clear what the couple mean to one another or what Ms. O.'s reservations are. They could have something to do with Mr. S.'s personality and unemployment, or with Ms. O.'s hang-ups about marriage, or maybe even with her desire to marry someone else.

When the priorities have been decided, the *goals* should be discussed. The practitioner should elicit from the client an image of what the results of the intervention program should be, for example, what they should look like or feel like. Mr. S. should be asked to describe his idea of a successful ending: what he should be able to do, to have, or to feel.

A minority of clients may be reluctant to make plans and goals. However, most clients are capable of pursuing a reasonable program if they understand it and if it is in line with their interests as they see them.

As we have seen in Chapter 7, a *contract* is a formal or informal agreement to identify what will be worked on. Contracts in interviews are not legally binding but have moral weight. Some agencies ask for written contracts as a means of control and for the sake of accountability. Some prefer the greater flexibility of a verbal and informal contract.

Middle Phase

The middle phase, shown in the three boxes that follow, advances the problem-solving process. Ideas and plans are generated and choices are made and revised about actions that may alleviate the problem. The middle phase moves into *implementation,* that is, putting the plan in action, observing its effects, revising it as necessary, and preparing for termination.

Interventions are actions that lead to change in the client's problems and circumstances. Judgments are formed about which interventions are realistic, proper, and acceptable to clients. Parallel judgments are formed by clients. Differences in the judgments of clients and practitioners can be explained by disparities in their knowledge, values, lifestyles, and aspirations.

The middle phase of intervention is highly individualized according to type of problem, client, and organizational purposes. This phase also varies depending on the recommendations contained in the particular model guidelines that are being followed. Decisions are made in the middle phase about what techniques to emphasize, what to omit, and what to add. Decisions may be made about the preferred order for using techniques. These decisions cannot be prescribed for all cases because they are made according to individual professional judgments. The basic middle-phase communication techniques reviewed here are building blocks from which more complex individualized communications can be constructed.

| **Middle Phase** | Discuss what to do
Introduce interventions
Pin down
Establish incentives
    and rationale
Get agreement
State time limits
Review
Give advice
Give guidance
Anticipate obstacles
Give encouragement
Analyze and overcome
    obstacles | | What would you like to do?
What would you like me to do?
    Or other people?
What can be done?
We should try this, in this way
    (tell, show, discuss).
In detail, we do this, like this, there, here,
    today, next week, with him or her or
    them, this way, this first, that last.
For these good reasons, because...
Is that okay? No? What else? Instead?
    Yes? okay!
Let's move along. Six interviews left.
■ How did you get along on
    those actions?
■ What stopped you?
■ What thoughts got in the way?
■ Who stopped you?
■ What conditions got in the way?
■ What did you need that you
    didn't have?
■ What scared you?
Let's see how we can change and
    avoid those obstacles.
I suggest you think of it this way;
    go about doing it like this; tell them
    that; ask them this.
■ How would that suit you?
■ Could you do it?
■ What can I do for you to help? |

Discuss What to Do. Interviews in the middle phase frequently begin with a review of what is being done, what the plan is, and what has transpired since the last contact. By the third interview, the practitioner and client have probably just finished making a plan and reaching an agreement or contract. The interview begins with a brief summary of the plan to fix it in mind. Then the following questions might be asked: "What would you like to do now?" or "What would you like me to do?" or "What can be done?" If the client and practitioner are past the third interview, there should be a brief review of the status of the work, followed by a discussion of obstacles. (See Chapter 8.)

The interventions, or changes in them, should be introduced by speech conventions such as "We could try this," or "I would suggest _____," or "Have you thought about this?" As the client waits for the practitioner to continue or starts to respond, the practitioner's speech tells, shows, and discusses. The practitioner didactically describes and explains the intervention.

The practitioner can describe the desired intervention plan to the client. She can discuss aspects with the client that are not well understood or are misunderstood, unclear, or anxiety producing. The thought that governs selection of the practitioner's speech is this: The purpose of the middle phase is to get results, to effect change, and to give help that is wanted. The whole aim of intervention is to reduce the problem by overcoming obstacles that stand in the way of potentially helpful activities.

Introduce Interventions

Name the Intervention.   The practitioner names the intervention so that it can be known, clarified in thought, and understood to have meaning, for example:

- We are starting this program to expand your family's means to help one another.
- What we are doing is rescheduling your play time.
- These activities are the preliminaries to job retraining.
- These are exercises recommended by your doctor to improve the flexibility of your wrist after your cast is taken off.
- These are prescribed medications for cutting down muscle contractions.

Naming the intervention usually involves phrases that reflect the intervention's purpose.

Describe the Intervention.   Describing the intervention means recounting and tracing the outline of the intervention. For example, the practitioner might tell the client, "The preliminaries to getting job retraining are checking what jobs will be available in the near future and finding out what training programs there are, what they cost, who will pay for them, how they match your interests and abilities, and how they might help your future income and advancement."

Explain the Intervention.   The practitioner should make the activities of the intervention as plain and intelligible as possible. Explanations might include who does what, in what order, with what alternatives, with what timing, and with what purpose. For example, the practitioner might say, "You should go to union headquarters and the state employment office. Get what information they have about job market prospects for the near future. Ask about the location and conditions for existing and planned retraining courses. Then you need to decide if they appeal to you. Talk it over with the union steward, your friends in the same boat, your family, and me." Details are put into this explanation to match with individual circumstances.

Pin Down.   It is advisable to fix the major ideas of the intervention in the mind. Thus they can be held onto, pictured clearly, and firmly perceived. This involves describing interventions of immediate interest in words and phrases.

Pinning down means discussing and giving information in detail. The practitioner should specify that this or that should be done, like this, in this manner, there or here, today or next week or after such and such, or before that, with her or him or them, this way, with this first and that last.

There is often a fear that going into such detail is boring or redundant. If the practitioner goes into unnecessary detail the client will show impatience. He will sigh, turn his head away, wrinkle up his brow, show displeasure, tap his foot, or twist up his body in the chair. Whether or not too much detail is being discussed can be checked out simply by asking the client.

Impatience with detail may not be a problem for some clients. Rather, they may be distressed by clear picturing of distasteful things that need to be done. If discomfort emerges, the practitioner has an opportunity to discuss it as an obstacle to overcome so that the client can get what she wants. For example:

P: Considering all that we have talked about, it seems to me that we are going to have to discuss your husband's illness with him directly.

C: Oh no!

P: Let me explain. You and I do not really understand what is wrong with him or how sick he is. We don't know what the clinic is doing or how he is reacting to the treatment.

C: That's true… But he won't come here. I don't even know if he's strong enough.

P: Then I could come to your apartment and see you there together.

C: But he will have a fit if he finds out I told anybody about this. He'll take it out on me. I can't stand that!

P: Do you feel you wronged him by asking us to help?

C: Not really—but maybe.

P: What is wrong about it?

Establish Incentives and Rationale.   In order to do something novel that may be unpleasant, frightening, or full of ambiguity, human beings need to have a compelling reason and some confidence in a reward. The actions have to be worth the trouble.

The purpose of problem-solving work is to reduce a problem so that it becomes less frequent, less intense, or of shorter duration. The client needs incentives and an acceptable rationale to undertake problem solving. The rationale is a foundation of thoughts and values, based partly on experience, that justifies what is about to be embarked on. To impart strength of will to a client in proceeding with an intervention that may be uncomfortable, discussion should be held to determine what is in it for him, what improvement is expected, and why the proposed activities are good and reasonable.

The incentives and rationale can usually be identified by starting with the target problem and picturing the conditions that can be expected when that problem is reduced. The basic incentive is to achieve the goal, that is, finding a job;

reducing tension; the satisfaction of a desired relationship with another person; the resources to house, feed, and shelter oneself and one's family; self-respect and a sense of well-being; or the skills for building self-confidence, meeting the right people, having the necessities of life, or developing a desired lifestyle.

It is best for the practitioner to phrase her part of the discussion in plain, straightforward terms that are familiar to the client, for example:

- Suppose you were to go through with these activities—what would you expect to get out of them?
- Do you think you would get those things?
- What difference would it make to you?
- Is the effort worth it, do you think?
- Is this program we have worked out reasonable to you?
- Well—I think it's reasonable, because you said you wanted this to happen.
- I think it's reasonable because most people feel that.
- I think it's reasonable because most people do not do that, and they stay out of trouble.
- It seems you are too dependent on your mother; it would be better if you weren't.
- You would like to be your own boss and you can be.

Get Agreement.   Often agreement is routinely reached throughout the discussion. Everything indicates that the client understands and accepts the program. Practitioners get confirmations of agreement when clients make positive facial expressions, nod, maintain eye contact, or move in closer.

It is not advisable, however, to take agreement for granted; it should be checked out in a verbal exchange. For example, the practitioner should ask:

- Is this all right?
- Are we going too fast?
- What reservations do you have?
- Shall we continue this?

Clients respond to such phrases mostly with head shakes or brief phrases such as: "OK," "No," or "I don't know." These are the signals that indicate the degree of closure of the discussion. If the client's answer is "OK," it is safe to proceed. An uncertain response is a signal to discuss more to get agreement. The likelihood of a client acting successfully on an intervention with which she disagrees is slight.

State Time Limits.   All intervention programs have time limits, although they may not be explicit. Some programs are limited by circumstances. For example, the time limits for a schooling or training program are set and publicly known from the beginning of the program.

Many interventions, however, do not dictate a specific ending time. In order for organizations to control costs, assign staff, and plan operations, it is still necessary to know approximately how much time will be used. There have to be planned endings so that the client can apportion her time, energy, and interests.

Except for programs with obvious limits, there are no established criteria for the optimum time necessary to find a job, recover or gain self-esteem, improve interpersonal skills, or get a child back from foster care. More and more agencies are making administrative recommendations about the length of time to be provided for such cases. In situations where agencies are responsible for long-term care such as foster home placement or institutional living for frail or sick elderly people, the long term is not an intervention as much as it is caretaking. Direct intervention takes place within the time allotted for caretaking work and can be limited.

The best time to bring up and discuss time limits is during the starting-up phase of an intervention program. This is also the time to advise a client about the allotted time for individual interviews. Sometimes a client asks right away, "How long will this take?" Whether he asks or not, the practitioner should introduce the subject by saying, "I want to tell you about how much time we will have for this work." The practitioner then goes on to say that it is the agency's recommendation that they use five interviews (or six, or eight, or twelve, as the case may be) over a period of two months (or three or four) to get the job done. The practitioner should add that these numbers can be reduced if the work goes fast, or they can be increased if necessary. The client should also be advised that he can come back at a later time if there is further need.

If an agency operates without time limits, this should be stated and the criteria for termination given. Most clients find such plain statements about time limits reasonable and welcome.

Once the statements of time limits have been made by the practitioner, clients usually keep track of the time. However, some clients may forget and should be regularly reminded of how much time is left. It has been a frequent observation of all types of clinicians that setting time limits provides an atmosphere that spurs activity.

Review.   It is advisable to review at every interview or at least at every other one. The review examines the problem condition at the start, identifies the major interventions attempted and their results, and confirms or changes the anticipated content for the remaining sessions. The review should be initiated right after the greetings or an inquiry about what is new. The review permits taking stock, or measuring results, so that practitioner and client can accelerate, slow down, or change a program that is not working.

The phrasing to elicit the review might be, for example, "Let's look at what has been going on here. When we started we agreed that we would concentrate on your finding a job as the first priority. Second, we would try to work on a better relationship between you and your wife. In the three weeks spent working on these problems, we have almost totally concentrated on the problem with your wife and have paid little attention to the job problem. That's how I see it. What do you think?"

The client replied that the problem with his wife did seem to be taking precedence. The practitioner asked for an assessment of progress with the marital conflicts. According to the client, these conflicts were abating; he gave details. The practitioner asked if he preferred putting the job problem aside so that the most concentration would still be on his marital situation. "No," he said, the job problem was uppermost. His savings were getting low. Soon he would have to confront going on welfare if he did not get organized to find a job. From that point, most of the interview time was spent on the priority problem of job hunting. The review thus obviously served to keep the intervention process from failing.

Give Advice.   Clients of all sorts seek advice. Many different kinds of people—those who are exceptionally dependent or ambivalent, or those who characteristically have a hard time making up their minds or feeling self-confident, but also well-organized and responsible people—all know from experience the value of a capable person's advice. Someone who is reliable can often throw light on a matter and provide assistance that people cannot provide for themselves.

Most people do not wish to project themselves as domineering or to make unwarranted intrusions into the lives of others. It used to be thought that advice given by a practitioner would encourage a dependent relationship that was unrealistic and might be harmful to the client. Although there is probably some truth to fears that giving advice can be domineering or weaken the client, much new insight into this subject has been uncovered. As a result of research into advice giving and data from practitioners who give a good deal of advice, it appears that fear is not necessarily justified. There is much to be gained from a reasonable amount of advice giving (Davis, 1975; Reid & Shapiro, 1969).

Surveys of client opinion show that clients sincerely seek advice and feel dissatisfied if they fail to get it. Clients do not necessarily follow advice exactly; however, they use it as a jumping off place to get started. They reorganize the advice in a way that feels right and makes the most sense to them. The advice triggers a process in which the client develops his own advice. That trigger is what the client really wants. Case 10.2 shows an example of a client's interpretation of advice.

CASE 10.2

EXAMPLE OF GIVING ADVICE

Mr. A. was receiving counseling for a marital problem. He and his wife had been drawing apart. She had developed open resentment about his long work hours that made him fatigued on evenings and weekends. Mr. and Mrs. A. had no time together, had stopped going out socially altogether, and had virtually stopped conversing except to say things like, "Where are the car keys?" After twenty-five years of a full and often happy home life, her distancing and his shyness about discussing it with her were causing Mr. A. extreme distress. He was blaming every-thing on "women's liberation."

Among other things, it was decided that Mr. A. must court his wife. He must "date" his wife, starting by taking her to an elegant place to dine. Mr. A. had been actively leading the discussion to make these decisions with the practitioner sup-porting him. Now, contemplating his first date with his wife, this capable, middle-aged, intelligent, and strong businessman asked the practitioner: "Where should I take her?"

Stumped, the practitioner thought about where she would like to go if she were his wife. She suggested a chic Chinese restaurant.

Next time she found out that Chinese food was not to the A.'s liking. How-ever, Mr. A. had taken his wife to a Bavarian restaurant in the suburbs that plays loud oom-pah music; they danced the evening away and had a great time to start off their reconciliation.

There are rules about advice giving. The practitioner should not give advice if it is motivated by the urge to make the client do something because the practitioner likes it. Advice should not be given unless the practitioner has exchanged enough ideas with the client for them to decide together what should be done. Also, before giving advice the practitioner should observe the nonver-bal cues that communicate a client's genuine and deep fear of going it alone. (This was the case with Mr. A.) If the practitioner is making a suggestion, then several possible ideas might be mentioned. This way the client is always se-lecting what to do and will be less likely to feel compelled to do any specific action.

Most particularly, a practitioner should not give advice when she does not know what the client should do. The practitioner should say straight out that she does not know and why she does not know. She can say that she will think about it, consult an expert, or read up on the subject so that she might give good advice later. Or she can refer the client to a good, reliable source that can be expected to have the necessary information.

A practitioner almost never knows what a client should do about major life decisions such as having a baby, giving up a child for adoption, getting married, leaving a spouse, changing jobs, or retiring. The practitioner and the client know that the pros and cons of such decisions involve predictions that are unreliable. A client who asks for advice about these major decisions is really asking to discuss the pros and cons in detail before taking the final leap into a decision. Practitio-ners are, however, free to give good advice, if they have it, about subparts to such questions. They can certainly give reasonable advice about a good restaurant or a good hour of the day for broaching a question to a spouse, employer, or land-lord. They can with sureness advise clients on such issues as disciplining children, planning and conducting weighty discussions with important people, or finding the best available resources for their problems.

The strongest form of advice is that shown in the illustration with Mr. and Mrs. A. "I think you should do this" was the advice that was communicated. Less force is exerted by stating the advice as a suggestion: "It seems to me that if it suits you it would be good to do this or think this." The weakest form of advising is to put emphasis behind one alternative that the client has already considered: "Of the several things you are thinking about, doing this seems the most promising." Strong advice should probably be reserved for putting a quick end to indecision that is pressing, highly anxiety producing, and only temporarily important.

Give Guidance/Anticipate Obstacles.   Some purposes of the middle phase are to accomplish target problem reduction, solve problems, and plan to overcome barriers that stand in the way. The type of change that is usually sought in human services is change in the complement of resources that can be brought to bear on a problem or change in the quantity and quality of social skills that an individual, family, or group possesses to improve well-being or quality of life.

Most of the interviewing techniques in this phase are those that teach, enlighten, and influence clients so that they can accomplish their goals. Giving guidance and its related process of anticipating obstacles are chief vehicles for problem reduction.

In the middle part of an interview, the emphasis is on pinning down the intervention program. Later in the series, the emphasis will be on getting the problem reduction actions to take place. The middle phase becomes a process of education and re-education. Giving useful guidance can help to identify and avoid obstacles. It is a means for increasing the efficiency of the whole process to save missteps. Guidance is leading a person through unfamiliar terrain and aiding him to reach a destination. The major communication in giving guidance is, "Let me show you *what, how,* and *in what manner.*"

After this introduction, the practitioner initiates discourse in which she directs the client in ways to put into effect the mutually planned steps of action. Clarifying—for example, who to talk to or what to say—may be in order. Giving thought to what something means, how something feels, or what to do with emotional reactions may also be necessary.

Speech used in guidance can be either direct or indirect. Direct speech is didactic, that is, instructive. Indirect speech consists of statements that confirm and emphasize the idea being discussed.

Guiding statements contain a great deal of information that informs clients where to go, how to get there, who to see, what to say, and what to do if an anticipated obstacle occurs. These instructional guides can be specific to the point of dotting every "i" and crossing every "t" if necessary. An example of this kind of guidance is shown in Case 10.3.

In addition to or as a substitute for didactic instruction there is rehearsal. The practitioner acts out the role of a person whom the client deals with. That other person may be a son, daughter, spouse, or friend or a teacher, doctor, lawyer, judge, or other authority. Such rehearsals give the client an opportunity to practice, to fix ideas in mind, to gain experience, and to obtain constructive criticism and suggestions on how to put his best foot forward.

The process of guidance is not complete unless the practitioner speaks about difficulties that can be expected and prepares the client for them to some extent. It is also necessary to alert clients that something untoward, unexpected, or adverse might happen and to tell them how to conduct themselves in that case.

There is great variation among clients in how much guidance they will need. It can, however, be assumed that practitioners will have to give verbal instruction and guided rehearsal to nearly everyone to a greater or lesser degree. Guidance should always be considered when a client is about to undertake a novel action for the first time and is anxious about doing well. Any client with a marked lack of experience or a mental impairment, such as Ms. D., will need maximum instruction.

CASE 10.3

EXAMPLE OF GIVING GUIDANCE

The client, Ms. D., is a chronically mentally ill young adult. She has recently been released from a six-week stay in a state mental hospital. She lives at home with her parents in impoverished circumstances. She is attending an outpatient clinic regularly for checkups on her reaction to medication and for help in making an adjustment in the community. She wants to get a job so she can have income and feel like "a real person," not sick and dependent. She is characteristically a frightened and shy person. She never seems to know the right thing to say to another person to get a desired response. The clinic has secured a reservation for her in a sheltered workplace located downtown. To get there she needs to take a twenty-minute ride on public transportation from her home.

Ms. D. is given the information about the reservation. She is told what kind of work is involved and that she can expect helpful supervision. Her remarks suggest that she does not feel comfortable going downtown or seeing strangers at the workplace office.

In order to assure that Ms. D. gets to the office, she has to be instructed which way to walk from her house to get on the right bus. She has to be coached on such subjects as what the sign on the bus will say so she knows she has the right one, how much fare and which correct change she needs to have ready, what will be the most comfortable place on the bus to sit if she has a choice, what will be the best place to stand if the bus has no seats, what sign to look for to know where she has to get off, where to go for coffee after the bus trip to get herself together for the interview, and the name of the person she will be interviewing with at the workplace office.

The practitioner and Ms. D. rehearse what to say in greeting the interviewer at the workplace. The practitioner suggests things the employment interviewer might say and questions that might be asked and rehearses answers with Ms. D.

Give Encouragement.   Giving encouragement fosters hope and inspires self-confidence. Encouraging statements can be important and powerful even when they are small words and phrases such as "un-huh," "oh yes," "that's right," or "go on," as long as they are uttered in an emphatic way.

In conventional speech, the previous common phrases convey a friendly and approving spirit. A fearful person may further benefit from hearing sentences that convey approval from the practitioner, such as:

- That's pretty good.
- Well done.
- Good thought.
- You're on the right track.

Encouragement can be furthered by statements that explain why the client's thought or deed is exemplary and why the practitioner thinks that the client can do even more. For example, the practitioner might say, "That was quite courageous of you to speak up in the meeting. It's probably fairly safe for you to do that again. Your supervisor was taken aback, but she responded politely and was interested. You did not get fired on the spot. That could happen, but it is unlikely. In fact it rarely happens even though people are always fantasizing about it. You were right, you know. Your fellow workers supported you. Of course they won't always do that; you have to decide whether something is worth the risk."

Encouragement is cognitive in the sense that it conveys information to the client. It is also affective in the sense that it conveys the practitioner's friendliness and caring.

Analyze and Overcome Obstacles.   The obstacles of concern in an interview are barriers to client attempts to carry out planned actions in real life. These obstacles exist in several areas. Some are in the mind of the client. They may be attitudes and mind-sets that make the client fearful, usually to an unrealistic degree. They may be adverse beliefs originating in the client's personality and lifestyle. Unless these mental obstacles are of recent origin, they are difficult to change. If they are of recent origin it is worthwhile to approach them by rational discussion, in which a practitioner points out the way the belief or attitude conflicts with known reality. Two examples of practitioner responses are:

- I thought your son had been cooperative in helping you until recently. What makes you change your mind about him now? What happened?
- I understand that most of the companies in your area of work are disorganized and pay poorly. Stories about that are written up in newspapers. What is going on that makes you think you are being personally singled out for humiliation?

Mental obstacles of long duration can be addressed directly if the client is willing and the practitioner has advanced skills. Faced with chronic mental attitudes the practitioner might find it advisable to concentrate first on conditions that are more changeable such as improvements in the environment, in living arrangements, in recreational outlets, and in skills to minimize conflicts with other people.

A major obstacle to intervention activity is the presence of hostile other people who have negative attitudes toward the client because of religion, sex, age, culture, or ethnic characteristics. Prejudice, discrimination, and unprovoked random attacks exist in society and are often misinterpreted as personal. A client may believe that he is responsible for a problem when in reality he is being victimized. Also, friends and relatives may not give anticipated closeness and support. They may be jealous, hostile, contemptuous, or enraged with the client because of their own problems. The client may live under financial and social restraints that in fact limit his ability to act in desirable ways and to conduct his life in a normal fashion.

It is necessary to find out what particular obstacle or set of obstacles is preventing the client from taking a planned action. Then the practitioner and client should make a special plan to cut down the negative effect of the obstacle and develop ways to help the client avoid it, confront it if necessary, get over it, or go around it. There is no way that is always preferable; for example, there is no virtue in facing up to something if it is ultimately better to avoid it. What matters is to hit upon a plan that will get the client over or around the obstacle so that the problem-reduction plan can take place.

The way to identify the obstacle is to review what the client has (and has not) done about it. The client may have put the action into effect and succeeded, or tried it out and failed, or not done it at all.

In case of failure or nonperformance, what needs to be asked is: "Tell me exactly what you did...and then what happened?...and then what did you do?" Thus we can draw out a specific picture of what events took place and how the client felt about them. With this information, a judgment can be made about the location of the obstacle and what it consists of. Then client and practitioner can approach the problem in a different way.

If the client is a nonperformer, the highest likelihoods are that she was frightened or that the plan was too hard, too easy, too unrealistic, or too vague. If nonperformance seems to be due to fear, the practitioner should make encouraging comments, give advice, establish incentives and a rationale, give didactic instruction, ask questions, and make comments that help the client express her fears so they can be viewed realistically. Then the intervention can be planned again to see if it will work next time.

If the intervention plan was inappropriate, it should be immediately revised, using the same techniques discussed earlier for establishing a plan initially. Case 10.4 shows an example of overcoming an obstacle.

Termination Interview

The termination interview, illustrated in the following three boxes, is a review of what has taken place in the intervention. The purpose is to fix events in mind so they may be called on in the future to guide in problem solving. There are five communications in a termination interview:

- This is what we accomplished.
- This is what we did not accomplish.
- This is what you did.
- This is what I did.
- Come back if you need to.

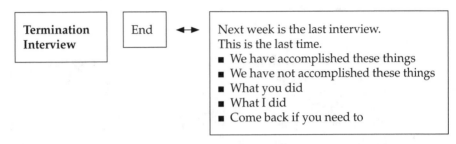

CASE 10.4

EXAMPLE OF OVERCOMING AN OBSTACLE

Mrs. T. must find an apartment to move into because very soon she will be evicted from her present quarters. She has an ill husband and two small children. Her present landlord refuses to accept welfare rent payments. Mrs. T. is not accustomed to taking action to meet and negotiate with businesspeople, and she is afraid. Her husband is housebound and cannot go out to negotiate with prospective apartment agents.

Preparing for the action, the practitioner has discovered Mrs. T.'s fears of being looked down on by building superintendents and her tendency to become ashamed and withdrawn. The practitioner has been encouraging and supportive, but Mrs. T. remains fearful.

The practitioner rehearses with her the best time of day to go out apartment hunting, plans for child care in her absence, what clothes she should wear to make herself feel her best, what she should say to the building agent, and what questions she should ask.

At the next interview, Mrs. T. says she did not go apartment hunting.

P: You were planning to go Wednesday?

Mrs. T.: Yes.

P: Well, let's go over what stood in your way.

Mrs. T.: You know, you know. I just can't.

P: I do know already how scared this makes you. But let's start from the top. You were going to leave the house at 10 A.M. Please go over what happened and what you were thinking from the time you got up until 10 A.M.

Mrs. T. then reconstructed the early morning. Her husband was mad because of being laid up. The kids made a mess over breakfast. All she had was a gulp of coffee. The current landlord pounded on the front door and yelled that they would have to appear in court next week.

The practitioner turns to Mr. T. and asks him if he could do all the household chores tomorrow and let Mrs. T. concentrate totally on getting herself together to go out to face building agents. Although grumpy about it, Mr. T. says he can and he will.

Problems may occur at termination. Some clients fail to show up for the final interview, apparently because the work is over and they have no interest in a summary. Some may develop separation anxiety and feel upset by the ending, preferring to avoid it. Practitioners may also feel distress over ending a sequence of interviews. On the one hand, they may criticize themselves for things they now wish they had done differently. Or they may have become genuinely fond of certain clients and hate to see them go. Sometimes a practitioner is proud of a client's accomplishments and of his own work and does not want the experience to end. The practitioner's feelings are important but not part of the client's situation, and they ought to be controlled. However, it is no cause for undue concern unless the practitioner allows his own feelings to engulf the client. Termination decisions are made according to the intervention model and agency policy.

CHAPTER 11

ADAPTATIONS OF TASK-CENTERED TREATMENT
Balance and Flexibility in Practice

INTEGRATION

Adaptations of the Task-Centered Treatment

Reid (1990) has described the use of the task-centered framework as an integrative device. He suggests that, during assessment, the practitioner draw upon any theories which may help elucidate and define the client's difficulty. He assumes that there is no one correct theory to make the assessment, that no one single theory will suffice for assessing the range of problems that practitioners ordinarily deal with, that what practitioners need are "'theory menus' that they can select from to find the theory or combination of theories that provide the best fit for the situation at hand" (p. 61).

In making an assessment within the framework of the task-centered model, one does not need a total, encompassing, sophisticated explanation of the problem. No matter how complex the assessment, for the most part it is a hypothesis. What is needed is "an identification of possible explanatory factors that may be amenable to change," states Reid (1990, p. 61). For many practitioners, psychodynamic assessment practices offer the richest, most interesting system with which to observe, explore, and speculate about the nature, characteristics, causes, and explanations of a problem. When moving from explanation to treatment, social learning theory, cognitive-behavioral treatment theory, available practice protocols such as IPT treatment for depression (see Chapter 3), and available practice wisdom may offer the most expeditious knowledge bases for charting the treatment.

Again according to Reid (1990), "the 'borrowed' theoretical understanding would not activate the full practice model connected to the theory but would rather color and shape the application of the task-centered approach" (p. 61). One is tempted, as a matter of fact, to construct protocols of classifications of borrowings, suggesting the multiple possibilities of combinations from the major practice theories to enlighten a series of potentially useful working explanations of a problem. To give in to that temptation would result in developing an imaginary supermodel that would resemble the author's favorite practices. Much better for readers to develop for themselves their own creative packaging of procedures chosen from the knowledge base that is valued by the practitioners.

When it comes to task development and implementation as the main treatment actions, the major source of information about the kinds of tasks to formulate (aside from one's own experience and that of the client) is the literature accumulated from the widest variety of viewpoints about what interventions have been undertaken and reported and their results. These reports come from every conceivable range of theoretical viewpoints and are nearly always translatable and assimilable into a formulation that can be slotted into the task-centered structure. The choice of implementation procedures can vary to make sense with the specifics and themes of the tasks.

Informal Convenience Approaches

There is yet another level of attention for flexible integration of the various approaches to brief treatment. We refer here to the intuitive creative intermixing that occurs simply by virtue of the practitioner being alert to new ideas, sensitive to the complexities of the job, and learning a new or novel approach without having the time or opportunity to do a serious study of the material. This kind of informal integrating is what seems to happen in the course of attending continuing education workshops, which are today offered in large numbers and for continuing education credits.

The learning objectives of continuing education, like the objectives for in-service training studies, are essentially to acquaint the participants with a survey of new or unfamiliar ideas and methods. Adult learners acquire new learning at a highly individualized pace. They seem to select and organize new learning in accordance with their own private objectives for themselves. Practitioners are nearly always motivated primarily to acquire new learning for use in particular circumstances, namely the needs of their own jobs. They will thus pick and choose from among the offerings of workshops those they recognize as being capable of attachment to the practice knowledge they already possess; and they will be interested in and pursue the new to the degree that it suggests possible solutions to practice problems they now have.

It is usually possible to evolve flexible incorporation of new techniques by reading, discussing with colleagues, doing a dry run of application in a discussion group, or even by oneself, and then trying out the new techniques in an appropriate case. Thereafter, if the new materials are deemed satisfactory, they will be tried out repeatedly, worked into the fabric of the practitioner's existing personal models, and refined repeatedly under a variety of circumstances. In the mind of an individual practitioner, but especially if the practitioner is part of a collegial group sharing experiences, the new additions to the repertoire will become smoothed out and the practitioner will feel comfortable about taking risks to implement new material. This way of integrating models is in truth real trial-and-error. It is informal, and it will be done only if convenient and if the practitioner feels secure.

Casual Applications

Casual applications refer to the almost accidental occurrences that may take place when one has recently read about an unfamiliar technique, or picked up a bit of information at a meeting. These integrations have serious drawbacks in that they permit to seep into one's repertoire behaviors and attitudes that are not well-founded, that are based on temporary or chic fads, and that lack genuine intellectual backing. However, on a casual basis, one is probably equally likely to run into new knowledge that is exciting, well-founded, and potentially highly useful. Care has to be exercised to evaluate the source of the new information, to make an informed professional judgment about the reliability of the source and the quality of the work done to develop the new technique. However, it has to be expected that in the ordinary course of professional life, we all run into thousands of bits of useful and useless information. It is not always easy to tell the difference when time for studying is limited.

All of the above schemes for designing integrated and eclectic forms of practice need to be worked out in an organized, planned fashion, take considerable time to develop, and are most practical when carried out in an organized way by a group of practitioners. The more formal approaches to integration are hard for an individual practitioner working on a large caseload with heavy pressures. A study of these formalized means of integrating models for an eclectic practice would serve individual practitioners well because they provide many ideas that could be experimented with on a partial basis by individual practitioners.

ADAPTING THE TASK-CENTERED APPROACH TO SETTINGS, CLIENT GROUPS, AND PROBLEMS: USING THE TASK-CENTERED MODEL FLEXIBLY

Firmly based on general problem-solving principles, the task-centered approach is able to take advantage of the relevance of problem solving to controlling the problems in living. It also readily fits a concentration on the client's own motivation. These characteristics, together with its systematic processes and empirical base, give the task-centered model general applicability. Nevertheless, it is always necessary in applying this model to adapt it to better fit particular settings, particular client groups, different problems, and the comfort and convenience of the practitioner.

There is a subtle but important distinction between integration of models and adaptation of a model. Integration is a process where the major action is to unite and blend two or more models or approaches. *Adaptation* of a unitary model refers to bringing one of them into correspondence with another, to improve its fit for a specific or new use or situation, often by modification. It could be argued that this is a distinction without a difference. The distinction may be fine, but it is real.

Like the processes of integration, informal adaptations of the task-centered approach (and, incidentally, of other approaches) are carried out constantly as practitioners select parts of various approaches, trying them out on a case-by-case basis and inventing novel procedures. The idea that adaptations should be systematically done and carefully studied and evaluated is a recent development, coming about in the course of the current emphasis on the legitimacy and necessity of planned eclecticism (Norcross, 1986).

Ideal, Systematic Adaptation

An ideal, systematic adaptation process would

1. *Consider risks and benefits.*
   - Taking a broad general look at the task-centered model, what would your hunches and beliefs be about its risks and benefits for the types of cases that comprise your practice?
   - What kinds of changes would you think would reduce the risks? Increase the benefits?
2. *Consider adaptation possibilities.* Still taking a broad general look, what changes would you make to increase the fit between the task-centered model and your own cases?
3. *Select three experimental cases.* Select cases to minimize bias: for example, the first three cases on Monday; or the first case on Monday, Wednesday, and Friday; or in any other manner that prevents making prejudgments on the suitability or nonsuitability of the case.
4. *Use the existing guidelines to handle the case.* It is advisable to use the guidelines as already in existence before making changes to check whether the expectation of a poor fit is actually the case. The guidelines may be found to work satisfactorily and need no alterations. The exception would be in settings where administrative requirements contraindicate one or more of the guidelines.
5. *Log the instances of gaps and misfits.* A sample log would include
   - Case identification
   - Date of occurrence
   - Guidelines used

- What was missing (gap)
- What was unsuitable (misfit)
- Other relevant information

6. *Design a revised guideline.* Referring to the adaptation possibilities considered in Item 2, and also to hypotheses generated in trying out the guidelines in Items 4 and 5, consider a range of alterations that could fill in gaps and improve the fit of the guidelines. Information on which to base the revision can be found in experience, in relevant research findings, and in the theory and guidelines of other models of practice. The source of the information should be stated.

7. *Try out the revised guidelines and log the results.* Repeat the revision process until the most satisfactory condition is obtained.

Informal Adaptation

Informal adaptation is bound to occur in the course of handling a case. Clinical judgment supersedes formal guidelines, except when that judgment leads to abandoning the model or turning it into some distinctly different entity. If possible, records should be kept of important informal adaptations so practitioners and their colleagues can study and replicate them.

Frequent Types of Adaptations

Adaptations include altering the order of the model, making substitutions, and providing two or more treatment sequences. The following sections describe each type of adaptation.

Altering the Order of the Model. The start-up and the first two steps of the task-centered model (that is, the referral or application and the identification of target problems, and the making of the contract) can be carried out in some other order when the circumstances would make it overly mechanical to comply fully with the order in the guidelines. In fact, experienced practitioners nearly always merge these steps. What is important to preserve the model's distinctive features is to be certain that the initial phases, that is, start-up and Steps 1 and 2, get done, regardless of order.

Of particular importance in rearranging the order are circumstances that come up in psychiatric clinics and in child welfare protective services. In psychiatric clinics, administrative regulations nearly always necessitate that the first order of business is diagnosis. This convention requires the assessment portion of Step 3, designed as part of the problem-solving effort, to be the first type of activity undertaken. However, in the course of securing the assessment information, the start-up, identification of target problems, and general features of the contract can be discussed and reviewed. Not many psychiatric clinics use a written contract, so that the proposed verbal contract can readily be woven into the full-bodied exploration that will constitute the assessment.

In child welfare protective services, the first order of business, according to prevailing interpretations of applicable laws and agency practices, is to investigate the possibility of child abuse and to make a decision on placement or home services. In these instances, the investigation, which has its own rules and guidelines, takes precedence over all the steps of the task-centered model. However, the task-centered model can be put into effect parallel to the investigation. Much of the information obtained from the client in the course of the investigation fulfills the requirements of the task-centered model's initial phases and so serves double duty. The addition of the contract may be helpful in such involuntary cases because it offers the client a measure of independence and respect that might otherwise be lacking in an authoritative process.

Making Substitutions.   It is always possible to substitute a procedure that serves the same or a similar purpose from another model. The caution that should be observed, however, is to avoid substituting an action that opposes the model. For example, one could not substitute open-ended, long-term treatment for a timed, goal-specific contract!

However, one could interpret the task development guidelines of the task-centered model as reflective discussion. The task-supporting procedures could be interpreted as sustainment, direct influence, exploration, and description. The provision of resources is environmental modification work. A good deal of the supporting of task performance can be seen as provision of interpersonal competencies.

Providing Two or More Treatment Sequences.   Sometimes termination is controlled not by the practitioner but by a court order or by a powerful administrative rule. For example, a client may be on probation for a time determined by the judge. A client may be in a court-ordered placement that he cannot leave without a formal release from a court. Aged persons may be held in long-term care because they cannot take care of themselves and have to live under institutional conditions. Such clients may have repeated episodes of service, usually for different problems because their living situation changes.

Adjusting the Model to Personal Style, Preferences, and Custom

Human service professionals have preferences for how to behave, how to sound, and what to emphasize in their work. They can become extremely uncomfortable if they are required to adopt a way of acting that grates against those preferences. Agencies also have customs, preferred terms, and ways of doing that they understand easily. There is no reason why practitioners or agencies must change their styles to use the task-centered model.

However, it must be noted that among the therapy disciplines old ideological struggles often take the form of conflict over terminology. The present period is seeing a diminution of these battles. The task-centered model, having been generated out of the revisionist trend of the 1970s, may sometimes speak in a language that offends the sensitivities of those who prefer another language. Although the language of the task-centered model conveys particular meanings, the various therapy languages tend to use different terms to convey the same or similar meanings. Therefore, it is not of prime importance to adhere to one language style rather than another, unless a language change alters the model's substance.

ADAPTING THE TASK-CENTERED MODEL TO PARTICULAR MODES AND SETTINGS

Involving Families and Other Important Persons

Contemporary family treatment is dated from the 1950s and has developed as an influential stream of thought and practice, relevant particularly for problems in which several family members, if not the whole family, are considered to be involved. Research in family treatment is a difficult undertaking and is not yet far advanced.

Adaptations of the task-centered approach to family problem solving are being developed (Fortune, 1985c; Mills, 1985; Rathbone-McCuan, 1985; Reid, 1985; Tolson, 1977). The essential strategy of family treatment within the task-centered approach emphasizes the identification of target problems and their subsequent reduction in accordance with the general guidelines already detailed in this book. Published reports on these developments show that practitioners who adopt the task-centered approach do so in an eclectic manner, influenced by communication and problem-solving training models, and by ideas about home tasks, in-session tasks, and environmental tasks. Reid (1985) and Mills (1985) have developed ways to expand the focus of the target problem to encompass issues in the problem context, thus to enhance the effect of the interventions, and possibly to have some influence on precipitating and maintaining factors. Rathbone-McCuan (1985) and Mills (1985) perceive a merging of crisis intervention with the task-centered approach under specific crisis conditions. The task-centered approach has been found to have a major strength in practice with older families and children because it fosters their participation rather than submerging their autonomous thinking and acting.

Levels of Family Involvement.   In using the task-centered model with families, the practitioner does not need to follow strict rules about who participates. Two levels of family involvement may pertain:

1. *Minimal or episodic involvement.* Occasional and collateral involvement of families is possible. There should be no prejudice or penalty to a client if relatives participate minimally or episodically. Family members may find it difficult to participate for various realistic reasons, aside from a reluctance to face issues and deal with problems. Working people often cannot take time from the job to attend treatment sessions. Fatigue and urgent interests may consume their off-work hours.

2. *Substantial involvement.* Some families want and agree to attend sessions regularly. Family involvement can be instrumental in providing services, practical problem-solving skills, and therapy. Family members may also be seen individually either for a series of sessions or intermittently. Married couples may be seen together in conjoint treatment.

Family interviews can be used to assess, to decide on priorities and duration, to divide up problem-solving activities (i.e., tasks) among family members, to increase the impact of the interventions, and to create flexibility in achieving desired goals.

Target Problem Identifications in Dealing with Families.   If feasible, target problem identification should be obtained from individuals, possibly in private, before issues are opened up to the group in the family meeting. Family members will often disagree about target problems. The practitioner can help members organize the array of target problems into clusters of those that seem reasonably related. When problems are clustered, disagreements are usually found to reflect contradictory or opposite perceptions of the same problems. These contradictory problem statements can be dealt with as if they are the same problem, only different sides to it.

The target problems on the present contract should be reduced to three. Additional problems should be put aside and may be taken up later. However, the processes of problem solving are such that these additional problems diminish and no longer need work after the work on the first three priorities has been accomplished. If there is an excess of urgent problems, they can be handled in parallel individual sessions or in any other manner that takes care of them expeditiously.

Important Others.   From time to time it will be desirable to include with a family significant other persons with whom the client and family are on intimate terms or closely involved. Caretakers would come under this category, for example, as would homemakers, landlords, or landladies. Still other important people might be aunts and uncles, cousins, neighbors, or spouse-companions.

Groups

Adaptations of the task-centered model for use with groups began with the original inception of the task-centered model. Fortune (1985b) has summarized the nature of these adaptations.

1. Forming groups so that the members' target problems and tasks are similar.
2. Using tasks that are the same or similar for each member.
3. Using visual aids (small charts or wall charts, for example) to clarify tasks and track them.
4. Interviewing some group members individually as well as in the group sessions.
5. Using specialized meeting formats to serve a purpose similar to that served by visual aids.

Fortune concludes that task-centered group treatment is adaptable for diverse populations in a range of institutional and community settings.

Child Welfare Practice

Rooney (1981) and Rzepnicki (1982) conducted practice research to generate systematically an adaptation of task-centered intervention applicable to work in child welfare. Rooney's model is developed for work with families separated because of child placement who have shown definite interest in being reunited. The model is considered to be a reunification process. Its unique adaptations include

1. *Limiting the permissible scope of target problems.* The target problems are defined only in connection with conditions blocking the child's return home to the natural parent or parents.
2. *Limiting the possibilities for interagency conflicts.* The practitioner maintains at least biweekly contact with all other agencies involved in the case to reduce adversary relationships and to enhance cooperation.
3. *Emphasizing parental visits.* Many parental visits with the child in placement are arranged, and on-the-spot counsel is made available.
4. *Monitoring regular task performance.* Visual aids and regular reviews in interviews are provided so that task performance can be monitored readily and kept on track with as little deviation as possible.
5. *Making access to practitioners easy.* Practitioners are available to help clients complete tasks to the maximum.
6. *Maintaining a high level of interaction among family members and attending to goals.* Tasks are formulated to maximize the family members sharing work and engaging in reciprocal tasks to achieve goals. In case of conflict between family members on strategy or targets, a reciprocal strategy should be used; that is, clients help one another but receive help directly in return for their focus or priority.

Rzepnicki (1982) developed a model that confined the target problem to expected barriers to achieving permanency for the child. This makes for an extremely closely focused practice. Case goals are addressed to reunifying the family (maintaining the child in the home or returning the child to the home) or achieving an alternative permanency plan. The Rzepnicki model resulted from a partial replication and further development of Rooney's work. The basic elements of the child welfare models as developed by Rooney and Rzepnicki are

1. *Target problems.* Target problems are limited to those conditions that, if not resolved, are harmful or likely to be harmful to the child.
2. *Social context assessment.* There is a thorough assessment of environmental deficiencies and personal and environmental strengths so that maximum effort may be given to remediable conditions that will ease the process of reunification.

3. *Joint case planning.* Coordination of effort of all agencies typically involved in foster care to maximize the service to the client.
4. *Clarification of responsibilities.* Accurate information should be provided to all the participants regarding what is expected of them by the agency, court, foster and/or natural parents, and each other. Legal sanctions, agency roles, and regulations should be communicated clearly and freely.
5. *Time limits.* Child welfare cases may last longer than other cases because problems may be very complex and courts make major decisions about time in care. Practitioners can monitor these cases and create several short contracts rather than enter into an unplanned, open-ended encounter.

Mental Health Settings

Law, custom, and history determine that the treatment of problems defined as mental illness is the domain of the medical profession, particularly psychiatry. A particular adaptation of the task-centered model can be made that should fit with this type of required practice (Brown, 1977 & 1980).

Start-up. The nature of mental health clinics is well known and their purpose is firmly understood in the human services system. There is little need to find out the referral source's goals or to negotiate an agreement on goals and resource availability. Except for the most unusual circumstances, clients are referred to mental health clinics for pretty much what mental health clinics do—diagnosis and treatment of mental illness or emotional disorder thought to resemble mental illness. For practical purposes, the start-up can be dispensed with.

Step 1: Client Target Problems Identified. Already having been classified as an actual or potential case of mental illness or disorder, the client may limit her attention to target problems such as personal traits, dysfunctional behaviors, moods, or cognitive confusion. However, she should not be discouraged or limited in the freedom to identify important problems of real-life circumstances. The problems the practitioner will be able to undertake will be constrained to those acceptable to the administration of the agency. These constraints on acceptable target problems have to be clarified and explained to the client if not readily understood.

In mental health clinics, the rapid early assessment needs to be expanded to permit the official psychiatric diagnosis according to the rules contained in the *DSM IV* (American Psychiatric Association, 1994), which covers clinical psychopathology, personality and developmental disorders, physical disorders, stressors, and appraisal of the client's highest adaptive capacity in the past year.

Step 2: Contract. The contract should be expanded to include drug therapy, psychotherapy, and any other type of therapy that will be provided by the clinic with the patient's agreement.

Step 3: Problem Solving.   An additional component, namely, provision of or support for a specifically psychiatric treatment plan having to do with drug therapy, psychotherapy, or other specified therapy is necessary in a mental health clinic setting. Large areas of overlap occur between what is customarily regarded as clinical therapy and what is called for in the guidelines of the task-centered model. The overlap is so great that in many instances the actual processes will be the same. When the processes are or appear to be different, they can be fitted into the problem-solving guidelines of the model, with those guidelines being rearranged and substitutions made to avoid unnecessary duplication of efforts.

Step 4: Termination.   Nothing in the task-centered termination guidelines is at variance with most mental health clinic practices.

Health Settings

As in the other settings discussed previously, problems being treated in health settings (hospitals or clinics) must be defined in a circumscribed fashion. Problems in health settings are confined to issues about the struggle to control the disease, the patients, the caretakers, the environment, the family, and work. Although these settings require no regular omissions from or additions to the task-centered model, the particular adaptation process is one of focusing. The sequences have to be focused on the patient's illness and medical recommendations for treatment. There is no escaping this focus in view of the all-embracing influence of the medical care institution (Epstein, 1983).

SUMMARY

It is always necessary to adapt the task-centered model to improve its fit in particular settings, with particular client groups, and with regard to different kinds of problems and the comfort and convenience of the practitioner. Formal, systematic adaptations offer the best route to creating effective adaptations consistent with maintaining the necessary essentials of the model. However, informal adaptations are continuously being made and should be recorded for later study and communication to colleagues. We have reviewed a number of studies that are directed toward developing model adaptations for child welfare, family treatment, groups, health, and mental health settings.

THREE TASK-CENTERED STUDIES

This section contains three adaptations of task-centered work: studies of work with surgical patients, with HIV/AIDS hospice patients, and with homeless individuals and families. Each of these is a single subject design study. Within the limitations of such studies, these projects illustrate the clinical usefulness and effectiveness of task-centered treatment in a variety of settings and with a wide variety of clients.

SURGICAL PATIENTS

Task-centered research within the hospital social work setting has been minimal. Wexler (1977) adopted the model in a pediatric hospital where crises frequently occurred and where the emphasis was on the family, not the individual. The first use reported of the task-centered approach was in a medical setting (Reid & Epstein, 1972). Reid (1992) described the potential usefulness of task-centered treatment in health settings but here we describe actual research to document the effectiveness of task-centered treatment with medical patients. This study and those that follow (Chapters 13 and 14) were primarily designed to accomplish clinical significance, that is, the workers' helpfulness to clients was paramount to the rigor of the research.

PREOPERATIVE INVOLVEMENT
WITH SURGICAL PATIENTS

From the point of view of the patient, surgery can be one of life's most frightening experiences. Operations considered minor by physicians may evoke severe anxiety reactions in the patient. "Will I survive?" "What will I be able to do afterward?" "How long of a recovery period?" and "Will it hurt?" are just a few of the concerns expressed by surgical patients. Surgery has become an acceptable means by which many disorders are corrected or eradicated.

This chapter is based on Debra Moriarty's MSW thesis research, which was supervised by Lester Brown.

The experience of surgery is unique in a patient's life. An individual's beliefs about health and illness can be classified into three major groups: the nonscientific system, the folk medical system, and the scientific system (Guerra & Aldrete, 1980). Most people live with more than one of these belief systems. The nonscientific belief system is based on religious or magical reasons. Illness is thought to be the result of another person or spiritual being. The second belief system, the folk medical system, is held by those that believe that diseases are defined as a disturbance in the laws of nature. Remedies are determined by the respected members of a society and passed from generation to generation. The last system, the scientific system, seeks to find rational empirical explanations for medical problems. Disease is believed to be the end result of the interaction of host (a human), an agent (parasite), and the environment (Guerra & Aldrete, 1980).

Many European Americans, African Americans, Asian Americans, Native Americans, and Latino Americans practice health activities that can be understood only in terms of these systems. Some share a concern for harmony and balance in nature. There may be a strong dependency on a god or a creator. Many Latino American groups believe in Curanderismo, which is the belief that illnesses can be cured by a Curandero(a) (a healer) who has been given healing powers by God (Guerra & Aldrete, 1980). It is necessary to be sensitive to ethnocultural characteristics in preparing patients for surgery. Clearly, patients' beliefs about their conditions are as significant as the views of the physician.

Anxiety about surgery is common, and it is an uncomfortable state of tension for any patient. It is infectious and communicated by both verbal and nonverbal cues. The patient does not usually share all of his concerns with his physicians. Indeed, some patients who seem calm to the physician may reveal anxiety to other health professionals. Social workers are in a unique position in the medical setting because they are trained to have an understanding of the psychological state of the patient and are in a crucial position to intervene with patients preoperatively.

The modern interest in the effects of psychological preparation of surgical patients dates to Lindemann (1941). In his study, fifty-one women from 20 to 55 years of age received a neuropsychiatric examination before abdominal surgery. The purpose of this study was to find out whether the amount of anxiety that the women experienced before surgery had anything to do with the postoperative course. Lindemann's (1941) study showed no significant relationship. However, in 1958, in a study of thirty people who were undergoing major surgery, Janis observed a relationship between the degree of fear manifested by the patients before an operation and the impact that this fear had on the patients' postoperative behavior. Janis (1958) found three patterns of coping with a potentially stressful situation: some patients showed a heightened level of anxiety about pain, mutilation by the surgeon, or even dying. The response was found to be a function of their personality structure. Other patients worried occasionally and were tense about specific concerns surrounding the surgery. Patients asked for information, and they were easily reassured. Postoperatively, they demonstrated good spirits and cooperated in their postoperative care. Thirdly, some patients exhibited an absence of anxiety. They demonstrated a high level of denial of the upcoming surgery and appeared to be invulnerable. After surgery, the latter became preoccupied with health concerns, were angry toward the medical staff, and refused even routine postoperative care.

Lindemann (1941) and Janis (1958) paved the way for additional research in this area. In 1964, Egbert and others completed an experiment with ninety-seven adult patients. This study demonstrated that patients given preoperative intervention consisting of patient education information and the teaching of a simple relaxation technique (deep breathing) showed better adjustment in the postoperative period than those that did not receive this intervention. Williams and others (Williams, Jones, & Williams, 1975) built on Egbert's work and demonstrated that the supportive type of preoperative involvement (one to two hours) was superior to a more cursory, brief approach.

Fortin and Kirouac (1976) found that patients who had been supplied with a broad range of information prior to surgery had a decreased analgesic utilization in the postoperative period. Also, communication with the patient by the anesthesiologist before surgery was recognized as another essential ingredient in psychologically preparing patients for surgery (Wallace, 1985).

Hypnosis was probably the first behaviorally oriented presurgical intervention used by the medical profession. Anderson and Masur (1983) pointed out that there have been studies showing the benefits of hypnosis, but also that mediating factors, such as relaxation, may cloud the benefits of this intervention (Bennet, 1985; Wilson, 1981). Stress inoculation serves as another cognitive/behavioral procedure that teaches people to prepare for and actively cope with stressors during medical treatment. Stress inoculation training has been applied successfully in a single case study to modify the maladaptive, depressive behavior of a cardiac patient facing open heart surgery (Blythe & Erdahl, 1986). Relaxation techniques and biofeedback taught to patients preoperatively also have been shown to decrease length of hospital stay, reduce the use of pain medication, and increase hospital recovery as compared to nonintervention groups (Alberts, Lyons, & Moretti, 1989). High anticipatory fear patients benefited the most from relaxation training, according to Wilson (1981).

Some general guidelines have been given for the most useful mix of presurgical intervention. Weiler (1968) asked open heart surgery patients which of the preoperative information given to them had been helpful. These patients reported that information about deep breathing, pain, oxygen, tubes, intensive care, and visiting hours as well as communication of information to relatives were most important to them. Lindeman and Van Aerman (1971) found that a structured presentation had a greater impact than unstructured approaches. There has been research suggesting that the most useful time for intervention is within two days prior to surgery (Christopherson & Pfeiffer, 1980). In Christopherson and Pfeiffer's study, patients who received information during this time had a significant decrease in anxiety from the presurgical period to the postsurgical period as compared to patients who received information three to thirty-five days preoperatively. Berkman and others (Berkman, Bedell, Parker, McCarthy, & Rosenbaum, 1988) evaluated the effectiveness of hospital social work preadmission screening and assessment with medical and surgical patients as compared to postadmission screening and assessment with the same population. Outcome variables included length of stay, readmission rates, posthospital home management, resource attachment, and satisfaction with hospital services (Berkman et al., 1988). The results showed preadmission patients reported better home management and a higher utilization of community resources. This preadmission screening also allowed social workers to alert physicians to psychosocial problems, which may have altered a physician's treatment plan for surgery (Berkman et al., 1988). Earlier screening and assessment with surgery patients may give social workers more time to use their discharge planning skills.

The majority of these studies revealed the efficacy of psychological preparation for surgery. Several studies showed that this preparation had positive outcomes on more than one measure. These studies, however, did not show consistent results for the same type of intervention. It seems that careful assessment of the psychological state of an individual is crucial before intervention. Three basic methods have been discussed: (a) sharing information about surgery with the patient, (b) teaching cognitive reappraisal to assist patients in dealing with anxiety-provoking thoughts, and (c) teaching some form of relaxation (behavior-oriented) technique.

Preoperative intervention, as shown through previous research, has resulted in a higher tolerance of pain, a more accepting attitude toward postoperative care, and earlier discharge from the hospital. For these reasons, psychological intervention by social workers with preoperative patients was considered for this study.

RESEARCH METHODOLOGY

This study was designed to look at the effectiveness of short-term task-centered treatment with problems encountered by elective surgery patients. The study used a quasi-experimental, single subject, multibaseline design (Barlow & Hersen, 1984). Single subject designs provide a technology for ongoing evaluation of interventions designed to meet identified social work goals. The multiple baseline design is useful in demonstrating the effectiveness of the task-centered intervention. Multiple baselines involve obtaining a stable baseline on two or more target problems and then sequentially introducing an intervention (task-centered) to the first target problem while recording baseline on the others. After the desired change has occurred in the first target problem, the same intervention is applied to the second and so on. Indeed, when clients present multiple problems, this design represents one way of dealing with them in some planned fashion, giving immediate action to those problems with the highest priority.

The study sample consisted of ten subjects randomly selected from elective surgery patients scheduled for surgery from November 1989 through January 1990 at Saint Joseph Hospital of Orange, California. Saint Joseph Hospital is a 500-bed private acute-care hospital in Orange County, California.

Subjects were randomly selected from a weekly surgery report printed by the Surgery Scheduling Department at Saint Joseph Hospital. Identifying information, including patient's name, telephone number, date of surgery, type of surgery, and medical insurance, was obtained from the hospital computer. Each subject's physician was contacted prior to the initial interview. None of the physicians contacted objected to the study. One physician requested that his patient not be contacted for two days, as the family was to discuss the need for surgery with the patient that night. Each subject was contacted by telephone one week prior to the scheduled surgery date.

A brief verbal explanation was provided to each subject, including an introduction to the practitioner and the facility/school, a description of the study and procedures, confidentiality, and the need for informed consent.

The initial interview consisted of four sections using a modification of the task-centered model format (Brown, 1980) to identify those issues of most concern to each respondent. The target problems were clearly specified and the level of associated anxiety was measured both during the baseline and during each intervention period.

Each client identified the two problems that were most important to him or her. These were labeled as Problem 1 (highest priority) and Problem 2 (second highest priority) for each client. Thus, Problems 1 and 2 were different for different clients.

In order to obtain a baseline prior to intervention, the respondent was requested to specify problem behaviors for the one week prior to contact by the practitioner, following the guidelines developed by Brown and Levitt (1979). Information regarding frequency, duration, location, and intensity of the behavior identified was obtained. Client self-anchored surgical anxiety scales were completed both before and after surgery, as well as self-anchored anxiety scales on each problem identified.

All study clients were then contacted twice during their hospitalization to continue to provide treatment on the target problems identified during the baseline interview. Task-planning activities were developed for the worker and client to do between sessions. Anxiety levels continued to be measured. Contacts with family, social agencies, physicians, and hospital personnel were recorded. Ratings of problem changes (using a ten-point scale) were assessed by both the client and practitioner. In more than one case, medical complications modified or delayed task achievement by clients. An additional session was also added for one client who spent one week in the Intensive Care Unit.

A closing interview was conducted one week after discharge from the hospital to determine the client's perception of changes in problems. Level of anxiety after surgery for each target problem continued to be measured. In this interview, the subject gave information on the perceived effectiveness of task-centered intervention.

At each client contact, the researcher used a modified, structured, written recording guide and assessment forms. These forms were used for each phase of the task-centered model. Data on problem status were obtained through client self-reports. Independent assessments by the practitioner with collaterals were made whenever possible.

The self-anchored score for anxiety, recorded on a five-point rating scale from "Little or no anxiety" to "Intense anxiety," allowed each client to report the intensity of anxiety about surgery and for each target problem. These scores were used as feedback to the client and the practitioner regarding problem change.

During the second and third sessions, a ten-point rating scale, ranging from "Problem greatly aggravated" to "Problem no longer present (completely alleviated)," was used to obtain a rating of problem change assessed by both the client and practitioner (Brown, 1980).

METHODS OF DATA ANALYSIS

The following methods for data analysis were implemented. Frequency distributions of the demographic characteristics of the ten surgery patients were recorded by hand. Problem types were classified into six different categories: Intrapersonal Conflict, Dissatisfaction with Social Relations, Difficulties with Formal Organizations, Inadequate Resources, Difficulty with Role Performance, and Self-Dissatisfaction (Reid, 1978). The difference in the scores for surgical anxiety and problem anxiety from preoperative involvement to final intervention were examined through nonparametric statistics (Nie, Hull, Jenkins, Steinbrenner, & Bent, 1975). Sign tests (Nie et al., 1975) were performed to compare problem-progress rating changes for both client and practitioner. The frequency distribution and the client and practitioner task progress means were compared for each problem (Nie et al., 1975).

CASE CHARACTERISTICS

Ages of study participants ranged from 60 to 80 years. Five women and five men participated in the study. One participant passed away before completing the study. Another subject had his surgery cancelled after admission to the hospital. Two of the study clients were Latino American; the others were European American. Half of the clients were married. Seven out of the ten clients lived either with family or spouse; three lived alone. Only one client had a psychiatric history. Nine out of the ten study clients had additional medical problems unrelated to the need for surgery. Length of stay in days for the study clients was about the average length of stay for all patients hospitalized with the same diagnosis at the hospital during the same time period. It is interesting to note that only the two Latino American clients had lengths of stay less than the average patient for that time period. (See Table 12.1.)

Table 12.2 shows how often each type of problem was rated as Problem 1 or Problem 2 by the clients. Intrapersonal Conflict was identified as Problem 1 by four clients—more than any other problem type. Inadequate Resources was iden-

TABLE 12.1   Client Planned Surgical Types, Frequencies, and Average Hospital Stays

| TYPE OF SURGERY | FREQUENCY | *Length of Stay (days)* *(November 1989 Through January 1990)* | |
		AVERAGE[a]	STUDY GROUP
Total hip replacement	3	8	8, 11, 8
Total hysterectomy	2	3	4, 3
Total knee	3	8	9, 9, 8
Colostomy closure	1	8	7
Colon resection/Ileostomy	1	10	14

Note: N = 10.

[a]Average length of stay for all patients hospitalized with the same diagnoses at Saint Joseph Hospital during the same time period as the study group.

tified as Problem 2 by four clients—more than any other problem type; it was also rated as either Problem 1 or Problem 2 more often than any other problem—by six clients.

COMPARISONS ACROSS CLIENTS

Comparisons were completed across clients for surgical anxiety and problem anxiety, problem change, task accomplishment, and follow-up information.

TABLE 12.2   Main Problem Types of Client Sample

MAIN PROBLEM CLASSIFICATION	PROBLEM[a]	FREQUENCY
Intrapersonal Conflict	1	4
	2	1
Dissatisfaction with Social Relations	1	1
	2	3
Difficulties with Formal Organizations	1	0
	2	1
Inadequate Resources	1	2
	2	4
Difficulty with Role Performance	1	0
	2	1
Self-Dissatisfaction	1	3
	2	0

Note: N = 10; total frequency exceeds 10 because all subjects reported at least two problem types.

[a]1 = given highest priority by client; 2 = given second highest priority by client.

Surgical Anxiety and Problem Anxiety

Surgical anxiety and problem anxiety were measured (five-point scale) preoperatively, during the second and third interactions and postoperatively. Statistically, sign tests were performed to show the difference between scores as measured at each contact for this sample. The differences in scores of anxiety between Time 1 and Time 2 were not significant (p < 1.00), yet the differences in anxiety scores between Time 1 and Time 4 were (p < .002) (Table 12.3).

Figures 12.1 to 12.10 show the changes in surgical anxiety and problem anxiety for each client. Cases 3, 4, and 10 had medical complications after surgery, which may have accounted for their increased scores at Time 1. For Clients 4 and 5, Problem 2 was not identified until Time 2. Client 5's medical complications may have accounted for his initial increase in anxiety for Problem 1, which was his inability to relax. Clinically, this client's level of anxiety decreased as he learned relaxation techniques. Figures 12.1 to 12.10 show the scores for surgical anxiety and problem anxiety for the ten cases at each contact.

The main problem was the one the client chose as having the highest priority. Nonparametric statistics (sign tests) were performed comparing Problem 1's anxiety scores for all cases. The differences in anxiety ratings were not significant between Time 1 and Time 2 (p = .375), but they were significant between Time 1 and Time 3 (p = .002) and between Time 1 and Time 4 (p = .003) (Table 12.4). This pattern was also seen with anxiety for Problem 2 for all cases. Between Time 1 and Time 2 the differences were not significant (p = .250), yet between Time 1 and Time 3 (p = .016) and between Time 1 and Time 4 (p = .008), they were. The trend of decreased ratings of anxiety tended to occur over both problems with each additional contact using task-centered treatment.

TABLE 12.3 Sign Test Results for Surgical Anxiety from Time 1 through Time 4

TIME OF MEASUREMENT	TWO-TAILED p	LEVEL OF SIGNIFICANCE
Time 1 Time 2	1.00	NS
Time 1 Time 3	.070	NS
Time 1 Time 4	.002	p < .05
Time 2 Time 3	.039	p < .05
Time 2 Time 4	.004	p < .05
Time 3 Time 4	.002	p < .05

Note: NS = nonsignificant.

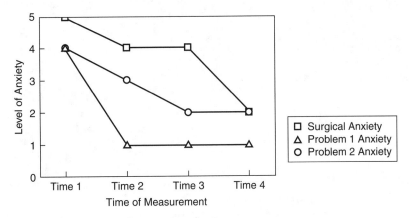

FIGURE 12.1   Levels of Surgical and Problem Anxiety at the Four Intervention Times for Problems 1 and 2: Client Case 1

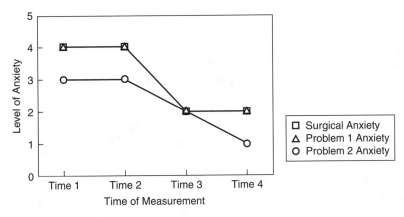

FIGURE 12.2   Levels of Surgical and Problem Anxiety at the Four Intervention Times for Problems 1 and 2: Client Case 2

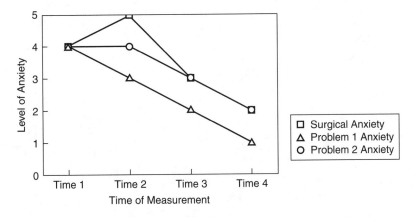

FIGURE 12.3   Levels of Surgical and Problem Anxiety at the Four Intervention Times for Problems 1 and 2: Client Case 3

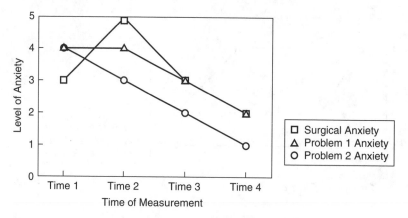

FIGURE 12.4 Levels of Surgical and Problem Anxiety at the Four Intervention Times for Problems 1 and 2: Client Case 4

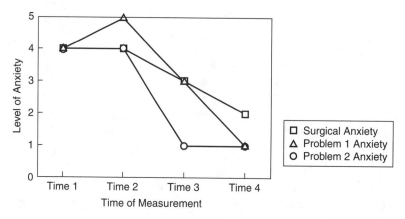

FIGURE 12.5 Levels of Surgical and Problem Anxiety at the Four Intervention Times for Problems 1 and 2: Client Case 5

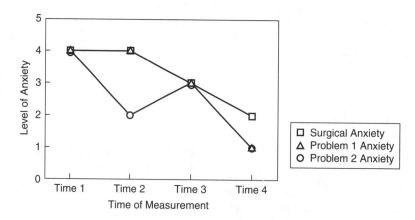

FIGURE 12.6 Levels of Surgical and Problem Anxiety at the Four Intervention Times for Problems 1 and 2: Client Case 6

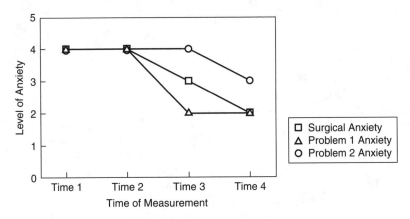

FIGURE 12.7   Levels of Surgical and Problem Anxiety at the Four
Intervention Times for Problems 1 and 2: Client Case 7

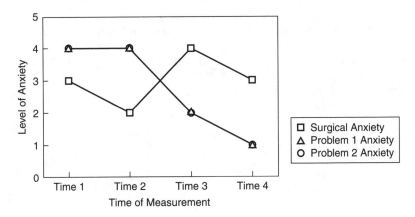

FIGURE 12.8   Levels of Surgical and Problem Anxiety at the Four
Intervention Times for Problems 1 and 2: Client Case 8

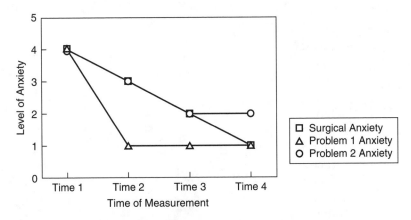

FIGURE 12.9   Levels of Surgical and Problem Anxiety at the Four
Intervention Times for Problems 1 and 2: Client Case 9

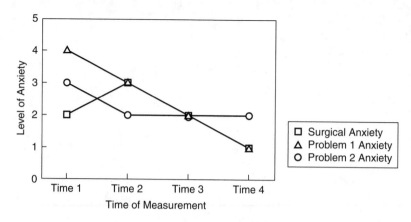

FIGURE 12.10   Levels of Surgical and Problem Anxiety at the Four
Intervention Times for Problems 1 and 2: Client Case 10

TABLE 12.4   Sign Test Results for Anxiety Related to Problems 1 and 2

TIME OF MEASUREMENT		TWO-TAILED p	LEVEL OF SIGNIFICANCE
Problem 1	Time 1 Time 2	.375	NS
	Time 1 Time 3	.002	p < .05
	Time 1 Time 4	.003	p < .05
	Time 2 Time 3	.008	p < .05
	Time 2 Time 4	.008	p < .05
	Time 3 Time 4	.062	NS
Problem 2	Time 1 Time 2	.250	NS
	Time 1 Time 3	.016	p < .05
	Time 1 Time 4	.008	p < .05
	Time 2 Time 3	.070	NS
	Time 2 Time 4	.004	p < .05
	Time 3 Time 4	.062	NS

Note: NS = nonsignificant.

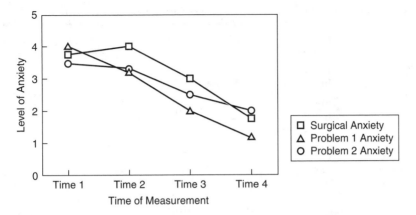

FIGURE 12.11   Mean Levels of Surgical and Problem Anxiety at the Four Intervention Times for Problems 1 and 2: Total Client Sample ($N = 10$)

The slopes of Figures 12.1 to 12.11 indicate an overall decrease in levels of anxiety over time for Problems 1 and 2 for all ten cases.

Problem Change.   Changes in targeted problems were measured by both the client and the practitioner. Change ratings were based on a ten-point scale: 1 = "Problem greatly aggravated"; 2 = "Considerable aggravation"; 3 = "Some aggravation"; 4 = "Slight aggravation"; 5 = "No change"; 6 = "Minimally alleviated"; 7 = "Some alleviation"; 8 = "Considerable alleviation"; 9 = "Substantial alleviation"; and 10 = "Problem no longer present (completely alleviated)." Brown (1980) and Reid (1978) both reported high levels of reliability for judgment in using this ten-point scale.

Sign tests were performed comparing rating changes evaluated by both the client and the practitioner for both Problems 1 and 2 (Table 12.5). Ratings by both the client and the practitioner showed similar results. Overall, there was a significant change from Time 1 to Time 4, from the point of view of both the client and the practitioner. This trend continued to support the decrease in anxiety previously mentioned for Problems 1 and 2.

Task Accomplishment.   To effect problem change, client and practitioner tasks were carried out between sessions during the problem-solving phase. A task was selected to address a particular target problem. For example, Client 9's target Problem 1 was that he had no one to assist him at home after discharge from the hospital. This problem resulted in the development of the following tasks:

1. Client will contact his insurance carrier to find out what his coverage is for home services or extended care placement.
2. The practitioner will explore costs of available options for discharge.
3. Client will prepare questions and notify social worker regarding home plan.
4. Practitioner will finalize arrangements with extended care facility for transfer.

TABLE 12.5   Sign Test Results for Progress Rating Changes for Clients and Practitioner

TIME OF MEASUREMENT		TWO-TAILED p	LEVEL OF SIGNIFICANCE
Problem 1 (client)	Time 2 Time 3	.070	NS
	Time 2 Time 4	.016	$p < .05$
	Time 3 Time 4	.062	NS
Problem 1 (practitioner)	Time 2 Time 3	.070	NS
	Time 2 Time 4	.016	$p < .05$
	Time 3 Time 4	.062	NS
Problem 2 (client)	Time 2 Time 3	.687	NS
	Time 2 Time 4	.062	NS
	Time 3 Time 4	.125	NS
Problem 2 (practitioner)	Time 2 Time 3	.375	NS
	Time 2 Time 4	.062	NS
	Time 3 Time 4	.125	NS

Note: NS = nonsignificant.

Table 12.6 indicates the number of tasks developed in each case for each problem. Overall, thirty-three tasks (60 percent) were assigned to the clients, and twenty-two tasks (40 percent) were assigned to the practitioner. Task progress ratings probably provide a better idea of the success of problem-solving actions than tallying the number of tasks. A five-point scale was used during each session when tasks were reviewed from the previous session: 0 = "No opportunity to carry out task"; 1 = "Minimally achieved" (or not achieved); 2 = "Partially achieved"; 3 = "Substantially achieved"; and 4 = "Completely achieved."

Tables 12.7 and 12.8 show mean achievement in each case for each problem. In some cases, only client or only practitioner tasks were assigned for problem resolution. For Client 7, physical limitations did not allow him the opportunity to follow through on an assigned task of attending a preoperative class. Tasks were assigned at different times during the four sessions.

TABLE 12.6   Number of Tasks Developed per Client and Practitioner

CLIENT	PROBLEM[a]	CLIENT TASKS	PRACTITIONER TASKS	TOTAL TASKS
1	1	1	—	1
	2	4	2	6
2	1	2	—	2
	2	1	—	1
3	1	2	3	5
	2	1	—	1
4	1	1	1	2
	2	3	1	4
5	1	3	—	3
	2	—	1	1
6	1	1	1	2
	2	2	2	4
7	1	1	3	4
	2	1	1	2
8	1	4	3	7
	2	1	—	1
9	1	2	—	2
	2	1	2	3
10	1	2	—	2
	2	2	—	2

Note: — = no task assigned.

[a] 1 = given highest priority by client; 2 = given second highest priority by client.

TABLE 12.7   Client Task Progress Means

CLIENT	PROBLEM 1 M	PROBLEM 2 M	OVERALL M
1	4.00	2.57	3.29
2	3.50	4.00	3.75
3	4.00	2.00	3.00
4	3.00	3.42	3.2.1
5	4.00	—	4.00
6	2.00	4.00	3.00
7	0	2.00	1.00
8	3.55	—	3.55
9	4.00	4.00	4.00
10	3.83	3.40	3.60

Note: — = no task assigned.

TABLE 12.8   Practitioner Task Progress Means

CLIENT	PROBLEM 1 M	PROBLEM 2 M	OVERALL M
1	—	4.00	4.00
2	—	—	—
3	3.50	—	3.50
4	4.00	4.00	4.00
5	—	4.00	4.00
6	3.00	4.00	3.50
7	3.86	4.00	3.93
8	3.86	3.00	3.43
9	—	3.75	3.75
10	—	—	—

Note: — = no task assigned.

In looking at the overall mean task progress ratings for the ten clients, it appears that the practitioner had greater success in carrying out tasks than the clients. However, even the clients tended to achieve tasks "Substantially" with the exception of Client 7, whose mean task rating was at the "Partially achieved" level.

Sign tests were performed comparing progress ratings for clients and practitioner. Results show there was not a significant difference in progress ratings between Time 1 and Time 3 (p = .250) or between Time 2 and Time 3 (p = .250) for the clients. For the practitioner, there was a difference between Time 1 and Time 3 (p = .031), but not between Time 2 and Time 3 (p = 1.000).

The practitioner noted obstacles to task accomplishment whenever a task was not completed. Once the client had trouble carrying out a task, the problem-solving action was revised to help ensure success. Any hospital system factors affecting treatment favorably or unfavorably were noted.

Difficulties in carrying out tasks were usually a result of the client's physical problems or a lack of support from others in a client's physical environment. These difficulties were most often overcome by the practitioner advocating for the clients within the medical system and by significant others supporting task achievement.

Follow-Up

Follow-up data of all the clients revealed that the clients felt that their situations were substantially improved and their anxiety had decreased, particularly in reference to the ten main problems. All client-reported reactions to the task-centered focus were positive.

SUMMARY AND CONCLUSIONS

This study showed Intrapersonal Conflict to be the major problem targeted as Problem 1 (highest in priority) and Inadequate Resources to be the main problem for Problem 2 (second highest in priority). Problems were targeted and prioritized by the clients, allowing the practitioner to be culturally sensitive. The problems identified by the two Latino American clients were not different from those defined by the European American clients. Preoperative surgical anxiety was high for all clients but decreased after surgery and with intervention. Problem anxiety also indicated an overall decrease over time for all ten cases.

The data provided evidence of the effectiveness of intervention with the study clients. Although the degree of change differed from one client to the next, all ten clients made progress toward problem resolution. Furthermore, change did not occur until the task planning and implementation sequence was initiated, suggesting that the initial contact alone did not result in problem alleviation.

The practitioner had greater success in task accomplishment than the clients. However, the clients achieved tasks "Substantially." Although these evaluations tended to be subjective ratings, there was considerable agreement between clients and practitioner regarding problem change and task achievement.

Follow-up data indicated the majority of the target problems improved. Surgical anxiety and problem anxiety had decreased. All ten clients expressed satisfaction with services provided and reacted positively to the task-centered focus of treatment.

This study demonstrated an effort to test task-centered intervention with elective surgery patients. It addressed some of the problems faced by patients preoperatively and postsurgery. Most of the subjects were elderly with numerous health problems. Seven out of the ten subjects lived with someone, either extended family or a spouse. This suggests that if an individual has another person in the home to assist even minimally, the chances of returning home faster after surgery are greater. Broken down by diagnosis, the length of stay for the study population was higher as compared with the average length of stay for the same time period and the same diagnoses at Saint Joseph Hospital. It is interesting to note that only the two Latino American clients had lengths of stay less than the average patient for that time period. Both clients had large extended families and went home sooner from the hospital. Latino American traditions tend to reinforce adult–child responsibilities for parents (Devore & Schlesinger, 1996), which may account for their earlier discharges.

Whenever possible, the problems were defined as the client perceived them. This allowed the practitioner to be culturally sensitive, minimizing the risk of attributing personality disorders to system-induced behaviors. Also, it is important to note that structured problem-oriented forms of treatment may work best with more disadvantaged clients (Brown, 1980). This study used random sampling, where the most disadvantaged clients were not necessarily targeted.

The main problem addressed for Problem 1 was Intrapersonal Conflict, followed by Inadequate Resources for Problem 2. Examples of Intrapersonal Conflict include internalization of stress-causing health problems; problems controlling anger; and depression relating to physical limitations caused by chronic illness. Problems with Inadequate Resources included financial difficulties and problems with finding adequate home care.

Overall, surgical anxiety before and after surgery, as well as problem anxiety for each problem identified, showed decreased ratings at each contact. The results suggested that preoperative anxiety is related more to emotion management worries than actual concerns about surgical procedure.

Changes in targeted problems by both the client and the practitioner were statistically significant from Time 1 to Time 4. This trend supported the decrease in surgical anxiety and problem anxiety. Because reliability of data was difficult to obtain through direct observation, whenever possible data were verified through another source (e.g., family members, medical records, etc.). From the results, it can be concluded that these clients showed progress in problem reduction. All problems that were identified improved. Furthermore, there appeared to be a relationship between task achievement and problem change ratings.

What was particularly helpful when using task-centered therapy in the acute hospital setting was the active involvement by the client, the detailed responsibilities outlined by both the practitioner and the client, and the clarity of the issues, making it possible to assess the problem outcome and resolution.

....

CHAPTER THIRTEEN

HIV/AIDS HOSPICE PATIENTS

WITH MISSAK PARSSEGHIAN

HOSPICE AND AIDS	TASK ACCOMPLISHMENTS
RESEARCH METHODOLOGY	SUMMARY
CASE CHARACTERISTICS	

In this study, task-centered social treatment was examined to see how helpful it might be in assisting acquired immuno-deficiency syndrome (AIDS) hospice patients with their problems. Because AIDS hospice patients have a limited life span and must address unfinished tasks, short-term treatment is the model of choice.

HOSPICE AND AIDS

In the past, hospices were mainly concerned with those dying of cancer. The AIDS epidemic started in the early 1980s; by the late 1980s, hospice programs started to care for AIDS patients (Torrens, 1985). The majority of the hospices providing care for AIDS patients were small homes with four to six beds (Kilburn, 1988). Von Guten and others (Von Guten, Martinez, Weitzman, & Von Roen, 1991) have suggested that hospice programs should care only for those who acknowledge their imminent death and are preparing for it. Recently, many AIDS hospice residents were able to return home due to the new "cocktail" (combinations of antiviral medications), which has successfully ridden some HIV-positive persons of any testable level of HIV in their bodies. Others have not been so fortunate.

Although AIDS and non-AIDS hospices have similarities, there are some important factors that are unique to each. If a program is set up to care for patients dying from differing conditions, the purpose will be more diffuse and the purpose will be seen less clearly by the community and by its own staff. The program will have to develop a broader range of services and capabilities and will not be able to provide its patients and staff with specifically designed programs for accomplishing objectives (Torrens, 1985).

One similarity between AIDS hospices and other hospices is that both cater to the terminally ill. Some other similarities can be found in the care being provided. The primary intent in all hospices is to provide symptom relief and maintenance of functions and quality of life (Von Guten et al., 1991).

One of the most obvious differences between AIDS and cancer hospices is the stigma associated with persons with AIDS. There are AIDS hospices in hospital settings. Due to the lack of education and the fears of hospital staff, the hospice sits as a separate entity without any in-house support services. Many of the residents of AIDS hospices seem to have no families. Those who do have families may have had their relationships with their families severed for many years. In the early stages of the AIDS epidemic, the significant other was pushed aside and was denied the basic rights that most spouses enjoy. The grief of significant others was not dealt with in the same way as the grief of family members of a cancer patient. Significant others did not have the benefit of treatment or support for their grief.

Due to the rising number of drug users with AIDS, many of the residents are homeless and do not have viable support systems. There are those who have adoptive families. In an AIDS hospice, many of the patients, while having supportive care providers and volunteers, die without family being present. Due to lack of funds, many AIDS hospice patients are cremated in a county morgue, with no funeral. Their ashes are simply discarded.

Contrary to AIDS hospices, cancer hospices have little or no stigma attached to them anymore. The majority of cancer patients have supportive families and enjoy the benefit of having insurance and funds for funerals. There have been instances in which cancer hospices have turned down AIDS patients due to the stigma attached or the specific care they require. Today, there are hospices that provide care for both AIDS and cancer patients.

Many people of color with AIDS in California do not have private health insurance and must rely on Medicaid (Medi-Cal) to fund their care. Because of the disparity in health care available under private insurance and Medicaid or Medi-Cal, a two-tiered system of health care delivery is emerging, with the public sector heavily overrepresented by minority group members (Benfer, 1987). Fortunately, there are AIDS organizations with hospices that provide great care and support. These hospices provide care for many of those with Medicaid or Medi-Cal, county indigents, and those with no insurance at all.

Social work in an AIDS hospice has many components. It is the social worker's responsibility to make clear to the patients all the criteria connected with being admitted to the hospice. It is possible at this stage for patients to go through denial. During these periods, the social worker assists the patients in coming to terms with their reality. The social worker comforts patients by informing them of what the hospice offers, how they will be cared for, and (most importantly) how every effort will be made by all staff members to provide the best possible care (Torrens, 1985).

Social workers and clients must work on many task-oriented issues. These range from completing a Supplemental Security Income (SSI) application, providing assistance to receive Medicaid, completing durable power of attorney forms so that a designated agent can carry out the patient's wishes, completing funeral arrangements, getting to and from a dentist for dentures or cavity repair, and setting up transportation for patient needs in the community (such as assistance with bus passes).

Social workers counsel patients in dealing with issues of depression, denial, anger, and acceptance of death (Krieger, 1988). The amount of work necessary with each patient depends upon where the patient is with the illness and how well the patient has accepted it (Krieger, 1988). Counseling of family, lovers, or friends occurs on a regular basis. Support groups for patients, families, lovers, friends, and volunteers are conducted by social workers.

In the last stages of AIDS, it is extremely important for the social worker to provide the necessary support to the dying patient. There are times when no words are exchanged; just being present is comforting. Upon a patient's death, the social worker works with the family, lover, and friends to assist them through the grieving process.

The task-centered model can be used as a case-management model and was chosen to target the specific problems of patients in the AIDS hospice in this study. Task-centered treatment can be used to help when hospice patients with AIDS experience helplessness, guilt, loss of control, denial, anger, depression, anxiety, and bereavement due to multiple losses. They may also experience legal, financial, social, and medical problems; loss of income; and unemployment and housing concerns (Ostrow, Sandholzer, & Felman, 1983).

RESEARCH METHODOLOGY

The study sample consisted of ten subjects. These subjects came from a variety of ethnic backgrounds.

A brief verbal explanation, which included introduction of the practitioner and the study, was given to each subject. A description of the study procedures was also provided.

A list of problems presented by the subject was narrowed down to no more than three problems. The central importance was in defining the problem so that it was congruent with the subject's own interests and perception (Epstein, 1988). Special attention was given to work in as structured and systematic a fashion as possible (Epstein, 1988).

A social worker met with each subject twice weekly or weekly for the length of the study. Tasks that were accomplished were discussed, and new tasks were implemented if and when new problems were targeted. New problems were prioritized and added to the contract, as specified and defined.

The study used a quasi-experimental single subject, multibaseline design (Barlow & Hersen, 1984). No control group was possible, so each subject acted as her own control. Previous occurrence of the problem was used as a baseline and, in essence, as a control for change. The majority of the subjects had three problems; two subjects had only two problems. Once problems were established, tasks were developed for solutions. All data were recorded using the recording guides developed for previous studies (Brown, 1980).

Graphs were used to show problem change for each subject's problem. Measures of change were generally taken at each interview. These data were used in the graphs. Task achievement was an additional measure in the effectiveness of intervention. These were rated using a five-point scale ranging from "No opportunity to carry out task" to "Completely achieved." Measures of problem change were rated by subject and practitioner on a scale ranging from 1 = "Problem greatly aggravated" to 10 = "Problem no longer present."

CASE CHARACTERISTICS

Subjects were seen according to need, ranging from twice a week to weekly. On each contact, task-centered methods were used. Subject characteristics are summarized in Table 13.1. Table 13.2 provides data on the main problem types reported by the study subjects.

Table 13.1 reveals that four of the study clients were African American, four were European American, and the remaining two were Latino American. There were nine males and one female. The clients ranged from 27 to 51 years of age. One was married, four were single, four were divorced, and one was widowed. Three had one child; one had two children; two had more than two children; and four had no children at all. Six of the ten clients had a history of drug abuse. All of the clients had the prognosis of less than six months to live.

Table 13.2 shows Depression as the most cited problem. These clients were all in a hospice and dying of AIDS—many with no family or friends to support them and many with backgrounds of drug addiction. Depression was normal at times. Lack of Funeral Arrangements and Lack of Legal Arrangements were the next two most frequently cited problems. Lack of Funeral Arrangements included the need to complete cremation and burial plans. Lack of Legal Arrangements included the need for completion of Durable Power of Attorney for Health Care and need for completion of wills. Not listed in the table are the least cited problems: Lack of Medi-Cal (Medicaid), Lack of Transportation, Lack of Socialization, Need to Contact SSI, Need to Celebrate Birthday, and Need of Family Counseling. Table 13.2 also shows the degree of problem change achieved for each major problem type.

TASK ACCOMPLISHMENTS

During the problem-solving stage, client and practitioner tasks were carried out to effect problem change. For example, Client 1's second priority Target Problem was that he did not have enough information on what was available as far as AIDS services in Kinshasa, Zaire. This information was vital for him so that he could decide

TABLE 13.1   **Demographics of Subjects**

DEMOGRAPHIC CHARACTERISTIC	FREQUENCY
Ethnicity	
African American	4
European American	4
Latino American	2
Gender	
Male	9
Female	1
Age	
Range: 27 to 51 years	
Marital status	
Married	1
Single	4
Divorced	4
Widowed	1
Children	
None	4
1 child	3
2 children	1
More than 2	2
History of Drug Abuse	
Yes	6
No	4

whether to stay in the hospice in the United States or to return home to his family. This problem resulted in the development of the following tasks: The practitioner contacted the AIDS Resource Center in Washington, DC, and obtained a referral to the World Health Organization. The practitioner contacted the World Health Organization in New York City, and obtained referral to the Global Program on AIDS in Geneva, Switzerland. The practitioner faxed a request to Global Program on AIDS for possible services in Kinshasa, Zaire, and received a return fax with a

TABLE 13.2   **Main Problem Types of Client Sample**

MAIN PROBLEM CLASSIFICATION	FREQUENCY	PROBLEM CHANGE
Depression	7	6
Lack of funeral arrangements	4	6
Lack of legal arrangements	4	8
Lack of contact with family	3	7

proper connection. The client wrote a letter to the regional office in Congo requesting information for AIDS services in Zaire.

Table 13.3 indicates the number of tasks developed in each case for each problem. Overall, 115 tasks were developed. Clients had thirty-six tasks (31.3 percent) and the practitioner had seventy-nine tasks (68.7 percent). In this setting (hospice), the clients were frequently too weak to carry out tasks and often needed the worker to help implement tasks. A five-point scale was used during each session to rate how much progress had been made on tasks since the previous session: 0 = "No opportunity to carry out task"; 1 = "Minimally achieved" (or not achieved); 2 = "Partially achieved"; 3 = "Substantially achieved"; and 4 = "Completely achieved" (Brown, 1980).

TABLE 13.3   **Number of Tasks Developed for Client and Practitioner**

CLIENT	PROBLEM	CLIENT TASKS	PRACTITIONER TASKS	TOTAL
1	1	2	3	5
	2	1	3	4
	3	2	3	5
2	1	0	4	4
	2	3	3	6
	3	1	3	4
3	1	3	3	6
	2	3	7	10
	3	1	2	3
4	1	1	2	3
	2	1	2	3
	3	0	2	2
5	1	1	2	3
	2	2	6	8
6	1	2	3	5
	2	0	2	2
	3	0	2	2
7	1	1	2	3
	2	0	4	4
8	1	1	2	3
	2	4	4	8
	3	0	2	2
9	1	1	3	4
	2	2	2	4
	3	1	2	3
10	1	1	2	3
	2	2	2	4
	3	0	2	2

Measures of problem change were rated by subject and practitioner on a scale ranging from 1 = "Problem greatly aggravated" to 10 = "Problem no longer present." For this study, the ratings of problem change shown on the graphs were from 5 = "No change" to 10 = "Problem no longer present," because no problems got a rating of "Worse" (4 or less on the ten-point scale). Figures 13.1 through 13.10 show the task progress achieved for each client, using only the 5 to 10 ratings.

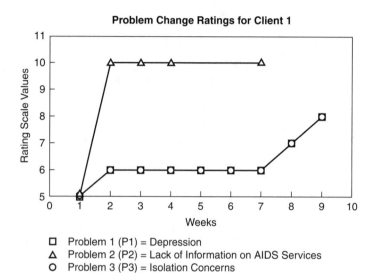

Problem 1 (P1) = Depression
Problem 2 (P2) = Lack of Information on AIDS Services
Problem 3 (P3) = Isolation Concerns

FIGURE 13.1   Task Progress for Client 1

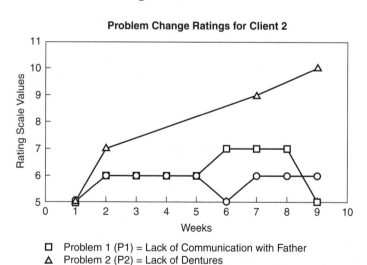

Problem 1 (P1) = Lack of Communication with Father
Problem 2 (P2) = Lack of Dentures
Problem 3 (P3) = Depression

FIGURE 13.2   Task Progress for Client 2

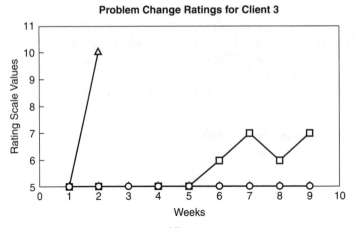

FIGURE 13.3   Task Progress for Client 3

Figures 13.4 and 13.5 show the greatest success in task achievement occurred for the completion of legal arrangements. There was less success with completion of funeral arrangements, as shown in Figure 13.3. Only two of the four were successful, as shown in Figures 13.4 and 13.10. Figures 13.1, 13.2, 13.3, 13.5, 13.7, and 13.8 show the progress achieved with depression.

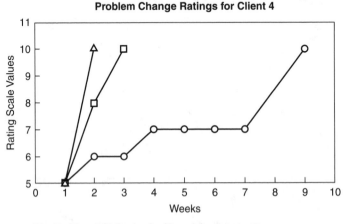

FIGURE 13.4   Task Progress for Client 4

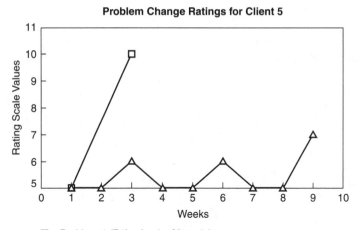

FIGURE 13.5   **Task Progress for Client 5**

Table 13.4 shows that nine of the ten clients had positive outcomes (complete, substantial, or moderate problem reduction), indicated by the + signs in the overall column. One client had no change for two of the three problems, due either to lack of support from the agencies involved or the inability of the client to act. The ones with minuses (–) are problems that were only minimally impacted. The zero (0) indicates no change in problem status.

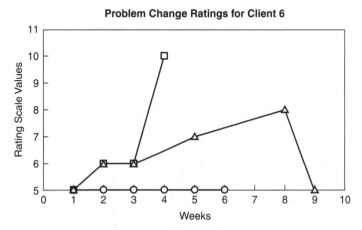

FIGURE 13.6   **Task Progress for Client 6**

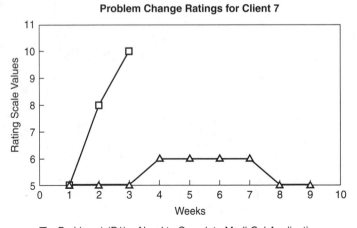

FIGURE 13.7   Task Progress for Client 7

Table 13.5 shows that the greatest success in problem accomplishment was the Lack of Legal Arrangements; next was Lack of Family Contact, then Depression; last was the Lack of Funeral Arrangements.

Table 13.6 shows that the majority of the clients were able to substantially accomplish their selected tasks. Only Client 6 had minimally achieved the tasks.

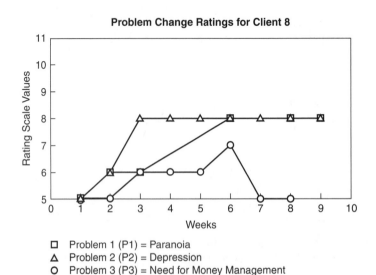

FIGURE 13.8   Task Progress for Client 8

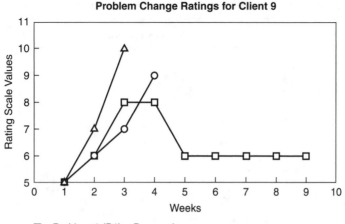

Problem 1 (P1) = Depression
Problem 2 (P2) = Need to Contact Family
Problem 3 (P3) = Lack of Legal Arrangements

FIGURE 13.9   Task Progress for Client 9

Table 13.7 shows that the practitioner was able to almost complete every one of his tasks for each client problem.

Tables 13.8 and 13.9 show a comparison of problem change by race/ethnicity and by drug use. Neither chi-square was significant. Race/ethnicity and drug use could not be shown to account for differences in problem change. The use of

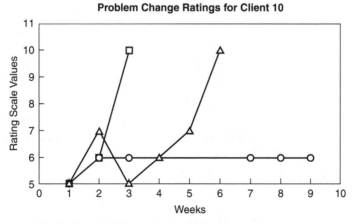

Problem 1 (P1) = Lack of Legal Arrangements
Problem 2 (P2) = Lack of Funeral Arrangements
Problem 3 (P3) = Death Denial

FIGURE 13.10   Task Progress for Client 10

TABLE 13.4   **Summary of Problem Achievement Scores for All Clients**

CLIENT	PROBLEM	ACHIEVEMENT SCORE	OVERALL SCORE
1	1	+	
	2	+	
	3	+	+
2	1	0	
	2	+	
	3	+	+
3	1	+	
	2	+	
	3	+	+
4	1	+	
	2	+	
	3	+	+
5	1	+	
	2	+	+
6	1	+	
	2	0	
	3	0	0
7	1	+	
	2	0	+
8	1	+	
	2	+	
	3	0	+
9	1	0	
	2	+	
	3	+	+
10	1	+	
	2	+	
	3	0	+

task-centered treatment appears to achieve problem change equally well, regard-less of the ethnicity of the clients. Previous drug use also did not appear to affect problem change.

SUMMARY

In this study, short-term, task-centered treatment was used to examine its use-fulness in solving problems of hospice residents. Task-centered casework was selected because of its proven effectiveness in previous studies. No prior studies have taken place using task-centered casework in a hospice setting.

TABLE 13.5   Summary of Specific Problem Accomplishments for All Clients

PROBLEM	CLIENT	ACHIEVEMENT SCORE
Depression	1	+
	2	0
	3	+
	5	+
	7	0
	8	+
	9	0
Lack of Funeral Arrangements	3	0
	4	+
	6	0
	10	+
Lack of Legal Arrangements	4	+
	5	+
	9	+
	10	+
Lack of Family Contact	2	0
	6	+
	9	+

The Moriarty (1990) study most closely resembles this study. Her patients achieved a significant degree of problem reduction as measured by her during the course of treatment and at the end of treatment. The present study used much the same methodology as Moriarty (1990).

In this study, task-centered therapy was tested for its effectiveness in solving problems of hospice residents. Subjects came from various backgrounds, including

TABLE 13.6   Client Task Achievement Mean Scores

CLIENT	P1 MEAN	P2 MEAN	P3 MEAN	OVERALL MEAN
1	3.00	4.00	2.00	3.00
2	0.00	4.00	2.00	2.00
3	4.00	2.00	0.00	2.00
4	4.00	4.00	4.00	4.00
5	4.00	3.00	*	3.50
6	3.00	0.00	0.00	1.00
7	4.00	1.00	*	2.50
8	2.00	3.00	1.00	2.00
9	1.00	4.00	4.00	3.00
10	4.00	4.00	0.00	2.65

*No problem (P) cited by client.

TABLE 13.7   **Practitioner Task Achievement Mean Scores**

CLIENT	P1 MEAN	P2 MEAN	P3 MEAN	OVERALL MEAN
1	4.00	4.00	4.00	4.00
2	4.00	4.00	3.00	3.67
3	4.00	3.00	2.00	3.00
4	4.00	4.00	4.00	4.00
5	4.00	4.00	*	4.00
6	4.00	3.00	2.00	3.00
7	4.00	2.00	*	3.00
8	3.00	3.00	4.00	3.34
9	3.00	4.00	4.00	3.67
10	4.00	4.00	3.00	3.67

*No problem (P) cited by client.

TABLE 13.8   **Problem Change by Race/Ethnicity**

RACE	PROBLEM 1	PROBLEM 2	PROBLEM 3
African American	9.50	7.50	7.00
White	7.25	8.25	6.67
Latino	10.00	8.50	6.00

TABLE 13.9   **Problem Change by Drug Use**

DRUG USE	PROBLEM 1	PROBLEM 2	PROBLEM 3
Yes	8.50	8.34	6.84
No	9.00	7.50	6.50

Peru and Zaire. Some of the residents had been homeless. Six of the ten had a history of drug abuse. Two of these six residents did not complete funeral arrangements due to an inability to realize their imminent deaths.

Due to the prognosis of having less than six months to live, many of the hospice residents were ill at times and were not able to carry out the tasks. For this reason, the practitioner carried out more than twice the number of tasks as the residents. Only one subject out of the ten was unsuccessful in completely achieving resolution or change for the problems because the agencies involved did not respond with needed services and because of the subject's lack of effort due to illness. Task-centered treatment did work in resolving most of the problems of hospice residents. Clinically, the results are significant. There were a total of twenty-eight problems, of which twenty-one had successful results. It took only ninety-five tasks to achieve these results.

······ ▬▬▬▬▬▬▬▬▬▬▬▬▬▬▬▬▬▬▬▬▬▬▬▬▬▬

CHAPTER FOURTEEN

HOMELESS FAMILIES AND INDIVIDUALS

WITH GLEN R. ALLEY AND WILLIAM COTTON

Shelter Network of San Mateo County is an agency that provides housing and case-management services to homeless individuals and families of this county adjacent to San Francisco. A relatively affluent area, this agency has for years been dedicated to the homeless of its county. The staff wanted training in providing task-centered case-management services. In exchange for training all of the staff, consulting for over a year, the staff readily agreed to implement a systematic study of the results of their efforts using task-centered treatment. This chapter is a summary of their efforts. The staff of the agency are the ones responsible for this research project; the lead author of this chapter provided the training and consultation.

LITERATURE REVIEW

Several factors contribute to providing homeless persons adequate care. Some of the reported factors to take into consideration are feelings of distrust, learned helplessness, and social disaffiliation (Sosin, Colson, & Grossman, 1988). Sosin

Michael Radding developed new agency forms to fit the task-centered model and directed the collection of data throughout this project.

et al. (1988) reported three possible events of homelessness that can affect the psychological well-being of an individual. First, the process of losing shelter, friends, roles, and family can produce psychological trauma in individuals. Second, the results of being homeless can be psychologically debilitating—the inability to cope with stress as the result of loss of control over one's life, safety, and normalcy. Third, being homeless may exacerbate psychological trauma among those who are susceptible (Sosin et al., 1988). Other factors affecting the well-being of the homeless are mental health and substance abuse issues.

The Community Mental Health Act of 1963 encouraged the de-institutionalization of chronically mentally ill individuals from large state-run facilities to community-based facilities. However, the funding for such programs was not provided. Of the approximately 600,000 homeless people in the United States, one-third may be suffering from a severe mental illness (Sosin et al., 1988).

One study on homelessness found that only 4 percent of the individuals had case managers. None of the participants had received outpatient mental health services during their periods of homelessness (Lamb, 1991). One theory suggests that the reason that homeless individuals have such a low compliance in mental health treatment is due to an inability to find help and/or use appropriate problem-solving skills (Lamb, 1991). Smith, Fisher, Cox, and Stocks (1989) theorized that the high rates for noncompliance among homeless individuals were also due to the previous mainstream assumption that "These people were best helped by being pushed, coerced, or told to change." They went on to report that, although the clients were able to make them, the changes were short-term at best. Reasons for these short-term gains were due to feelings of frustration that resulted in "turning off," or "turning against whoever was pushing them" (Smith et al., 1989).

The trauma of becoming homeless can result in feelings of mistrust due to higher levels of victimization, as well as decreased levels of support through social networks (friends and family). These factors combined with other variables may account for low help-seeking behaviors or resistance to utilizing services.

Approaches geared toward working with the homeless population have centered on combinations of social action, community-based clinics, and group settings. An example of this was a project/study conducted by Sachs and Newdom (1999). They assisted a small New England town in organizing the homeless population there. The major concern was securing shelter and rent control for this population in spite of opposition by the town council. In the end, Sachs and Newdom were able to obtain nightly shelter through the town hall until a more permanent shelter was established on a full-time basis. One of the unintended benefits of this was to enlist assistance from the community. "Some of the churches mobilized to help with food, clothing, and other needs beyond what had been done in the past" (Sachs & Newdom, 1999). Although other resources were encouraged to assist, at no time in the study was there a mention of a focused approach regarding case management for distributing needed resources. In addition, there was no discussion with the clients regarding their desired goals toward change.

Other approaches to work with the homeless have included group therapy with the goal of assisting members in changing self-image as well as developing the new patterns of behavior. The approach included the use of basketball as a medium to enable young homeless men to develop feelings of empowerment and cohesion. Accordingly, it was theorized that these individuals would be able to apply these feelings toward developing improved problem solving and coping skills (Pollio, 1995). Another example is a project/study that was conducted in Honolulu to assist homeless mothers and their children. The goal of this project was to "reduce familial conflicts by enhancing the participants' interpersonal problem-solving skills" (Daniels, D'Andrea, Omizo, & Pier, 1999). This study found that both parents and children were able to use these skills to decrease stress. But, once again, that lack of resources also impacted the participants.

Working with the homeless requires the stimulation of a range of new behaviors by individuals and families (Lewis, 1992). As with the previous study, Lewis presents several strategies for interviewing and assisting homeless individuals/ families in developing a more positive self-image and behavioral change, but does not address issues regarding resource provisions such as case managers. In addition, no information is presented regarding research findings as to the success of using such an approach.

What appears to be essential in working with the homeless is the use of case management to obtain desired resources. In addition, not every individual receiving interventions will require the same services. What seems to be the most logical intervention is a case-management approach. A homeless person's or family's situation is shaped by a number of factors: work, school, economy, discrimination, and others. The amount of stress generated by being homeless may bring on a range of dysfunctional behaviors which must be overcome if their homeless situations are to change (Lewis, 1992). It would be difficult at best using a traditional cookie-cutter approach in serving this client population. A more appropriate approach is the use of case-management techniques.

Rose and Moore identified five case-management functions that apply: (1) outreach to or identification of clients, (2) assessment of needs, (3) service or treatment planning, (4) linking or referring clients to appropriate resources, and (5) monitoring cases to ensure that services are delivered and used (Rose & Moore, 1995). However, as shown previously, a homeless individual and/or family may be presented with several problems. Both the worker and the client need to decide which problem(s) take priority. A task-centered approach toward case management makes most sense here.

The benefits of this approach are as follows: (1) it is a problem-solving method of intervention, (2) it is highly structured, which means that the procedures for implementing the model are specific, (3) it focuses on solving problems as perceived by clients, (4) it is time limited, (5) it is theoretically open and thus can be used with many theoretical orientations, (6) change occurs through the use of tasks, which are activities designed to ameliorate the identified problems, (7) it is present oriented, and (8) it is based upon empirical research that has been tested and found to be effective (Tolson, Reid, & Garvin, 1994).

RESEARCH METHODOLOGY

This study used a single subject AB design, sometimes referred to as a case study design (Bloom et al., 1999; Kazdin, 1981). This design provided evidence about change that occurred contiguous to an intervention, even if it could not provide the causal evidence preferred in experimental studies. Replicating the use of task-centered treatment in over a hundred cases, with a variety of individuals and families and having good baseline data, repeated measures, and clear outcomes control for most of the internal validity problems that exist in such studies. Although not an experimental study, this study may provide the clearest evidence to date of the effectiveness of the task-centered approach in real social work settings and not the arbitrary or "sterile" environment of a separate research project. All of the cases in one agency for one year were evaluated and the findings are reported here.

Baseline data were obtained related to the client identified problems before any task planning and implementation were done. For this project, clinical evidence of change, albeit inexact, subjective, or less than perfect, was the desired goal. Clients and workers achieving their stated goals and being satisfied with their work together was of more importance than a more rigorous and exacting experimentally designed study.

FINDINGS

There were 128 single individuals or families seen by nine workers during the year long study. Of these clients, 178 adults and 147 children made up the sample of those seen by Shelter Network for services. The largest group of clients were Latino American, followed by European American and then African American. Native Americans and Asian Pacific Americans made up the remainder.

Client Backgrounds

The clients had been homeless anywhere from one day to over one year. Most had been homeless for six months or less. For most, 55 percent, it was also their first time being homeless. Eviction followed by job loss and family breakup accounted for most of the homelessness (59 percent). Rent increases, domestic violence, substance abuse, illness, mental health problems, and imprisonment accounted for the remainder. A majority reported no problem with substance abuse (56 percent). The remainder acknowledged that this had been a problem. Although thirty-eight clients had been arrested before, only twenty-eight were ever convicted of a crime, most for misdemeanors. Priority for housing was granted to forty-seven of the clients for any one of the following reasons: pregnancy, having infants, sleeping in a car or on the street, and medical issues. Housing was provided by Shelter Network in a range of units: a large residence that housed single adults, a converted motel for families, and transitional apartments all in different areas of the county.

Procedures

Over one week's time, all of the staff (case managers and support staff) were trained in the use of task-centered practice, using didactic instruction, videotapes of cases, discussion, and reading. The staff was then to try the model with a new client. A few weeks later, training resumed which focused on more detailed examination of problem specification, task planning and implementation, and an exploration of any kinks the staff identified when they tried the model. Staff supervisors received additional training in supervising task-centered work.

In preparation for the study and the staff's use of the task-centered approach, the agency's record-keeping system was redesigned to match the proscribed steps in the task-centered model—based on task-centered recording guides used by Brown (1980) and originally designed by Epstein (1988). The new record-keeping guides provided a means to collect data that fit perfectly with task-centered treatment and with the agency's needs. Staff input was obtained throughout the process to insure that they were comfortable with the ways in which they would record the work they did with clients.

Staff

The agency staff was a mixture of women and men with some college work, bachelor's degrees, and three MSWs. Before training was agreed to, the staff had to decide that they wanted it. They were given several chapters of Epstein's *Helping People* (1988) in order to read about the model before they decided about the training. They decided unanimously to receive the training, and they requested participation in researching the effectiveness of their work.

Instruments

The instruments used were an intake form and three different recording guides, each of which mirrored a phase of the task-centered model. The Initial Phase Recording Guide documented the initial phase of the model: targeting and specifying the problems, contracting, previous problem solving, etc. The Middle Phase Recording Guide was used for each task-planning and implementation interview. Using a five-point scale, which ranged from "Task not done" to "Task completely achieved," task achievement was rated during these interviews by clients and workers. The final interview, when service ended, was recorded in a Final Interview Recording Guide. In this interview, both client and worker provide ratings of client change, using a ten-point scale ranging from "Problem deteriorated" to "Problem totally resolved."

Target Problems

Problems targeted by the clients totaled 425. Needing permanent housing was the most targeted problem (97) followed by needing employment and job training.

The other problems targeted frequently were health, childcare, needing higher income, legal assistance, insufficient savings, emotional issues, and transportation. Being closer to a school, needing parenting skills, needing a change of address, applying for public assistance/disability, credit problems, moving furniture, needing to work for program or jail time, and English training were all targeted by one or few clients. Residents suggested 90 percent of the problems; workers and clients or others suggested the other 10 percent.

Tasks and Task Achievement

The clients and workers developed 1,591 tasks as means to solve the clients' identified problems. Over 72 percent (1,146 tasks) were suggested by clients or clients with the worker. Workers suggested 23 percent or 362 tasks. Others suggested the remaining tasks. Clients were moderately, substantially, or totally committed to achieving the 1,424 total tasks. Most of the remainder had minimal commitment. For five tasks, there was no reported commitment. Middle interviews with the clients provided 3,154 updates on task achievement. At each update, clients and workers reported their progress on task achievement. Clients reported moderate to complete achievement on 84 percent of tasks. Sixteen percent were minimally achieved at reporting times. Workers reported almost exactly the same: 85 percent were moderately to completely achieved and 15 percent were minimally achieved.

Client tasks were primarily centered around efforts to deal with the majority of problems reported. Efforts to arrange permanent housing and obtain employment accounted for about 40 percent of the tasks developed. Worker tasks primarily were making referrals and arranging temporary housing. These worker tasks accounted for almost 8 percent of the tasks. The remainder of the tasks were devoted to the following, in descending order of frequency: follow-up on legal issue, follow-up on job training/education, follow-up on referrals, keeping appointments, arranging childcare, following budget/saving money, discussing and dealing with emotions, reviewing newspaper advertisements, health care, credit issues, practicing English, payments on debts, appointments to see children, and miscellaneous one-time tasks.

Problem Change

Although task achievement is presumed to bring about problem resolution, this is not always the case. As can be seen, most of the tasks were achieved at a moderate to complete degree. Residents and the caseworker at the end of service rated problems, usually when the client moved into permanent housing. Residents were more negative about outcomes than the workers. Clients rated about 48 percent of the problems as completely resolved; caseworkers rated 52 percent as completely resolved. Those problems that were moderately to substantially resolved and so rated by clients make up about 31 percent; workers rated 33 percent in these categories. Clients rated no change in problem status 14 percent of the time; for caseworkers this was 11 percent. Deterioration in problems identified occurred in clients' perceptions in about 7 percent of problems; caseworkers saw deterioration in about 4 percent. Regardless of which views one prefers, problem status changed in positive directions about 80 percent of the time, which is consistent with previous task-centered research studies on problem reduction.

Mandated Service Components

Besides the task-centered problem solving, some residents also participated in twelve-step programs. If any history of substance abuse appeared in a person's history, participation was required. Any misuse of substances was grounds for dismissal from the programs and temporary housing.

All residents had a requirement to have a savings account. These funds were put in accounts for them, so the residents would have generated the monies needed for security deposits when permanent housing became available.

DISCUSSION

A positive feature of Shelter Network is that the case managers worked where the clients lived, so appointments were rarely missed. They might be shifted if a client needed to make an appointment elsewhere, but clients and workers were very accessible during the period of service.

It might be fruitful to have an idea of the kind of case that was impossible to resolve using task-centered methods (and probably any other voluntary form of service provision). One very smart middle-aged man had lived for several years in large boxes that he had reorganized into a small structure. He decided that he would like a more permanent arrangement, with a bathroom, and applied to Shelter Network for services. His primary problem was not having income. This client had a graduate degree in the hard sciences, lost his aerospace industry job, and became homeless. At some point, he also became a member of a secret religious group. His religious beliefs required that he receive, in payment for work, food, shelter, clothing, and the few other necessities for a normal life. He could not receive monies for his work, only the necessities for daily living. The religious beliefs he shared minimally, because they were secret and known only to other religious group members. From his story and his behavior, it was believed that he would be eligible for SSI disability (psychiatric). However, he refused to apply, because that would be accepting monies for no work. An effort was made to find a place that might provide shelter and food in exchange for work, but there was no success. Efforts continued during his stay to resolve the work/money dilemma, but there was no way to do so. At the end of his time in the residence, he thanked them for trying and returned to his former abode. To those of us who spoke with him, his beliefs were not unreasonable. Yes, there was a certain amount of paranoia, perhaps a delusional system, but his notion of food and shelter for work was also reasonable. However, very few if any places can offer such an employee that kind of remuneration. One can't readily be forced to accept psychiatric disability; trying to force him to work was also beyond the scope of any case manager.

The clients reported in this study are not unlike those reported earlier in this volume. They were experiencing problems in daily living. Some had substance abuse problems; some had mental health issues. Domestic violence affected a few. These individuals and families, with few exceptions, were not extraordinarily "different" people. They were people caught in complicated situations, needing help, but, for the most part, reasonable about the options for receiving help and about working hard to get out of their particular homeless situations.

For the most part, the problems that the homeless presented to Shelter Network caseworkers were generally easier to deal with than the one particular failure just described. Almost all of the problems presented were manageable and could be dealt with as long as the clients and staff all contributed to the problem-solving efforts. The task-centered model provided structure for their problem solving but it was their efforts that made their work together as successful as it was.

Alberts, M., Lyons, J., & Moretti, R. (1989). Psychological interventions in the pre-surgical period. *International Journal of Psychiatry in Medicine, 19* (1), 91–106.

Allen, F. A. (1981). *The decline of the rehabilitative ideal: Penal policy and social purpose.* New Haven, CT: Yale University.

Alley, G. R. (1999). Personal communication.

Alley, G. R., & Brown, L. B. (2000). *Task-centered diabetes problem solving support group: A study.* Paper presented at the Biennial NASW Conference, Baltimore, MD.

Alley, G. R., & Brown, L. B. (In press). Cultural sensitivity and social work practice. *Journal of Sociology and Social Work.*

Alter, C., & Evens, W. (1990). *Evaluating your practice: A guide to self-assessment.* New York: Springer.

American Psychiatric Association. (1994). *Diagnostic and statistical manual of mental disorders* (4th ed.). Washington, DC: Author.

Anderson, K., & Masur, F. (1983). Psychological preparation for invasive medical and dental procedures. *Journal of Behavioral Medicine, 6* (1), 1–40.

Ashford, J., LeCroy, C., & Lortie, K. (1997). *Human behavior in the social environment: A multidimensional perspective.* Pacific Grove, CA: Brooks/Cole.

Bailey-Dempsey, C. (1993). *A task-centered approach to resolve school failure.* Unpublished doctoral dissertation, State University of New York at Albany.

Barlow, D. H., & Hersen, M. (1984). *Single case experimental designs: Strategies for studying behavior change* (2nd ed.). New York: Pergamon.

Bass, M. (1977). Toward a model of treatment for runaway girls in detention. In W. J. Reid & L. Epstein (Eds.), *Task-centered practice* (pp. 183–194). New York: Columbia University.

Basso, R. (1986). *Teacher and student problem-solving activities in educational supervisory sessions.* Unpublished manuscript, Wilfrid Laurier University, Faculty of Social Work, Waterloo, Ontario, Canada.

Bauer, G. P., & Kobos, J. C. (1987). *Brief therapy: Short-term psychodynamic intervention.* Dunmore, PA: Jason Aronson.

Beck, A. T., Rush, A. J., Shaw, B. F., & Emery, G. (1979). *Cognitive therapy of depression: A treatment manual.* New York: Guilford.

Becker, H. S. (1966). *Social problems: A modern approach.* New York: Wiley.

Bednar, R. L., & Kaul, T. J. (1978). Experiential group research: Current perspectives. In S. L. Garfield & A. E. Bergin (Eds.), *Handbook of psychotherapy and behavior change: An empirical analysis* (pp. 769–816). New York: Wiley.

Bennett, H. (1985). Behavioral anesthesia. *Advances, 2* (4), 11–21.

Benfer, D. (1987). Health care policy issues related to AIDS: Lessons learned from the Henry Ford Hospital experience. *Henry Ford Medical Journal, 35* (1), 52–57.

Bergin, A., & Garfield, S. (1994). *Handbook of psychotherapy and behavior change* (4th ed.). New York: Wiley.

Bergin, A. E. & Lambert, M. (1978). The evaluation of therapeutic outcomes. In S. L. Garfield & A. E. Bergin (Eds.), *Handbook of psychotherapy and behavior change: An empirical analysis* (pp. 139–190). New York: Wiley.

Berkman, B., Bedell, D., Parker, E., McCarthy, L., & Rosenbaum, C. (1988). Preadmission screening: An efficacy study. *Social Work in Health Care, 13* (3), 35–41.

Berlin, S. (1983). Cognitive-behavioral approaches. In A. Rosenblatt & D. Waldfogel (Eds.), *Handbook of clinical social work* (pp. 1095–1119). San Francisco: Jossey-Bass.

Berlin, S. (1990). Dichotomous and complex thinking. *Social Service Review, 64* (1), 46–55.

Blatt, S. (1999). Personality factors in brief treatment of depression: Further analyses of the NIMH-sponsored treatment for depression collaborative research project. In Janowsky, D. (Ed.) *Psychotherapy indications and outcomes* (pp. 23–45). Washington, DC: American Psychiatric Press.

Blizinsky, M., & Reid, W. J. (1980). Problem focus and outcome in brief treatment. *Social Work, 25* (1), 89–98.

Bloom, M., Fischer, J., & Orme, M. (1999). *Evaluating practice: Guidelines for an accountable practitioner.* Boston: Allyn & Bacon.

Blythe, B., & Erdahl, S. (1986). Using stress inoculation to prepare a patient for open heart surgery. *Health and Social Work, 11,* 265–273.

Bromley, M. A. (1987). New beginnings for Cambodian refugees—or further disruptions? *Social Work, 32* (3), 236–239.

Brown, L. B. (1977). Treating problems of psychiatric outpatients. In W. J. Reid & L. Epstein (Eds.), *Task-centered practice* (pp. 208–227). New York: Columbia University.

Brown, L. B. (1980). *Client problem solving learning in task-centered social treatment.* Unpublished doctoral dissertation, School of Social Service Administration, University of Chicago, Chicago, IL.

Brown, L. B. (1996). An ethnic-sensitive approach to empirical school social work practice. In Constable, R., Flynn, J., & McDonald, S. (Eds.), *School social work: Practice and research perspectives* (3rd ed.). (pp. 387–399). Chicago: Lyceum Books.

Brown, L. B. (Ed.). (1997). *Two spirit people: American Indian lesbian women and gay men.* New York: Haworth.

Brown, L. B., & Alley, G. R. (1999a). *Seeing in true colours.* Unpublished paper, Department of Social Work, California State University, Long Beach.

Brown, L. B., & Alley, G. R. (1999b). Beyond stereotypes: Do we only see what we want to see? *Proceedings of the National Conference, Beyond Stereotypes,* University of South Carolina.

Brown, L. B., Alley, G. R., Radin, M., & Cotton, W. (1999). *The effectiveness of task-centered case management with the homeless at Shelter Network of San Mateo County, California.* Unpublished report, Departments of Social Work and American Indian Studies, California State University, Long Beach.

Brown, L. B., & Levitt, J. (1979). A methodology for problem system identification. *Social Casework, 59,* 408–415.

Brown, L. B., Oliver, J., & Klor de Alva, J. (Eds.). (1986). *Sociocultural and service issues in working with Hispanic American clients.* Albany, NY: Rockefeller College Press, State University of New York at Albany.

Brown, L. B., Sarosy, S., Quarto, G., & Cook, T. (1997). *Gay men and aging.* New York: Garland.

Budman, S. H. (1981). *Forms of brief therapy.* New York: Guilford.

Budman, S. H., & Gurman, A. S. (1988). *Theory and practice of brief therapy.* New York: Guilford.

Butler, J., Bow, I., & Gibbons, J. (1978). Task-centered casework with marital problems. *British Journal of Social Work, 8,* 393–409.

Butler, R. N., & Lewis, M. I. (1982). *Aging and mental health.* St. Louis: Mosby.

Camasso, M. J., & Camasso, A. E. (1986). Social supports, undesirable life events, and psychological distress in a disadvantaged population. *Social Service Review, 60* (3), 378–394.

Castel, R., Castel, F., & Lovell, N. A. (1982). *The psychiatric society.* New York: Columbia University.

Christopherson, B., & Pfieffer, C. (1980). Varying the timing of information to alter preoperative anxiety and postoperative recovery in cardiac surgery. *Heart and Lung, 9* (5), 854–861.

Cohler, B. J. (1982). Personal narrative and life course. In P. B. Baltes & O. G. Brim, Jr. (Eds.), *Life span development and behavior* (pp. 205–241). New York: Academic Press.

Comptroller General of the United States. (1973). *Report to the Congress, social services: Do they help welfare recipients achieve self-support or reduce dependency?* Social and Rehabilitation Services, Department of Health, Education, and Welfare, Washington, DC.

Corcoran, K., & Fischer, J. (1987). *Measures for clinical practice: A sourcebook.* New York: Free Press.

Cormican, E. (1977). Task-centered model for work with the aged. *Social Casework, 58,* 490–494.

Cummings, N. A. (1990). Brief intermittent psychotherapy throughout the life cycle. In J. K. Zeig & S. G. Gilligan (Eds.), *Brief therapy: Myths, methods, and metaphors* (pp. 169–184). New York: Brunner/Mazel.

Cummings, N. A., Dorken, H., Pallak, M. S., & Henke, C. (1990). *The impact of psychological intervention on healthcare utilization and costs: The Hawaii Medicaid project.* South San Francisco: Biodyne.

Daniels, J., D'Andrea, M., Omizo, M., & Pier, P. (1999). Group work with homeless youngsters and their mothers. *Journal for Specialists in Group Work, 24* (2), 164–185.

Davanloo, H. (1978). *Basic principles and techniques in short-term dynamic psychotherapy.* New York: SP Medical and Scientific Books.

Davis, I. P. (1975) Advice-giving in parent counseling. *Social Casework, 56,* 343–347.

Devore, W., & Schlesinger, E. (1996). *Ethnic-sensitive social work practice.* Boston: Allyn & Bacon.

Dewey, J. (1933). *How we think.* Lexington, MA: D.C. Heath.

Diekring, B., Brown, M., & Fortune, A. E. (1980). Task-centered treatment in a residential facility for the elderly: A clinical trial. *Journal of Gerontological Social Work, 2* (3), 225–240.

Dixon, S. L. (1987). *Working with people in crisis* (2nd ed.). Columbus, OH: Merrill.

Donohue, K. (1996). *Developing a task-centered mediation model.* Unpublished doctoral dissertation, State University of New York at Albany.

D'Zurilla, T. J., & Goldfried, M. R. (1971). Problem solving and behavior modification. *Journal of Abnormal Psychology, 78* (1), 107–126.

Edelson, M. (1988). *Psychoanalysis: A theory in crisis.* Chicago: University of Chicago

Egbert, L. D., Battie, G. E., & Welch, C. E. (1964). Reduction of postoperative pain by encouragement and instruction of patient. *New England Journal of Medicine, 270* (4), 825–827.

Elkin, I., Shea, T., Watkins, J. T., Imber, S. D., Sotsky, S. M., Collins, J. F., Glass, D. R., Pilkonis, P. A., Leber, W. R., Docherty, J. P., Fiester, S. J., & Parloff, M. B. (1989). National Institute of Mental Health treatment of depression collaborative research program: General effectiveness of treatment. *Archives of General Psychiatry, 46,* 971–983.

Elmer, E. (1981). Traumatized children, chronic illness, and poverty. In L. H. Pelton (Ed.), *The social context of child abuse and neglect* (pp. 185–227). New York: Human Sciences.

Epstein, L. (1965, December). Casework process in crisis abatement. *Child Welfare, 44,* 551–555.

Epstein, L. (1977). A project in school social work. In W. J. Reid & L. Epstein (Eds.), *Task-centered practice* (pp. 130–146). New York: Columbia University.

Epstein, L. (1983). Short-term treatment in health settings: Issues, concepts, dilemmas. In G. Rosenberg

& H. Rehr (Eds.), *Advancing social work practice in the health care field* (pp. 77–98). New York: Haworth.

Epstein, L. (1985). *Talking and listening: A guide to the helping interview.* Columbus, OH: Merrill.

Epstein, L. (1988). *Helping people: The task centered approach.* St. Louis: C. V. Mosby.

Ewalt, P. (1977). A psychoanalytically oriented child guidance setting. In W. J. Reid & L. Epstein (Eds.), *Task-centered practice* (pp. 27–49). New York: Columbia University.

Fisch, R., Weakland, J. H., & Segal, L. (1982). *The tactics of change.* San Francisco: Jossey-Bass.

Fischer, J. (1976). *The effectiveness of social casework.* Springfield, IL: Charles C. Thomas.

Fisher, R., & Ury, W. (1981). *Getting to yes: Negotiating agreement without giving in.* Boston: Houghton Mifflin.

Fisher, S., & Greenberg, R. P. (Eds.). (1977). *The scientific credibility of Freud's theories and therapy.* New York: Basic Books.

Ford, D. H., & Urban, H. B. (1964). *Systems of psychotherapy: A comparative study.* New York: Wiley.

Fortin, F., & Kirouac, S. (1976). A randomized controlled trial of preoperative patient education. *International Journal of Nursing Studies, 13,* 11–24.

Fortune, A. E. (1977). Practitioner communication in task-centered treatment. Unpublished doctoral dissertation, University of Chicago.

Fortune, A. E. (1979). Problem-solving process in task-centered treatment with adults and children. *Journal of Social Service Research, 2,* 357–371.

Fortune, A. E. (1981). Communication processes in social work practice. *Social Service Review, 55,* 93–128.

Fortune, A. E. (1985a). Planning duration and termination of treatment. *Social Service Review, 59,* 647–662.

Fortune, A. E. (1985b). Treatment groups. In A. E. Fortune, *Task-centered practice with families and groups* (pp. 33–44). New York: Springer.

Fortune, A. E. (1985c). Families and family treatment. In A. E. Fortune (Ed.), *Task-centered practice with families and groups* (pp. 117–128). New York: Springer.

Foucault, M. (1973). *Madness and civilization: A history of insanity in the age of reason.* New York: Vintage/Random House.

Franklin, D. L. (1985). Differential clinical assessments: The influence of class and race. *Social Service Review, 59,* 44–61.

Frieswyk, S. H., Allen, J. B., Colson, D. P., Coyne, L., Gabbard, G. O., Horwitz, L., & Newson, G. (1986). Therapeutic alliance: Its place as a process and outcome variable in dynamic psychotherapy research. *Journal of Consulting and Clinical Psychology, 54* (1), 32–38.

Gambrill, E. (1983). *Casework: A competency-based approach.* Englewood Cliffs, NJ: Prentice-Hall.

Gardner, H. (1985). *The mind's new science: A history of the cognitive revolution.* New York: Basic Books.

Garfield, S. L. (1980). *Psychotherapy: An eclectic approach.* New York: Wiley.

Garfield, S. L. (1986). An eclectic psychotherapy. In J. C. Norcross (Ed.), *Handbook of eclectic psychotherapy* (pp. 132–162). New York: Brunner/Mazel.

Garfield, S. L. (1989). *The practice of brief psychotherapy* (2nd ed.). New York: Wiley.

Garfield, S. L., & Kurtz, R. (1976). Clinical psychologists in the 1970s. *American Psychologist, 31* (1), 1–9.

Garfield, S. L., & Kurtz, R. (1977). A study of eclectic views. *Journal of Consulting and Clinical Psychology, 45* (1), 78–83.

Garvin, C. D. (1974), Task-centered group work. *Social Service Review, 48,* 494–507.

Garvin, C. D. (1981). *Contemporary group work.* Englewood Cliffs, NJ: Prentice-Hall.

Garvin, C. D., Reid, W. J., & Epstein, L. (1976). Task centered group work. In R. W. Roberts & H. Northern (Eds.), *Theoretical approaches to social work with small groups* (pp. 238–267). New York: Columbia University.

Gelles, R. J., & Cornell, C. P. (1985). *Intimate violence of families.* Beverly Hills, CA: Sage.

Germain, C. B., & Gitterman, A. (1980). *The life model of social work practice.* New York: Columbia University.

Germain, C. B., & Gitterman, A. (1987). Ecological perspective. In *Encyclopedia of social work.* Silver Springs, MD: National Association of Social Workers.

Gibbons, J., Bow, I., Butler, J., & Powell, J. (1978). Client reactions to task-centred casework: A follow up study. *British Journal of Social Work, 9* (2), 203–214.

Gibbons, J., Butler, J., & Bow, I. (1979). Task-centered casework with marital problems. *British Journal of Social Work, 9* (2), 393–409.

Gibbons, J. S., Butler, J., Urwin, P., & Gibbons, J. L. (1978). Evaluation of a social work service for self-poisoning patients. *British Journal of Psychiatry, 133,* 111–118.

Gil, R. M., & Brown, L. B. (1985). Social work practice with Hispanic groups. In L. B. Brown, J. Oliver, & J. J. Klor De Alva (Eds.), *Sociocultural and service issues in working with Hispanic American clients* (pp. 89–102). Albany, NY: Nelson A. Rockefeller College of Public Affairs and Policy, State University of New York at Albany.

Golan, N. (1978). *Treatment in crisis situations.* New York: Free Press.

Goldberg, E. M., Gibbons, J., & Sinclair, I. (1984). *Problems, tasks, and outcomes.* Winchester, MA: Allen and Unwin.

Goldberg, E. M., & Stanley, J. S. (1978). A task-centered approach to probation. In J. King (Ed.), *Pressures and changes in the probation service* (pp. 59–83). Cambridge, England: Institute of Criminology.

Goldberg, E. M., & Warburton, R. W. (1979). *Ends and means in social work.* London: Allen and Unwin.

Goldstein, H. (1986). Toward integration of theory and practice: A humanistic approach. *Social Work, 31* (5), 352–357.

Green, R., & Ephross, P. (1991). *Human behavior theory and social work practice.* Hawthorne, NY: de Gruyter.

Greif, G. L., & Lynch, A. A. (1983). The eco-systems perspective. In C. H. Meyer (Ed.), *Clinical social work in the eco-systems perspective.* New York: Columbia University.

Guerra, F., & Aldrete, A. (1980). *Emotional and psychological responses to anesthesia and surgery.* New York: Grune and Stratton.

Gustafson, J. P. (1981). The complex secret of brief psychotherapy in the works of Malan and Balint. In S. H. Budman (Ed.), *Forms of brief therapy* (pp. 83–130). New York: Guilford.

Hanrahan, P. (1986). Task-centered system: Review of the research. Unpublished manuscript.

Hari, V. (1977). Instituting short-term casework in a long-term agency. In W. J. Reid & L. Epstein (Eds.), *Task-centered practice* (pp. 89–99). New York: Columbia University.

Hersen, M., & Turner, S. M., Eds. (1985). *Diagnostic interviewing.* New York: Plenum.

Hinsie, L. E., & Campbell, R. J. (1970). *Psychiatric dictionary.* New York: Oxford University.

Hofstad, M. O. (1977). Treatment in a juvenile court setting. In W. J. Reid & L. Epstein (Eds.), *Task-centered practice* (pp. 195–202). New York: Columbia University.

Hogarty, G. D. (1989). Metaanalysis of the effects of practice with the chronically mentally ill: A critique and reappraisal of the literature. *Social Work, 43* (4), 363–374.

Horowitz, B., & Wolock, I. (1981). Maternal deprivation, child maltreatment, and agency intervention among poor families. In L. H. Pelton (Ed.), *The social context of child abuse and neglect* (pp. 137–184). New York: Human Sciences.

Howard, K. I., Kopta, S., Krause, M., & Orlinsky, D. E. (1986). The dose-effect relationship in psychotherapy. *American Psychologist, 41* (2), 159–164.

Jackson, A. A. (1983). *Task-centered marital therapy: A single case investigation.* Unpublished doctoral dissertation, University of Alabama at Tuscaloosa.

Jahoda, M. (1953). The meaning of psychological health. *Social Casework, 34,* 349–354.

Janis, I. (1958). *Psychological stress: Psychoanalytical and behavioral studies of surgery patients.* New York: Wiley.

Janowsky, D. (Ed.). (1999). *Psychotherapy indications and outcomes.* Washington, DC: American Psychiatric Association.

Jayaratne, S. (1978). A study of clinical eclecticism. *Social Service Review, 52* (4), 621–631.

Jayaratne, S. (1982). Characteristics and theoretical orientations of clinical social workers: A survey. *Journal of Social Service Research, 4* (2), 17–30.

Johnson, H. C. (1986). Emerging concerns in family therapy. *Social Work, 31* (4), 299–307.

Jonas, H. (1966). *The phenomenon of life.* New York: Harper & Row.

Jones, D. L. (1985). African-American clients: Clinical practice issues. In J. Oliver & L. B. Brown (Eds.), *Sociocultural and service issues in working with Afro-American clients* (pp. 63–75). Albany, NY: Rockefeller College Press, State University of New York at Albany.

Kadushin, A. (1990). *The social work intervention: A guide for human service professionals.* New York: Columbia University.

Kadushin, A., & Martin, J. (1988). *Child welfare services* (4th ed.). New York: Macmillan.

Kanfer, F. K., & Saslow, G. (1969). Behavioral diagnosis. In C. M. Franks (Ed.), *Behavior therapy: Appraisal and status* (pp. 417–444). New York: McGraw-Hill.

Kanter, J. S. (1983). Reevaluation of task-centered social work practice. *Clinical Social Work Journal, 11* (3), 228–244.

Kazdin, A. (1981). Drawing valid inferences from case studies. *Journal of Consulting and Clinical Psychology, 49* (2), 183–192.

Kendell, R. E. (1975). *The role of diagnosis in psychiatry.* London: Blackwell Scientific Publications.

Kilburn, L. H. (1988). *Hospice operation manual.* Washington, DC: National Hospice Association.

Kilgore, D. (1995). *Task-centered group treatment of sex offenders: A developmental study.* Unpublished doctoral dissertation, State University of New York at Albany.

Kirk, S. A., & Greenley, J. R. (1974). Denying or delivering services? *Social Work, 19* (4), 439–447.

Kitsuse, J. I., & Spector, M. (1973). Toward a sociology of social problems: Social conditions, value judgements, and social problems. *Social Problems, 20* (4), 407–419.

Klerman, G. L., Weissman, M. M., Rounsaville, B. J., & Chevron, E. S. (1984). *Interpersonal psychotherapy of depression.* New York: Basic Books.

Kolevson, M. S., & Maykranz, J. (1982). Theoretical orientation and clinical practice: Uniformity versus eclecticism? *Social Service Review, 56* (1), 120–129.

Koss, M. P., & Butcher, J. N. (1986). Research on brief psychotherapy. In S. L. Garfield & A. E. Bergin (Eds.), *Handbook of psychotherapy and behavior change* (pp. 627–670). New York: Wiley.

Koss, M. P., Butcher, J. N., & Strupp, H. H. (1986). Brief psychotherapy methods in clinical research. *Journal of Consulting and Clinical Psychology, 54* (1), 60–67.

Krieger, I. (1988). An approach to coping with anxiety about AIDS. *Social Work, 33* (3), 263–264.

Lamb, H. R. (1991). Factors contributing to the homeless among the chronically and severely mentally ill. *Hospital and Community Psychiatry, 41* (3), 301–305.

Lambert, M. J., Shapiro, D. A., & Bergin, A. E. (1986). The effectiveness of psychotherapy. In S. L. Garfield & A. E. Bergin (Eds.), *Handbook of psychotherapy and behavior change* (3rd ed.) (pp. 157–211). New York: Wiley.

Larsen, J. A., & Mitchell, C. T. (1980). Task-centered, strength-oriented group work with delinquents. *Social Casework, 61,* 154–163.

Lemon, E. C. (1983). Planned brief treatment. In A. Rosenblatt & D. Waldfogel (Eds.), *Handbook of clinical social work* (pp. 401–419). San Francisco: Jossey-Bass.

Levenstein, P., Kockman, P., & Roth, H. (1973). From laboratory to real world: Service delivery of the Mother-Child Home Program. *American Journal of Orthopsychiatry, 43,* 72–78.

Levinson, H. L. (1977). Termination of psychotherapy: Some salient issues. *Social Casework, 58* (8), 480–489.

Levy, R. R. (1983). Overview of single-case experiments. In A. Rosenblatt & D. Woldfogel (Eds.), *Handbook of clinical social work* (pp. 583–602). San Francisco: Jossey-Bass.

Lewis, W. M. (1992). *Practical counseling techniques: Helping homeless people: Unique challenges and solutions.* Alexandria, VA: American Association for Counseling and Development.

Lidz, C. W., Meisel, A., Zerubavel, E., Carter, M., Sestak, R. M., & Roth, L. H. (1984). *Informed consent: A study of decision-making in psychiatry.* New York: Guilford.

Lieberman, M. A., Yalom, I. D., & Miles, M. B. (1973). *Encounter groups: First facts.* New York: Basic Books.

Lindeman, C., & Van Aerman, B. (1971). Nursing intervention with the presurgical patient—The effects of structured and unstructured preoperative teaching. *Nursing Research, 20* (4), 319–332.

Lindeman, E. (1941). Observations on the psychiatric sequelae to surgical operations in women. *American Journal of Psychiatry, 98* (7), 132–139.

Longres, J. (1995). *Human behavior in the social environment.* Itasca, IL: Peacock.

Lorion, R. P., & Parron, D. L. (1985). Countering the countertransference: A strategy for treating the untreatable. In P. Pedersen (Ed.), *Handbook of cross-cultural counseling and therapy* (pp. 79–86). Westport, CT: Greenwood.

Luborsky, L. (1984). *Principles of psychoanalytic psychotherapy: A manual for supportive-expressive treatment.* New York: Basic Books.

Luborsky, L., Crits-Christoph, P., Mintz, J., & Auerback, A. (1988). *Who will benefit from psychotherapy? Predicting therapeutic outcomes.* New York: Basic Books.

Macy-Lewis, J. A. (1985). Single-parent groups. In A. E. Fortune (Ed.), *Task-centered practice with families and groups* (pp. 92–100). New York: Springer.

Maddi, S. R. (1980). *Personality theories: A comparative analysis.* Homewood, IL: Dorsey.

Malan, D. (1976). *Frontier of brief psychotherapy.* New York: Plenum.

Maluccio, A. D., & Marlow, W. D. (1974). The case for the contract. *Social Work, 19,* 28–36.

Mann, J. A. (1981). *A casebook of time-limited psychotherapy.* New York: McGraw-Hill.

Marshall, P. (1987). Task-centered practice in a probation setting. In R. Harris (Ed.), *Practising social work* (pp. 119–134). Leicester, England: University of Leicester School of Social Work.

Mays, D. T., & Franks, C. M. (1985). *Negative outcome: What to do about it.* New York: Springer.

McCarty, L. M. (1978). A protective service caseworker performance scale. *Child Welfare, 52* (3), 149–155.

McGoldrick, M., Pearce, J., & Giordano, J. (1996). *Ethnicity and family therapy* (2nd ed.). New York: Guilford.

Merton, R. K. (1971). Social problems and sociological theory. In R. K. Merton & R. Nisbet (Eds.), *Contemporary social problems* (pp. 793–845). New York: Harcourt, Brace, Jovanovich.

Meyer, C. H. (1983). Selecting appropriate practice models. In A. Rosenblatt & D. Waldfogel (Eds.), *Handbook of clinical social work* (pp. 731–749). San Francisco: Jossey-Bass.

Mills, P. R., Jr. (1985). Conjoint treatment within the task-centered model. In A. E. Fortune (Ed.), *Task-centered practice with families and groups* (pp. 161–171). New York: Springer.

Moriarty, D. (1990). *Task centered therapy with surgical patients.* Unpublished master's thesis, California State University, Long Beach.

Morrow-Howell, N., Lott, L., & Ozawa, M. (1990). The impact of race on volunteer helping relationships among the elderly. *Social Work, 35* (5), 395–404.

Mortland, C. A., & Egan, M. G. (1987). Vietnamese youth in American foster care. *Social Work, 32* (3), 240–245.

Mullen, E. J. (1983). Evaluating social work's effectiveness. In M. Dinerman (Ed.), *Social work in a turbulent world* (pp. 63–75). Silver Springs, MD: National Association of Social Workers.

Mullen, E. J. (1985). Methodological dilemmas in social work research. *Social Work Research and Abstracts, 21* (4), 12–20.

Mullen, E. J., Dumpson, J., & Associates (Eds.). (1972). *Evaluation of social intervention.* San Francisco: Jossey-Bass.

Naleppa, M. (1995). *Task-centered case management for the elderly in the community: Developing a practice model.* Unpublished doctoral dissertation, State University of New York at Albany.

Naleppa, M., & Reid, W. (1998). Task-centered case management for the elderly: Developing a practice model. *Research in Social Work Practice, 8* (1), 63–85.

National Association of Social Workers. (1987). *Encyclopedia of social work* (Vol. 1, 18th ed.). Silver Spring, MD: Author.

Neighbors, H. W., & Taylor, R. J. (1985). The use of social service agencies by Black Americans. *Social Service Review, 59,* 258–268.

Nelson, B. J. (1984). *Making an issue of child abuse: Political agenda setting for social problems.* Chicago: University of Chicago.

Newcome, K. (1985). Task-centered group with the chronically mentally ill in day treatment. In A. E. Fortune (Ed.), *Task-centered practice with families and groups* (pp. 78–91). New York: Springer.

Newman, F. L., & Howard, K. T. (1986). Therapeutic effort, treatment outcome, and national health policy. *American Psychologist, 41* (2), 181–187.

New York Times. (1990, May 17), 1.

Nie, H., Hull, C., Jenkins, J., Steinbrenner, K., & Bent, D. (1975). *Statistical package for the social sciences* (2nd ed.). New York: McGraw-Hill.

Norcross, J. C. (Ed.). (1986). *Handbook of eclectic psychotherapy.* New York: Brunner/Mazel.

O'Connor, R. (1983). *A study of client reactions to brief treatment.* Unpublished doctoral dissertation, University of Chicago.

O'Connor, R., & Reid, W. J. (1986). Dissatisfaction with brief treatment. *Social Service Review, 60* (4), 526–537.

Oliver, J., & Brown, L. B. (Eds.) (1983). *Sociocultural and service issues in working with Afro-American clients.* Albany, NY: Rockefeller College Press, State University of New York at Albany.

Orlinsky, D. E., & Howard, K. I. (1986). Process and outcome in psychotherapy. In S. L. Garfield & A. E. Bergin (Eds.), *Handbook of psychotherapy and behavior change* (pp. 311–384). New York: Wiley.

Ostrow, D., Sandholzer, T., & Felman, Y. (1983). *Sexually transmitted diseases in homosexual man: Diagnosis, treatment and research.* New York: Plenum.

Othmer, E., & Othmer, S. C. (1989). *The clinical interview: Using DSM-III-R.* Washington, DC: American Psychiatric Press.

Parad, H. J., & Parad, L. G. (1990). *Crisis intervention: Book 2.* Milwaukee, WI: Family Service Association of America.

Pardes, H., & Pincus, H. A. (1981). Brief therapy in the context of national mental health issues. In S. H. Budman (Ed.), *Forms of brief therapy* (pp. 7–24). New York: Guilford.

Parloff, M. B., & Dies, R. T. (1977). Group psychotherapy outcome research, 1966–1975. *International Journal of Group Psychotherapy, 27,* 281–319.

Parloff, M. B., Waskow, I. E., & Wolfe, B. E. (1978). Research on therapist variables in relation to process and outcome. In S. L. Garfield & A. E. Bergin (Eds.), *Handbook of psychotherapy and behavior change: An empirical analysis* (pp. 233–282). New York: Wiley.

Parsseghian, M. (1993). *Task-centered practice with HIV/AIDS hospice patients.* Unpublished master's thesis, California State University, Long Beach.

Patterson, C. H. (1986). *Theories of counseling and psychotherapy.* New York: Harper & Row.

Pedersen, P. (Ed.). (1985). *Handbook of cross-cultural counseling and therapy.* Westport, CT: Greenwood.

Pelton, L. H. (1981). Child abuse and neglect and protective intervention in Mercer County, New Jersey. In L. H. Pelton (Ed.), *The social context of child abuse and neglect* (pp. 90–136). New York: Human Sciences.

Perlman, H. H. (1957). *Social casework: A problem-solving process.* Chicago: University of Chicago.

Pincus, A., & Minahan, A. (1973). *Social work practice: Model and method.* Itasca, IL: Peacock.

Pinkston, E. M., Friedman, B. S., & Polster, R. P. (1981). Parents as agents of behavior change. In S. P. Schenke (Ed.), *Behavioral methods in social welfare* (pp. 29–40). Hawthorne, NY: Aldine.

Piven, F. F. (1981). Deviant behavior and the remaking of the world. *Social Problems, 28* (5), 489–508.

Pollio, D. (1995). Hoops group: Group work with young "street" men. *Social Work with Groups, 18* (2/3), 107–122.

Pomeroy, E. C., Rubin, A., & Walker, R. J. (1995). Effectiveness of psychoeducational and task-centered group intervention for family members of people with AIDS. *Social Work Research, 19* (3), 142–152.

Pope, B. (1979). *The mental health interview: Research and application.* New York: Pergamon.

Proctor, E. K., & Rosen, A. (1983). Problem formulation and its relation to treatment planning. *Social Work Research and Abstracts, 19* (3), 22–27.

Rathbone-McCuan, E. (1985). Intergenerational family practice with older families. In A. E. Fortune (Ed.), *Task-centered practice with families and groups* (pp. 149–160). New York: Springer.

Reid, W. J. (1975). A test of the task-centered approach. *Social Work, 20* (1), 3–9.

Reid, W. J. (1978). *The task-centered system.* New York: Columbia University.

Reid, W. J. (1981). Family treatment within a task-centered framework. In E. R. Tolson & W. J. Reid, (Eds.), *Models of family treatment* (pp. 306–331). New York: Columbia University.

Reid, W. J. (1985). *Family problem solving.* New York: Columbia University.

Reid, W. J. (1990). An integrative model for short-term treatment. In R. A. Wells & V. Giannetti (Eds.), *Handbook of brief psychotherapies* (pp. 55–77). New York: Plenum.

Reid, W. J. (1992). *Task strategies.* New York: Columbia University.

Reid, W. J., & Bailey-Dempsey, C. (1995). The effects of monetary incentives on school performance. *Families in Society, 76,* 331–340.

Reid, W. J., Bailey-Dempsey, C., Cain, E., Cook, T., & Burchard, J. (1994). Cash incentives versus case management: Can money replace services in preventing school failure? *Social Work Research, 18,* 227–238.

Reid, W. J., & Epstein, L. (1972). *Task-centered casework.* New York: Columbia University.

Reid, W. J., & Epstein, L. (Eds.). (1977). *Task-centered practice.* New York: Columbia University.

Reid, W. J., Epstein, L., Brown, L. B., Tolson, E., & Rooney, R. H. (1980). Task-centered school social work. *Social Work in Education, 2* (1), 7–24.

Reid, W. J., & Hanrahan, P. (1982). Recent evaluations of social work: Grounds for optimism. *Social Work, 27* (4), 328–340.

Reid, W. J., & Shapiro, B. (1969). Client reaction to advice. *Social Service Review, 43,* 165–173.

Reid, W. J., & Shyne, A. (1969). *Brief and extended casework.* New York: Columbia University.

Roberts, A. R. (1990). *Crisis intervention handbook: Assessment, treatment and research.* Belmont, CA: Wadsworth.

Roberts, R., & Nee, R. (Eds.). (1970). *Theories of social casework.* Chicago: University of Chicago.

Roberts, R., & Northern, H. (1976). *Theories of social work with groups.* New York: Columbia University.

Roe v. Wade, 410 U.S. 113 (1973).

Rooney, R. H. (1977). Adolescent groups in public schools. In W. J. Reid, & L. Epstein (Eds.), *Task-centered practice* (pp. 168–182). New York: Columbia University.

Rooney, R. H. (1978). *Separation through foster care: Toward a problem-oriented practice model based on task-centered casework.* Unpublished doctoral dissertation, School of Social Service Administration, University of Chicago.

Rooney, R. H. (1981). A task-centered reunification model for foster care. In A. N. Maluccio & P. A. Sinanoglu (Eds.), *The challenge of partnership: Working with parents of children in foster care* (pp. 135–150). New York: Child Welfare League of America.

Rooney, R. (1992). *Strategies for work with involuntary clients.* New York: Columbia University.

Rose, S., & Moore, J. (1995). Case management. In R. Edwards (Ed.), *Encyclopedia of social work* (19th ed.) (pp. 335–340). Washington, DC: National Association of Social Workers.

Rosen, A., Proctor, E. K., & Livne, S. (1985). Planning and direct practice. *Social Service Review, 59* (2), 161–177.

Rothery, M. A. (1980). Contracts and contracting. *Clinical Social Work Journal, 8* (3), 179–187.

Rubin, A. (1985, November). Practice effectiveness: More grounds for optimism. *Social Work, 30,* 469–476.

Rzepnicki, T. (1982). *Task-centered intervention: An adaptation and test of effectiveness in foster care services.* Unpublished doctoral dissertation, School of Social Service Administration, University of Chicago.

Rzepnicki, T. L. (1985). Task-centered intervention in foster care services: Working with families who have children in placement. In A. E. Fortune (Ed.), *Task-centered practice with families and groups* (pp. 172–184). New York: Springer.

Rzepnicki, T. L. (1991). Enhancing the durability of intervention gains: A challenge for the 1990s. *Social Service Review, 65* (1), 92–111.

Sachs, J., & Newdom, F. (1999). *Clinical work and social action: An integrative approach.* New York: Haworth.

Salmon, W. (1977). A service program in a state public welfare agency. In W. J. Reid & L. Epstein (Eds.), *Task-centered practice* (pp. 113–122). New York: Columbia University.

Schuerman, J., Rzepnicki, T., & Littell, J. (1994). *Putting families first.* Hawthorne, NY: de Gruyter.

Shea, M., Elkin, I., & Sotsky, S. (1999). *Patient characteristics associated with successful treatment: Outcome findings from the NIMH treatment of depression collaboration research project.* In Janowsky, D. (Ed.), *Psychotherapy indications and outcomes* (pp. 71–90). Washington, DC: American Psychiatric Press.

Sheafor, B. W., & Landon, P. S. (1987). Generalist perspective. In *Encyclopedia of social work.* Silver Springs, MD: National Association of Social Workers.

Sherman, E. A., Neuman, R., & Shyne, A. W. (1973). *Children adrift in foster care: A study of alternative approaches.* New York: Child Welfare League of America.

Sidel, R. (1986). *Women and children last: The plight of poor women in affluent America.* New York: Viking.

Sifneos, P. E. (1987). *Short-term dynamic psychotherapy: Evaluation and technique.* New York: Plenum.

Siporin, M. (1975). *Introduction to social work practice.* New York: Macmillan.

Smith, G., Fischer, D., Cox, H., & Stocks, B. (1989). Street-linked therapy. *Journal of Strategic and Systemic Therapies, 8* (2 &3), 26–37.

Smith, M. L., Glass, G. N., & Miller, T. T. (1980). *The benefits of psychotherapy.* Baltimore, MD: Johns Hopkins University.

Solomon, B. (1976). *Black empowerment: Social work in oppressed communities.* New York: Columbia University.

Sosin, M. R., Colson, P., & Grossman, S. (1988). *Homelessness in Chicago: Poverty and pathology, social institutions and social change.* Chicago: University of Chicago.

Spector, J., & Kitsue, J. I. (1974). Social problems: A reformulation. *Social Problems, 21* (2), 145–159.

Spivack, G., Platt, J., & Shure, M. B. (1976). *The problem solving approach to adjustment.* San Francisco: Jossey-Bass.

Stein, T. J. (1981). *Social work practice in child welfare.* Englewood Cliffs, NJ: Prentice-Hall.

Stein, T., Gambrill, E., & Wiltse, K. T. (1977). Contracts and outcomes in foster care. *Social Work, 22* (2), 148–149.

Stiles, W. B., Shapiro, D. A., & Elliot, R. (1986). Are all psychotherapies equivalent? *American Psychologist, 41* (2), 165–180.

Strean, H. S. (1978). *Clinical social work theory and practice.* New York: Free Press.

Strupp, H. H. (1986). Psychotherapy: Research, practice, and public policy (How to avoid dead ends). *American Psychologist, 41* (2), 120–130.

Strupp, H. H., & Binder, J. L. (1984). *Psychotherapy in a new key: A guide to time-limited dynamic psychotherapy.* New York: Basic Books.

Sulloway, F. J. (1979). *Freud: Biologist of the mind.* New York: Basic Books.

Sundberg, N. D. (1977). *Assessment of persons.* Englewood Cliffs, NJ: Prentice Hall.

Taylor, C. (1977). Counseling in a service industry. In W. Reid & L. Epstein (Eds.), *Task-centered practice* (pp. 228–234). New York: Columbia University.

Taylor, C., & Rooney, R. (1982). Personal communication.

Taylor, R. J., Neighbors, H. W., & Broman, C. L. (1989). Evaluation by Black Americans of the social service encounter during a serious personal problem. *Social Work, 34* (3), 205–214.

Thio, A. (1978). *Deviant behavior.* Boston: Houghton Mifflin.

Thoits, P. (1985). Negative outcome: The influence of factors outside therapy. In D. T. Mays & C. M. Franks (Eds.), *Negative outcome in psychotherapy and what to do about it* (pp. 267–273). New York: Springer.

Thomas, E. J. (1983). Problems and issues in single-case experiments. In A. Rosenblatt & D. Woldfogel (Eds.), *Handbook of clinical social work* (pp. 583–602). San Francisco: Jossey-Bass.

Thomas, E. J. (1984). *Designing interventions for the helping professions.* Beverly Hills, CA: Sage.

Thomlinson, R. J. (1984). Something works: Evidence from practice effectiveness studies. *Social Work, 29* (1), 51–56.

Tolson, E. R. (1977). Alleviating marital communication problems. In W. Reid & L. Epstein (Eds.), *Task-centered practice* (pp. 100–112). New York: Columbia University.

Tolson, E. R. (1988). *The metamodel and clinical social work.* New York: Columbia University.

Tolson, E., & Brown, L. B. (1981). The relationship between drop out rates and students' practice skills in task centered casework. *Social Casework, 62,* 308–313.

Tolson, E., Reid, W., & Garvin, C. (1994). *The generalist model of social work practice.* New York: Columbia University.

Torrens, P. R. (1985). *Hospice programs and public policy.* Chicago: American Hospital Publishing.

Toseland, R. W., & Coppola, M. (1985). A task-centered approach to group work with older persons. In A. E. Fortune (Ed.), *Task-centered practice with families and groups* (pp. 101–114). New York: Springer.

Trotter, C. (1999). *Working with involuntary clients.* Thousand Oaks, CA: Sage.

Videka-Sherman, L. (1988). Metaanalysis of research on social work practice in mental health. *Social Work, 33* (4), 325–338.

Von Guten, G., Martinez, J., Weitzman, S., & Von Roen, J. (1991). AIDS and hospice. *American Jounral of Hospice and Palliative Care, 8* (4), 17–19.

Walsh, F. (1982). Conceptualizations of normal family functioning. In F. Walsh (Ed.), *Normal family processes* (pp. 3–42). New York: Guilford.

Wallace, L. (1985). Surgical patients' expectations of pain and discomfort: Does accuracy of expectation minimize post-surgical pain and distress? *Journal of Pain, 22,* 363–373.

Weiler, M. (1968). Postoperative patients evaluate preoperative instruction. *American Journal of Nursing, 70* (1), 1465–1467.

Weissman, A. (1976). Industrial social services: Linkage technology. *Social Casework, 57* (1), 50–54.

Weissman, A. (1977). In the steel industry. In W. J. Reid & L. Epstein (Eds.), *Task-centered practice* (pp. 235–241). New York: Columbia University.

Weissman, A. (1979). *Linkages and referrals.* Unpublished doctoral dissertation, University of Maryland at Baltimore.

Wells, R. (1982). *Planned short-term treatment.* New York: Free Press.

Wells, R. A., & Giannetti, V. J. (1990). *Handbook of the brief psychotherapies.* New York: Plenum.

Wexler, P. (1977). A case from a medical setting. In W. J. Reid, & L. Epstein (Eds.), *Task-centered practice* (pp. 50–57). New York: Columbia University.

Whan, M. W. (1979). Accounts, narrative and case history. *British Journal of Social Work, 9* (4), 489–500.

Whan, M. W. (1986). On the nature of practice. *British Journal of Social Work, 16* (2), 243–250.

Williams, J., Jones, J., & Williams, B. (1975). The psychological control of preoperative anxiety. *Psychophysiology, 12* (1), 50–54.

Wilson, J. (1981). Behavioral preparation for surgery. *Journal of Behavioral Medicine, 4* (1), 79–102.

Wing, J. K. (1978). *Reasoning about madness.* Oxford, England: Oxford University.

Wise, F. (1977). Conjoint marital treatment. In W. J. Reid & L. Epstein (Eds.), *Task-centered practice* (pp. 78–88). New York: Columbia University.

Wodarski, J. S., Marcy, S., & Malcolm, F. (1982). Using research to evaluate the effectiveness of task-centered casework. *Journal of Applied Social Sciences, 7,* 70–82.

Wood, K. M. (1978). Casework effectiveness: A new look at the research evidence. *Social Work, 23* (6), 437–458.

Woods, M. E., & Hollis, F. (2000). *Casework: A psychosocial therapy* (5th ed.). New York: Random House.

Yalom, I. D. (1985). *The theory and practice of group psychotherapy* (2nd ed.). New York: Basic Books.

INDEX

Personal problems, 34–35, 64, 99, 108, 189, 232
  indeterminate quality of, 9–10, 12, 16, 27, 31–32, 63
Pfeiffer, C., 283
Phobias, 60, 84, 85
Pier, P., 315
Pilkonis, P., 58, 61
Pincus, A., 52, 229
Pinkston, E. M., 185
Piven, F. F., 9
Planning process, 12, 80, 143, 227, 264, 269
  for client task performance, 95, 100, 107–108, 178, 190, 207
  developing a, 12, 43–45, 66, 254
  discharge, 185, 284–285, 293, 297
  for multiple problems, 284, 297
  piecemeal, 177
  problem solving, 74, 183
  time-limited treatment, 16, 45, 56, 67, 70, 83
  treatment/intervention, 38, 165–167, 169–170, 189–190
Platt, J., 177
Pollio, D., 315
Polster, R. P., 185
Pope, B., 243, 246
Postoperative behavior, 282–284, 288, 297–298
Poverty, 1, 11–19, 28, 31–32, 61, 149–150, 246
Powell, J., 99
Practical interventions, 44, 66, 68, 77
Practitioner, 129–130, 141, 143, 145, 158, 237, 259
  characteristics, 56–57, 65–67, 76, 115
  congruence, 147, 162, 231, 252
  role of, 139–140, 146–157, 162, 170–171, 174, 205
Practitioner tasks, 93, 95, 98, 100–101, 106–107, 170, 174–181, 188–190
  implementation examples, 193, 221–222, 224, 226
  revision, 219
  in task-centered studies, 293–296, 302, 304, 309, 312
  types of, 215
Prejudice, 9, 15–16, 30, 104, 106, 153, 264
Preoperative involvement, 281–284, 297, 298
Presenting problems, 6, 26, 40, 49
Presurgical intervention, 283–284, 288, 297
Priorities, 9, 231, 243, 248, 274, 295
  client, 124, 151, 154–155
  determining, 151–155
  establishing, 127, 250–253, 259
  guidelines for selecting, 171
  mandated, 151, 152–154, 155, 157, 171
  methods, 151–152

multiple problem planning, 284, 285, 287, 296–297
  target problems, 128, 147, 169–173, 188–189
  in task-centered studies, 301, 315–316
Problem, 6–32, 53, 128, 230–231, 233, 267–268, 270. See also Mandated problems; Target problem
  altered, 215, 216, 218
  basic, 6, 11
  boundaries, 127
  classification, 22, 60, 102, 134–135, 144, 155, 286–287, 303
  crisis, 127, 145–146, 235
  deep/long-standing, 127, 140, 145
  environment, 3, 7–8, 18, 21, 65
  focal, 6
  frequency, 46, 144, 198, 199, 200
  history, 102–103, 130, 204
  interpersonal conflict, 3, 7–8, 13, 16–17, 47, 99
  intrapsychic, 3, 7, 8
  measuring, 217–218
  naming, 12, 22, 23, 94, 115, 123
  new, 215, 230
  presenting, 6
  progress rating change, 286–287, 293, 295, 297–298, 302–310, 312, 317–319
  real, 6, 215, 276
  requests, 6
  social context, 7–8, 10, 12–21, 200–201
  specifying, 102, 115, 124, 301, 317
  trivializing, 127, 141, 144–145, 168
  types, 56, 58, 85, 87, 90, 302, 303
  underlying, 6, 11, 18, 21, 47, 75, 142
Problem definition, 5–14, 21, 40, 71, 78–80, 132, 250
  by age, 12, 27–29, 30, 32
  assessment, 18, 24, 108, 158, 162, 195–196
  assumptions, 128–130
  boundaries, 134–135, 143–144, 145, 147
  classification, 102, 134–135, 144, 155, 286–287
  client, 89, 93, 105, 124, 129, 162–163
  client selection criteria, 75, 82–83, 84
  for clinical work, 22–32
  complexity of, 9, 12, 144, 173
  cultural/ethnic, 29–30, 202
  describing, 12, 22–23, 115, 123, 126, 162–163
  dilemmas of, 8–12, 32
  environmental deficits, 30–32, 65
  explicit, 120, 122, 124
  focus, 22–25, 32, 83–84, 87
  by gender, 27–29, 30, 32
  general orientation to, 130–134
  impasse resolution, 8, 141–142, 162, 170
  implicit, 118, 119, 124
  importance of, 5–8, 11, 78

models, differences in, 51
  multiple-person case, 172–173
  by naming it, 12, 22–23, 94, 115, 126, 134, 144, 147, 160, 163, 192
  personal, 9–10, 12, 16, 32, 99
  poverty, 12, 13–17
  practical judgment and, 24–25, 32, 63, 148
  practitioner's role, 129, 146–157, 162
  priorities, 151–155, 171
  in problem-solving approach, 74
  psychopathology and, 25–26
  rapid early assessment, 76, 78, 93
  referrals, 8, 17, 28, 93, 111, 113, 115, 118
  refining, 194
  relativity of, 9, 10–12
  search process, 137–145, 162
  social, 7, 8, 10, 12–22
  socioeconomic status, 12, 27–29, 32
  specifying, 12, 22, 23, 126, 147–149, 155–157
  task-centered approach, 19–20, 32, 301
  underlying problems, 26–27, 32
Problem identification, 8–22, 99, 128, 147, 152, 189, 298. See also Identification
  client facilities, 135–146, 178, 285, 315, 316, 319
  in complex conditions, 134, 200
  practitioner's role in, 99, 146, 152
  in treatment sequence, 93, 100, 127
Problem reduction, 144, 191–194, 298, 307, 310–311, 318–319.
  circumventing obstacles, 255–256, 261, 264
  steps in, 94–95, 192–193
  of target problems, 173, 174, 177, 178, 206, 261, 273
  task-centered model, 8, 92, 95, 101, 108, 190
Problem search process, 137–145
  dilemmas, 139–140
  mandated, 138–139
  rationale, 138
Problem solving (PRBS), 29, 63, 75, 79–80, 103, 129, 144. See also Intervention; Treatment
  alternative strategies for, 117, 204–205
  as brief treatment model type, 72–73
  cognitive-behavioral approach, 35, 47–48, 51, 67
  crisis intervention, 48, 67
  eclecticism, 50–51, 61, 67
  family approaches to, 48–49, 56, 67, 201
  group approaches, 49–50, 67
  implementing interventions, 183
  interviewing style, 238, 239, 253
  methods, 45–51, 54, 67
  obstacles to, 40–41
  paradigm diagram, 174
  planned, 45, 56, 67, 74, 75, 101, 133, 183